S0-AUO-058

"DO YOU LOVE ME?"

Jesus Questions the Church

"DO YOU LOVE ME?"

Jesus Questions the Church

Michael H. Crosby

ORBIS BOOKS

Maryknoll, New York 10545

The Catholic Foreign Mission Society of America (Maryknoll) recruits and trains people for overseas missionary service. Through Orbis Books, Maryknoll aims to foster the international dialogue that is essential to mission. The books published, however, reflect the opinions of their authors and are not meant to represent the official position of the society.

To obtain more information about Maryknoll and Orbis Books, please visit our website at www.maryknoll.org.

Nihil Obstat, January 20, 2000
Daniel Fox, OFMCap., Minister Provincial
Province of St. Joseph of the Capuchin Order

Copyright © 2000 by Michael H. Crosby

Published by Orbis Books, Maryknoll, NY 10545-0308.

All rights reserved.

Scripture quotations from *The New Revised Standard Version of the Holy Bible* (Nashville: Catholic Bible Press, 1993).

Greek renderings based on D. Dr. Alfred Schmoller, *Handkonkordanz zum greichischen neuen Testament*, text nach Nestle (Stuttgart: Privilegierte Württembergische Bibelanstalt, 1949).

No part of this publication may be reproduced or transmitted in any form or by any means, electronic or mechanical, including photocopying, recording, or any information storage or retrieval system, without prior permission in writing from the publisher.

Queries regarding rights and permissions should be addressed to: Orbis Books, P.O. Box 308, Maryknoll, NY 10545-0308.

Manufactured in the United States of America

ORBIS/ISBN 1-57075-236-2

For Mary Kremer, OP

My Dear Friend and Collaborator

CONTENTS

Part II: Peter and the Beloved Disciple

PREFACE

In the way it is structured, John's gospel can be used by a contemporary reader to address two problems facing the institutional church today. The first half of the gospel challenges the way religions (especially religious leaders) can become so preoccupied with institutional preservation that they fail to be centered on Jesus Christ. The last section shows two different approaches to Jesus Christ as prefigured in Peter and the Beloved Disciple. John's gospel clearly opts for the latter as being the ideal way discipleship should be exercised by all within every religion and institution that identify themselves with Jesus Christ.

"John" cannot be read without contextualizing the writings in the communities to which they were addressed. In the first eleven chapters of John's gospel we find Jesus replacing an entrenched institution's sacred sites with himself, its holy feasts with his message, and its inviolable days with his creative work of restoring the world to an entirely new way of life, light, and love. The last chapters contrast, in the figures of Peter and the Beloved Disciple, how this replacement-theology is expressed in the different communities that will identify with these figures. On the one hand, Peter seems unable, until the very end, to manifest a faith based on his own personal experience of the risen Christ. On the other hand, we find highlighted the Beloved Disciple "remaining" with Jesus as an example of what it means to be centered on him. This challenges those who "remain" with Jesus to walk in his truth and light rather than any human expression of it and to live in his love by loving one another. The more desirable disciples seem identified with the Beloved One who "remains" with Jesus until the time he returns. The first letter of John is convinced that time, that "hour," is at hand (1 Jn 2:18).

In probing the language of John's corpus, it seems there were internal tensions within the Johannine community (as evidenced in the letters) and outside tensions (as evidenced in the gospel). The gospel's first part (1:19–12:19) contrasts the Johannine community with the Jewish synagogues. Here the Israel of God is replaced with Jesus (and those who believe in him).[1] In the final chapters (13:1-21:25) the story-line of the gospel reveals tensions the Johannine community faced vis-à-vis what we know now to be the more dominant Petrine community. On the one hand, it found itself confronted with this increasingly dominant (and dominating?) force of other Christians as it sought to be linked to Jesus Christ and to live in mutually sustaining love. On the other, it was not strong enough to sustain the love demanded of it in the face of the ever-extending power and influence of the Petrine group. Furthermore, because of its own internal tensions, as evidenced in the letters, it found itself at a critical point. Consequently, the Johannine community was struggling to survive. Bruce Malina notes:

> In sum, the whole of John abounds in statements, scenes, and behavioral descriptions that are redolent of "love," that is, of group attachment, of the interpersonal dimension of language—in sum, of intimacy. The story of Jesus moves in the direction of greater intimacy between Jesus and his own. In fact, in the end, the focal personage in the story with whom the audience would identify is the disciple whom Jesus loved, the beloved disciple (13:23; 18:15-16; 19:26; 20:2; 21:7, 20).[2]

Malina's insights are particularly helpful to me as I witness the contemporary dominance of the Petrine/Apostolic approach to "church." Too often it is promoted in ways that seem to suffocate the very possibility of another way of being "church," a way that, as in John's time, should exist side-by-side with the Petrine approach rather than be viewed in competition with it, much less as a threat to it. At the same time, I find that the contemporary communities that might identify with the Johannine way of being church are often more busy critiquing "Peter" than witnessing to the love which is what the wider world still seeks.

In an effort to articulate this struggle to be faithful to the love command of John within its own ranks and in a church demanding another kind of fidelity to Peter, I developed a retreat around "Questions Jesus Asks Us." The first time I shared my reflections on John was at a retreat at the Dominican Retreat Center in Dover, Massachusetts. Aware that John demanded a heart-trip more than a head-trip, I sought help from my Dominican friend, Mary Kremer, as to how I might communicate the message. Process is her field as an educator.

Following her advice, I developed a process for Dover. However, halfway through the retreat, I felt the process was not working as I had hoped. I called Mary to discover what I might be doing wrong. After I had described what I was doing, Mary asked: "Mike, how much time are you giving them to reflect on their own after you have shared your reflections?"

"About ten minutes," I said.

"That's not enough at all," she responded immediately. Her next question got to the heart of any effective way of eliciting a response from any adult: "On this retreat, what do you want to happen for them? Do you want to offer them inspiration, education, or transformation?"

When I answered, "transformation," she said emphatically, "Then you must give *them* time to integrate it and struggle with it themselves."

Since what we know today as the gospel according to John seems to have been written for a community to reinforce its members individually and collectively vis-à-vis the dominant Petrine/Apostolic church, I believe transformation is more possible when people read these reflections in a group, continually finding contemporary applications. Whatever the style of reflection/action, it will be very important for the participants to remember their effort is being blessed. This we know from John's account of the consoling words of Jesus spoken in the last part of the Farewell Discourse. Jesus' promise should nourish all of us in our effort to be open to the questions he asks us in each of this book's chapters through the fullest meaning of what reader- and audience-response theory[3] invites us to do: "I ask not only on behalf of these, but also on behalf of those who will believe in me through their word, that they may all be one. As you, Father, are in me and I am in you, may they also be in us, so that the world may believe that you have sent me" (17:20-21).

Knowing that Jesus prays for us and intercedes for us continually before the "Father," we now can ask this same Father, in Jesus' name, for what we need (16:26). Through my reflections on John's corpus I am beginning to listen much more closely to the questions Jesus asks me. I am also knowing the power I receive when I ask my questions in Jesus' name. My hope is that this may be the same gift the reader will receive from reading this book.

Finally, besides thanking Mary Kremer again, I want to thank Sr. Thomasina Cattafe, RSM for taping my retreat at Dover and for Ms. Liz Wisniewski for transcribing the tapes and helping in the editing of this book.

DO YOU NOW BELIEVE? (16:31)

The Question at the Heart of the Farewell Address (14:1–17:26) and John's Prologue (1:1-18)

"I have said these things to you in figures of speech. The hour is coming when I will no longer speak to you in figures, but will tell you plainly of the Father. On that day you will ask in my name. I do not say to you that I will ask the Father on your behalf; for the Father himself loves you, because you have loved me and have believed that I came from God. I came from the Father and have come into the world; again, I am leaving the world and am going to the Father."

His disciples said, "Yes, now you are speaking plainly, not in any figure of speech! Now we know that you know all things, and do not need to have anyone question you; by this we believe that you came from God."

Jesus answered them, "Do you now believe? The hour is coming, indeed it has come, when you will be scattered, each one to his home, and you will leave me alone. Yet I am not alone because the Father is with me. I have said this to you, so that in me you may have peace. In the world you face persecution. But take courage; I have conquered the world!" (16:25-33)

John 16:25-33 and its core question are near the center of Jesus' Farewell Discourse (14:1– 17:26). For those of us struggling to know who Jesus might be for us in a church that often seems to act as though it has all the answers, these three paragraphs offer a direction.

First of all, Jesus talks about a day and an hour when he will no longer speak to his disciples "in figures, but will tell you plainly of the Father" (16:25). Then, because they have believed that Jesus is the one who came into the world from God and have loved him, they will be able to ask in his name (16:26-28). Hearing his words, his disciples now think he is "speaking plainly, not in any figure of speech." Now they no longer "need to have anyone question" him. They simply believe he has come from God (16:29-30). Jesus responds to their certitude with a question that exposes their lack of insight—or their inability to witness to their faith when the crunch will come: "Do you now believe? The hour is coming, indeed it has come, when you will be scattered, each one to his home, and you will leave me alone" (16:31-32).

I believe the contemporary church, especially in its Roman Catholic expression, is quite scattered. Too often, I feel, the result is that Jesus is being left "alone" as we argue in our disparate "homes." "Plain speaking" seems taboo. The result is fear. Consequently, "figures of speech" become the dominant mode of expression for people trying to be faithful to the message of John's gospel. They find themselves—in a church with the answers—as a community of believers with many questions.

Our Ideology Colors Our Questions

In the honor/shame culture that gave rise to the gospels, questioning characterized many of the exchanges that took place, especially among males as they competed with each other for social standing. Marcus Fabius Quintilian lived (35–100) at the same time John's gospel seems to have been written (85–100). Writing of that era, he noted that most people asked questions, not to elicit information, but to reinforce their already-established positions. Questions were asked to stump one's opponents, to embarrass them, to shame them, and to express contempt for adversaries, or to provoke the anger of real or perceived challengers by challenging their name or dignity. Finding this cultural pattern in the scriptures, Jerome Neyrey notes that such questions "only occasionally" represent "a disinterested quest for information."[1]

Since this book's chapters on John revolve around various questions Jesus asks (the hearer and/or reader), it is important that we be open, that the goal of our quest not be to reinforce our ready-made answers, but to find Jesus' questions speaking to our hearts.

Now, as in the days of the Johannine community from which the fourth gospel arose, our stance or location in the world—personal as well as social—colors our questions. It also influences our interpretations of others' questions. Our stance involves ways in which we approach and interpret almost everything in life—including the scriptures. Depending on where we stand (geographically, psychologically, sexually, culturally, etc.), our questions of the scriptures, as well as our interpretation of them, will consciously or unconsciously reflect our world view. While we (especially if "we" are white males with a Western European perspective) may insist on the "objectivity" of our interpretation, anyone not white or not male or not conditioned by European thought processes may find that our interpretation often reveals a historical bias that unwittingly says more about our social location than it does about the text. The fact that I am an able-bodied, white, male, heterosexual, North American, Roman Catholic cleric belonging to a large religious order circumscribes, if not defines, my understanding of the text quite differently than if I were an Ethiopian Coptic lesbian single mother.

"Where I sit is how I stand." Where I sit also cannot be separated from the culture that has provided my seat. This is important to remember, especially for people like me who represent the dominant groups in society. Our ways of communicating often accept culture as a given rather than as a force that might be critiqued. According to the priest-anthropologist Gerald Arbuckle, culture "is a pattern of shared assumptions, expressed in symbols, myths, and rituals. This pattern has been invented, discovered, or developed by the group as it has struggled to cope with problems of external adaptation and internal cohesion. The group considers these assumptions valid and seeks to teach them to new members as the correct foundation for perceiving, thinking, feeling, and acting."[2]

What Arbuckle describes as culturally conditioned and communicated "assumptions" which a dominant group defines as "the correct foundation" or "truth" I will be calling *ideology*. Arbuckle notes: "On the basis of these assumptions ["ideology"], people develop rule-bound institutions and standardized behavior patterns in response to their need for order and predictability in relationships." Given this reality, it will be important to understand the cultural and cosmic significance of the first part of John's gospel (1:19–12:19). Here Jesus undermines the heart of his culture's "shared assumptions" and "rule-bound institutions" that were "expressed in symbols, myths, and rituals." These "truths" demanded "standardized behavior patterns" which Jesus overturned and replaced with himself as truth itself. This book examines the consequences for those who, faced with a similar ideology in the Petrine/Apostolic thrust of today's church, seek to identify with Jesus via the Johannine community.

While trying to be faithful to good scholarship, this book is not meant to offer a scholarly exegesis of each word or even every passage in John. Rather, it represents the result thus far of my struggle as a reader of this "word" living in my "world." My "world" is defined for me by my social location in the United States of America as a Roman Catholic priest. Here I am called to live in a love that has been grounded thoroughly in faith. In this sense, I agree fully with Raymond Brown who has stated of John and the questions Jesus asks in the fourth gospel: "The question most appropriate to the Gospel concerns the relation of the believers to God, through and in Jesus."[3] The ultimate question is: "Do you believe?"

Reader-Response and the Author of John's Gospel

In John, "believing" represents authentic hearing and seeing. It involves hearing the text and acting on it as well as reading the text and making it part of one's life and that of one's group. It entails what we read about in 1 John: "What we have heard, what we have seen with our eyes, what we have looked at and touched with our hands, concerning the word of life" (1 Jn 1:1). The way we allow these revelations of God to reside deeply in our lives comes, not with any answer (apart from Jesus who is the answer insofar as he is the way, the truth, and the life [14:6]), but by remaining with the questions. What matters for the reader today is not so much how Jesus questioned the first disciples, but how Jesus questions *us* in our particular social location. Each question is meant to elicit a response. How we engage will be called "reader-response" communication.

"Reader-response" theory began in the United States in the mid-to-late 1960s. In the early 1980s it began to be applied to the scriptures. One of the first in the United States to apply the theory to John's gospel was R. Alan Culpepper.[4] Since a reader-response approach revolves around the identity and tasks of the author(s) and the reader(s), Culpepper's task—as is the charge of anyone serious about John's gospel—first involved determining the identities of the gospel's author and audience.

In terms of the authorship of the gospel and letters attributed to "John,"[5] I grew up believing that (1) the fourth gospel was written by John the Evangelist; (2) John the Evangelist was John the Apostle; and (3) John the Apostle-Evangelist was the "Beloved Disciple." This theory (a "fact" then) was reinforced in cult. The triptychs above many altars in Catholic churches depicted Christ crucified and, at the foot of the cross, his mother and John with book and quill in hand. However, I now understand the gospel of "John" quite differently in terms of authorship. Rather than John the Apostle with quill-in-hand, evidence points to no less than three different authors, editions, or redactions with the Beloved Disciple appearing only in the final version.[6] Consequently, it is very difficult to know who the real human author(s) or source may have been.[7]

It seems that, because of the Beloved Disciple's significance, a community developed around him and/or his inspirational figure after Jesus' death/resurrection.[8] In contrast to the communities that developed around Peter and the other apostles (like Thomas,[9] or Paul, or even Apollos [1 Cor 1:12]), this group struggled to be faithful to the person and teachings of Jesus as communicated by the Beloved One. Building on the pioneering insights of Johannine scholars like Louis Martyn and Raymond Brown, Kevin B. Quast has shown that John's community was a dynamic but beleaguered group struggling to maintain its unique identity.[10] The Community [School] of the Beloved Disciple felt itself under siege from three sources. On the *outside,* the Jewish synagogues had evicted Christians from membership. The exclusion of Christians had developed to the point that the Jewish ritual included a prayer against them. *Within* the Christian community, the Johannine community found itself in tension vis-à-vis the increasingly hierarchical approach represented in the Apostolic orientation of those house churches that had come together around the persons and memories of Peter and the other apostles. *Within itself*, as the letters evidence, conflicts were producing ever-increasing tensions.

Most scholars believe this alternative community identifying with the Beloved Disciple gave rise to the corpus of Johannine writings which contained the gospel and the three letters attributed to "John." At the same time, it tried to implement in its life the words contained in these writings. In this sense, through the word enfleshed in it, the community became both the author and the audience.

For this reason, this book will view the Community of the Beloved Disciple as both author and audience, writer and reader, of the Johannine corpus. Aware of concerns about authorship, I will be stressing the role of the "reader." The first "readers"[11] were those for whom the Johannine corpus was directly intended: the Johannine community. By returning to the disciples' statement that Jesus now "spoke plainly," the reader today realizes that the words cannot be limited only to a dialogue that took place at some historical time—as at the "last supper" between the disciples and Jesus. They also reflect the struggle between "belief" as understood by the community of the Beloved Disciple and "belief" as interpreted by those defined by the Petrine viewpoint. Raymond Brown highlights the value of this way of reading the present into the past by writing:

> When later on the disciples make the claim, "We believe that you came forth from God," Jesus' skepticism is obvious: "So now you believe? Why, an hour is coming, and indeed already has come, for you to be scattered, each on his own, leaving me all alone" (16:29-32). Even after the resurrection, the scene with Thomas indicates that the faith of the Twelve can stand improvement (20:24-29). In fact, Thomas' delayed confession of Jesus as "My Lord and my God" may be paradigmatic of the fuller understanding of Jesus' divinity to which, John hopes, the Apostolic Christians may ultimately be brought.[12]

While many interpreters of John stress the "reader" who existed at the time the Johannine corpus was written, this "historical" or "intended reader" is not the "reader" I have in mind in this book. My "readers" are those today who struggle with questions Jesus asks, who seek to discover how we who identify with the Beloved Disciple in a church identified with Peter might be faithful in a loving way. My "readers" are those persons and/or that community of persons John's Jesus envisioned who would "believe in me through their word" (17:20). Since I am writing this book primarily for the contemporary reader, for purposes of spirituality rather than theology, and for a popular audience more than for academics, I refer to these persons engaging the text of John and reading this book of mine as "the reader."[13] As such reader/disciples we too need to return to the challenge of John 16:25-33 and allow Jesus to question us regarding our belief. A deeper examination will help in interpreting John's relevance to us today.

The Structure of John's Gospel

Under the rubric of believing in Jesus as the core of the gospel (and the letters as well), we can outline the final structure of John's gospel as we have it today in the following way:

1:1-18   **PROLOGUE:** A summary of the role of God's Word of Life and Light in a world of darkness.

1:19–12:19   **PART ONE:** Jesus' "own" do not receive him. Jesus, the Word, reveals himself to the world and his own. They do not believe in him (= receive him). However, a core group of disciples believe in him; they remain with him.

1. 1:19–4:54	Jesus' search for true believers takes him outside Judaism's temple and rituals.	
2. 5:1–10:42	Jesus' growing threat to established/entrenched religion: replacing its feasts.	
	a. 5:1-47	Jesus, the New Moses, replaces the Sabbath Feast.
	b. 6:1-71	Jesus, the Bread of Life, replaces the Passover.
	c. 7:1–8:59	Jesus, the Living Water and Light of the World, replaces water and light rituals.
	d. 9:1–10:21	Jesus, the Healer of Humanity (blind from birth), exposes the blindness of religion's leaders.

Jesus' Plain-Speaking and the Key Johannine Figure of Speech

Given the fact that the reader of John will be the contemporary reader, we thus are invited by the Johannine paragraphs at the beginning of
this chapter to discover where our faith may be colored by "plain speaking" as well as by "figures of speech." In a special way we need to begin
by examining two ways of speaking used in John that have become contemporary sources of conflict: the notion of God as "the Father" and the
meaning of *hoi Ioudaioi*.

Plain Speaking about "The Father"

In this passage Jesus says he will speak to his disciples "plainly of
the Father" (16:25). In the few lines that opened this chapter (16:25-33),
Jesus speaks of God as his "father" 6 times. John uses this image as the
main title of God 118 times. In our "world," where male words imaging
God can be so divisive and the source of much "scattering," we might
well ask: "What did Jesus really mean when he called God 'Father'?" As
Dorothy A. Lee sees it: "The question is whether the central Johannine
image of God as father supports patriarchy (literally, 'father rule')."[14]

To call another "father" meant many things in the Roman-ruled Mediterranean world that encompassed Judaism. In the wider "world," to publicly call anyone but one's blood by the title "father" was seen as subversive. "Father" was the dominant title of the Roman ruler. It "resonated
with the image of empire as patriarchal family and emperor as father. It
was particularly apt as a title by which the persecuted could invoke God's
power," Mary Rose D'Angelo has written. She continues,

> The Roman order was perhaps the "fact" that loomed largest on
> the horizons of ancient Christianity and Judaism, and the as-
> sumption of the titles *parens patriae* and *pater patriae* was a
> major step in the emergence and solidification of the new world
> order Augustus constructed as the basis of his rule.
>   The title was awarded to Julius Caesar late in his life, possi-
> bly at the urging of Cicero; it functioned to establish a relation of
> *pietas* between Caesar and the Roman people.[15]

Having noted that both Jewish and Christian piety saw "father" as the
highest and most appropriate title for God, a title that reflected anti-
imperial notions, D'Angelo concludes: "The imperial context is also the
context of Jesus' life and, even more, of his death. The designation of

God as father, if indeed it was important to Jesus, was important because of what it communicated to his hearers. . . . If indeed the title 'father' was important to Jesus, it may have been in the context of spiritual resistance to imperial pretensions."[16] Assuming this to be the case, I will also continue to refer to "the Father" in this text with the hope that its subversive element will always be understood by the reader.

If, at the time of Jesus, "father" represented an image connected to Jesus that threatened to subvert the "world" system of his day, in our own time, the notion of God as "mother" represents an image that threatens to subvert the "world" of many organized religions, especially Catholicism. Just consider the threat that inclusive language of God represents, especially to those in the hierarchy who are intent on preserving the male, clerical model of the church! The deep resistance of the Roman Curia to the use of "inclusive" language in the liturgy in the United States is a case in point. Any disinterested observer would recognize that the issue behind the controversy is not liturgical language inclusive of women; it is how far women will be included in the liturgy itself.

Moving from the wider world to that of the family, the image of "father" implies an intimacy based on familial ties of love and responsibility. It also involves notions associated with wisdom piety which viewed the soul as descending from God. Given John's stress on Jesus doing the work of the "Father," it seems to suggest that he is a kind of apprentice or the one who has inherited the family business. Thus the "work" of the Father is that of Jesus (5:17).[17] This represents the deepest familial notion: it involves the way the lineage must be continued.

Unlike the traditional image of "father" that upheld patriarchically-exclusive dynamics, Jesus' image of "Father" in John invites a radical alternative. Now his Father loves Jesus' disciples because of their faith in Jesus that makes them willing to model their lives on his love (16:27). Now, in their mutually-shared Spirit, Jesus will be with all those who remain identified with him and provide access to one of the many dwelling places ("remaining" places) in his Father's house (14:2f).

Examining the Johannine "Figure of Speech"
around the Notion of hoi Ioudaioi

The Greek equivalent for "the Jews" is *hoi Ioudaioi.* "The Jews" is the way the New Revised Standard Version (NRSV) of the Bible, which I am using here, translates *hoi Ioudaioi.* From John's references to people like John the Baptist, Jesus' own disciples, Jewish leaders like Nicodemus, and friends like Mary, Martha, and Lazarus, the fourth gospel is clear that not all of "his own people did not accept him." Consequently, the "his own" (*idioi*) represented in the "world" that rejected him cannot be identified only with the historical figures in the text, with certain religious leaders, with a certain kind or representative grouping of "the Jews,"[18] or even with "the Johannine Jews." Because this phrase has so many contextual connotations, a disservice is done when these contexts are not considered.

At times, the phrase refers to geography ("the Judeans"), or to some grouping of "the Jews" (the religious authorities, those who were divided over their allegiance to Jesus, or those representing unbelief in or opposition to Jesus), or to some geographic-based grouping (the religious leaders of Judea). Given these nuances, Culpepper writes, "by translating *hoi Ioudaioi* as "the Jews" in this context, the NRSV and other translations produce a reading that makes little sense."[19]

At this point, I think it is important to listen to those who point to the anti-Jewish (if not anti-Semitic) bias found in John. One of the clearest and most helpful reviews I have found has been that of Tina Pippin in her "'For Fear of the Jews': Lying and Truth-Telling in Translating the Gospel of John." First she asks: "What is the ethical responsibility of translators who each hold a fragment of the blame [for Christian hatred of Jews expressed in the gospel of John] each time they translate?"[20] Then she shows how much exegesis has been overly apologetic. Finally, she ponders a series of questions that must be asked by anyone serious about John's gospel and the way it has been used by cultures as ideological justification for hatred of and violence toward the Jews—as well as any other group they choose to scapegoat:

> Many scattered questions arise as I face the rhetorical power of this gospel: Is the abusive rhetoric part of the appeal of this gospel? Is there a translation option to offer? Is replacement of *Ioudaioi* or the offering of alternative possibilities to be recommended? What if the translator left it blank, untranslatable? Would others fill in the bank with equally unacceptable options? Who are candidates to be children of the devil and not from God? Hitler added options to this hate speech: Roma (Gypsies), homosexuals, political dissidents. Is there a group that is legitimate to hate? The Gospel of John provides the site to talk about the larger problems of Christianity/ies and its sacred, authoritative texts. The act of demonization is not unique to Christianity, but is the Johannine message fuel for polemic and violence against the Jews?[21]

Examining possible ways to translate John's *hoi Ioudaioi*, Pippin (following Daniel Harrington[22] and Padraic O'Hare[23]) concludes that the words should not be translated. This has led me to decide never again in this book to translate *hoi Ioudaioi*.[24] While this might assuage my uneasiness about the image, I also must ask myself how we might understand *hoi Ioudaioi* not only in the context of early Christianity but especially in our own time.

Elizabeth Harris has shown that "his own" who did not receive the Word (1:11) is really "every person coming into this world" who is defined by its ideology rather than that of the Word.[25] If this is the case, then, as far as the contemporary reader is concerned, John's use of the term *hoi Ioudaioi* represents the wider, cosmic struggle that is elicited by the presence of Jesus in the world of any era. Consequently, "his own" not accepting him can be found in contemporary *hoi Ioudaioi*, those defined by the cultural attitudes and ideological stances represented in today's world, especially that part of the "world" that sanctions violence, especially religious abuse, against any group that is not one's own. In this sense I agree with Heinrich Schneider's conclusion regarding *hoi Ioudaioi*: "Ultimately the group stands for the forces opposed to Jesus, which are the forces of darkness. It is obvious that we are not dealing with an ethnic group, but with a dramatic theological symbol. . . . We would miss the full significance of this symbol if we considered the Jew in John only as a historical figure. 'The Jews' are an ever-present reality and threat to any worship of God in spirit and in truth."[26]

The "World" in John's Writings

At the very time when the disciples say they now hear Jesus speaking "plainly, not in any figure of speech," Jesus answers them with the question: "Do you now believe? The hour is coming, indeed it has come, when you will be scattered, each one to his home, and you will leave me alone. Yet I am not alone because the Father is with me. I have said this to you, so that in me you may have peace. In the world you face persecution. But take courage; I have conquered the world!" (16:31-35).

The First Century "World" of John's Readers

John uses the word *kosmos* seventy-eight times in his gospel. In this particular passage he uses it four times: "I . . . have come into the world; again, I am leaving the world" (16:28) and "In the world you face persecution. But take courage; I have conquered the world!" (16:33).

In the "world" of John, religion was embedded in the social institutions from the basic unit of the household to the empire itself. This is important to remember as we probe John's meaning of the "world." At times it just refers to the world in a neutral way, without judgment. Other times it connotes a more positive meaning. In the main, however, it represents a negative notion.

In its negative sense, the "world" symbolically and theologically represents all those forces (including religious ones in their cultural embeddedness) which not only oppose God's word but can be actively hostile to it, especially in its human manifestation in Jesus the Christ. The "world" represents wherever (and in whomever) relationships make no "place" for God's word to dwell. It represents those social and cultural forces in society that not only have organized themselves without God, but also appeal to religion and its protective mantle as a way of ensuring this opposition. This is the "darkness" that cannot or will not comprehend the light. It is that part of creation which rejects its creator, which stands against the light, which is unwelcoming and/or resistant to the word. It may present itself as being of God, but, because of its own institutionalized biases, it will not or cannot recognize its life-source (1:10). In this negative sense, according to Robert Kysar, the "world" stands as a symbolic representation of the realm of unbelief, "the area in which there is total rejection of the truth of God revealed in Christ. It is used in conjunction with judgment and with Satan (as in 9:39; 12:31; and 16:1). It symbolizes that way of being, that way of living, which is opposed to God and the divine plan of salvation for humans."[27]

In this sense, the "world" comprises those cultural forces discussed earlier, especially religious institutions and ideologies which consciously or unconsciously can make no room for the living God: "He was in the world, and the world came into being through him; yet the world did not know him. He came to what was his own, and his own people did not accept him" (1:10-11). As Walter Wink says, in its structural sense, the "world" refers to a religious system that "is unaware of its alienation from God"[28] (18:20). While the first part of the gospel makes clear that this refers to the Jewish institutions, the last part shows how the "world" can also be a church overly linked to Peter, a church that, as a result, fails to remain grounded, like the Beloved Disciple, in Christ.

The Twenty-first Century "World" of John's Readers

In contemporary language, the "world" hostile to Jesus in John expresses what the 1971 Synod of Roman Catholic Bishops called the "network of domination, oppression and abuses which stifle freedom and which keep the greater part of humanity from sharing in the building up and enjoyment of a more just and more communal world."[29] This "world" does not mean our planet; rather, it represents the planet's people, especially in its officialdom, who stand opposed to God. As in the time of Jesus, when religion was embedded in all societal structures, this officialdom often is connected to recalcitrant religious leaders organized in a group. Those members who have come under the power of the group's ideology stand in need of conversion. Thus, the Bishops prophetically wrote in 1971: "Scrutinizing the 'signs of the times' and seeking to detect the meaning of emerging history, while at the same time sharing the aspirations and questions of all those who want to build a more human world, we have listened to the Word of God *that we might be converted to the fulfilling of the divine plan for the salvation of the world.*"[30]

I believe that the "sin of the world" revolves around its various "isms." According to the anthropologist Gerald Arbuckle, "isms" are especially dominant in cultures of prejudice toward one's own group over-and-against others. A key "ism" of Jesus' time was ethnocentrism. Arbuckle explains how such enthnocentrism worked then. The dynamics are still at work in our "world."

> On the assumption of racial, national, religious, sexual, or social superiority, people act to protect or 'enhance their status. Violence, even wars, result from ethnocentric jealousy. Jews looked on Samaritans as racially inferior people, and vice versa. When Jesus [spoke]... many of his listeners must have become enraged with jealousy. Jesus had to be marginalized, they felt; otherwise, his teachings would undermine the racial supremacy of the Jewish people.[31]

Today, wherever "isms" define institutions, people easily get characterized, not as persons, but according to their particular grouping, e.g., according to sex and race, age and power, as well as by ethnic group, national origin, religious persuasion and/or sexual orientation. The community's resources (which are controlled by the group in power) will be allocated in a way that encourages the control of information and technology by those with power at the expense of others. When this occurs within a developed nation, for instance, materialism in the form of consumerism will give rise to economic imperialism. When "isms" dominate leadership within a religion, clericalism will be the consequence.

When religious ideology is used to reinforce the existing social arrangements or "isms" within any religious institution, religion becomes a justification for the abuse of power by religious elites. Truth is on its side alone; anything not under its power is suspect or even untruthful. One must be right; those disagreeing are "outside" truth and salvation.

The World That Jesus Conquers

Facing such ideological forces—which might be called any darkness within or without that keeps the light of the Christ from illuminating the world—the community's members might easily experience discouragement. Despite the influence and force of this "world," the followers of Jesus, however, are to take courage. Why? Because Jesus has overcome the world (16:33).

"Overcoming the world" means emerging victorious and justified after a trial, tribulation, or test. For Jesus' audience, courage will arise to the degree that his followers are ready to testify on his behalf in the midst of their own trials, tests, and tribulations. As long as John's readers remain faithful to Jesus' word, they too can claim the victory that was his even as they continue to struggle in the world. The promise made to the first disciples becomes operative whenever people of faith engage the text in a way that makes them challenge their "world." It is in this sense that Gail O'Day writes:

> John 16:33 is the most telling temporal statement in the farewell discourse and the most revealing of the way the farewell discourse holds together narrative form and theological content. The fourth evangelist uses *temporal figures* to evoke *theological reality*. John 16:33 gives narrative embodiment to the realized eschatology that is so characteristic of the Fourth Gospel. It shows how God's new age has entered the present. Jesus' announcement, "I have conquered the world," asserts that the "future" victory is in fact the present reality. Jesus' victory over the world is not to be deferred to a then and there, but is always available in the here and now. This victory colors the whole discourse. The reason that Jesus can speak with such confidence to the disciples about their future is that it is the risen Jesus who speaks, the Jesus who has already conquered the world.[32]

Like the Beloved Disciple in John's gospel, so too the persons and/or groups desiring to make the gospel the core of their lives in "the world" will be the ones to whom Jesus can speak plainly, without any figure of speech. These will be the ones to whom Jesus entrusts his word. These will become the community of beloved disciples who make room in their homes for his word.

John's gospel serves as an appeal to all communities of readers to have courage in face of persecution from without and divisions from within. If they are going to survive in such a world, with its institutionalized sin expressed in its brand of "Judaism" (which we call "isms" today) and its ideology (*Ioudaios*), John's readers of any era need to discover how these attitudes can creep into their own community, understand their dynamics as death-dealing, recall the vision of unity that Jesus desired, and convert from their scatteredness and individualism to become the beloved community entrusted with the word to be witnessed in whatever world they are called to transform. In the face of the dominant ideology sustaining the "world" which they must reject, John's community must speak another language. On the one hand it must separate itself from the "world"; on the other, its language of love must offer communion and union to all who would embrace it.

As we—and especially those of us who are part of the Petrine church —grapple with the message of John's gospel for our world today and do so while remaining faithful, Jesus' question "Do you now believe?" should stand as a challenge to each of us. It challenges us to be the beloved disciples and to gather with our gifts to keep from being scattered (*skorpizein*) in the face of the infrastructure's influence and control. "Do you now believe?" will be the question challenging us as we struggle with the Johannine text throughout the chapters of this book. The response to this question of Jesus will be determined by the way we, as readers, allow his questions to resonate in us and our gatherings. Only in small, faith-based communities where members are free to question will we find a new way of living, an alternative to the Petrine-dominated approach to community that too often seems more intent on its prerogatives than on the proclamation of Jesus himself.

Part I

JESUS AND ENTRENCHED RELIGION

ONE

WHAT ARE YOU LOOKING FOR? (1:38)

The Question of John 1:19–4:54

In our contemporary, consumer-driven society, we are used to hearing the question: "What are you looking for?" At a deeper level, "What are you looking for?" refers to far more than the meeting of material needs. It speaks to our search, our longings, and our deepest desires. When this question comes to us from Jesus, it means: "What do you want in life?" and "What are you seeking from me for your life?" Even more deeply, the question bespeaks an invitation: "May I help you?"

"What are you looking for?" (1:38a) are the first words Jesus utters in John's gospel. John the Baptist was "standing with two of his disciples." He recognized Jesus and proclaimed him "Lamb of God" (1:35-36). When his two disciples heard him say this, they turned from being with him to Jesus. At this Jesus himself "turned and saw them following." He said, "'What are you looking for?' They said to him, 'Rabbi,' (which translated means Teacher), 'where are you staying?' He said to them, 'Come and see.' They came and saw where he was staying, and they remained with him that day" (1:37-39a).

John uses the word *zētein* at least twenty-nine times in the gospel. The notion of seeking, particularly the search that brings people to Jesus (and, more important, Jesus' search for authentic faith from them), colors the first chapters in John (1:19–4:54). While the meaning of the term *zētein* is not always clear, the "search" it entails often involves the action of turning—either toward Jesus or away from him.[1] Given this book's interest in looking at the questions Jesus asks, in hearing them addressed to us as readers, we might begin by asking ourselves: How open are we to "turn" when we hear Jesus question us, especially when he asks us life's basic question: "What are you looking for?"

Structuring John 1:19–4:54 around the Quest

This book revolves around questions Jesus asks in John's gospel. Authentic questions have to do with genuine quests. John Painter distinguish-

3

es between "quest" stories and "rejection" stories in John. Quest stories are meant to lead the reader-as-questor into a deeper openness to or acceptance of the one who asks the questions. In contrast, rejection stories involve a question put to Jesus by those who are closed or entrenched in their ways or ideology. Such queries do not arise from a basic acceptance of him grounded in trust; they involve challenges and tests that expose the questioners' hardness of heart. According to Painter, "In the rejection stories a position opposed to Jesus is brought into confrontation with him. The action of the story does nothing to change the position of the opponent. Its purpose is to justify the alienation of the reader [to the objector] because of the action taken by those represented by the opponent."[2] When John wants to portray those opposed to Jesus, he often uses their questions to expose their ideological stance as reflecting institutional entrenchment.

In my experience, people whose questions are raised in an effort to justify institutional arrangements defined by the "isms" of the world still reflect this entrenchment. Nothing anyone says or does will change their position. They reinforce their "isms" with an ideology that justifies existing institutionalized dynamics of control. Often this is done in the name of God, truth, or some higher power. In terms of the contemporary "world" in which today's reader engages John, when such ideology reflects a mind*set* of the left or the right (politically speaking), free markets or distribution mechanisms (economically speaking), or liberal or conservative positions (religiously speaking), or when the position of a person, a group, or a collective of persons and groups is entrenched, there can be no possibility of dialogue. You either support the dominating ideology (which sustains the "isms" in the institution) of the status quo and are "one of us" or you are "one of them." And if you are "one of them" you can be rejected and "invalidated"; you can be put "outside the temple" (see 9:22; 12:42; 16:2).

Besides identifying and outlining the "anatomy" of the quest/rejection stories, John Painter also finds a chiastic structure in John. Many people have written about "chiasms" and "chiastic structures" which can be found in the scriptures.[3] In such literary arrangements, there is a relationship, or connection, or parallel between the first and the last (sentences, sections, etc.), the second and second last, the third and third last, and so on. These dyads often converge on some central notion. The core passage or section reveals the heart of the meaning contained within the wider whole.

A chiastic structure holds together the quest stories in 1:19–4:54. These stories have to do with people's quest for Jesus. At the center of all these human quests can be found a divine quest, which is expressed in the cleansing of the temple (2:13-22). The Word enfleshed in Jesus comes to his own[4] in a quest for true worship(ers). In uncovering the structure of the text this way we see revealed a key insight in John: true seekers will be those whose search centers not on their own interests, but on being open to worship God in spirit and in truth. Adapting Painter, we can chiastically structure this pattern quite clearly:

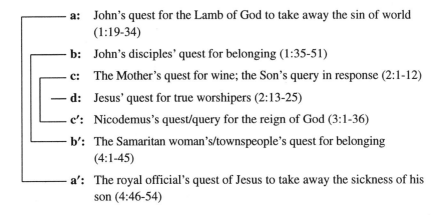

a: John's quest for the Lamb of God to take away the sin of world (1:19-34)

b: John's disciples' quest for belonging (1:35-51)

c: The Mother's quest for wine; the Son's query in response (2:1-12)

d: Jesus' quest for true worshipers (2:13-25)

c': Nicodemus's quest/query for the reign of God (3:1-36)

b': The Samaritan woman's/townspeople's quest for belonging (4:1-45)

a': The royal official's quest of Jesus to take away the sickness of his son (4:46-54)

a. John's Quest for the Lamb of God to Take Away the Sin of the World (1:19-34)

John 1:19-51 seems to indicate possible tensions and rivalries that existed between the Johannine community and remnants of the Baptist's own community of disciples which was trying to maintain an identity of its own.[5] The setting is "in Bethany across the Jordan where John was baptizing" (1:28). Here "priests and the Levites" sent by *hoi Ioudaioi* approach John (1:19). A few verses later, another group shows up: those "sent by the Pharisees" (1:24). The fact that both groups were "sent" contrasts these authorities with God who sent Jesus into their "world." While Jesus was sent to invite, these groups were sent to test.

In a fascinating article, "Will the Court Please Call in the Prime Witness? John 1:29-34,"[6] J. D. Charles argues that this opening passage reflects the trial-like setting of the entire gospel. John's gospel is not, however, merely the record of a historical trial involving Jesus and his opponents. We as readers are also put on trial by the characters and dynamics represented in the text itself. An experience I had in late 1992 made me quite aware of how sinister such dynamics can be.

Around Christmas, newspaper revelations alleged that a few friars in my province of Capuchin Franciscans had been charged with pedophilia and other related acts of sexual impropriety. Because I had been in a position of leadership during the time when the main perpetrator had committed his deeds—which now had come to light (but about which I then knew nothing)—I was subpoenaed to testify about my recollection of events surrounding the allegations.

From the beginning of my deposition, it became clear that the lawyers for the victims and others alleging abuse were not questioning me in a genuine search for truth. As their inquiry progressed, I soon realized that the perpetrators and alleged perpetrators were not the only ones on trial. As a member of their community, and as a former leader in that community, I was on trial as was the entire province.

Early on, the prosecuting lawyer had stated that his goal was not only to get guilty verdicts for the defendants; he wanted to "bring down" the place where the main violations had allegedly occurred. He wanted to destroy our province.[7] In this forensically charged setting, it became virtually impossible to feel that his questions were raised in an honest search for truth. He was entrenched in his position; he had an ideological stance; his questions of me were asked to reinforce his already-determined point of view. His mind was made up. His job, his reputation, his name depended on it.

My two depositions (given before all criminal charges were dropped —as well as all civil claims, due to settlements that had taken place before the crimes and allegations had become public knowledge) have helped me recognize the difference between questions grounded in trust and those that are meant to test. The former find the questioner spiritually open to a response. The latter reveal the inquirer as ideologically blinded. The difference between the two helps me understand the first part of this section of John's gospel where we find both kinds of questions—those based on trust and those meant as tests.

John uses two words for "to question": *erōtan* and *aitein*. While not always the case, it does seem that, when questions arise from a genuine search, or inquiring, the word *aitein* is used.[8] When questions arise from self-interest, the word *erōtan* usually appears.[9] When a question is self-serving, it gets asked in much the same way that questions get asked at an inquest. The goal of the question is not to elicit a genuine response. Rather, its purpose is to test an opponent in a way that reinforces the questioner's pre-conceived idea, stance, or ideology. On the other hand, when the question is asked as part of the effort arising from a genuine quest, it evidences a trust-based search for the truth. The first type of question involves an implicit or explicit challenge to the opponent's authority; its purpose is to test. The second type of question reveals an implicit or explicit willingness to submit to another's authority; it is based on trust.

When a query is grounded in insincerity or cynical motivation on the part of the questioner, the very environment of the questioning takes on the characteristics of a trial. One goal is sought: to triumph over the witness. Conversely, when a question is a sincere and open request on the part of the questioner, the dynamics involved in the questioning lead to genuine testimony offered by a faithful witness.

J. D. Charles is not alone in saying that the entire gospel of John represents one extended trial scene or inquest between Jesus and his opponents.[10] The dynamics of the two sides can be charted by the kinds of questions posed in John's gospel, whether arising from openness or opposition:

QUESTION

AITEIN	ERŌTAN
QUEST	QUERY
TRUSTING	TESTING
TESTIMONY	TRIAL
INVITATION	INQUISITION
INQUIRY	IDEOLOGY
ACCEPTANCE	REJECTION
INTIMACY	BETRAYAL

Jesus' response to the two kinds of approaches to him (entrenchment or encounter) will be elusiveness or engagement. The response of the reader will have parallels as well. Either we will be led to reject Jesus in one form or another or to deepen our commitment to "remain with" him in a way that gets expressed in authentic witness (*martyria/martyrs*). Paul S. Minear's insights into the meaning of being a testifier or witness, based on the Greek *martyrs*, help us understand the implications for Johaninne discipleship then and now. He writes:

> According to a recent Gallup poll, not more than one in eight church members in American admits any readiness to make a major sacrifice for religion. Whether or not that is accurate, we all view the martyr as an exceptional person.
>
> I use the term to call attention to four basic meanings of the Greek word cluster *martyrs*, of which the English word martyr is a transliteration.
>
> 1. *Martyrs* is a person who sees something happen and who reports to others what has been seen.
>
> 2. In the case of prophecy, a *martyrs* is a person who sees and hears invisible and inaudible things and who reports to God's people what has been seen and heard.
>
> 3. In the case of legal procedures, whether actual or metaphorical, a *martyrs* is a person who is hailed before a court and who is called on to give a testimony that will result in acquittal or conviction of criminal charges.

4. All three of the above meanings lie behind the development of a fourth: A *martyrs* is a person who, on trial for life, refuses to recant faith and who willingly accepts death as the price of fidelity.[11]

Such was the witness of John. In a world where religion too often accommodates itself to the prevailing culture, to the point that it no longer invites authentic witness from its members, especially its youth,[12] it seems refreshing when we still find young people willing to take "a stand" for their convictions about Jesus Christ.[13] John the Baptist was such a young man. His heroism came at a price. He "was a man sent from God . . . as a witness to testify to the light, so that all might believe through him" (1:6-7). The purpose of his witness was to make straight the way of the Lord (1:23). John's orthodoxy was proved in his orthopraxy. He didn't just talk religion; he manifested its authentic power in his life. He had a role: to prepare for the Messiah. Now that the Messiah had come, John's role was basically over. This brings us to the next section in our chiasm.

b. John's Disciples' Quest for Belonging (1:35-51)

"The next day," the evangelist declares, John was with "two of his disciples." Seeing Jesus walk by, the Baptizer declares: "Look."

John's "looking" is not just visual. It involves something more. This is clear when he points to Jesus not as "there," but as "here": "*here* is the Lamb of God" (1:35-36). The possibility of becoming connected to Jesus is not something far away, but quite present; not something in the distant future, but now. When John points out Jesus, the two disciples begin to follow him. At this, "Jesus turned and saw *them*." The word for "to see" (*theasthai*) used by John here means "to gaze on" or "to discern with the eyes." It suggests contemplating another, coming to know another, becoming engaged with another. The possibility of something more coming from this encounter begins when the first words Jesus speaks in John's gospel take the form of a question: "What are you looking for?"

In asking the question, the implication is that the disciples are on some kind of a search. In fact, the phrase in Greek means, what do you *seek?* The question is an invitation to John's readers as well. Mark Stibbe notes that the words in Jesus' question "are important because they alert the reader at the earliest stage to one of the primary motifs of the gospel, which is 'seeking Jesus,' an action which the narrator presents as the ultimate religious quest (John 14.6)."[14]

John's disciples respond to Jesus' "What are you looking for?" with a question of their own: "Rabbi, where are you staying?" (2:38b). "Where do you stay" might, at first glance, appear to be a conversation opener, like "Where are you from?" Or it might bespeak the disciples' desire to go with Jesus simply to talk with him and to find out more about this one John has called Lamb of God and Son of God. However, especially since "to remain with" (*menein*) is the same expression John uses to connote Jesus' union with God and our union with him, "Where do you stay?" reveals the desire at the core of all peoples' hearts to be grounded in that which represents the absolute, the source of meaning for their lives. It also represents John's way of saying that "remaining with" Jesus establishes an evident alternative community to the surrounding ways of living in the "world." What the disciples seek is some kind of connectedness, some relationship, some community, some way of being with Jesus. "Staying" in John is not about a place as much as about a way of abiding with another.

The way John sculpts Jesus' response makes it clear that, while we may be thinking of developing our connectedness to God around a place ("where" do you stay?), the "where" is not as important as the "with whom." "He said to them, 'Come and see.' They came and saw where he was staying, and *they remained with him* that day" (1:39). They, who began by searching for a place, find that their search leads them to a person: "They remained with him." "Where do you stay?" may be the theological question we ask at the beginning of our spiritual journey—when we "enter" marriages, consecrated life, the priesthood, etc. However, "remaining with" the God-revealed-in-Jesus-Christ is where we find the journey must be grounded and directed if we are to find true spiritual fulfillment.

What does it mean to "remain with" Jesus for those of us who have "entered" or are "in" the church today? I have found this question haunting me for the past several years. It has led me to do much reading and writing, seeking and consulting, listening and learning from the insights of others on the spiritual path. Some of this has been helpful, while some has been more of a hindrance—at least to me.

Today, while many people increasingly seem to be alienated from religion in many of its organized and/or institutional expressions, peoples' search for intimacy with God and meaning continues unabated. When the likes of *Time* and *Newsweek* feature Jesus on their covers or run articles about "The Search for the Historical Christ," their sales rise dramatically. Newsstand sales of *U.S. News & World Report* increase by 20 to 40 percent when Christ or other religious subjects appear on its covers.[15] Despite the alleged self-centeredness of many in the generation behind mine (the "boomers") and the one behind theirs (Generation X), I continually meet members of these groups seriously seeking engagement with some kind of higher power. An analysis of their approach to God has been well summarized in Wade Clark Roof's *A Generation of Seekers*.[16] He discovered that while many people no longer unquestioningly subscribe to the tenets of their parents' religions, their faith-search is leading them to cross denominational lines and move beyond religious boundaries previously considered taboo.

The first two disciples who follow Jesus are one who goes unnamed[17] and Andrew. John notes that Andrew was Simon Peter's brother (1:40), an indication of the significance of Peter in the community at this time. Andrew "finds" his brother and brings him to Jesus. Whether he comes eagerly or otherwise John doesn't tell us. However, we are told that Simon gets renamed by Jesus "Cephas (which is translated Peter)" (1:40-42). Demonstrating John's stress on the centrality of Jesus and the need for disciples to "remain with" Jesus rather than with Peter (or anyone else), nothing further is said about the meaning of the new name; this is markedly different from what we find in the Synoptics (especially Matthew). While John acknowledges Peter's uniqueness in the wider church, he has no need to underscore it as seems to be the case today. Any place that Peter—or any other disciple—holds must be subservient to that of Jesus.

"The next day," the community of disciples gets expanded. Jesus "finds" Philip. Philip was from Bethsaida, the town of Andrew and Peter. He, in turn, "finds" Nathaniel. Now, however, the dynamic moves beyond simple seeking and sighting, questions and answers. John begins to make it clear that any seeking and sighting must involve more than ordinary "seeing" and that questions and answers must lead to a relationship.

By the time John's first chapter ends, Jesus has been called virtually every name attributed to him in the entire corpus of the Synoptic gospels. The significance of the fact that John begins the gospel featuring the titles it takes many chapters in the Synoptics to reveal—and then goes beyond these—was brought home to me a few years ago.

This time my search had led me to a talk by a very well-known member of the U.S. hierarchy. He was the seventh of nine speakers in a nine-month grouping of talks entitled "The Jesus Series." This had been organized, in part, to address questions raised by "The Jesus Seminar," a group of scripture scholars trying to determine the historical accuracy of words and deeds attributed to Jesus.

Because I had been struggling with the identity and role of this "Jesus" in my own life, I genuinely looked forward to what the bishop would say. He began his talk on "Christ and the Church" by noting the various titles given to Jesus in the first chapter of John's gospel: The Word with God, Jesus Christ, Only Son, the Messiah, the Lamb of God, the One Who Baptizes with the Holy Spirit, the Son of God, Rabbi (which translated means Teacher), the Messiah (which is translated Anointed), the one "about whom Moses in the law and also the prophets wrote," "Son of Joseph from Nazareth," and King of Israel. Noting that the image of Jesus revealed in all the many chapters of the Synoptic gospels is fully presented in John's first chapter, he went on to say that this was John's way of "taking the theology of Jesus further" than christology to his ecclesiology, from his understanding of the Christ to that of the Church.[18]

My initial reaction of pleasure at his insights soon dampened. Within five minutes the topic had changed. We moved into the epistles of Paul and their notions about Christ's mystical body, the church. This was followed by talk about "the church" from the perspective of "the Fathers," Robert Bellarmine, and the documents of the Vatican Council. As he proceeded he talked about "the church" as ontically connected to Christ in the Spirit, about "the church" as a "perfect society," etc.

I left the presentation deeply disappointed. I had come wanting to hear about "*Christ* and the Church" from this highly respected Roman Catholic churchman. After just a few minutes devoted to Jesus, what I basically heard about was "the church." It made me wonder if I'd ever heard anything from a Jesus-centered Catholic ecclesiastic.[19] I recalled the plaintive words spoken to me by a young adult minister I met some years ago: "You know, Mike, the more I listen to what seem to be the priorities of the leaders of our church and then look at what seem to be the priorities of Jesus Christ, I'm coming to the conclusion that I don't know if I any longer can find Jesus in the church." That night's talk revolved around "the church." I left still searching for Jesus.

What I was looking for was not what I found in the bishop's talk. Disappointed, I left with my question, "Who is Jesus?" still unresolved. I was helped in my quest when I read a quote from Carolyn Osiek in which she made it clear that my question was not to be taken lightly: "In short, while in the other Gospels Jesus calls attention to the absolute claims of the reign of God and evangelizes all who will listen so that they can be attentive to it, in John the person of Jesus functions as central focus that draws all things to himself. Jesus is the full revelation of God, or at least as full as human understanding can absorb."[20]

I know that good christology cannot be separated from ecclesiology and I know that we cannot speak of Jesus without "the Christ." However, I have often found myself asking why it is that so many Catholics are leaving the institutional church to seek for this elusive Jesus and finding him in a "'bible-believing' church."[21] How is it that young people today can make statements like this one made by an intern in my office: "It wasn't until I got out of Catholic high school before I learned that being a Christian means I'm a disciple of Jesus and not just a Catholic"?

As I try to find some sort of balance between "Jesus" and "Christ," I find that the fundamentalists tend to stress "Jesus" while we in Catholicism are preoccupied with "Christ." Those of a more literal persuasion seek an encounter with a Jesus who touches them personally. Those who are professionals in the mainline churches argue details having to do with the historical figure of Jesus or with the understanding of a believing community centuries ago. I find the results of these approaches striking when they are contrasted:

JESUS	/	CHRIST
WORD	/	SACRAMENT
FAITH IN	/	WORKS
BAPTISM	/	EUCHARIST
PERSONAL RELATIONSHIP	/	GRACE
INDIVIDUAL	/	HIERARCHY
PERSONAL BELONGING	/	INSTITUTIONAL BELONGING

The fact that I left the bishop's lecture dissatisfied with the seeming inability of so many contemporary ecclesiastics to truly lead people to Jesus Christ instead of or, at least, along with (which would be better) "the church," brings me to remark on the one title in this chapter that Jesus gave himself. At the end of the first chapter Jesus says to Nathaniel: "Very truly, I tell you, you will see heaven opened and the angels of God ascending and descending upon the *Son of Man*" (1:51). This title serves as a Johannine climax regarding the identity of Jesus as the Christ. John first introduced Jesus as Word in the act of creating the world (1:1-4). The new genesis revealed in the Word made flesh to dwell among us (1:14) and explained in the titles attributed to Jesus by others now reaches its zenith with Jesus' self-identification of himself as "Son of Man."[22]

c. The Mother's Quest; the Son's Query (2:1-12)

Chapter 2 begins by featuring another quest arising from a human need: "On the third day there was a wedding in Cana of Galilee, and the mother of Jesus was there" (2:1). John goes on to tell us that "Jesus and his disciples had also been invited" (2:2). In the first-century Mediterranean world defined by codes of honor and shame, social stratification and conventions determined (1) the selection of marriage partners; (2) the marriage bond itself which the partners celebrated; (3) the immediate conjugal families involved; and (4) the extended family of relationship beyond the immediate families of the bride and groom.[23] While John does not describe the exact connection of Jesus, his mother, or his disciples to the wedding group, it can be assumed that at least some of them (probably Mary and Jesus) fit categories three or four above. Indeed, John Pilch notes that, "the fact that Mary and Jesus do not hesitate to interfere in this wedding to remedy the shortage of wine (John 2:4-7) strongly suggests that they were related to the wedding party. It would be very shameful for non-relative guests to interfere in a wedding."[24]

At an unexpected time the wine gave out (3:3a). The mother of Jesus said to him, "They have no wine" (2:3). At first glance, this might seem to be simply the statement of a fact. However, since no statement in John is simple, it probably reflected social dynamics that were about to come into play if something didn't happen and happen quickly: the hosts would be dishonored if the invited guests were not to have enough of that key ingredient of all weddings—the wine. John uses the word *gynē* to note Jesus' riposte or put-down of his mother in his response. "And Jesus said to her, 'Woman (*gynē*), what concern is that to you and to me? My hour has not yet come'" (2:4).

Free from the overlay of today's mariologies and popular piety, John's story-line describes the dynamics that probably reflect more closely the actual event: women were anonymous. Their sons addressed them not as persons with whom they shared intimacy ("Mother"), but functions: "Woman." Given their unequal standing, Jesus' title for his mother was what any respecting son used for a woman of that culture. Mary's challenge, "They have no wine," receives Jesus' sharp response: "Woman [reminding his mother of her place], what concern is that to you and to me?"

No matter how it is interpreted, Jesus' response to his mother reveals some kind of culturally-laden distance that existed between mothers and their sons. Its very abruptness "draws a sharp line between Jesus and his mother."[25] And while this distance might reflect culturally-conditioned mother-son dynamics, the reader is invited to recognize that theologically, between the one he calls "Father" and himself, no distance at all exists: "My hour has not yet come." As we have already seen, in Jesus, the "hour" represents that moment of intimacy between the Father and the Son wherein the work of God is to be fulfilled.

Jesus' mother then utters her final words in John's gospel. She tells the servants "Do whatever he tells you" (2:5). For current Catholicism—which often seems to be characterized by Marian devotees who appear to be more concerned with private communiques than with divine revelation, with praying the rosary (which doesn't contain this passage as one of its mysteries) than with care about those in need, with quoting what Mary says to her "beloved priests" more than with what she says to the evangelical reader—Mary's "Do whatever he tells you" serves the Johannine purpose of concentrating his whole message on the person of Jesus.

The rest of the story, as they say, is "history." The best wine is served "now" (2:10). The "not yet" becomes the "now." John declares that this "first of his signs (*sēmeion*)" also "revealed his glory" (*doxa*). While this glory intimates Jesus' divine connection, it also produces an effect in his disciples: "they believed in him." In a culture defined by honor and shame, Jesus had saved the bridegroom from disgrace by providing the wine. This "first of his signs" elicits from his own followers an honor directed toward Jesus: they believed in him. The first of the signs, worked on "the third day," anticipates the final sign worked on the third day as well. In both cases, the result is belief on the part of the disciple.

d. Jesus' Quest for True Worshipers (2:13-25)

The core of John's chiastic structure for 1:19-4:54 centers on Jesus' cleansing of the temple. While the other sections indicate various peoples' search in relation to Jesus, here Jesus exposes the corruption of a temple which has become defined by economic interests. In its place he will "raise up" himself as the new temple in which seekers can find identity and meaning. All the Synoptics place this event at the end of Jesus' life and ministry. John's placement of it at the beginning is clearly not meant to serve historical accuracy as much as to make a deeper, theological statement.

For *hoi Ioudaioi* the temple was God's house, the divine dwelling place. But, by this time, the temple also had become a place of enormous economic significance to its officialdom and those of the empire with whom officials colluded. Upon entering the temple, Jesus "found people selling cattle, sheep, and doves, and the money changers seated at their tables. Making a whip of cords, he drove (*exeballein*) all of them out of the temple, both the sheep and the cattle. He also poured out the coins of the money changers and overturned their tables" (2:14-15).

Contrary to the popular conceptions about this event, Jesus did not simply "cleanse" the temple. The word used for the redirection of this place of worship that had been defiled goes deeper. The temple was, as we can see from the Latin word which has its roots in *exeballein*, exorcized. Thus, Jesus' first contact with the main structure of organized religion involves/demands an exorcism of its demonic dimension. The purpose for which the temple had been built—worship of God—had been replaced by the purpose which always has compromised religion from the beginning until now; the bottom line had become the market. "Stop making my Father's house (*oikos*) a marketplace" (2:16). The temple (*hieron*) had become another kind of house (*oikos*) and the religion of the house was now to make money (*oikonomia*).

Having degrees in economics as well as theology, I have found that the main obstacle to authentic religious observance invariably involves some kind of economic bottom line. Religion gets coopted by the marketplace. I discovered this in my first assignment as a young priest in Milwaukee. In my first three years in a "changing parish," one thousand white families left as blacks moved in. No amount of preaching openness and reconciliation could touch the white peoples' fears and anxieties about their property values. In fact, instead of the biblical command to love one's neighbor, property values had become their bottom line. After five years in the parish, I realized that I was unable to preach the "bottom line" of the gospel when people's ideology was being expressed in a culturally defined worship that had come to exalt property over persons. Considering myself a failure, I left to work in the area of social justice, thinking that, if I addressed the structural bottom line of economics itself, a kind of institutional change of heart might more easily bring about change in individuals.

At the Justice and Peace Center in Milwaukee, which I joined in 1973, I ran into the same obstacle—but in an even more subtle way. There, as I began attending shareholder meetings, I found religion actually being replaced by the market. Representing my own province and other church groups, I would attend annual meetings of corporations and propose that their fiscal bottom line be brought into balance with their moral one. Inevitably I'd be told by shareholders: "Go sell your stock." Others would say: "You have no business being here. Go back and stick to the pulpit." Such experiences made it clear for me that, in my "world," the "Father's house" (*oikos tou patros*) had been replaced indeed by another house (*oikos*): the *oikonomia* itself.

That this "bottom line" has become the new religion is clear from a book published as I was writing this book, *Lead Us into Temptation: The Triumph of American Materialism.* In it James B. Twitchell shows quite convincingly that, in our urbanized and secular society, consumerism and materialism have replaced traditional religion. Where our ancestors "went to church" to find meaning and magic, we go to the mall. We are not being led there unwillingly, Twitchell insists: "We are not victims of consumption ... 'getting and spending' is what gives our lives order and purpose."[26] The liturgy for this new religion that has become increasingly globalized is advertising. As "buying and selling" once infiltrated the temple, so now the materialistic creed has infiltrated our churches as well. Not only are we preachers fearful of raising questions about the exploitative nature of present-day capitalism, we cooperate with it. A 1999 Canadian survey of churches reported that half of them actually have had to capitalize on this phenomenon: they have become addicted to gambling-related monies just to survive.[27]

That Jesus was searching for true worshipers is clear from the recollection of his disciples noted by John: "Zeal for your house will consume me" (2:17). While our economy thrives on increasing market share and those whose bottom line is the market are zealous for *oikonomia* in the form of increased dividends and cheaper prices—regardless of the cost to other people or the planet—zeal for his Father's house, and to prepare a place there for his followers, constituted Jesus' search.

Jesus' purging of the the temple with its religion embedded in economics now became a threat to the survival of the "people," but, most especially, the authorities. These authorities had already shown that they would strike back if the temple were to be threatened, as had happened when the Jewish high priest had led an army north to destroy the Samaritan temple when it had been perceived as a threat. Now, in Jesus, a greater threat faced the temple's teachers.

Seeing Jesus' purging of their place of "worship," the religious leaders do not respond with a genuine inquiry about what they might do to change their ways. Rather, their query is a challenge: "What sign can you show us for doing this?" (2:18). Possibly they had not yet heard about Cana; possibly they didn't care. Whatever. In response to their challenge, Jesus retorts: "Destroy this temple (*naos*), and in three days I will raise it up." Now, in the form of another query from the leaders, the questioning continues: "*Hoi Ioudaioi* then said, 'This temple (*naos*) has been under construction for forty-six years, and will you raise it up in three days?'" (2:18).

John tells the reader that "he was speaking of the temple of his body." However, Jesus' words elicited two reactions. In light of the resurrection of his body, "his disciples remembered that he had said this; and they believed the scripture and the word that Jesus had spoken" (2:22). Others' "belief" would remain based on the "signs" (2:23). But to those demanding signs Jesus would not "entrust himself," for he knew what was in the heart of everyone (2:24). Their search for Jesus stopped at signs. In the disciples who believed in the scriptures and his words, Jesus had found true worshipers. For him, true worship involved making him the bottom line.

In this story John clearly shows that the time has now come when God will not be found in a temple-turned-traitor nor in the entrenched and economically-laden religion identified with it but in Jesus and those who participate in his body by professing faith in him.

c'. Nicodemus's Quest/Query for the Reign of God (3:1-36)

The account of Nicodemus's encounter with Jesus is one of the best-known stories in John's gospel. Far from being a mere narration of a religious leader's search for Jesus in "the night," John's description of this representative person of the past was meant to speak to the reality of his community of the 90s as well. In the dialogue between Nicodemus and Jesus, C. K. Barrett reminded us over twenty years ago, "we are made to hear not a conversation between two persons but the dialogue of church and synagogue, in which (according to the Christian view) the former completes and fulfills the latter, which is in consequence superseded."[28] In a parallel vein, we can add that Nicodemus represents the "crypto-Christians" at the time of the Johannine church who were unable to publicly profess their faith in Jesus Christ. Today that group might be those whose need for acceptance in institutional religion keeps them from speaking out regarding their belief in how Jesus would act in today's world and circumstances.

The account begins when "a Pharisee named Nicodemus, a leader of *hoi Ioudaioi*" comes to Jesus by night (3:1). The mention of "night" evokes a darkness defining Nicodemus himself. It represents his inability to "understand" in a way that will lead him to witness publicly to Jesus before the members of his own religious leadership group. It represents his fear of being excluded from their midst. Even though he himself was a temple leader, this fear controlled him. It reminds me of the bishop who told me (privately) of the trepidation of so many U.S. bishops today to publicly profess what they believe for fear of being ostracized or marginalized by their peers—who also live in fear.

Nicodemus, acknowledging Jesus' authority, addresses him with a title of honor: "Rabbi, we know that you are a teacher who has come from God; for no one can do these signs that you do apart from the presence of God" (3:2). While greeting Jesus with the title due a person of higher stature, the fact that Nicodemus then says "we know" (*oida*), indicates that he either comes as a representative of the teachers of Israel (3:10) or identifies himself as part of this group. Although he acknowledges that "these signs" Jesus has performed (yet only one has been performed—at Cana) could not have been done "apart from God," some force keeps Nicodemus from bringing himself to submit to this higher power he has found in the person of Jesus. His "knowing" is intellectual rather than something based on intimacy.

Dismissing Nicodemus's bestowal of honor, Jesus challenges his acknowledgement that "no one" could do the signs Jesus did without coming from God by countering: "Very truly, I tell you, no one can see the kingdom of God without being born from above (*anōthen*)" (3:3). Nicodemus interprets being born "from above" in a literal way and asks: "How can anyone be born after having grown old? Can one enter a second time into the mother's womb and be born?" (3:4).

If baptism represents a decision on the part of the baptized to enter into the earth's womb-waters to come out committed to live in the world according to the model of life proposed by the baptizer, Jesus' baptism involves an entirely new way of life that must be lived by entering the reign of God. Now it becomes clear that the baptism Jesus prescribes must come not just through water, but through the Spirit as well (1:31-33). If, in the beginning, the Spirit hovered over the waters to make things new, being born again demands "being born of water and Spirit" (3:5).

Having heard, but not understanding (unwittingly or intentionally) what Jesus has said about being "born of the Spirit" (3:8), Nicodemus asks a third question of Jesus: "How can these things be?" (3:9). Jesus responds with a further question. It is a question that might well be asked of every one of us professors of religion, theologians, and preachers in our contemporary "Israels": "Are you a teacher of Israel, and yet you do not understand these things?" (3:10).

The follow-up sentence of Jesus in John makes clear that the story of Nicodemus is not simply the story of an encounter between Jesus and a certain closeted cleric. The use of "we" as well as "I" is not meant to convey a magisterial tone. Rather, it reflects the fact that the Johannine community had come to identify itself and its baptism (and its public witness dimension) with Christ in a way that challenged the "crypto-Christians." These might have been the would-be disciples who intellectualized about Jesus or who declared their discipleship but wanted to keep it secret, probably for fear of being excluded from the synagogues. They might have been those who were of the Petrine orientation but found in its approach patterns that deviated from the other-oriented love stressed by the Jesus Christ of the Beloved Disciple yet were afraid to speak out for fear of exclusion as well: "Very truly, I tell you *we* speak of what *we* know and testify to what *we* have seen; yet you do not receive *our* testimony..." (3:11). Not open to act on the testimony offered, those defined by this world (earth-bound) do not believe what speaks to them of the realm above (see 3:12-13). And, if they are not grounded in the realm above, it is impossible for them to give evidence of it below.

At this point, John makes an interpolation. Jesus' words here constitute two of the best-known passages in the entire gospel. Following his assertion that "just as Moses lifted up the serpent in the wilderness, so must the Son of Man be lifted up," Jesus speaks the oft-quoted (and oft-misquoted or misunderstood) words: "For God so loved the world that he gave his only Son, so that everyone who believes in him may not perish but may have eternal life" (3:16).

Probably more ink has been spilled and more debates and conflicts have been waged among Christians regarding this passage than any other scripture passage. Indeed, today, "John 3:16" is not just a scripture passage; it has become a regular feature, hanging as a banner from the stands at almost every major televised sporting event in the United States. Paradoxically, despite our nation's saturation with the verse, a 1994 Barna Research Group survey found that 65 percent of the wider population still did not know what the John 3:16 actually said. More surprisingly, "while 'born-again' Christians—those who say they have made a personal commitment to Jesus and believe they are going to heaven as a result of confessing their sins—fared better than their nonborn-again counterparts, they still had low scores, with only 50 percent understanding John 3:16."[29]

Despite the fact that some question whether Jesus ever actually spoke the words,[30] they are in the text. Furthermore, millions of people have centered their lives around what they (and others) have believed these words to mean. At the same time, others have been threatened with eternal damnation if they do not abide by the verses. Still others remain confused by what they mean. In fact, this one sentence may be one of the most disputed scripture texts in the Bible. It also has become one of the most abused scriptural passages as well as an instrument of religious abuse.

Many times people get so caught up with debates about "who can be saved" based on this passage that they forget how it begins. This was brought home to me very clearly at my Capuchin Franciscan province's provincial chapter in June, 1999. Jerry Johnson, one of our simply professed brothers, was in my small reflection group. When we began discussing salvation and John 3:16 came up, Jerry said: "If someone came to me and said: 'Jesus Christ came into the world to save you and everyone else from your sins,' it really wouldn't make much sense to me. But if someone came and said that Jesus Christ came into the world to show us how much God loves each one of us, that's something that would make all the sense in the world to me."

If we juxtapose 3:16-18 with 3:19-21, we see that God's love for the "world" demands a response from those who live in it. Building on this notion, Mark Stibbe writes:

> If vv. 16-18 present a brief portrait of God, vv. 19-21 present a frank, realistic and decisive portrait of humanity. The verdict (*krisis*) in v. 19 is that people preferred darkness (*skotos*) to light (*phōs*). Here there is irony in the fact that people loved darkness more than light. The word for "loved" is the same as in v. 15 for God's love (*agapaō*). People love darkness because their evil deeds can remain hidden rather than be exposed. However, humanity is faced with a choice: to do evil (*ho phaula prassōn*) or to do the truth (*ho de poiōn ten alētheian*). Those who do evil are of the darkness, but those who do the truth are of the light.[31]

Living in light means living in love (see 1 Jn 2:9-11). In the next section we get a glimpse of an outsider who found in Jesus light, love, and living water.

b′. The Samaritan Woman's/Townspeople's Quest for Belonging (4:1-45)

Mainly because the Synoptic gospels are totally silent about any ministry of Jesus in Samaria, many have concluded that this scene had its true setting, not in the ministry of the historical Jesus, but in the environment of the Johannine community. Just as Jesus' encounter with Nicodemus was meant to reflect problems the Johannine community had with "crypto-Christians," so John's process of reading his ecclesiology into his christology seems to be evidenced here. But just as John could project back from his community to the time of Jesus, so too we can project forward to Jesus' disciples today. It is important that we do this, especially when we consider those whom mainline Christians tend to exclude from their company and institutions.

While having common roots in Moses and sharing faith in the five historical books attributed to him in the Hebrew scriptures, Jews and Samaritans shared little or nothing else (except mutual suspicion and hostility). Samaritans had descended through intermarriage between the Israelites of the Northern Kingdom and pagan colonists brought in by the Assyrian conquerors. Thus their religion was Mosaic but overlaid with pagan accretions. They worshiped God on Mount Gerizim because, about one hundred years before this, *hoi Ioudaioi* had destroyed their temple. As with the Bosnians (Catholic) and the Serbs (Orthodox) and the English-speaking and French-speaking in Quebec, mutual suspicion and historical mistrust dominated dynamics between the people of the two groups.

The story begins by noting that, on Jesus' trip from Judea to Galilee, "he had to go through Samaria" (4:4). At this time, two routes connected Judea and Galilee, the shorter through Samaria and the longer via the other side of the Jordan. The fact that Jesus *had* to go through Samaria seems less a matter of human demand than of "Johannine necessity," less a geographic description than an ideological sign. Jesus had to go through this alien geographic territory to show that the fullness of his message was unfettered by any traditional or human categories. Driven in this way, Jesus' journey brought him to Sychar, near the place Jacob had given Joseph. It was the site of "Jacob's well." Since it was about noon, Jesus decided to sit by the well.

Everything starts off as expected. The traditional cultural patterns and social customs governing interactions between men and women, Jews and Samaritans, serves as the context for the opening encounter. A Samaritan woman comes to draw water. Jesus, the male, using the imperative, says to her, "Give me a drink." The Samaritan woman says to him, "How is that you, a Jew, ask a drink of me, a woman of Samaria?" For the reader unfamiliar with Jewish ways and mores, John parenthetically remarks: "Jews do not share things in common with Samaritans" (4:7, 9).

That Jesus, the Jew, initiates the conversation shows that he is not one to be controlled by cultural and social norms, much less by the religious conventions meant to uphold them. Indeed, Jesus seems to ignore the traditional patterns which demand that men keep women "in their place." In the narration of this unique story, John seems to sum up Jesus' overall approach to women: He calls them in a way that leads to their belief in him and their resulting public ministry in spite of male dynamics oriented to keep them in their traditional roles.[32]

While it is true that Jesus' request for a drink gets expressed as a demand, reflecting the male treatment of women as servants in that era, the woman does not react by drawing away from Jesus. Rather, she reminds him of society's boundaries between Jews and Samaritans. At this, Jesus invites her to go deeper, to recognize who it is who is asking. He is no ordinary "Jew." His request for a drink should really have elicited a deeper question from her: "If you knew the gift of God, and who it is that is saying to you, 'Give me a drink,' you would have asked him, and he would have given you living water" (4:10).

When people become so used to dipping for water stored in a cistern, the promise of living water must be very inviting. However, since religious notions of *hoi Ioudaioi* were embedded in the very culture, again the woman returns to the traditional cultural patterns—as well as a superficial way of understanding. She replies, "Sir, you have no bucket, and the well is deep. Where do you get that living water? Are you greater than our ancestor Jacob, who gave us the well, and with his sons and his flocks drank from it?" (4:11-12).

Linking this story with the "water and Spirit" that enables people to be born again, Jesus now elaborates on the "living water" that only he can provide: "Everyone who drinks of this water will be thirsty again, but those who drink of the water that I will give them will never be thirsty. The water that I will give will become in them a spring of water gushing up to eternal life" (4:13-14). The woman's response now echoes every reader's deepest longing: "Sir, give me this water, so that I may never be thirsty or have to keep coming here to draw water" (4:15). Where hers was a superficial reaction, the reader's searching heart knows what the words really mean: In Jesus the cistern can bring forth abundant life.

Jesus' response to the woman's request is an example of one of John's literary devices: a total change of subject. Rather than commenting on her request for the "living water" that he has told her he can provide, he says: "Go, call your husband, and come back" (4:16). After denying that she has a husband and hearing Jesus agree with her—but from an entirely different perspective—the woman realizes this Jewish man is able to probe the depths of peoples' ways. She moves from calling him "Sir" to acknowledging him as "a prophet" (4:19).

Despite a gradual change in her heart, the woman still appears trapped by her culture's religio-cultural patterns. She reverts to the "them" and "us" exchanges Jews and Samaritans used in their challenge-riposte repartees: "Our ancestors worshiped on this mountain, but you say that the place where people must worship is in Jerusalem" (4:20). From the context it is likely that, while the two of them spoke, Jesus and the woman could see the ruins of the Samaritan temple that had been destroyed some 150 years before. As the narrative develops in this geographical setting, it becomes clear that its story line goes deeper than discussions about any physical ruin. It involves another kind of boundary, that of a decaying religion and its dying spirit in the face of life.

The woman's comments about the traditional places for worship of God serve as a lead-in to Jesus' rejection of geographically-defined (and disputed) sites. True worship demands the transfer of loyalties and "bottom lines" once identified with specific institutions, "isms," and ideologies to a higher power. Jesus declares: "The hour is coming when you will worship the Father neither on this mountain nor in Jerusalem." The Johannine concept of worship as an internal "prostration" (*proskunein*) serves as a critique of all those forms of worship which stress rituals without heart. Not confining the worship of God to any geographic place (Jerusalem or the Mount near Sechem) or institutional leaders ("ancestors") connected to those places, true worshipers will worship "in spirit and truth." The God that religion often identifies by place and group now will be found in "spirit, and those who worship him must worship in spirit and truth" (4:21-24).

The woman's response to Jesus indicates she has begun to recognize in him someone more than just another Jew or even a prophet. That something "more" does not make her defensive. Rather, it leads her to raise a point about her messianic hopes: "I know that Messiah is coming" (and, for the reader who doesn't know what the Jewish term means, John notes of the Messiah that he "is called Christ"). "When he comes, he will proclaim all things to us" (4:25).

Just when things are moving toward a possible profession of faith from the woman, we get a Johannine "Just then." John tells us "Just then his disciples came." They bring with them their cultural taboos and religious mores. "They were astonished that he was speaking with a woman, but no one said [to her] 'What do you want?' or [to Jesus] 'Why are you speaking with her?'" (4:27). However, if the disciples, who have been with him all this time, are still overly bound by their cultural stereotypes, the woman rises above hers. In so doing she leaves her water jar, goes back to the city, and says to the people (conveniently forgetting Jesus'

Jewishness): "Come and see a man who told me everything I have ever done! He cannot be the Messiah, can he?" (4:29).

Her invitation to her townspeople, "Come and see," echoes Jesus' own words to his first disciples (1:46). The fact that John places Jesus' words on her lips indicates that he sees her as a true disciple. Despite the fact that Jesus had exposed her very soul, he did it in a redemptive way that empowered her to believe. With her question "He cannot be the Messiah, can he?" the woman moves from being an individual having an audience with Jesus to becoming a representative of every one of us who reads what happened. Here is a person who has come to the well doing "business as usual." After her encounter with Jesus, she leaves her water jar (v. 28), just as the first male disciples left their primary mode of work. She then becomes a witness of faith to others who are involved in their "usual business," and she witnesses in a way that makes them become seekers as well.

On hearing the woman's witness, "they left the city and were on their way to him" (4:30). They went "on their way *to him*," not to Sechem. The priority now becomes clear. In John, faith is defined not by place but by a person. Furthermore, unlike Jesus' disciples (of a Jewish background which limited the way men and women interacted), the Samaritans were not bound by the Jewish rabbinic codes regarding the treatment of women in public, religious, and legal spheres. However ignoble she may have been in the eyes of some Jews who would have regarded her as an intrinsically incompetent witness, the woman was not questioned or challenged by the villagers (4:28-30). This indicates that her witness was sufficiently credible for them to believe in her.[33]

"Many" believed in him because of the testimony of the woman (4:39). "Through her testimony," the goal of bringing others to Christ had begun to be realized. These "many" more had come to Jesus because of the woman's word. Now they believed in him, not because of her testimony, but because of their own experience. Hearing him had led them to know that this was "truly the Savior." While Nicodemus heard Jesus declare that "the world might be saved through him" (3:17), these people could acknowledge publicly what Nicodemus could not: "We know that this is truly the Savior [not just of the Samaritans or even *hoi Ioudaioi*, but] of the world" (4:41-42). What the many Samaritans professed echoes what John had written earlier as a summary of Jesus and John's gospel about him. It touches on the universal as well as the cosmic implications of Jesus:

> The true light, which enlightens everyone, was coming into the world. He was in the world, and the world came into being through him; yet the world did not know him. He came to what

was his own, and his own people did not accept him. But to all
who received him, who believed in his name, he gave power to
become children of God, who were born, not of blood or of the
will of the flesh or of the will of man, but of God. (1:10-13)

In this passage from the Prologue, the word for world, *kosmos*, is
used for the first time by John, and it appears twice. The next time it appears is at the beginning of the body of the first section of the Johannine
narrative. John the Baptist refers to Jesus as "the Lamb of God who
takes away the sin of the world" (1:29). In his meeting with Nicodemus,
Jesus declares: "For God so loved the world that he gave his only Son,
so that everyone who believes in him may not perish but may have eternal life" (3:16). Now the term *kosmos* is used for the fifth time here at
Sechem, with people rejected by those who considered themselves true
religionists. The cosmic and universal dimension of Jesus gets acknowledged by outsiders: "We have heard for ourselves, and we know that this
is truly the Savior of the world" (4:42). The universal implication of
Jesus' salvation—for the world—becomes clear. Rudolf Schnackenburg
notes:

> The Samaritans, who are regarded by the Jews as half Gentile,
> appear as representatives of the non-Jewish world. If Jesus is the
> "savior of the world"—a sonorous title that emphasizes the uni-
> versal significance of the person of Jesus—the boundaries of the
> Jewish way of thinking and Jewish religiosity (cf. 4:21-24) have
> been crossed and a broad horizon for all humankind is opened.[34]

In the first century, "savior" was a term used for people honored by
others, people such as teachers, philosophers, or leaders of some kind.
However, in John's cultural world, the phrase "Savior *of the world*" was
used exclusively of the Roman Emperor.[35] To call anyone else by this imperial title was tantamount to subversion. The allegiance of the Samaritans who transferred to Jesus the title used by the head of the current ruling power, Rome, contrasts with the attitude of the members of Jesus'
own "household," who knew what they had to lose if their belief were to
result in accepting the baptism that would take away their sin and the sin
of the world. For the reader of any era, the challenge is the same: belief
in Jesus as "Savior of the world" has economic, political, and religious
consequences.

In a 1998 visit to Vienna, Pope John Paul II alluded directly to this
fact when he addressed fifty thousand people assembled in Heldenplatz
(Heroes' Square), the site where several hundred thousand Austrians
greeted Hitler after the Anschluss in 1938. There the Pope reminded his

audience: "Sixty years ago a man declared himself the Savior. The new saints carry another message: Salvation is not in man, but in Christ."[36]

In the face of any imperial magisterium or any sovereignty, be it secular or spiritual, political or papal, John's gospel makes one thing clear: Jesus alone reigns. He is the savior, the one who makes the world whole. Those who proclaim him by this title in effect have transferred any ultimate allegiance they may have given to any other "savior" in the world to him alone. In so doing they stand as subversive to any power that would ever again assume, in theory or behavior, that title.[37]

a'. The Royal Official's Quest of Jesus to Take away the Sickness of His Son (4:46-54)

The final section of this first triadic structure in John finds Jesus going "from that place to Galilee." While some had definitely sought Jesus and even testified on his behalf, the wider "world" had not. So he left "that place." "That place" in Jesus' "world" had not received him. In Galilee he was welcomed because "they had seen all that he had done in Jerusalem at the festival; for they too had gone to the festival" (4:43-45). The specific place where he arrived was "Cana in Galilee where he had changed the water into wine" (4:46a). Thus, Jesus completes his first journey as recorded in John. He began in Cana; he now returns there.

The royal official who comes to Jesus there is representative of "the world" that exists beyond *hoi Ioudaioi*. Once again John makes it clear that, as with Nicodemus and *hoi Ioudaioi*, there are always exceptions to the "theys" that we tend to lump into one category. As Nicodemus was a religious official, this man is a "royal official," someone connected to the empire quite directly. Both represent individuals within authoritative systems who recognize a higher authority and acknowledge it by deferring to the higher power they find in Jesus. However, unlike the religious official who was not able to "understand" (3:10), the royal official was able to understand the implications of this in a way that affected his whole world, i.e., his son, himself and, indeed, his whole household.

By ending this section with the story of the royal official submitting himself to Jesus (and thus acknowledging Jesus as savior of "the world"), John suggests how the reader is to respond: The savior of the world, the one who makes the world whole, invites acknowledgment. Although Jesus initially challenged the royal official who came to him with a need, "Unless you see signs and wonders you will not believe," (4:48), given this second sign, the royal official did believe "and his whole household" as well. This contrasts with those officials of religion who see signs and wonders and still do not believe. Whether readers will respond in the pattern of the royal official or the religious official will be up to them.

TWO

DO YOU WANT TO BE HEALED? (5:6)

The Question of John 5:1-47

Until now in John's gospel Jesus has been free of serious conflict
with anyone. At the most a few misunderstandings have occurred. Even
after his cleansing of the temple (2:13-22), he is not directly challenged
(as he is in the Synoptics); rather, *hoi Ioudaioi* only query him about the
authority behind his actions (see 2:18-20). However now, in chapter 5, all
hell breaks loose.

The healing of the man outside the temple in a way that enabled him
to be brought back into it—and the fact that this was done on the sabbath
—resulted in the temple leaders' resolution to kill Jesus. Their decision
was not so much to take his life as to save their own within a system that
demanded their loyalty to protect itself. While the man was healed, the
sickness in their own religious system was exposed. In protesting Jesus'
sabbath healing, they showed themselves to be violating the very purpose
of the sabbath they had been ordained to preserve.

John's story about the opposition between Jesus and the leaders of
the past reflects not only the dynamics between the early community and
the Jewish temple, but also the conflict the Johannine community was experiencing with the religious leaders of the wider church. The chapter as
we have it now likely existed as part of a wider collection of sabbath
healing stories dealing with issues of authority and power between members of the Community of the Beloved Disciple and the Petrine group
whose leaders seem to have adopted the very same power dynamics of
hoi Ioudaioi that had been rejected by Jesus.

The story begins with a healing on the sabbath (5:2-9). It ends with
the argument between Jesus and the crowds about their intent to kill him
for working the cure on the sabbath and making himself "equal to God"
(5:18; 7:19-23). In this story the core issue raised by the author has to do
with how the healing of one person exposes the entrenched disease in the
wider body. Jesus' work of healing not only restores individuals who are
paralyzed, it touches the nerve that exposes the paralysis of the entire system, a paralysis that must also be healed. Indeed, if Rudolf Schnacken-

burg is correct that John highlighted the sabbath theme deliberately "as an act of provocation,"[1] this first truly public act of healing by Jesus will be a subversive act, an act of provocation exposing the sickness of the system itself.

The chapter begins with John saying "After this" (meaning after all that has taken place thus far in the previous four chapters), "there was a festival." It was a festival "of *hoi Ioudaioi*." In other words there is already a sense of being separated from the things of *hoi Ioudaioi*. The sense is: "It is *their* festival, not *ours*." Exegetes differ as to which feast was being celebrated.[2] For the reader, the nature of the festival does not matter. What matters is that Jesus' action takes place on the sabbath, the holiest day of the week, a day that is the source of more "dos" and "don'ts" for the average Jew than any other.

John begins by noting that Jesus came into Jerusalem and went to this pool where "many invalids lay" (5:3). The English word the NRSV has chosen for *asthenountōn,* "invalid," points well to the predicament of the "blind, lame, and paralyzed" of that society—or any other culture of that time. Among these was a man who had been ill for thirty-eight years. While no specific illness is ascribed to him, he suffered from something that made him an "invalid." John's failure to give the man a name or a diagnosis might enable the reader to better identify not only with the invalid but with his pathology as well. While the nature of his sickness not described as blindness, lameness, or paralysis, one thing we can say about this invalid is that he seems to have been poor, since his mat (*krabattos*) was a resting place for beggars. We also know from the story as it develops that his poverty had led him to become a beggar—and this further "invalidated" him in that society.

In the Mediterranean culture of Jesus and the community of the fourth gospel, all sickness reflected societal taboos, and physical invalids were social invalids as well. They were "in-valid-ated" by their religion-embedded world. This world was defined by family ties which included one's immediate family as well as more distant kin. It also extended to wider social institutions grounded in familial and kinship units. In such a culture, invalids were the marginalized and rejected of society, its refuse. People with physical ailments threatened a society which perceived itself as being well. And, just as society quarantined me when I got the whooping cough in the 1940s, so first-century society alienated its sick members to keep its "healthy" members from contamination. Personal disease threatened the social order. Individuals exhibiting deviation from the norm had to be segregated to maintain that order.

The connection between individual pathology and social invalidation must be grasped if we are to understand the dynamics involved not only at the personal level, but, more important, at the cultural level of social relationships related to sickness and disease in chapter 5 and elsewhere in the gospel.

The Anthropology of Being an Invalid

A growing number of scholars have recently begun examining scripture in terms of the cultural context of the environment that gave rise to the texts. Almost all of these scholars are indebted to the pioneering work of the cultural anthropologist Mary Douglas.

Douglas found that sickness, such as that described in the scriptures, carried with it corporate as well as individual implications, that there was a connection between physical ailments and cultural pathology. In cultures such as that of Jesus, the natural body and the corporate body, the individual and the collective, reproduced and reinforced reciprocal images of one another. The social order was an extension of the individual, and, on the micro-level, the individual expressed the macro-level of the group. In a well known passage Douglas declares:

> The human body is a model which can stand for any bounded system. Its boundaries can represent any boundaries which are threatened or precarious. The body is a complex structure. The functions of its different parts and their relations afford a source of symbols for other complex structures. We cannot possibly interpret rituals concerning excreta, breast milk, saliva, and the rest unless we are prepared to see in the body a symbol of society, and to see the powers and dangers credited to social structures reproduced in small on the human body.[3]

If social structures are reproduced at the micro-level in the human body, the human body reflects the macro-level of the social structure. Thus, to find diseases and cures, illness and healing, sickness and wellness in one without examining their source or manifestation in the other is to ignore the complexity of meaning these stories had for first-century hearers or readers of the gospel. Invalids such as those consigned to the porticoes of the temple cannot be considered apart from the cultural institutions in which their religion was embedded. This culture had defined them as "invalidated," without honor, and thus unworthy to enter into the inner places of the temple. Conversely, the invalidation projected on the invalid was often designed to keep the invalid in that condition, because a system that considers itself "healthy" and "whole" must have scapegoats to convince itself of its own wholesomeness and integrity.

The scripture scholar who has done more than anyone else to connect anthropological insights about people's disease with cultural perspectives of the first-century Mediterranean world is John Pilch. While Pilch acknowledges his indebtedness to Mary Douglas, he has also been influenced by the works of Allan Young[4] and Ronald Frankenberg,[5] medical anthropologists whose research has uncovered different classifications of pathology. I have found these classifications to be quite helpful in understanding the story of the man at the pool.

John's world considered pathology (always connected to sin) in terms of three interconnected, ever-larger concentric circles: disease, illness, and sickness. While we might not find perfect a conjunction with words used for pathologies in John, I find meaning in seeing the three terms expressed as *nosēma, astheneia,* and a derivative of the latter, *asthenountōn.*

Nosēma (5:4 [used only here in John]), or *disease,* refers to physical conditions in terms of the biomedical model. It identifies abnormalities in the structure or operations of various organs and systems of organs. To use an example from our own culture, a doctor would look at AIDS as a disease that is transmitted through blood transfers.

Astheneia (4:46; 5:5, 7; 11:1, 2, 4, 6), or *illness,* has to do with the way a pathology is experienced and understood by the patient. It identifies the condition in terms of the person's perceptions and experience of the disease, especially in light of how that disease is understood by the person's wider circle of family, friends, and acquaintances. In our culture, many people with AIDS would be reluctant to reveal that they have the disease because of the ways this wider circle might react to the "why" and "how" of the disease rather than the "what."

Asthenountōn (5:3; 6:2), or *sickness* ("sick ones") serves as a cultural tool for socializing both disease and illness;[6] this is what truly makes one an "invalid." It identifies disease by redefining the symptoms of the biomedical model and identifies illness by focusing on the underlying dynamics of people with this condition in terms of their social interactions. When cultural anthropologists apply the sickness model to persons with AIDS, they view them as a subgroup within a wider system that defines them in terms of aberrations and reacts to them in fear as social outcasts.

Sickness, to use the words of Frankenberg, relates to the "cultural performance" (how one "does" in a particular culture; how the culture gives the disease and/or illness meaning) of the one suffering the disease and illness.[7] He notes:

> To me sickness is the key concept since it provides the social and cultural framework for the anthropologist to analyze the social consequences of illness and disease that are in this sense secondary. Disease depends on the existence of the social organization of biologists and the medically trained, and illness on a socially constructed sense of self, which certainly does not exist in

the same form in all societies. Sickness as cultural performance can be analyzed in all societies even if a specific performance may be the denial of disease and the absence of illness.[8]

In the New Testament world, those who were sick were "treated" not as people with viruses and in need of vaccines and vaccinations, but as people whose social relations were askew. Proper treatment for such people would be to quarantine them, to isolate them from others. In the face of sickness, society did not ask "what" might be the cause. It sought a "who," someone to blame (the person's own sin or inherited sin, or evil spirits). The sick became society's scapegoats. On them was placed everyone's fear of being contaminated. Consequently, they could be excluded from "the world."

Do You Want to Be Made Well?

Within this cultural setting, "Jesus went up to Jerusalem" from Galilee (5:1). In an aside[9] which also reveals that John's audience might not have been familiar with Hebrew, the author states: "Now in Jerusalem by the Sheep Gate there is a pool, called in Hebrew Bethzatha, which has five porticoes" (5:2).

According to Craig Koester, this pool was considered to have healing powers like the Greco-Roman healing shrines to the gods Ascleppius and Serapis. If this was the case, the author might have been suggesting that the temple itself was diseased so seriously and its religious corruption was so malignant that the people had turned to Hellenistic healing practices to compensate for the lack in their own religious system.[10] A parallel exists today when people increasingly seek alternative ways to find healing in their lives in face of the bankruptcy of their own religious institutions whose leaders can only loudly caution against such alternative ways as being alien to traditional practice.

John's mention of the long number of years that the man had been sick indicates that he suffered from something chronic. "When Jesus saw him lying there and knew that he had been there a long time, he said to him, 'Do you want (*thelein*) to be made well (*hygiēs*)?'" (5:6). The word Jesus uses points not to a particular disease but to the condition that created the ill-health in the first place. Had Jesus limited himself to healing the man's sick body, it's likely the word *therapeuein* (for "cure" [5:10]) would have been used. Knowing this invalid's sickness rests in the deeper invalidation of his society, Jesus goes beyond asking if the man wants to be "cured." He asks if he wants to be "made well."

Instead of responding to Jesus' question, the man explains why he is diseased: "Sir, I have no one to put me into the pool when the water is stirred up (*tarassein*); and while I am making my way, someone else steps down ahead of me" (5:7). The man's personally and socially disvalued state is further complicated by a failure in his underlying social relations. His response reveals an admission to colossal cultural failure: "Sir, I have no one to put me into the pool when the water is stirred up" (5:7). If his kin have abandoned him, that is too bad, John Pilch notes. However, if he has made no friends in a culture where survival depends upon making friends, that is a worse shame.[11]

Because he had been sick for thirty-eight years, the man is so accustomed to being an invalid that he isn't able to perceive what it would mean for him—as well as for his social relations—to be validated. Maybe, deep down, he is afraid to be well. As Mark Stibbe has noted, "People who have been sick for that length of time often become so dependent on others that the very idea of healing, which of course means relinquishing such dependence, is threatening."[12]

Stibbe's insight makes me think of "Francis Baker."[13] I first met Francis in the early 1980s. He seemed to be an engaging young man. However, as I got to know him better, he began telling me of the pain he carried within him as a result of a very pathological family situation. Everything he could remember about his childhood revolved around the experience of being "invalidated" by his father. Mr. Baker was recognized as an upstanding Catholic, but a side of him the public did not see hid a compulsive gambler, a person filled with rage, and a parent who physically and emotionally battered his offspring.

Mr. Baker fathered many children. By the time Francis was born he took an almost immediate dislike of him. He treated Francis very differently from the way he had treated the other children. He'd put him on the porch in the middle of bitterly cold winter nights without a coat and he would raid his paper route monies to pay off his gambling debts. He even thrust Francis's hand into the lit burner on the stove.

For almost fifteen years, I heard Francis relate the litany of such past incidents with as much power as though they had just happened. In his mind, he was "sick" because of the "illness" of his parents. The rage revealed a deep bitterness toward his father (and anger at his mother for her apparent enablement of the father's behavior).

Eventually, however, finally tired of being eaten up by his resentments, Francis decided to embark on a serious effort to embrace Twelve Step Spirituality into his life. He got through the first three steps: he recognized his powerlessness and the fact that his life was unmanageable; he came to realize that a power greater than his could deliver him from his pathological resentment; and he made a conscious choice to turn his life over to the care of God as he had come to understand this God to be. Now he realized he had to address his resentments, to take the fourth and fifth steps: to do a complete moral inventory and then to admit to himself and to another the exact nature of the wrongs he had committed.

There came a point where Francis told me to be ready for a phone call so that he could take the fifth step. Not long after this, I got the call. He was ready, and he wanted to know when I would be available. When we found the right time, he called me in Milwaukee and began with an exact inventory of all the things about which he was resentful. However, as he shared the account of the violence done him as a child, his description seemed to me to be colored with the same anger and resentment that I had heard time after time before.

Aware of this, I took a risk and interrupted the flow of Francis' train of thought. "Francis," I said, "can I ask you something?"

"Sure, Mike," he said. "What do you want to ask?"

"Well, Francis," I answered, "I know I should just let you tell me everything, and I do want to hear it all. But how I'm hearing you tell me these things about your father and mother doesn't sound any different from the way you've told me this before. It seems like the same anger and resentment of the past is still with you." Suddenly, I remembered the gospel story about the man at the pool, and I found myself recalling it for Francis.

"Do you remember the story of the invalid at the pool, the man who had lain there for thirty-eight years?"

"Yes," he answered.

"Well, Francis," I continued, "the story has it that this man was stuck there as an invalid all those years. And then Jesus came and asked him: 'Do you want to be healed?' For some reason, I'm reminded of this passage as I listen to you tell me all about the pain that's paralyzed you all these years."

After a short interval, I decided to take another risk: "Francis, I'm wondering if you could imagine yourself as the man hearing this question: 'Do you really want to be healed?' What will happen to you, to your self and to your relationship with your parents, if you really get healed?"

There was a long pause at his end of the phone. "Oh my gosh," he said. "I don't know what I'd do. I've carried this pain for so long. I don't know how I'd live if I were to be free of my resentments." And then, after another pause, Francis said: "Mike, I don't think I'm really ready to be healed. We'll have to wait to do that fifth step. Is that okay with you?"

The Man Diseased, Ill, and Sick Is Cured, Made Well, and Restored

In response to the man's rationale for his continued pathology, "Jesus said to him, 'Stand up, take your mat and walk.' At once the man was made (*egeneto*) well (*hygiēs*)..."(5:8-9a). The use of the word *egeneto*, "made," with *hygiēs* might lead a reader familiar with Greek to recall images of the first creation when order was brought from chaos. As in the beginning, when the Word entered the world and all was made well so that God could have a sabbath rest, so now John's statement about the former invalid cannot be limited to what happened to his body alone. Through his restoration the body of creation itself experienced a new kind of transformation. Like creation itself, he has been "made well," restored from his chaotic state to wholeness. Furthermore, his individual healing has helped make creation whole. Now cured, he is restored to health: "He took up his mat and began to walk" (5:9b). He can now be an upright member of the community.

In a culture concerned about *curing* diseases and *healing* illnesses, Jesus questioned whether the man wanted to be *hygiēs*, made well or whole, of his disease. Any healing of this invalid who had been "invalidated" by society would have consequences on his standing in his society, in his world. If he were to be "made well," he would not just be cured or even healed; he would no longer be "invalidated" by society but restored to it fully whole. Thus, when Jesus said, "Stand up, take your mat and walk," he was validating him to participate in an upright manner in his world.

The chart below, while not being slavish to the Greek words which classify pathologies, highlights the interplay of the dynamics that took place in the man when he moved from being an invalid and, therefore, "invalidated," to being cured in a way that made him whole:

LEVELS OF BEING INVALID(ATED)	LEVELS OF BEING MADE WHOLE
DISEASE (*nosēma*). "Where does it hurt?"	CURE (*therapeuein*). The symptoms are gone.
ILLNESS (*astheneia*). "Who is to blame?"	HEALING (*hygiēs*). Being made well.
SICKNESS (*asthenountōn*). "How does it affect society?"	MADE WELL (*iasthai*). Relationships made right.

Had John ended the story with this "sign" (*sēmeion*), there would be nothing more to say about this chapter. But, in fact, the story continues as the author reminds the reader: "Now that day [on which he was made well] was a sabbath" (5:9c). Because of this, *hoi Ioudaioi* challenged the man.

Pathologically blinded by their legalistic interpretation of the sabbath, the religious officials were unable to recognize fulfillment occurring before their eyes. Looking at this man, they could see only that his *disease* had been *cured*. Not only did his *healing* take away his *illness*; the fact that he had been *made well* threatened their control over *sickness* itself. All this threatened to undermine their very system which in many ways depended on people being diseased. Reacting to this threat, they challenged "the man who had been cured (*therapeuein*), 'It is the sabbath; it is not lawful for you to carry your mat'" (5:10).

Sabbath "work" covered different activities, such as planting and plowing, weaving and kneading, which were prohibited. In following Jesus' orders to transport his bed, the man was violating the last of the thirty-nine classes of work by carrying an object from one place to another. The religious leaders react to his being made well by seeing him, not as someone who has been restored to society, but as an accomplice in doing something that should not have been done on the sabbath. Thus, they further invalidate him as one who has broken the law: "It is the sabbath; it is not lawful for you to carry your mat" (5:10).

Unable to accept responsibility for his own behavior as a person now healed, the man shifts the accountability to the one who healed him. "He answered them, 'The man who made me well (*hygiēs*) said to me, 'Take up your mat and walk.'" And, like all inquisitors who query a person on trial (and this is part of the overall trial dimension of John's gospel), "they asked him, 'Who is the man who said to you, 'Take it up and walk?'" (5:11-12).

At this point John—as the omniscient author—declares: "Now the man who had been healed (*iasthai*) did not know who it was" (5:13a). This Greek word for healing, *iasthai*, is unique in the gospel. Here *iasthai* means "to be restored to right relationships." Such restoration represents the deepest healing of all: to be made whole, to be one with family, to be part of all creation. The healed man didn't know exactly who it was that had healed him, John explains, "for Jesus had disappeared in the crowd that was there" (5:13b). Here, as elsewhere in John, Jesus is somewhat elusive. In time, John tells us, "Jesus found (*hereuskein*) him in the temple." He who had lain for years "invalidated" and kept outside, among the five porticoes, now was inside, in the temple, experiencing a new validation from the one who had made him whole. Finding the man, Jesus said: "See, you have been made well! Do not sin (*mēketi hamartane*) any more, so that nothing worse happens to you" (5:14).

At face value, it would seem that here Jesus is parroting the cultural standards that identify sickness with sin (9:2, 34) when he says: "You have been well; do not sin any more." Indeed the statement *is* confusing. And if it is confusing in the text, the attempts of scripture scholars to explain it have been even more so. I have found only one satisfying possibility; it comes from Jeffrey Staley. The man's sin was not linked to his physical condition but to his non-witness regarding the one who made him whole:

> It would appear, then, that the healed man understands Jesus' ambiguous *"Mēketi hamartane"* as somehow a response to his

previous conversation with "*hoi Ioudaioi*," for he seems to return immediately to his interrogators with the new information, "Jesus [i.e., not just anybody] was the one who made me well." And since the narrator had earlier said that many of the people in Jerusalem had believed in Jesus precisely because of his signs (2:23; 3:1-2; 4:45), ironically, the healed man's intentions should be understood positively (cf. 11:45-46; 12:9-11, 17-18). Only the reader and Jesus know enough not to trust the level of belief in the Jerusalemites (2:24; 3:10; 4:1-3, 48). As a result of the healed man's proclamation, however, "*hoi Ioudaioi*" begin to stalk Jesus —because he was doing "these things" on the Sabbath.[14]

For John, the "sin" of those whose lives have been changed by their encounter with Jesus is their fear to testify publicly to their new-found faith in him. Personal faith without social witness is no faith at all. In a parallel way it can be said that "sin" exists when those who have been restored by Jesus to right relationships are unable to give evidence of their faith in face of challenges by the religious leaders. John says in the very next sentence that the one now made whole became an evangelist of the good news: "The man went away and told *hoi Ioudaioi* that it was Jesus who had made him well" (5:15).

Hearing his testimony, *hoi Ioudaioi* turned from challenging the recipient of the healing to attacking the healer himself. Their attack takes the form of *diōkein*. The word *diōkein* can be translated as "to be zealous"; it can also mean "to persecute." "Therefore *hoi Ioudaioi* started persecuting Jesus, because he was doing such things on the sabbath." Their zeal-expressed-in-persecution is echoed in Saul's breathing threats on the way to Damascus (Acts 9:1-9). It is echoed down through the ages in the zeal of every religious leader who, to preserve a sick religious system, persecutes the very ones who might contribute to making it whole.

Healing the body of this invalid was not valid ("invalid") according to the body of the law regarding sabbath observance—as interpreted by the body of the religious leaders. The cultural implications of being made well now become clearer. The implications for the reader are opening up, since, in reader-response, "every character is a trap of a certain kind, one which the writer would like his readers to fall into."[15] With the response of *hoi Ioudaioi* John lays bare the underlying social and systemic disease that resists healing. In the process he is entrapping us so that we can find parallels in our own lives and structures. Where might we still be entrenched in our religious ways that keep us from being healed?

Earlier—and also in the temple—Jesus had identified himself with the Father when he liberated the temple from its pathological patterns (2:13-16). He did this in such a way that "his disciples remembered that it was written, 'Zeal for your house will consume me'" (2:17). Now, with the healing of the invalid during a day on which such work was prohibited by the law, Jesus' zeal to do God's work is met with a parallel zeal on the part of *hoi Ioudaioi* to persecute him: "For this reason *hoi Ioudaioi* were seeking all the more to kill him, because he was not only breaking (*lyein*) the sabbath, but was also calling God his own Father, thereby making himself equal to God" (5:18).

This is the first time we are offered such a high christology. Although being equal to God is what Jesus' opponents say of him, it serves John's purposes.[16] Their characterization of Jesus as "making himself equal to God" will become a major basis of debate between him and *hoi Ioudaioi* as the rest of the gospel evolves. "They regard this as arrogant pretense," Raymond Brown notes, "but the Johannine Jesus 'makes' nothing of himself. He simply *is* the Son and the Father has turned over all things to him, so that whoever refuses to honor the Son refuses to honor the Father (5:19-23)."[17]

The same word used for Jesus' breaking of the sabbath is that used earlier by Jesus in speaking about tearing down (*lyein*) the temple. That statement had elicited John's comment that Jesus was referring to the restoration in his own body (2:21). If Jesus' zeal had led him to make whole the temple and to do the kind of healing that cleansed the law from its obfuscations to get to the heart of *shalom*, it is little wonder that the leaders, sensing the beginning of the peoples' transferring of honor from them to Jesus, would double their efforts to persecute him for violating the sabbath.

This passage contains one of the few instances in which John's gospel mentions "honor" directly. Jesus sees himself as being worthy of honor as is the Father. Consequently, those who dishonor him do "not honor the Father who sent him" (5:23). Not surprisingly, Jesus' opponents find such words a challenge to their own honor. In a culture which considered honor to be a commodity in limited supply, one's honor came at another's expense. Jesus' claim of honor for himself would be interpreted as transferring to him the honor due to the religious leaders. This constituted a real challenge, not just to their honor, but to their very life in the community.

The Sabbath and Shalom: Ushering in the New Creation

In the Aramaic of Jesus' day, according to J. Duncan M. Derrett, *holos* involved a kind of wholeness. In Greek the parallel word was *hygiēs*. In either language the image of Jesus making the man whole on the sabbath suggests notions connected with *selim* or *shalom*. Being made whole or being made well was part of the purpose of the *shabath* whose ultimate goal was *shalom*.[18] People restored to health were seen to be in "a *state* of complete well-being and not merely the absence of disease or infirmity." When Jesus healed the body of the man on the sabbath, *hygiēs* was being produced, and not just for an individual. It was a sign that the sabbath itself was achieving its purpose. The restoration of the corporate body resulting in *shalom* was clearly at hand. In terms of this cultural/ meaning model, not only was the body of the man restored, but creation itself was made more whole, brought to a fuller sense of well-being, achieving its *shalom*.

This insight into biblical *shalom* as representative of the fullness of health was captured in 1996 in a powerful document prepared by the Catholic Health Association of Canada:

> Of all the biblical words related to health, healing and whole-ness, the one around which most of the others are formed is *shalom*. In the Old Testament, this term receives its meaning in the context of the exodus, the defining event in which God re-veals his intent to save and heal Israel and give it *shalom*. Yah-weh sees the suffering of his people and hears their cry.
>
> *Shalom* extends to all of creation. "All of creation is one, every creature in community with every other, living in harmony and security toward the joy and well-being of every other crea-ture." Such a vision suggests that *shalom* and salvation share similar meanings. In fact, the Hebrew word *yeshe*, which is most often translated "salvation," also expresses a broad, holistic con-cept which may more properly be translated as "health." Throughout the Hebrew Bible, what is at issue is the problem of human brokenness and how we can be restored to health and wholeness...
>
> Healing has to do with restoring our bonds with the deepest parts of ourselves and experiencing harmony within ourselves, with society and the Earth. It is at these deeper levels that soul lives. One of the challenges we face today is to bring soul back into our discussion of health and healing. It means paying atten-tion to the inner life, developing, and in some instances recover-ing, ways of feeding and nurturing the soul.[19]

The religious leaders were keepers and interpreters of the sabbath for the good of the souls (*ruah*) of the people. Their own economic liveli-hood (= health) depended on maintaining their status and control over these souls. With Jesus doing such healing, and on a sabbath, their whole system—which depended on others' sickness (= sins)—was being threat-ened. Consequently, they immediately perceived the imperative need to

rid themselves of the threat to their system: "Therefore *hoi Ioudaioi* started persecuting (*diōkein*) Jesus, because he was doing such things on the
sabbath" (5:16).

The reaction of the Jewish leaders to Jesus' action of bringing health
to the invalid can be found at any level of our world when one person's or
group's "health" (survival) depends on preserving sickness in others. The
tobacco industry, for example, depends on people's addiction that it might
stay well (= profitable). Thus, it was not surprising to find in a 1997 internal tobacco document reference to the fact that, in 1982, a worker at the
Tobacco Institute, the lobbying group of the tobacco industry at that time,
had attacked efforts of anti-tobacco education programs which were telling
school children that smoking was dangerous and could lead to disease.
Citing "potential problems" for the industry posed by such programs, she
warned that the strategies meant to show individuals the hazards to health
of smoking "could be hazardous to the tobacco industry's health."[20]

We have seen that *diōkein* means "to persecute." This is what the
leaders started to do in reaction to Jesus' doing "such things on the sabbath." But *diōkein* can also mean "to prosecute." Thus, from now on,
court-room forensics begin to dominate. The prosecution waged by Jesus'
accusers elicits from him his only defense: He "answered them, 'My Father is still working, and I also am working'" (5:17). For Jesus to refer to
his activity of healing on the sabbath as "working" is to identify it with
God's work.

To understand the context for Jesus' response, one must begin by examining the links between work and law, as well as between sabbath and
shalom. For authentic Jews, Hebrew law arose from Israel's creation-
based faith.[21] For *hoi Ioudaioi,* the God of the law was the Creator of the
world. While sabbath law acknowledged the human need for a non-work
day, it was founded on a deeper recognition of God as Lord of the sabbath
and author of creation itself. An offense in the realm of the law thus had
consequences not only in the social realm, but also in the cosmic realm.
The law was established as a means by which the original divine work of
ordering chaos at the cosmic level (creation) might be actualized in the
social sphere (creatures) in order that harmony might prevail.[22]

Aware of the creative purposes of work, the leaders had to have intu-
ited, at the very least, that Jesus' self-defined "work" of healing the invalid not only called into question their exercise of religion, but also undermined the social order over which they presided. If their order was
subverted, their whole "world" was threatened. As in any sick organization, the health of one part threatened the entire whole. It was in the interests of their own "health" that Jesus' healing had to be stopped immediately. Furthermore, since Jesus identified his work with that of God, it
meant that their interpretation of God would no longer be "valid." Conse-

quently they themselves would be "invalidated." This can be the only rationale for their reaction which John states quite clearly: "For this reason *hoi Ioudaioi* were seeking all the more to kill him, because he was not only breaking the sabbath, but was also calling God his own Father, thereby making himself equal to God" (5:18). Not only was Jesus unilaterally undermining the law of the sabbath, which had been ordained for the good of the social body as well as the cosmic body, he was "making himself equal to God" and determining that his "work" was that of God.

In his soliloquy of 5:19-47, Jesus makes a charge geared to unmask the underlying reason for his opponents' entrenched obduracy. First of all, they have been so blinded by their own limited approach to the scriptures that they "do not have the love of God" in them (5:42). Second, they have been so desirous of maintaining their honor with and glory from each other (5:41, 43-44a) that they do not "seek the glory that comes from the one who alone is God" (5:44). When religious leaders are so concerned about preserving their laws, it is often hard to find God's love in them. And when they are so preoccupied by maintaining their own reputation with members of their own group, it is not likely that the glory of God will get much more than lip service.

In his final summation, Jesus appeals to the one through whom the law of the sabbath came to Israel: he appeals to the testimony of Moses himself. Because of their obduracy, Jesus has no need to accuse them. Their accuser is Moses, on whom they have set their hope (5:45). Because the hour that is coming for the final accusing is "now here" (5:25), they now stand accused before God, not by Jesus but by the one who prefigured Jesus. Since Moses is the one in whom they say they believe, and since Moses, "wrote about" Jesus, not to believe in Jesus' word invalidates their belief in Moses. If their belief in Moses is bogus, so is their interpretation of his word, especially since his word was about this Word called Jesus: "If you do not believe what he wrote [about me], how will you believe what I say?" (5:47).

The final message is clear, be it to *hoi Ioudaioi*, the opponents of the Johannine community who struggled with representatives of an Apostolic group that seemed to interpret the "word" in a way that gave more authority to the position of its leaders than to the One who gave them that authority, or the reader today who struggles with similar concerns: many times our obsession with our "law" finds us and our leaders missing the whole point of the law—the need to believe in *the* Word whose healing at all levels of the world brings about the ultimate purpose of the sabbath—*shalom.*

THREE

DOES THIS OFFEND YOU? (6:61)
DO YOU ALSO WISH TO GO AWAY? (6:67)

The Questions of John 6:1-71

By this point in John's gospel, Jesus has cleansed the temple. He has undermined the interpretive power of the religious leaders with regard to the type of healing that can take place on the sabbath. In the process, he has exposed the deeper sickness that infects religious systems that purport to be grounded in God but have turned to religious idolatry that glorifies the institution's prerogatives. In chapter 6—which takes place in the context of another "feast," the highest feast of Passover—we find more controversy between Jesus and his opponents. An exposition of this chapter helps us with the meaning of what we know to be Eucharist today.

In some contemporary ecclesial communities—especially in Roman Catholicism—we find much complaining, many disputes, and increasingly open breaks about matters related to the Eucharist (see 6:41, 52, 60-61). On the one hand we find debates about who can preside (married men, women, active homosexuals, and even men who are alcoholic or allergic to gluten); on the other, many people have "gone away" over issues related to who can fully participate (divorced and remarried people, non-Catholics, those who disagree on ecclesiastical decrees related to women's role in the church, and even those who belong to such groups as Call to Action).

In my travels I have found quite a few places where arguments occur around issues such as "who will preside" and "who can receive." Yet, at a wider level I find that the average Catholic, much less the average Christian, has little understanding of what the Eucharist really entails as I find it envisioned in the sixth chapter of John.[1] This dearth of insight is everywhere. It is found even among highly educated Catholics—as I learned years ago at a parish in a major Midwestern city.

Our province had been asked to minister at "St. Timothy's." Its parishioners are highly educated in their particular fields. Unfortunately, as I learned during a parish visit, their education often stops at the church door on Sundays when they come to celebrate the eucharistic liturgy.

40

I had been asked by the Capuchin pastor "to preach on the Eucharist" at a mid-morning Mass. I decided I'd begin by finding out where the people "were coming from" regarding their understanding of the Eucharist and their sense of being part of its celebration. So I went straight to the pews and, after explaining that I had been asked to preach on the Eucharist, asked the congregants: "When you receive the Eucharist, who is it that you receive?"

After a long pause, a middle aged man raised his hand. He said: "When I receive the Holy Eucharist I receive the body and blood, soul and divinity of our Lord and Savior, Jesus Christ, whole and entire in each and every part." This *Baltimore Catechism* definition had been ingrained in this man and in millions of us for generation upon generation since its first appearance in the 1800s. He could still recite the phrase from memory.

"Wow," I said, surprised at his response. "I haven't heard that definition in years." After praising him, I asked for an elaboration on what the definition meant. "Exactly who is this Jesus Christ that you receive in the Eucharist whole and entire?"

Perplexed at my question, he repeated: "Well, the Jesus Christ I receive in the Eucharist is the body and blood of my Lord and Savior, whole and entire, in each and every part."

"That's right," I said. Then I pressed on: "Who is this Jesus Christ?" Pointing to the crucifix behind me, I asked, "Is it Jesus on the Cross in that flesh, or is it Jesus Christ risen from his death on the cross?"

"It's Jesus Christ risen, because Christ has died, Christ *is risen*," came someone's reply.

"Great, but when we receive the *risen* Christ, are we brought into relationship with anyone else?" Further prodding elicited from the parishioners "God." By this they meant the one Jesus called "Father." Gradually they decided that, if we have two members of the Trinity, "the Holy Spirit" must be in the Eucharist too.

"Is there anyone else to whom we become connected with the risen Jesus when we celebrate Eucharist?" I asked.

After an even longer pause, a young person said, "I think Mary's in there too."

"You do?"

"Yes."

"Well you are right if you mean that she and all the other members of the communion of saints are identified with the risen Christ and, to this degree, are related to him in the Eucharist too. Won't we be praying in a few minutes to God to "grant also to us, your children, to enter into our heavenly inheritance in the company of the Virgin Mary, the Mother of God, and your apostles and saints?" I went on. "Okay, with Jesus risen from the dead as the one we receive in the Eucharist, we also receive the other members of the Trinity and are linked with the communion of saints. But, is there anyone else we receive as well?"

From the far back of the church a hand was raised. A woman said, "I think my neighbor is in there too."

"You do?" I asked, and she nodded back. Then I asked the congregation: "How many of you agree with her that, when you receive the Risen Lord in the Eucharist, you also are brought into relationship with each other?"

About 25 percent of the hands were raised.

"How many of you don't think you receive each other in the Eucharist?" Now about 50 percent of the hands were raised.

Realizing there were some who didn't feel at ease declaring themselves, I laughingly asked: "How many of you don't know what to believe?"

That day I realized the importance of the first disciples' question of Jesus regarding his explanation of what we know as Eucharist today: "This teaching is difficult; who can accept it?" (6:60). Even more, I became convinced of the awesome significance of Jesus' counter-questions: "Does this offend you?" (6:61) and, to the twelve: "Do you also wish to go away?" (6:67).

Maybe the wish is not to "go away," but to better understand what the Eucharist really entails. The rest of this chapter attempts to examine the sixth chapter of John that we might come to a fuller understanding of this mystery of our faith.

John's Chapter 6: Understanding What Real Presence Means

Over thirty years ago, at my province's theology center in Marathon, Wisconsin, I began my journey from a *Baltimore Catechism* understanding of the Eucharist by delving into a newly revised commentary on John that had just been released. It was Raymond Brown's popular study, *The Gospel of St. John and the Johannine Epistles.*[2] What I learned back then still serves me well today in trying to understand and explain what Eucharist means. While I will be faithful to Brown's basic structuring in this chapter, I have nuanced it a bit differently. And while the vast majority of exegetes limit any possible eucharistic notions only to 6:51c-58 if at all,[3] preferring the whole to represent a high christology with only the last part having eucharistic overtones, I see the whole chapter offering an understanding of the "real presence" that is at the heart of all eucharistic gatherings. The more I have understood reader-response as involving how we appropriate the text in our lives today, the more this approach to the whole chapter from the perspective of the real presence makes sense to me.

I divide chapter 6 into two parts, 6:1-24 and 6:25-71. The quest stories of 6:1-24 contain the narratives about the feeding of the 5,000 (6:1-15) and the boat narrative wherein Jesus appears to his disciples and eludes the crowds who want to "make" him king (6:16-24). The rejection stories of 6:25-71 feature the discourses on the bread of life in its two forms (his word and his flesh [6:25-59]) and the divisions the discourse elicits (6:60-71). Everything, it seems, is used by John to articulate dimensions of the real presence of Jesus that is meant to abide in the community of believers.

Feeding the Five Thousand (6:1-15)

"After this Jesus went to the other side of the Sea of Galilee, also called the Sea of Tiberias" (6:1). That John refers to Tiberias as a "sea" rather than the lake that it is says more about his theological purposes than his sense of geography. Referring to the water as a "sea" with Jesus' going to the other side evokes images of the the crossing of another sea centuries before in a way that brought life out of death and manifested the real presence of God with Israel (see Ex 14).

Despite the fact that only two accounts of healing have been presented in the gospel thus far (with only the healing on the sabbath described as public), John notes: "A large crowd kept following him, because they saw the signs that he was doing for the sick" (6:2). John has made a point of placing Jesus' signs in the context of Jewish festivals to portray Jesus transforming and replacing them (2:13f; 4:43-44; 5:1f; see 7:2f; 10:22 [previous and following]; 12:1f). He notes that now that the Passover, "the festival of *hoi Ioudaioi*, was near" (6:4), Jesus went up the mountain and sat down there with his disciples" (6:3). Because Passover was identified with Moses, it is quite likely that John's placement of Jesus on "the mountain" rather than "a mountain" is meant to recall Sinai and the Passover meal Moses authorized for Israel. As the people followed Moses, so now "the crowd kept following" Jesus. Wes Howard-Brook points out that people's following of Jesus, especially at this Passover time, meant the religious leaders were losing their authority over them: "The crowd following Jesus across the sea to the other side is expressing its collective desire to offer allegiance to a different religious leadership. The fact that these people are in the wilderness at Passover rather than where the official religion expected them to be—in Jerusalem—reveals their lack of loyalty to the Judean status quo."[4]

Once he is seated with his disciples, Jesus tests Philip: "Where are we to buy bread for these people to eat?" (6:5b). Philip was from Bethsaida, the capital of Gaulanitis, which was located on the northern shore of the Sea of Galilee. Its name means "fishing village" (see Mk 6:45).[5] Jesus wonders aloud if Philip can figure out what to do.

If the crowds had followed Jesus on their own volition, why would Jesus feel obliged to provide food for them? Would he be dishonored if these guests, uninvited as they might be, were not fed? I don't think so.

Driven by a divine necessity, he recognizes the opportunity to provide not just food, but a sign: "he knew what he was going to *do*" (6:6b). With "five barley loaves and two fish," all that could be produced from the "five thousand in all," Jesus set about to surpass the action of Elisha who had wondrously fed one hundred men (2 Kgs 4:42-44) centuries before.

After ordering the crowd to be seated (*anapiptein*, as for a meal), the ritual (which was already enshrined in the memorials of the Johannine community) was enacted. "Then Jesus took (*lambanein*) the loaves, and when he had given thanks (*eucharistein*), he distributed (*diadidonai*) them to those who were seated; so also the fish, as much as they wanted" (6:11). Unlike the Synoptics' versions, John's version is the only one in which Jesus does "eucharist" in the way he gives thanks. Similarly, in a significant deviation from the Synoptics, Jesus himself distributes the loaves and fish to the thousands. In this form of Eucharist he becomes personally present to everyone. And, finally, in a wonderful twist of words, only after "they were satisfied" (implying that none were excluded and all got enough) does Jesus in John's version "command" the disciples: "Gather up (*synagein*) the fragments (*klasmata*) left over, so that nothing may be lost" (6:12).

The earliest word for "church" was *synagōgē*. For the first time we find in John a connection between the gathered community and the fragments left over. Here an ecclesial image gets linked to a eucharistic one: one body is another; all have been gathered together in the power of a deeper manifestation of Jesus' real presence.

Once the people "saw the sign that he had done, they began to say, 'This is indeed the prophet who is to come into the world'" (6:14). Having identified Jesus as part of the Mosaic prophetic tradition, they moved to make him their king instead of the detested Herod Antipas, the client king of Caesar. Why submit to one who takes food from you when you can have one who gives it to you—without taxation? Wes Howard-Brook comments:

> The Jewish desire to be rid of Roman rule overrode nearly every other goal in the minds and hearts of Palestinians from Galilee to Judea. As Craig Koester notes, "Roman rulers regularly placated the populace with distributions of bread or grain." The Roman "feeding" has been replaced with a Jewish "meal"! This multitude responds to Jesus' actions with the "correct" interpretation: he is the messiah, the one who will set Israel free! This is the meaning of the "prophet who is to come into the world"—the one predicted by Moses (Deut 18:18) to speak God's word as Moses' successor.[6]

The peoples' messianic expectations are not shared by Jesus. Aware that the crowd was looking for a messiah or king who would feed their stomachs rather than satisfy their souls, Jesus "withdrew again to the mountain by himself" (6:15).

The story of the multiplication has taken place on "the mountain" (6:3f). Now John notes that Jesus "withdrew again to the mountain by himself" (6:15). How can you "withdraw to" a place where you already are? Is this apparent discrepancy evidence of another redaction? Were there different traditions brought together by someone who didn't connect the beginning with the end? While we will never know, we do know that the image of "withdrawal" in the gospels often is used in conflictual settings. Jesus "withdraws," not so much to escape the actions of the people, such as their efforts to make him "king," but as a strategic maneuver enabling him to return for a deeper kind of engagement. The people have followed looking for a sign, the sign has been given, they want to make Jesus king, he withdraws. The elusive Christ will not be present for those looking for him to fill their stomachs. He will do the finding and make himself present to those who have faith. This brings us to the next section.

The First Sign of the Real Presence:
Jesus Appears to His Disciples in the Boat (6:16-24)

Now that the ritual breaking of the bread has taken place, we next find Jesus manifesting himself to his disciples as they row in their boat. The boat is the context for the real presence, the appearance of Jesus. For Catholics, everything about the Eucharist revolves around the notion of the real presence. Unfortunately, this image has been held captive too often in the Roman Church by ideological notions limited to transubstantiation on the one hand and poor theology on the other.

The first section finds the disciples in the boat, often seen as a symbol of the church itself. "When evening came, his disciples went down to the sea, got into a boat, and started across the sea to Capernaum. It was now dark, and Jesus had not yet come to them" (6:16-17). In the verse before this passage, Jesus has withdrawn. Now John makes it clear that any personal experience of Jesus' presence lies beyond the power of anyone except himself. He remains elusive to his own disciples in the boat, to say nothing about those still on the shore.

The image of darkness adds to the sense of being alone. It also recalls for the reader what happened "in the beginning" when the word came into the heart of the "world's" darkness (1:1f). Possibly imaging the original chaos, John notes: "The sea became rough because a strong wind was blowing. When they had rowed about three or four miles, they saw Jesus walking on the sea and coming near the boat" (6:18-19ab). The last time these disciples "saw" Jesus was in the ritual breaking of the bread and distribution of the fish. Now, in an image that shows his power over chaos itself, they "see" him walking on the sea, nearing them in the boat.

Their reaction reflects that human response many have had to a manifestation of divine presence: "They were terrified" (6:19c). At this Jesus "said to them, 'It is I; do not be afraid'" (6:20).

Jesus' words: "It is I" (*egō eimi*) are his self-appropriation of the divine name, the real presence of the Divine One. The words are the same as those originally revealed by God to Moses on Sinai: YHWH. Unlike Mark's version, which makes Jesus' sea crossing an epiphany with Jesus floating past the boat like a ghost (Mk 6:48-50), John's version makes the event a theophany, a manifestation of God's presence. This is reminiscent of Exodus 3:14 where God's name is revealed in the words "I AM." Peter Ellis finds this echoing of the divine name so important to John's story of Jesus that he places this text (6:16-21) at the very center of a chiastic structuring of the entire gospel. As such it represents the "new exodus" in which "Jesus walks on the sea, declares 'I am he' and brings the new Israel to the other shore of the sea."[7]

Not only does Jesus do something here beyond human capacity (walking on water), he reveals in his very power to do so that he is linked with God's own power. This is the first time the disciples are faced with Jesus making his real presence felt by the use of the divine name. Their response to this manifestation of the divine presence in their boat, their community, is echoed in the desires of everyone seeking to experience that presence in their lives: "They wanted to take him into the boat" (6:21a).

The two verbs John uses for the disciples' response to the real presence of divinity in their midst (after their initial fear) have strong eucharistic overtones. The first denotes desire: "they wanted" (*thelein*). From the beginning of this book, we have stressed the role of desire, of "wanting," of willingness to seek Jesus Christ to be the center of our lives and the heart of that boat called "church." The second verb used to describe the disciples' response to the divine "I am" is "to take" (*lambanein*): "They wanted to take (*lambanein*) him into the boat." As Jesus had "taken" the loaves and given them to the disciples and the five thousand, so now they wanted "to take" him into the boat. They wanted to remain in his real presence.

A more accurate translation, with definite contemporary overtones of the Eucharist for disciples, renders the text: "They wanted *to receive* him into the boat." "Receiving" Jesus resonates with those who want to receive him in his full eucharistic presence. The next verses of John will extend the dimensions of this presence from the boat-group (6:16-25) to his word (6:26-51b) and, finally, to Jesus' flesh and blood itself (6:51c-59).

Requesting a Sign: Bread Come Down from Heaven for Life (6:25-34)

Jesus had come to the disciples in the boat even when they were not specifically looking for him. Meanwhile, the crowd "got into the boats and went to Capernaum looking for Jesus" that they might question him about his presence there. The crowd's query of Jesus ("When did you come here?") evokes from him an exposé of their motivation. They have come, under the guise of wanting a sign, hoping for more bread. The messiah they seek is not one of faith but one who will give them full stomachs. Such a search, he tells them, is too limited: "Do not work for the food that perishes, but for the food that endures for eternal life, which the Son of Man will give you. For it is on him that God the Father has set his seal" (6:26-27).

Given the subsistence diet on which first-century peasants lived, it might appear that Jesus was very insensitive to upbraid them for seeking him because he fed them. The equivalent would be my announcing at our "Loaves and Fishes" meal in Milwaukee: "It would be better for you to go upstairs to Eucharist than to come downstairs here for a meal." But this is not the point that Jesus is making. While we readers are aware of who Jesus really is, the crowds were not. They knew nothing of Jesus' walking on the water, much less his self-identification with God (*egō eimi*). So, picking up on Jesus' words about "work," they ask him which works in particular they must do.

Jesus makes it clear that the real "work" everyone must perform is not to be identified with manual labor, with multiplying bread and fish, or with any other "works." It ultimately is a grounding in and expression of faith: belief in the One sent by God (6:28-29). Returning again to their desire for some kind of sign, despite the fact of the ritual feeding that should have been fresh in their minds (if not in their stomachs), "they said to him, 'What sign are you going to give us then, so that we may see it and believe you? What work are you performing? Our ancestors ate the manna in the wilderness; as it is written, "he gave them bread from heaven to eat"'" (6:30-31).

At this point the reader will recall what Jesus had said earlier to the disciples when they asked about food in its physical form: "I have food to eat that you do not know about" (4:32) and "My food is to do the will of him who sent me and to complete his work" (4:34). Now, to the crowd, he speaks in a similar vein but, for the first time, begins linking the notion of food with his own real presence. Responding to their quoting from the tradition, Jesus declares: "Very truly, I tell you, it was not Moses who gave you the bread from heaven, but it is my Father who gives you the true bread from heaven. For the bread of God is that which comes down from heaven and gives life to the world" (6:32-33).

Again, not having experienced Jesus' walking on water, the crowd perceives his words only at face value. They have not experienced the sign of the "I AM." Thus, because they are still operating within the mind-set of a "world" that links Moses with the gift of manna and which believes that the Messiah will give the people bread at Passover time,[8] the crowds petition: "Sir, give us this bread always" (6:34). In response to their request, John puts into the mouth of Jesus a theology about bread that will be beyond their comprehension (6:35-59).

The Second Sign of the Real Presence:
Jesus' Word as the Bread of Life (6:35-51b)

At this time in Jewish theology, especially its wisdom tradition, the manna of the desert which nourished the people had been identified with God's word itself. Sirach 24:21 had promised the people seeking Wisdom: "Those who eat of me will hunger for more, and those who drink of me will thirst for more." Alluding to this theological image, Jesus responded to the crowd's request for "this bread always" by challenging them to move from thinking of bread in terms of something physical to thinking of it as his real person and presence: "I am the bread of life. Whoever comes to me will never be hungry, and whoever believes in me will never be thirsty" (6:35).

Despite the fact that the people have come to Jesus and have "seen" him, they do not believe (6:36). He has come down from heaven to do the will of the Father which is to "lose nothing of all that he has given" Jesus. The Father's will for those who see Jesus and believe in him is to give them eternal life and he "will raise them up on the last day" (6:37-40). As God's word came down from heaven and would not return empty until it accomplished that for which it was sent (Is 55:10-11), so Jesus has come down from heaven, sent by God, and will not return empty because he will lose nothing of all that has been given to him and will "raise it up on the last day" (6:39).

While most Protestants find the real presence in God's word realized in Jesus Christ in the scriptures, many Catholics have little appreciation of this manifestation of the real presence. This lack of appreciation often extends even to priests. One liturgist I know recalls the time he spoke at a diocesan convocation of priests. He was asked to reflect on the manifestations of the real presence of Christ in the liturgy. The priests had no problem with the traditional understanding which identified the real presence with the consecrated bread and wine as Jesus' real flesh and blood ("transubstantiation"). They didn't even have a problem believing in the real presence of Christ found among the baptized gathered in the assembly. But what created a real stumbling block for them came when the liturgist, following the ritual itself, linked the real presence of Jesus, the fulfillment of the law and prophets, with the proclamation of the word as it takes place in the readings or the homily. If our own religious leaders have problems believing in the real presence of Christ in the word, it should not be surprising that "*hoi Ioudaioi* began to complain about him because he said, 'I am the bread that came down from heaven'" (6:41).

Jesus responds to the complaints by reiterating what he has already said: "No one can come to me unless drawn by the Father who sent me; and I will raise that person up on the last day" (6:43-44). He then expands on Isaiah's prophetic words: "They shall all be taught by God" (see Is 54:13). He declares that anyone who "has heard and learned from the Father comes to me" and notes that no one has "seen the Father except the one who is from God." The way to see the Father they cannot see is by coming to the One whom they can see. Finally, he concludes by saying: "I tell you, whoever believes [in me] has eternal life" (6:47).

For Israelites used to identifying God's word and purposes with their own institutions, Jesus reference to "all" who come to him being taught by God and "whoever" believes in him having the promise of eternal life was virtually incomprehensible. How could God's word addressed to them quite exclusively be now for "the world"? Did this mean that Jesus would be the source of life not only for them, but for all who would come to him and abide in his teaching? Jesus makes it clear that this is exactly what he means. He summarizes his position by declaring that he is the bread that gives life: "I am the living bread that came down from heaven. Whoever eats of this bread will live forever; and the bread that I will give for the life of the world is my flesh" (6:51).

The Third Sign of the Real Presence:
Jesus' Flesh and Blood for Life (6:51c-59)

If any section of John's gospel reflects the evolution of the Johannine community's understanding of the eucharistic presence of Jesus within its midst, it is this one. John Pilch writes that "the Eucharistic overtones were probably the result of Christian rethinking of this topic added at a late stage in the final edition of the Fourth Gospel."[9] From the high christology of a eucharistic theology, John moves the conversation to a deeper level.

Hoi Ioudaioi, able to consider the "bread" in a Mosaic sense only, cannot grasp what Jesus is saying because a definite shift now has taken place in Jesus' words and imagery. The bread that once was himself and his word is now his flesh (*sarx*). So *hoi Ioudaioi* murmur and complain among themselves: "How can this man give us his flesh to eat?" (6:52). Either because he overhears them or because he knows the hearts of people (2:25), Jesus proclaims the words that have come to be among the most important (and disputed) in John's gospel:

I tell you, unless you eat the flesh (*sarx*) of the Son of Man and drink his blood (*aima*), you have no life in you. Those who eat my flesh and drink my blood have eternal life, and I will raise them up on the last day; for my flesh is true food and my blood is true drink. Those who eat my flesh and drink my blood abide in me, and I in them. Just as the living Father sent me, and I live because of the Father, so whoever eats me will live because of me. (6:53-57)

I find it interesting that fundamentalist Protestants have little problem taking literally John 3:16 about belief in Jesus Christ bringing "eternal life" while the passage means little to the average Catholic. Yet, at the same time, Catholics accept literally Jesus's words in John 6:53 which mean little or nothing to many Protestants: "Unless you eat the flesh of the Son of Man and drink his blood, you will have no life in you. Those who eat my flesh and drink my blood have eternal life." The day that both passages become part of the active faith of all Christians will be a happy day indeed.

As noted earlier, there has been disagreement as to whether Jesus' reference to his flesh and blood should be taken in a christological sense or in a eucharistic sense. If the christological interpretation is used, Jesus' flesh and blood become essential identifiers of him who was crucified on the cross. When the eucharistic sense prevails, the Johannine Jesus' references to the bread as his *flesh* and the drink as his *blood* echo the Synoptics' notion of the bread and the wine-cup as eucharistic identifiers. Rather than opting for a purely christological interpretation of the whole chapter or a eucharistic dimension toward its end, Francis Moloney links both notions. He concludes:

> The reader is asked to be receptive to the revelation of God that will take place in broken flesh and spilled blood (vv. 53-54), a never failing (v. 35) nourishment that the Son of Man will give (v. 27). But the Christian reader asks: Where do I encounter this revelation of God in the flesh and blood of the Son of Man? By means of the underlying eucharistic language the author insinuates an answer: it is in the Eucharistic celebration that one can encounter the flesh and blood of Jesus the Christ.[10]

We encounter the flesh and blood of Jesus the Crucified Christ by our identification with him through the blood and water which flowed from his side (19:34). This blood and water give birth to and constitute the community of believers, most particularly when the comunity celebrates its identification with Christ in his eucharistic presence. The community of believers (19:35) who have been formed into the body and blood of Christ by the Spirit, who gather to celebrate his real eucharistic presence in their midst, are those who "will look on the one whom they have pierced" (19:37).

The word John uses to describe eating (*trōgein*) generally refers to crunching with the teeth—a truly physical process of mastication (6:54, 56, 57). Similarly, the word for drinking (*pinein*) does not mean to "drink in" in the sense of "taking in" but refers to the physical process of imbibing. Such words were used by the Johannine community's writer to help it understand itself-in-ritual in a form that would distinguish it from outsiders. Anthony Blasi notes that while this ritual served as "a liturgy that bears some resemblance to that of the wider Christian community," it "seems calculated to 'turn off' non-Christians: 'He who munches on my flesh and drinks my blood has eternal life, and I will raise him on the last day.' (6.54)" Such words, he concludes, helped establish a unique and genuine identity for the Johannine Christians: "From the Johannine perspective this genuineness is a matter of being in communion with Jesus and divinity" (see 6:56-57).[11]

For a people who did not eat certain forms of flesh or imbibe any animal blood, the very concept of munching on Jesus' flesh and drinking his blood would have been abhorrent. Indeed, I myself find it abhorrent to think in these categories if Jesus' "flesh" and "blood" are identified with his body on the cross rather than his risen and and glorified body. The degree of my resistance to the notion of "munching" was brought home to me when a friend told me of an incident involving him and a friend.

"James" tries to participate in the Eucharist on a daily basis. His co-workers know that he tries to "get in" a Mass before work or during the noon hour. Once, at an out-of-town convention, a Protestant co-worker, "Frank," asked if he could go to Mass with him. James was glad to oblige. On the way, Frank asked: "Would it be okay if I'd go to communion?"

"Well, it'd be okay with me as long as you agree with us Catholics about what you are doing," James said to Frank.

"What is it you believe you are doing?" came Frank's reply.

Looking at me with great sincerity, James said, "I told him: 'When we take the host we believe we are actually chewing on the flesh of Jesus and when we take the cup we are really drinking his blood.'"

"Ugh," I said. "That's gross!"

When James registered surprise, I tried to explain to him my understanding of "eat my flesh" and "drink my blood." Eating or "munching" on Jesus may be his command, but what he called his "flesh" now is not the same, I said, "as yours or mine. Drinking of Jesus may be what we've been told to do, but his blood is not that which was poured out on the cross."

"First of all, James," I said, "we've got to realize who this Jesus is today and what, therefore, his body and blood are all about. We are not 'receiving' the physical body and blood of Christ Crucified but that of the Christ who died but is now risen."

"Oh, I get it," he said. "It's like we say in response to the priest's words after the consecration, 'Let us proclaim the mystery of faith: Christ has died, Christ *is risen*.' So, we're sharing in the life of the risen Christ."

"Exactly," I said. Then I mentioned that, according to Raymond Brown, consuming someone's body and blood in the Hebrew idiom meant to accept that whole person into oneself. I concluded: "Jim, I think this is the only way we can understand the 'real presence' of Christ in this sacramental form."

One important element that my friend James did manage to convey to Frank—an element that also characterized the early Johannine community—was the way in which belief in the real presence of Jesus makes this ritual a kind of "border ritual." It is different from the Passover ritual of *hoi Ioudaioi* and it separates the community from the wider society. By believing in Jesus as the bread of life and participating in the ritual of eating his flesh and drinking his blood, the members set themselves apart from life in this "world" on its terms. They realize in ritual that they have already entered "everlasting life."[12]

Jesus concludes by describing himself in eucharistic images that touch on another Mosaic connection: "This is the bread that came down from heaven, not like that which your ancestors ate, and they died. But the one who eats this bread will live forever" (6:58). If we eat the bread that is his flesh and drink from the cup that is his blood we have already entered into eternal life. Unlike the Israelites who needed the manna each day to survive, those who eat his flesh and drink his blood abide (*menein*) in him forever. "Remaining with" Jesus represents the deepest relationship possible, the most profound form of really being present to another, that of intimacy.

Having finished narrating Jesus' words, John notes: "He said these things while he was teaching in the synagogue at Capernaum" (6:59). Until now the reader has been told only that the crowd "went to Capernaum looking for Jesus" (6:24). Now we learn that the ensuring discourse and debate took place "in the synagogue" at Capernaum. Why would the author make note of this fact, especially after the discourse on the bread of life is concluded? Is it for the same reason we have been and will be reminded after two different healings that they took place on the sabbath (5:9; 9:14)? Is John perhaps saying that Jesus is replacing what is at the heart of the most sacred for *hoi Ioudaioi* with himself? I think so.

The events in this chapter—the multiplication of the loaves, the walking on water, the bread of life discourse—took place when "the Passover, the festival of *hoi Ioudaioi* was near" (6:4). John now makes it clear that Jesus not only has fulfilled the purposes of Passover, he has surpassed them. He has replaced them with his own real presence. And, since the synagogue was the center of Israel's worship, now those who come to him and believe in him will constitute the true worshipers. For *hoi Ioudaioi* the synagogue is a place of worship. For the Johannine community, the synagogue is the community at worship.

Who Believes in This Elusive Mystery of Faith? (6:60-71)

We have seen that the ritual of taking, blessing, and distributing the loaves was a prelude to an understanding of the real presence of Jesus in the various forms sculpted by John in chapter 6. The first form of Jesus' real presence is in the community of disciples that "receives" him in the boat (6:16-24). The second is in himself as word, in his teaching (6:25-51). The final form of the real presence is in the sacramental form of bread and wine become his body and blood for the life of the world (6:52-59).

Until Jesus refers to his flesh as bread and his blood as drink, it is only the *hoi Ioudaioi* who murmur about him and his teaching (6:41). When Jesus says his flesh must be eaten and his blood drunk, this notion of his real presence elicits complaining from his own disciples. They say: "This teaching is difficult; who can accept it?" (6:60). In a more literal fashion, they say, "This word is *sklēros*." This does not mean they find Jesus' teaching difficult to understand or comprehend. No. They find it hard, harsh, unacceptable. Aware that his disciples are complaining, Jesus asks them a direct question about what he has said: "Does this offend you?" (6:60-61). Because it does, many return to their former ways of life (6:66).

Today, especially among more traditional Catholics whose understanding of the Eucharist is still defined by limited notions identified with the *Baltimore Catechism*, I have found a new kind of murmuring and offense regarding the Eucharist. It has little or nothing to do with identifying Christ's real presence in its third form, namely his body and blood as bread and wine that is food and drink for the believer. Perhaps this is because the fights over transubstantiation have subsided and people are willing to accept this form of the real presence of Jesus as a mystery of their faith. But when faced with other forms of the real presence of Jesus, they are offended.

At the beginning of this chapter I recalled an incident that took place at a parish in which the majority of the people at a Eucharist found it difficult to "believe" that the real presence of Jesus also exists in the members of the community itself. However, if we say that (1) we "belong" to the church, and (2) we are members of the body of Christ, and (3) the church is the body of Christ, and (4) the body of Christ is the Eucharist, then we must have eyes to see that, (5) when the risen Christ comes to us, we also receive the members of his risen body, all the communicants in the church. This connection between the church, the body of Christ, and the Eucharist can be charted in three simple dyads:

We belong to:		We are members of:		We are part of:
THE CHURCH	=	THE BODY OF CHRIST	=	THE EUCHARIST

Despite this truth, many Catholics not only refuse to believe that the consecrated body and blood of Jesus Christ which they "receive" includes the members of his body and blood who are their partners in the "boat" called the church, they want to evict from "their synagogues" all those who promote such teaching. I discovered this some years ago when I gave a retreat at an affluent parish in Florida.

As I concluded each homily at the "Sunday Masses," I related the story of a man who had expressed in a very powerful way his understanding of the communal dimension of the real presence of Jesus in the Eucharist. "You know, Mike," he said, "I truly believe I am a member of the body of Christ and I believe in the Eucharist as the body and blood of Christ. Therefore, when I'm in the pew and you say the words of consecration, I also hold out my hand and say to myself as a baptized member of the church: 'This is my body. This is my blood.'"

It wasn't long before the phones were ringing. The priest who had come to give the parish retreat, some were "murmuring," was a heretic. He was saying that, in the risen Christ, we receive each other in the Eucharist. When I heard of their "complaining," I asked to meet with them. The dozen or so people who appeared for our meeting each brought along a copy of the *New Catechism of the Catholic Church*. There was not a Bible in sight.

According to some scholars, the word "murmuring," suggests division within a community over the interpretation of scripture.[13] This particular meeting evidenced a high degree of murmuring, not only over my explanation of scripture, but also over tradition. I was called a schismatic and accused of being disloyal to the teachings of the Holy Father. I responded by saying that, while I might not agree with the pope on all matters of discipline, in matters of faith, such as understanding what the Eucharist really entails, we were totally in sync. They didn't believe it.

Unable to convince them about the real presence of Christ in the community, I referred to Paul's first letter to the Corinthians. In this letter he speaks of abuses at the Lord's Supper, noting that when Christians come together to celebrate the ritual performed by Jesus but do not act like members of his body they show "contempt for the church of God" (1 Cor 11:22). Finally, I used his concluding argument as mine: "Examine yourselves, and only then eat of the bread and drink of the cup. For all who eat and drink without discerning the body, eat and drink judgment against themselves" (1 Cor 11:28-29).

They were unimpressed by the word of God in Paul and said, "That's not what it means." As I was trying to explain that Paul had meant what he said, one of the members who had shown some degree of openness to my reflections during my morning and evening conferences was paging through her *Catechism*. Suddenly she announced that she had found a section connecting the Eucharist with the unity of the church. Referring to 1 Corinthians 10:16-17, which links the bread with the body and the body with the members, number 1396 in the *Catechism* quotes St. Augustine:

> If you are the body and members of Christ, then it is your sacrament that is placed on the table of the Lord; it is your sacrament that you receive. To that which you are you respond "Amen" ("yes, it is true!") and by responding to it you assent to it. For you hear the words, "the Body of Christ" and respond "Amen." Be then a member of the Body of Christ that your *Amen* may be true.[14]

As she read this statement from the *Catechism,* the majority of the people in the group sat stunned. When she finished, a woman who had been adamant about the fact that I was a heretic said emphatically, "I don't believe it."

The woman found this teaching hard, harsh, unacceptable. In response to the first disciples who reacted in a similar fashion (about an understanding of his teaching which she willingly endorsed), Jesus asked a question and posed a follow-up question: "Does this offend you? Then what if you were to see the Son of Man ascending to where he was before?" Realizing that his teaching has offended his disciples, Jesus suggests another sign that might make them believe: his resurrection. But his question is really rhetorical. He is getting nowhere. Thus he concludes: "It is the spirit that gives life; the flesh is useless. The words that I have spoken to you are spirit and life" (6:61-64a). On the one hand, his flesh is spirit; thus it can be consumed. On the other hand, however, flesh itself is useless if it remains without that Spirit whom he has promised to send the Johannine community.

After telling his unbelieving disciples, "The words that I have spoken to you are spirit and life," Jesus goes on to say, "but among you there are some who do not believe" (6:63-64). Then John immediately adds: "For Jesus knew from the first who were the ones that did not believe, and who was the one that would betray him" (6:65).

In my mind, the contemporary form of betrayal of the body and blood of the risen Christ in its eucharistic expression is that which gets expressed in the way we undermine each other as his members and then celebrate the ritual of communion. When Catholics are most insistent that they are "munching" on the real flesh of Christ and drinking his blood in celebrating the Eucharist, but can't "stomach" their neighbors, the betrayal Jesus prophesied gets fulfilled. It gets fulfilled when they would much rather visit shrines that contain receptacles holding consecrated hosts alleged to have bled than to "recognize Christ in the poorest, his brethren," as the *Catechism* says. In the words of St. John Chrysostom, "You have tasted the Blood of the Lord, yet you do not recognize your brother [or sister]. . . . You dishonor this table when you do not judge worthy of sharing your food someone judged worthy to take part in this meal."[15]

John writes, "Because of this many of his disciples turned back and no longer went about with him." The phrase translated here as "turned back" literally means, "returned to the things of the past," namely "the world." With so many of his disciples leaving, Jesus asks (in the first mention of them as a group) the twelve, "Do you also wish to go away?" (6:66-67).

Data shows that, since the Vatican Council, many disciples may not have consciously "gone away" because of issues related to the Eucharist or what it means to be a eucharistic community. Yet some have left the boat because of the chaos it's been in. Other have gone because they have found the church's equivalent of *hoi Ioudaioi* in the Petrine office intransigent about seemingly anachronistic issues related to the Eucharist, such as who can preside. Rather than continue complaining or disputing with the leaders, they have simply "gone away." While the split with Jesus described in the gospel probably reflects a schism in the Johannine community (about eucharistic celebrations vs. foot washings as the rituals to celebrate the real presence), such schisms and splits continue today.

As the Johannine community faced its own internal schisms it could never forget the words Simon Peter spoke on behalf of the twelve, the Apostolic Community of John's day, as well as its own belief. Pointing not to himself but to Jesus as *the* teacher, Peter declared: "Lord, to whom can we go? You have the words of eternal life. We have come to believe and know that you are the Holy One of God" (6:68-69). For the first time in John's gospel someone connected to Jesus is able to understand that Jesus' words come not from him, but from God. It is because Jesus' words are grounded in God that they are able to offer eternal life for those who believe. To hear such an assertion from one who spoke/speaks on behalf of the whole community ("we have come to believe and know") is refreshing indeed.

FOUR

WHY DO I SPEAK TO YOU AT ALL? (8:25)

The Question of John 7:1–8:59

Not too long ago I was visiting some family members. We got into a heated discussion about people in prisons and what got them there. Living in Milwaukee with jails on two sides of our friary and having worked for a time in a prison, I've had some experience. However, someone in the group kept challenging me as to why people ended up incarcerated. After an extended exchange, he said: "I know for a fact that everyone in prison goes there just to get three meals a day and a bed at night." Exasperated, all I could say was: "Why do I even talk with you?"

This experience gave me some insight into what Jesus must have felt when he uttered a similar question at the end of the conflict with his opponents that is described in chapters 7 and 8: "Why do I speak to you at all?" (8:25).

Most Johannine commentators consider chapters 7 and 8 as one unit (with the exception of 7:53-8:11 which is considered an addition). Various reasons are offered for combining the two chapters: the events in both take place in the temple during the Jewish festival of Booths, they relate to the same themes, and both chapters have a distinctively forensic, trial-like flavor. Furthermore, from beginning to end, we clearly see the efforts of the religious leaders to rid themselves of this threat to their established system and their entrenched ways of thinking.

John begins by noting that "the Jewish festival of Booths was near" (7:2). Booths, or Tabernacles, was considered the most prominent of the main feasts of Judaism. Along with Passover and Pentecost (Weeks), it was one of the three main feasts that involved making a pilgrimage to Jerusalem. Passover commemorated the Exodus and Pentecost honored the Torah. Booths was the harvest festival (Dt 16:13) that helped Israel recall its time in the wilderness when its people had pitched tents for shelter. By the post-exilic period, this feast had become associated with the end times.

In Zechariah's prophecy, the feast of Booths was associated with light and living water (Zec 14). Water and light ceremonies, plus the ritual of positioning oneself to face each of the four directions of the temple's walls, were central to the celebration of this feast. These elements should be recalled as we consider the context for Jesus' words in the temple. It is also important to recall that, by the time of John's final redaction, the temple had been destroyed. Through the images he chooses, John will be trying to show that Jesus is the living temple, the one who replaces the temple that had been destroyed historically; it is now to be replaced ideologically (2:19).[1] Not only will Jesus be the temple, he will be its living waters, its very life.

Chapter 7 begins with a phrase meant to link what is to come with what has already been said: "After this . . ." (*meta tauta*). While this phrase may be a familiar Johannine literary tool to bridge two unconnected stories, here the stories are connected. What has gone before—the "this" of "after this"—includes Jesus identifying himself with the temple (2:19) and declaring that true worship will no longer be associated with it (4:21); his healing on the sabbath and putting himself in confrontation with the religious leaders (5:1-47); and finally his proceeding, during Passover, to proclaim that he himself will be the bread promised to Israel's ancestors (6:1-71). Now, in chapters 7 and 8, during another major feast, "the Jewish festival of Booths" (7:2) we will find that the controversy between Jesus and his opponents escalates. Affronted by his deeds and challenged by his words, the crowd and *hoi Ioudaioi* have become so incensed that Jesus has to take precautions for his safety: "After this Jesus went about in Galilee. He did not wish to go about in Judea because *hoi Ioudaioi* were looking for an opportunity to kill him" (7:1).

The World's Works as *Evil*; Evil-as-Violence

After being challenged by his own brothers (who did not believe in him) to go to Judea (7:3-5), Jesus says: "My time (*kairos*) has not yet come, but your time is always here. . . . Go to the festival yourselves. I am not going to this festival, for my time has not yet fully come" (7:6, 8). In terms of chronological time, Jesus' response to his brothers' challenge makes perfect sense. However, in between the two sentences John places on Jesus' lips other words that at first glance seem out of context: "The world cannot hate you, but it hates me because I testify against it that its works are evil" (7:7).

Now is the *kairos*, the time for the lines of demarcation between Jesus and "the world" to be clearly drawn. Highlighting the trial-like atmosphere that pervades the whole gospel, Jerome Neyrey declares that the "events narrated in John 7-8 fit into this larger pattern in the Fourth Gospel of the trials (forensic) and tribulations (honor challenges) of Jesus: he is charged and put on trial, and judgments are rendered concerning him. This Gospel can, then, be said to narrate the tribulations of Jesus in terms of a forensic trial proceeding."[2] Neyrey's insights are particularly appropriate when we find summarized in this one sentence what the underlying debate will be about: though he has come into the world from God to do the good works of God, the world will not receive him because "its works are evil" (7:7).

An examination of the forensic dynamic in these two chapters between Jesus and his opponents (at times his brothers, at other times *hoi Ioudaioi*, the people of Jerusalem or the crowd, and at still other times the temple police, the chief priests, and the Pharisees) reveals that the charges are quite one-sided. Jesus dominates the scene; he denounces and indicts his opponents. These sentences contain some of the most virulent and violent statements in all the gospels. Jesus acts as prosecutor, leveling one charge after another against his opponents. At the same time he acts as judge. The result is clear: they stand condemned.

The progression and interconnection of the differences Jesus outlines between those who abide in his word and *hoi Ioudaioi*, statements made in 8:31-47, offer stark contrasts. These reflect some of the strongest biases against *hoi Ioudaioi* in the entire gospel. The differences between the world's "works" and those of Jesus are extreme. In the remaining paragraphs I will consider some of the more striking differences. They can be outlined as follows:

WORLD'S WORKS	JESUS' WORKS
Of the Devil	Of the Father
Evil	Good
Seek Own Glory	Seek God's Glory
Demonize Jesus	Demonize His Opponents

CHILDREN OF THE DEVIL	CHILDREN OF THE FATHER
Live in Darkness	Live in Light
Are Liars	Live in Truth
Are Slaves	Are Free
Want to Kill	Desire God's Will
Die in Sin	Believe I Am He
Have No Place for the Word	Make a Home for the Word
Judge by Human Standards	Judge by the Father's Standards
Live from Below	Live from Above

John's use of the term "evil" (*ponēros*) is quite deliberate. It appears only three times in his gospel. In the first instance, Jesus declares that "judgment" results from the fact that "the light has come into the world, and people loved darkness rather than light because their deeds were evil"

(3:19). Another time the word *ponēros* is used is in the Farewell Discourse. Here Jesus prays not that God will take his followers "out of the world, but [that he will] protect them from the evil one" (17:15). The NRSV here seems to personify *ponēros*. What this means will become clearer when we examine the final section of chapter 8 and see how *hoi Ioudaioi* demonize Jesus (8:48), thus exposing their own deceit and revealing their own "demonization."

Elaine Pagels was one of the first to show how the early Christians, under siege from a host of sources, characterized their opponents in demonic terms.[3] Unlike the Synoptics who speak of Satan or Beelzebub as some kind of extra-terrestrial figure, John personifies Satan in those human forces and institutions that oppose Jesus (i.e., "the world" [in its negative meaning] and *hoi Ioudaioi*). According to Pagels, Satan expresses human conflict and characterizes "human enemies within our own religious traditions."[4] In this sense, *hoi Ioudaioi* who oppose Jesus are not just adversaries or even enemies; they are instruments of Satan working within religious institutions. Satan's works are evil; therefore, Jesus must testify against their corporate expression.

Scholars do a great disservice to John when they try to undermine the contemporary applicability of Pagel's insight by limiting it to the Johannine world of the first century. Demonization of a group's enemies is a phenomenon that seems to be as old as humanity itself and that has contemporary manifestations. Ralph K. White, in his examination of the three major wars of the twentieth century involving the United States, has shown that the first step in any conflict between groups begins when the ideology of each "side" is based on the demonization of the other. He calls this the "diabolical enemy image."[5] Moving beyond White's application to wars between nations, we find the diabolical enemy image at work when people opposing abortion call their opponents "baby killers," when gays are called degenerate, when those critical of capitalism's excesses are termed unpatriotic, when those wanting to abstain from sex before marriage are ridiculed as weird, and when those who cannot in conscience accept some of their religious leaders' teaching as dogma are branded as "disloyal."

Besides using demonic terms for his opponents, John's Jesus said that the world's works were "evil." A study by Roy F. Baumeister comes closest to presenting a contemporary expression of the dynamics of evil that existed between Jesus and *hoi Ioudaioi*. In *Evil: Inside Human Violence and Cruelty*, Baumeister portrays evil as the purposeful inflicting of harm or suffering on human beings. Purposeful inflicting of harm or "evil-as-violence" is exactly what we see in chapters 7 and 8 of John as *hoi Ioudaioi* seek at various times to kill Jesus. The insight that makes Baumeister's study so relevant for our purposes is his stress on the perpetrator of violence's gain rather than the victim's loss. Contrary to studies correlating violence with low self-esteem, Baumeister declares that the case is just the opposite: "Dangerous people...consist mainly of those who have favorable views about themselves. They strike out at others who question or dispute those favorable views....Most of the aggressive people I have known were...conceited, arrogant, and often consumed with thoughts about how they were superior to everyone else."[6] Anyone doing reader-response today can easily think of contemporary examples.

In addition to the evil-as-violence which arises to protect a personal or group ego, the author cites two other major causes of evil: the desire for material gain coupled with a lack of scruples about the means for achieving this gain and a distorted idealism wherein "noble ends are often seen as justifying violent means." When this happens, "the victims don't get much mercy."[7]

With regard to the evil stemming from a desire for material gain, we need not limit material gain to possessions and property only. "Material gain" can also refer to the wealth of power and prestige. In a church in which leaders are not aggrandized by material wealth but by power and prestige, religious leaders can experience great temptation to do evil. Thus we find some religious leaders so preoccupied with careerism[8] that they abdicate thinking for themselves. They only repeat the "party line" of their superiors. In the process they become pawns in the hands of often-times unscrupulous higher religious superiors who themselves have become controlled by an ideology defined by power and control. In the end, violence is done. Evil prevails.

Violence in the "World" of Contemporary Capitalism

This type of violence and evil is not limited to religious institutions; it can be found in many manifestations of modern-day capitalism. While I find it most obvious in the tobacco companies,[9] I believe they are merely extreme representatives of the shadow side of an economic system which has done much good but which also has been called "savage" by Pope John Paul II. The very existence and the livelihood of many of the executives, workers, and stockholders in the tobacco companies depends on a kind of capitalization of evil. This takes form in the selling of a product which, if used as intended, can cause only sickness and death. If evil is that which does violence and if violence is any force that inflicts injury, these companies and their "works" represent a powerful force of evil in our world today. When investors in such companies know that most of their dividends come from that which causes sickness and death and don't care, then indifference, the ultimate result of violence and evil, pervades their hearts—and their "bottom lines."

The words of Jesus about certain works in this "world" being evil took on new meaning for me some years ago. It was the day I attended the annual meeting of Philip Morris, home of the Marlboro Man and Virginia Slims. After the meeting I recalled the text of John 3:19-21:

> And this is the judgment, that the light has come into the world, and people loved darkness rather than the light because their deeds were evil. For all who do evil hate the light and do not come to the light, so that their deeds may not be exposed. But those who do what is true come to the light.

Violence is evil when power is used to control others. It is the ultimate evil when people are willing to be part of a dynamic that takes life, when they are complicit in strategies to kill or eliminate life. Thus, while we speak of the "evil" of abortion, of assisted suicide and euthanasia, we also recognize the evil in an economic system that makes money by selling that which does violence. When "whistle-blowers" expose the wrong being done, they risk their jobs and sometimes even their lives.

Because Jesus knew *hoi Ioudaioi* were looking for an opportunity to kill him, he could testify against the world that its works were evil. The opponents of Jesus were seeking him in order to do violence to him. When violence takes possession of our individual or corporate souls, we can actually *seek* (consciously or unconsciously) to harm those who oppose us. In his analysis of the eight uses of the word for seek (*zētein*) in chapter 7 alone, Jerome Neyrey states:

> "Seeking" Jesus, then, means either to "seek to arrest" him or to "seek to kill" him; even seeking to arrest him serves as the prelude to killing him and so comes to the same thing. "Seeking" in John 7 is tantamount to murder. So from the narrative point of view this audience is either unbelievably obtuse as to the public controversy over Jesus, or it is lying when it says it does not know what Jesus means about "seeking" him. We favor the latter interpretation for two reasons. In 7:20 the judges and critics of Jesus already lied by asking "Who seeks to kill you?" When the narrator has clearly informed his readers that they are in fact "seeking to kill him" (7:1); Jesus knows this and so asks the question, "Why do you seek to kill me?" (7:19). Moreover, Jesus will shortly expose many of his audience as sons of the devil, who is both liar and murderer *from the beginning* (8:44). Hence, we read the crowd's question in 7:35-36 as a lie about murder; they are "seeking" Jesus to arrest and kill him, but now they are lying about it.[10]

Today we routinely hear lies and denials from spokespersons of corporations about corruption and from governments about graft and influence-peddling. The same type of thing can happen, though more subtly, in religion. One example is when church teaching makes an about-face but will not acknowledge it as such, be it with Galileo, teachings having to do with marriage, private property and democracy, or even the death-penalty.

Violence in "The World" of the Church

What contemporary meaning lies behind the evil-as-violence expressed in John's words noting "no one would speak openly about him for fear of *hoi Ioudaioi*" (7:13)? When the United States Catholic bishops were unable to agree on a document related to women in the church, they settled instead for a statement on domestic violence. In it they describe violence—"in any form"—as "never justified" and sinful. At times, they say, it is a crime. They find that violence is connected with abuse, and they define abuse as "any kind of behavior that one ... uses to control another through fear and intimidation."[11] Further, they show how religion can undergird violence when scripture passages are "used selectively" to promote or rationalize violence.

Increasingly I find women and men asking why the bishops' own words about violence on the "domestic" level aren't being applied to violence on the "ecclesiastical" level as well. They are asking whether the scriptures are being "used selectively" to support dynamics that keep people from sharing in the very body and blood of Christ, to provide "scriptural" justification for the view that it is God's will that only men are to be ordained and that these men, in the Latin Rite, are to be celibate.[12] That "no one would speak openly about him for fear of *hoi Ioudaioi*" because they might be expelled from the synagogue has its contemporary expression in our religious "world" when ecclesiastical leaders state that anyone disagreeing with their teaching related to women and the priesthood will be considered to be "outside" the church.

Another way the evil, violence, and abuse continue in religious systems is when the people are divided in spite of the apparently united front of the leaders. In John's gospel this occurs in the debate "the crowd" has about Jesus when some say "He is a good man" while others say "No, he is deceiving the crowd." When the people fight among themselves, the leaders split themselves off. I find it interesting that, when the leaders do intervene, it is usually to clamp down on issues relating to internal power structures and sexual dynamics within the church rather than to deal with external issues relating to social justice. Meanwhile, issues that undermine the integrity of the community can go unaddressed. The status quo (and the control of the leaders) can continue.

Seeking God's Glory vs. Self-Glory

Once in the temple, "Jesus began to teach" (7:14). Whatever he said created incredulity among *hoi Ioudaioi*. They were astonished (*thaumazein* [see 3:7; 4:27; 5:20, 28]). They doubted how someone so unlearned (in the type of education connected with them [7:15]) could "have such learning." He had not come through their system. He was not speaking the party-line. Who had taught him? From whence, therefore, came his authority? In their system, no valid learning existed unless it came from a recognized teacher.[13] So their first query about Jesus' "learning" sets the stage for what will be an ongoing challenge-riposte between them and Jesus until the end of chapter 8 (7:19, 20, 23, 25, 28, 35f, 42, 47, 51; 8:19, 22, 25, 33, 43, 46, 48, 53, 57).

Jesus rebuts their charge by declaring that the source of his teaching is not himself but the one who sent him. Anyone committed to doing God's will would recognize that his teaching is God's, not his own (7:16-17). Then, in a clear challenge to their corporate code of honor, he declares: "Those who speak on their own seek their own glory; but the one who seeks the glory of him who sent him is true, and there is nothing false (*adikia*) in him" (7:18).

Unless one is aware of the cultural dynamics behind these words, it is easy to miss the levels of meaning involved. What we have here, and throughout chapters 7 and 8, is a culturally-defined dynamic that involves challenges to Jesus' honor by *hoi Ioudaioi* and his defense of that honor. While the specific word for "honor" (*timē*) does not appear here, Jesus' reference to "glory" (*doxa*) is its equivalent. Jerome Neyrey points out: "'Glory' (*doxa*) is often and correctly translated as reputation or fame; it means 'public opinion' quite simply, that is, 'honor' (for *doxa*/glory as a synonym of honor, see Rom 16:25-27; Eph 3:20-21; Jude 24-25; 2 Peter 3:18). As Jesus states the case, ambitious *achievers* seek honor for themselves, while those with *ascribed honor seek honor* for the ascriber." Thus Jesus ascribes all honor/glory to his Patron/Father who sent him.[14]

Slaves to Sin via the Lie vs. Living in Freedom via the Truth

After this, in what had to be understood as another challenge to their honor as well as to their integrity, Jesus says he is "true." He is without any *adikia* or untruth, falsity, or injustice. In 8:31 and subsequent verses he picks up the same theme. Unlike his opponents, he is free because he speaks the truth. They are enslaved because their "truth" is a lie. It therefore enslaves them.

Even though they are a dominated people and, therefore, enslaved to Rome, *hoi Ioudaioi* insist that, because they are descendants of Abraham, they have never been slaves to anyone (8:33, 39). In response, Jesus introduces into the mix the notion of sin: "Everyone who commits sin is a slave to sin" (8:34). Their sin is that, though they claim to be free in terms of religion, they are not; they are slaves to their own willed blindness. "At this point," Carolyn Osiek writes (with insights that can ring true for religious authorities of any era),

> the author is telling us that there are two kinds of unfreedom which block the passage to freedom. The first is reliance on status. Jesus' hearers say, "But we have our credentials; we are born into the right religion, the right tradition; we got our degrees from the appropriate schools; we know who we are; we know our heritage." In other words, they are entrenched in their triumphalism: "We are not going to be enslaved by anything, because we come from the right towns and we can rely on our status."
>
> Jesus cuts through their self-assurance by introducing the second lack of freedom: "The one who sins is a slave to sin." In John's Gospel, sin does not consist of little things, nor even of big things, that we do and have to undo. Rather, here sin is a refusal to see the truth. It is not an *inability* but a *refusal* to see the truth.[15]

If those who are entrenched in the word (*logos*) of their own "truth" refuse to change, it is understandable that they will need to eliminate from their midst anyone else's truth by declaring it false. Whether this applies to the religious leaders of Jesus' day or ours, the dynamic is the same.

To *hoi Ioudaioi* convinced of their own freedom because of their descent from Abraham, Jesus says that, if they were truly Abraham's children, they would be *doing* what Abraham did—which was to believe in his *logos*. Because they refuse, they remain in their own *logos* and, to that degree, are slaves to sin (8:34). This makes them unfree and, therefore, the illegitimate offspring of Abraham (8:41). Also, because they don't believe in the one in whom Abraham believed, they are children of evil itself (see 8:44). Consequently they are also children of the lie.

What does it mean to be "children of the lie"? While this phrase may remind some readers of Scott Peck's book, *People of the Lie*, they may be wary of viewing scripture through a psychoanalytic and, quite possibly, overly subjective lens. Yet Michael Willett Newheart has shown in a recent collection of essays on John that "recent literary studies in the Fourth Gospel seem to be paving the way for psychological analysis."[16]

Even though M. Scott Peck is no theologian or scriptural exegete, he is a recognized popular interpreter of the human psyche of people as well as of North American culture. Peck's insights into what it means to be "people of the lie" have much to offer those seeking a contemporary understanding of the dynamics that elicited such vindictiveness from Jesus. Peck argues that "the concept of evil has been central to religious thought for millennia. Yet it is virtually absent from our science of psychology. ...The major reason for this strange state of affairs is that the scientific and the religious models have hitherto been considered totally immiscible—like oil and water, mutually incompatible and rejecting."[17]

In *People of the Lie: The Hope for Healing Human Evil*, Peck links evil with the lie itself, just as Jesus does in chapters 7 and 8 of John. We have already noted how, in order to save their system, *hoi Ioudaioi* set in motion a plan to kill Jesus. Making a scapegoat of one's "enemy" is the best way to ensure that enemy can be killed. "A predominant characteristic," Peck notes "of the behavior of those I call evil is scapegoating. Because in their hearts they consider themselves above reproach, they must lash out at anyone who does reproach them. They sacrifice others to preserve their self-image of perfection."[18] When religion is added to this dynamic, it can be close to demonic.

Michael Willett Newheart calls such a dynamic the "shadow" at work. He writes:

> "The Jews," then, evoke fear and anger from characters in the narrative, and the reader feels the same emotions toward them. They carry the reader's shadow, the sum total of what one refuses to acknowledge about himself or herself. The reader, therefore, projects the archetype of the Self onto Jesus and the shadow onto "the Jews." The reader must read the narrative, then, with a divided consciousness: alienation toward "the Jews" through anger and fear, and identification with Jesus through love, peace and joy.[19]

What does it mean for *hoi Ioudaioi* to be children of the lie? What kind of "father" is really being revealed here? It seems from the context that we are not talking about blood genealogy but about bad ideology. I find one of the best descriptions of the dynamics being played out in this challenge-riposte in Gil Bailie's *Violence Unveiled*. Despite disagreeing with him on his understanding of the source of violence,[20] I concur with his notion of the fuller meaning of *logos*. His explanation of it approximates what I have been calling "ideology." He writes:

> The term "father" as the evangelist uses it here refers to a social law of gravity that predetermines the pattern (the *logos*) of social developments in the ordinary course of cultural history. No doubt first-century Judaism was a patriarchal society, but the term "father" in these verses refers to the organizing principle of conven-

tional culture regardless of its religious concepts or its peculiar form of social organization. What the Johannine Jesus calls the "father"—the father of lies and the murderer from the beginning —has virtually nothing to do with the male parent whom we call father.[21]

While Bailie's next paragraph personifies the devil as a diabolical figure, those more familiar with John's identification of the diabolical with collective forces in "the world" can grasp the point:

> Jesus argues that those to whom he is speaking are neither the children of Abraham nor of God for, he says, "you want to kill me when I tell you the truth" (8:40). Those to whom Jesus is speaking have not been able to persevere in his *logos*. They have merely "believed" in him, while unwittingly remaining loyal to a "father" whom they mistakenly think is Abraham or God, but whom Jesus recognizes as a diabolical figure. The evidence for Jesus' claim that his listeners are in the grip of this diabolical figure consists of one thing: they want to kill him.[22]

Justification for killing ultimately rests in different interpretations of truth. Differences about "truth" are grounded in people's differing *logoi*. The violence that results in the will to kill stems from unresolved conflicts, which arise from different perspectives of good and evil, different interpretations of truth. *Hoi Ioudaioi* were trying to kill Jesus because they were not remaining in the truth; they were slaves to the logic of the lie. Over each system of *logos*, Bailie concludes, "there presides a *father*."[23] One has been and will remain "a murderer from the beginning and does not stand in the truth, because there is no truth in him. When he lies, he speaks according to his own nature, for he is a liar and the father of lies" (8:44). The other has been and will remain the source of Jesus' identity and veracity: the God of life.

Judging by Human Standards vs. Judging by God's

As part of his challenge to their honor, Jesus questions his opponents about how they practice truth and justice according to their interpretation of the law: "Did not Moses give you the law? Yet none of you keeps the law. Why are you looking for an opportunity to kill me?" (7:19-20).

Hoi Ioudaioi have already decided that Jesus must be eliminated violently (5:18; 7:1). However, the people seem genuinely surprised to hear Jesus say such a thing. Instead of *hoi Ioudaioi* answering his challenge with their own riposte, John says it was the "crowd [who] answered."

They say: "You have a demon! Who is trying to kill you?" (7:20). The de-monization of the enemy, the first step in scapegoating, has now infected the thinking of the crowd, not just that of the religious leaders.

At this Jesus recalls the previous reaction of *hoi Ioudaioi* to his heal-ing of the "invalid-ated" man who had been at the pool for thirty-eight years (5:2-18). He links his "work" of healing restoration with the true purpose of the law that came from Moses. According to that law, circum-cision of a man's penis—which identified him in his body as belonging to a wider corporate body—made the males of Israel perfected in a way that made the wider social body, the collective whole, free from contamina-tion. The circumcision of the individual's body-part was meant to rein-force the ultimate goal of the Mosaic law: to bring the created order—individual, communal, collective, and cosmic—into closer conformity with the plan for the world intended by God from the beginning. This conformity between the cultural order and the cosmic order, as the Psalms reminded the people (see Pss 35; 85; 97), was meant to ensure that justice as right relationships would bring about the original creative plan of God. Consequently, while Jesus' healing of the invalid on the sabbath *appeared* to the religious legalists to have invalidated Jesus as a God-ordained heal-er, he challenged them not to "judge by appearances, but judge with right judgment" (7:24). In addressing the way his opponents were judging—by externals rather than justice—Jesus now was undermining the criteria by which these religious leaders were judging.

Anyone judging rightly would recognize in his restoration of the in-valid the creative work of God. Thus Jesus connected his healing of a man's "whole body" with fulfilling the very purpose of the sabbath: the restoration of the whole collective body in *shalom*. If their law, meant to uphold the order of Israel by sabbath observance, allowed the leaders to perform a circumcision on a part of the body—a ritual intended to sym-bolize the making "whole" of a man—couldn't they see that his healing of the whole body symbolized the fullest purpose of the sabbath—the es-tablishment of a new order for creation itself? He answered them:

> I performed one work, and all of you are astonished. Moses gave
> you circumcision (it is, of course not from Moses, but from the
> patriarchs), and you circumcise a man on the sabbath. If a man
> receives circumcision on the sabbath in order that the law of
> Moses may not be broken, are you angry (*cholan*) with me be-
> cause I healed a man's whole body on the sabbath? Do not judge
> by appearances, but judge with right judgment. (7:21-24)

The word for anger that John's Jesus uses here to describe his hear-ers' reaction is *cholan*. Ordinarily anger arises from a sense of being disrespected, attacked, or deprived of something considered to be one's right. However, anger in the form of *cholan* is not just an emotional reaction to perceived or real threats; it arises from a place deep within one's being. It represents an underlying resentment stemming from a kind of envy or jealousy toward another who is feared as a threat to one's world. People with *cholan* end up having their perception clouded. With objectivity impaired, clear judgment is impossible. Consequently, only appearances—for instance, Jesus' healing on a sabbath which appears to be the breaking of a law—are all that can be judged. Rather than judging from *cholan*, Jesus challenged them, they should judge objectively, in the light of that toward that which all law was ordered: the new realm of Jubilee's *shalom.*

Jesus' arguments would fall on deaf ears. Like the religious leaders before them, these religious leaders would never proclaim—much less submit to—the vision of Jubilee, because to do so would be a threat to their very existence as those who stood to benefit most from their alliance with the ruling powers of the day.[24]

Living Water and Light vs. Sin and Darkness

During the first six days of the festival of Booths, each day began with a procession to the Pool of Siloam to gather water. The water was brought back through the Water Gate and carried to the altar. There the presiding priest poured the water and some wine into two vessels on the altar and allowed them to overflow onto the altar itself. On the seventh morning, the ritual was more dramatic: the procession to the altar was repeated seven times.

Thus, on this most important of all seven days, the last, Jesus "cried out, 'Let anyone who is thirsty come to me, and let the one who believes in me drink. As the scripture has said, "Out of the believer's heart shall flow rivers of living water."'" (7:37b-38). Although this text has been translated in different ways, it is clear that John here means to portray Jesus proclaiming himself as the source of everything sacred that this ritual represents for Israel. No longer will people need to process with the priests to the altar; now they can "come to" Jesus directly. Those who come to him and place their faith in him will have living waters flowing from their hearts. This "living water" will be Jesus' own Spirit whom believers will receive once he has been glorified (7:39).

Jesus' dramatic words created "a division (*schisma*) in the crowd" (7:43). On the one hand, some seemed able to make the connection between Jesus' words and the ritual setting; they proclaimed him as "really the prophet" (7:40). Others went further, saying: "This is the Messiah" (7:41a). On the other hand, their very profession of faith in him elicited more skepticism from others because of their conviction that the Davidic Messiah would come from Bethlehem in Judea and they knew Jesus had come from Galilee (7:41b-42).

Having subverted the ritual of the feast of Booths which involved the pouring of the water by identifying his own Spirit as "living water," Jesus then turned upside down the second of the great rituals, namely light. He declared: "I am (*egō eimi*) the light of the world. Whoever follows me will never walk in darkness but will have the light of life" (8:12).

What the law has been for Israel, Jesus is now for the world. The law the Pharisees are trying to use to judge Jesus cannot, therefore, apply. His light, he himself, is the law from God. Now no longer do those struggling to find God need to do so with rituals of water and light. By identifying with Jesus they can experience his living water in themselves and live in his light. This light is no longer to be isolated in a temple; it exists for "the world." Jesus is the light "the world" cannot provide on its own. The rabbis referred to the law as a lamp or a light to guide the steps of Israel (Ps 119:105).[25] For religious leaders who found their light in the law (and their interpretation of it), Jesus' words could only be understood as seditious.

The Authorities' Teaching vs. The Teacher's Authority

Although the temple police had been sent quite a bit earlier to arrest Jesus (7:32), we have heard nothing of what happened to them. Now they reappear before the chief priests and the Pharisees. But they come with empty hands, without the intended prisoner. The religious leaders demand to know why (7:45). The reply of the temple police indicates that they are more closely linked with the people than with the plots of the priests. They have become so much a part of the crowd that they are quite taken by this Jesus: "Never has anyone spoken like this!" (7:46).

After remonstrating with the police for being taken in by this deceiver (note the diabolical-enemy image), the religious leaders put up for their gendarmes a united front. They ask: "Has any one of the authorities or of the Pharisees believed in him?" We know that at least one "authority," Nicodemus (as well as other crypto-believers referred to by Nicodemus in his use of "we") came to Jesus, although at night.

In many ways this scene reminds me of the united front put up by the National Conference of Catholic Bishops on various matters, especially the controversial birth control issue. While they indicate to the crowds (the laity) that it is their common teaching that artificial birth control is mortally sinful, some bishops (at the bishops' meetings) challenge such teaching. However, evidencing the degree of fear and intimidation that exists in this body, most keep silent, even though they know such teaching is leading people astray. Bishop Kenneth Untener refers to these crypto-Catholic leaders in noting what happened when he challenged the body's "teaching" on birth control. In 1992, he recalled:

> At the bishops' meeting a year ago I got up and said I don't know how we can say the logic of our teaching on birth control is compelling because we know it's not. Yet we were prepared to pass a statement with a paragraph asking people who disagreed to reexamine their position.
>
> So I said I don't know how we can pass this paragraph knowing what everybody in this room silently knows and engage in this conspiracy of silence. This is the sign of a dysfunctional family.
>
> Well, I must have had 20 or 30 bishops come up to me individually in the hallway and thank me for saying that. The trouble is they all looked over their shoulder before they did it.[26]

Until now the bishops have been more muted in their rejection of such truth from one of their members than were *hoi Ioudaioi*. They merely distance themselves from the likes of Untener.

The conclusion of the chief priests and the Pharisees about "this crowd" who believes in Jesus (which seemingly now includes the temple police) is twofold: (1) they don't know the law and (2) they are accursed. Robert J. Karris explains that "those who do not know the law" in John 7:49 were understood by the rabbis as the "people of the land." They might not have been poor but they were marginalized in the system by the religious authorities because they did not have formal training in the law.[27] In a parallel contemporary vein, this attitude is like that of bishops who have no qualms in telling the laity that the law says they are accursed if they practice artificial birth control, even though these very same bishops don't believe this themselves. As John will show of such leaders, they themselves stand judged.

Toward the end of his debate with his various opponents, after declaring that they are "from below" while he is "from above," Jesus is challenged with a query about the source of his identity: "Who are you?" Having manifested himself in works and words, the frustrated Jesus merely responds with the question that set the theme of this chapter: "Why do I speak to you at all?" (8:25). This question on the lips of the Johannine Jesus is a formal expression of the fact that he has given up ever trying to change them. Now Jesus puts them on trial even as he continues his defense. He charges, "I have much to say about you and much to condemn" (8:26a). In the same breath he defends himself: "The one who sent me is true, and I declare to the world what I have heard from him" (8:26b). He then moves on to speak about what it means to be a true child of Abraham, living in the truth rather than being a slave to the lie (8:31-43).

Everything—charges and countercharges, challenges and ripostes, accusations and defense—now comes to a fever pitch regarding the central issue of Jesus' identity and where he is from. In the process, the identity of *hoi Ioudaioi* becomes clear, and their origin is seen to be not only sin, but "the father of lies" (8:44). However, it would be an oversimplification to identify this "devil" as existing outside *hoi Ioudaioi*. Indeed, their plotting is a revelation of the demonic that exists whenever the word and works of Jesus are violated in any form. This occurs not only when they are patently rejected, but also when they are taken out of context, selectively interpreted to reinforce previously-entrenched cultural positions, or isolated from equally significant passages found elsewhere in scripture.

FIVE

WOMAN, WHERE ARE THEY?
HAS NO ONE CONDEMNED YOU? (8:10)

The Questions of John 7:53-8:11

The account in John's gospel traditionally called "The Woman Taken in Adultery" has always been problematic. Just its name—usually some variant on "the adulterous woman"—has posed difficulties. Questions about its title, however, are overshadowed by two other concerns: a structural one and an interpretative one. Structurally, exegetes wonder whether the story should be in John's gospel at all. Indeed, it is absent from the earliest reliable manuscripts of John's gospel.[1] Interpretatively, some question what it really means while others take issue with its evident anti-woman bias. One result of these concerns is that the story rarely gets discussed.[2] Often it's lucky to be relegated to an appendix.

There is no denying that problems exist relating to this story. However, not to investigate it because of its problems does a disservice to us as contemporary readers, since the story is in the text as we have it. Consequently, I will address the problems first and then try to show the story's relevance to the reader today.

Problems Related to the Story Traditionally Called
"The Woman Taken in Adultery"

1. *The naming of the story sets a bias.* If you were to ask anyone the title of this story, it would be a rare person who wouldn't respond with some version of "the adulterous woman." In the words of Gail R. O'Day, such a naming represents "the power of interpretive interests to read the text against its own shape."[3] The "power of interpretive interests" represented in Western European, white, male, clerical types like myself has shaped the way the text has been received in the wider community for centuries.

In the introduction to this book I noted how the fact that I am an able-bodied, white, male, straight, educated, North American, Roman Catholic cleric colors the way I think. This bias does not get shed when I approach the gospel of John. Any interpretation I do, even trying to be as objective as I can, will be reflected through the lens of my social location. I've called this subtle and hidden standpoint "ideology." Since popular understanding of the scripture texts traditionally has been proferred by others who share variations of my stance (with some exceptions representing Anglo-Saxon male Protestants), it's not surprising that the original naming of this story (which seems to have been identified with Augustine) has been "set" in the culturally-dominated transmission of it. O'Day contends that, as exegesis has presented the woman in a way that has continued her (and other women's) marginalization, so the early church and those (males) who interpreted the text tried also to marginalize the story itself. In short, patriarchal prejudices created and sustained the textual and canonical margir ʌʲty of the text.

2. *The story seems out of place in John's gospel.* The passage we have today was omitted from virtually every early manuscript. While versions of all the other stories in the gospel can be found in the various sources (codici), there are no traces of this story. It seems to have found its way into John at a much later date. In the Greek Church it was not recognized as canonical (legitimated as part of the official text) until the Middle Ages. Although early writers in the Latin Church, like Augustine, mentioned it and Jerome included it in the Vulgate, Raymond Brown notes that commentaries on the text did not appear in the West until 900.[4] Consequently, most academic commentators simply offer no commentaries of any significance regarding the text.

Another argument for exclusion of this passage now found between chapters 7 and 8 is that it just doesn't fit well. If one were to excise the text of this story, it wouldn't be missed at all. C. H. Dodd states that since the two chapters are really "a collection of miscellaneous material" and "a series of controversial dialogues, often without clearly apparent connection,"[5] he finds no need for the story here.[6] While I disagree with Dodd and have tried to show in the previous chapter that a basic unifying theme is Jesus' identity and origin in contrast to that of *hoi Ioudaioi*, Dodd's argument that the two chapters are simply a collection of stories ought to speak to the story's inclusion rather than its exclusion. If chapters 7 and 8 are a collection, why shouldn't this story be included too?

Another argument against the story's placement in the fourth gospel is that it seems more suited to the gospel of Luke. Indeed, given the Lukan sensitivity to women, there is good reason for seeing this as a more proper placement. Some have even suggested where it might "fit" into the Lukan narrative—after Luke 21:38 which states that "all the people would get up early in the morning to listen to him in the temple." The connection is appropriate because John 8:2 begins by saying, "Early in the morning he came again to the temple. All the people came to him and he sat down and began to teach them." It would seem logical, then, that the story would fit perfectly at this point in Luke's narration.[7]

Yet another argument has to do with style. It just doesn't seem to reflect some of John's key patterns. Furthermore, the key features of this story are not found elsewhere in the gospel. One of the main patterns used by John, especially in his narratives involving character and story development, is repetition in the form of circular theme development, recurrence, and chiasm. Here any repetition or duplication is lacking. The story just moves from point "a" to "b" and "c" without parallels of balance.[8]

One of the strongest arguments revolves around the story's terminology,[9] particularly in the use of the phrase "the scribes and the Pharisees" to describe those who brought the woman to Jesus. The joint presentation of scribes with Pharisees simply cannot be found anywhere else in John, yet it is so common in the the Synoptics that it has become part of the *lingua franca* of secular society.

Why the Text Should Be Included
in Any Serious Reader-Response Study of John

Where does all this leave us? How can this book of mine be viewed as credible, much less reviewed as creditable in the "academy," if it includes a serious discussion of this piece? My answer lies in the kind of methodology I am using: reader-response. Reader-response theory differs from other theories in its approach to the text. In the historical-critical method I learned thirty years ago, a method that involves form criticism and redaction criticism, one asks how a text got where it is and why one writer places it in one place and another places it somewhere else (or not at all). Reader-response theory begins with a basic assumption about the text itself. This assumption is a variation on the saying: *What you see is what you've got.* You work with what's before you.

While John 7:53–8:11 may not have originated in the Johannine community, it now stands as part of the faith community's "received text" of the scriptures. It is part of its tradition as well, in the fullest sense of what tradition means: the very origin of and ongoing environment within which the scriptures exist. This wider notion of tradition giving rise to and cultivating the scriptures has been well-articulated by Sandra Schneiders: "Tradition is the actualization in the present, in and through language, of the most valued and critically important aspects of the community's experience, or, more precisely, of the community's experience of itself as it has been selectively appropriated and deliberately transmitted."[10] Thus, whether or not this passage can be found in early documents is not as important as the fact that it is now part of what the faith community considers the inspired text itself. The value of this rationale for inclusion is attested to by the fact that, when the Revised Standard Version was first published in 1952, the story was not included in the text; it was relegated to the margin. This created such an uproar among the believing community that it was reinstated (in brackets) in the next printing. This brings me to a corollary point: the issue of canonicity.

"Canonicity" refers to the official list of books considered by the church as God's inspired word. Building on the materials originally included in St. Jerome's "Vulgate" translation of the scriptures, the Council of Trent finally decreed in 1546 that there were forty-five books in the First Testament and twenty-seven in the Second which would be considered inspired. While the need for such a decree arose because of Protestant and Catholic differences over some books in the Greek scriptures (the Septuagint) not found in the Hebrew, there were no serious differences over the gospels or what were considered any parts of them.

Sandra Schneiders shows that the establishment of the canon, "including the composition of its books," was a work of tradition. The scriptures arose through the community's tradition and the canonicity of the scriptures was the work of tradition. She concludes:

> The scripture thus traditionally established became the norm of ongoing tradition, which, nevertheless, remains the indispensable context of the Bible's interpretation. The canon as a whole and its parts as canonical are in dialectical hermeneutical relationship to each other at the literary level, while the whole of scripture and the whole of tradition realize the same type of relationship at the level of the Church's life.[11]

The fact that John 7:53-8:11 was absent from original manuscripts seems non-disputable, but, in light of the fuller meaning of tradition for readers of faith, it also seems non-significant. Acknowledging the tradition already in place that accepted the story as "historical," Jerome included the passage in his translation of the Bible into Latin. This inclusion effectively determined its canonicity, at least for the Latin Church. Thus, it cannot be disputed that the story has become part of the received canon as we have it today with its placement where it is in John 7:53–8:11.

In addition to the fact that the story and its placement are part of the canon, a further reason can be given for its inclusion in chapters 7 and 8. The linguistic characteristics and the theme link it with the trial-like setting of these chapters. Rather than detracting from the other sections of chapters 7 and 8, it fits quite well. It also highlights Jesus' mercy in contrast with what may be considered an overly-harsh treatment of the woman by the religious leaders. As Barnabas Lindars has shown, these two chapters revolve around accusations and judgments.[12] The religious leaders are determined to challenge Jesus so that they can ultimately kill him. This is their goal in 7:53–8:11; hence the story's "fit."[13]

A final rationale for the inclusion of this story is provided by the liturgy of the ecumenical churches, in particular the Sunday readings. While I would hope that the "faith response" that this book is attempting to elicit might resonate with all Christians, I assume that the majority of those reading it will come from the Roman Catholic tradition. This Johannine text is significant enough to merit inclusion as a gospel for one of the Sundays of the church's calendar year. It is proclaimed throughout the world every Fifth Sunday of Lent when the churches celebrate the "C Cycle."

Interpreting the Text

Most homilies dealing with this text seem to concentrate on the woman's sin, or concerns about the way Jesus seems to "tolerate" a serious sin, or speculation as to why Jesus would write on the ground or what he wrote.

From my perspective, such conjecturing may be quite creative, but it is ill-conceived and often as contrived as it is questionable. When people concentrate on why Jesus responded to his opponents' challenge by writing or debate what or why he wrote, they miss what John raises as the main point of the story (8:6), to say nothing of Jesus' verbal response to his challengers. I find such speculation to be a disservice, a deviation from the very important issues that can be uncovered when one sets out to do a more objective reading of the text. It is to this task that I now turn.

The Woman "on Trial" for Her Act of Adultery (7:53–8:5)

The story begins by noting that, after Jesus' debates with "the crowd," the "chief priests and Pharisees," and, of course, the seemingly ever-present *hoi Ioudaioi*, "went home" (7:53). No reason is given for this abrupt departure, except that the highest authorities—the chief priests and the Pharisees—have been frustrated in their efforts to have Jesus arrested (7:45-48) and have been challenged by one of their own, Nicodemus, to give Jesus a hearing before condemning him (7:50-51).

As they went to their homes, Jesus went to the Mount of Olives. Why? We are not told and will not try to speculate, since this is the first and last reference to this place in John's gospel (although it is mentioned by Luke that, "he would go out and spend the night on the Mount of Olives, as it was called" [Lk 21:37]). Perhaps the reference in John to Jesus' going to the Mount of Olives is just to get him back "to the temple" at a specific time, "early in the morning" (8:2). "All the people" came to him there, on the turf of the religious leaders. With everyone present "he sat down," as was the custom of Jewish teachers (but noted nowhere else of Jesus in John's gospel) "and began to teach them" (8:2).

The image of people coming to Jesus and his sitting down and teaching them suggests that he is someone in whom the people have invested authority. Sitting down to teach was what established and respected rabbis did. The impression is clear: The people—in fact, "all" of them—are moving their allegiance from the temple authorities to Jesus. The reaction of the religious authorities, who previously have experienced at least some dissension in their ranks (7:48-52), seems quite normal: envy at the success of Jesus and a sense of being dishonored in the process.

In the introduction to this book, I discussed anthropologist Gerald A. Arbuckle's view of the culture of Jesus as a "culture of prejudice." This culture was grounded in notions of scarcity: one's gain was another's loss. Consequently, if the honor from others ("the people") expected for one's self or one's group were to be redirected to another, this would be seen as a threat to one's own honor. Envy would probably follow. If power in the form of control and the authority to elicit obedience from others were in short supply and "the people" were to transfer their allegiance to someone else's influence and teaching, envy would be sure to follow. Arbuckle writes:

> Envy is the sadness a person feels because he or she lacks what someone else has and either desires it or wishes that the other did not possess it. It is a potentially destructive emotion; if it is uncontrolled, the envious not only wishes the envied person, relationship, or thing ruined but in fact may destroy that which is envied. Envy appears when the higher gifts, successes, or possessions of another are seen as reflecting poorly on the self. Envy involves feelings of inferiority, covetousness, or ill will toward the envied person.[14]

In cultures where honor/shame codes characterize relationships, envy defines the dynamics among persons and groups when one's honor is threatened. "While not wishing to reduce the entire conflict between Jesus and the Pharisees, Scribes, etc., to issues of envy, nevertheless, in a world where all goods are thought to exist in limited supply and where there is intense competition for honor, we expect *challenges* to claims," Jerome Neyrey explains.[15] Why? To lose honor is a shameful thing.

When the honor of one's self or group is at stake, action must be taken to protect it. Numbers 5:11-29 had made it clear that, if "a spirit of jealousy" were to come on a husband whose wife had defiled herself, he could bring her to the priests. They would then perform rituals to determine her innocence or guilt. However, in John's story, the jealousy and envy are associated with the priests, the religious leaders themselves. Now they are about to be dishonored, not for their approach to the woman in her adultery, but for their own infidelity.

In the contemporary situation of our church, when power and control are perceived to be in short supply, the organizing relationships among various persons (women and men, cleric and lay) are worked out so that positions of honor are ensured for members of one group over another, even when this may be at the expense of the overall good of the people the church is supposed to serve. This leads to "isms," social arrangements reinforced by ideologies of racism and sexism, nationalism and clericalism. Arbuckle notes some things that can happen when "isms" define the relationships in institutions:

> Today, within the church, the struggle against cultures of prejudice continues, though there is a little more sensitivity to their discriminatory and unjust consequences. For example, the centuries-old patriarchal culture obstructs within many local churches an honest sharing between the sexes that would further building of the Kingdom. Male evangelizers can be so jealously committed to retaining their status that even scriptural texts are manipulated to support their dominative positions in evangelization.[16]

With the issue of power at stake between the religious leaders and Jesus, the scene is set for the actors to appear before Jesus. "The scribes and the Pharisees brought a woman who had been caught in adultery" (8:3a).

In a culture grounded in notions of honor and shame, codes were written to enable society to function optimally. Sexual relationships between men and women in Israelite society were governed by codes of conduct that were designed to protect men's honor and to minimize their shame. The First Testament established strict codes concerning adultery. Leviticus 20:10 and Deuteronomy 22:22-29 describe in detail what should be done in cases of violation of the commandments stated in Exodus 20:14 and 17 and repeated in Deuteronomy 5:18 and 21: "You shall not commit adultery; you shall not covet your neighbor's wife." The latter commandment reveals clearly the bias in favor of the male.

Like murder and idolatry, adultery in first-century Israelite culture constituted a grave sin. Though the manner of death for adultery is not mentioned in Leviticus 20:10 and Deuteronomy 20:22, sentences of stoning for this sin were common during the first century. Later, in the period of the Mishna, adulterers were sentenced to strangling. Whatever the form of execution, adultery constituted a public crime punishable by death.

In John, anonymity is often used as a tool to help the reader enter the text more easily. In this story, however, the anonymity of the woman is cultural. She has no name, no voice, no defense, no purpose except to serve a man's sexual and functional needs and to be an object of his proprietary interests. She is not a person but property, not a subject but an object, not an individual with rights but a tool for others' agendas.

Since women were considered men's property, a man convicted of adultery was punished not only because he had infringed on another man's property, but because he had dishonored that man. Since a woman had no rights, only the rights of the married man could be violated. A wife and her partner committing adultery could violate the rights of her husband, but the wife had no rights which her husband could violate. As noted by Hisako Kinukawa, who herself comes from a culture highly defined by notions of honor and shame, a man committing adultery "was punished because he had affected the honor and property of the other male party, not the rights of the woman."[17]

Adultery was defined as a man having genital relations with (1) a married woman, (2) a betrothed virgin, or (3) a nonbetrothed virgin. If a man committed adultery with a virgin who was not betrothed, the law demanded that, to protect the honor of her patriarchal household, he marry her and never be able to divorce her (because then she would have become a source of shame to her family). The punishment for adultery was death for both parties (Lev 20:10), with stoning as the usual means of death (see Ez 16:40). Since there were no ways of determining if a man was a physical virgin at the time of espousal and marriage, but it was believed that there were for women, a woman found to be non-virginal at the time of legal intercourse could have charges brought against her. "They shall bring the young woman out to the entrance of her father's house and the men of her town shall stone her to death, because she committed a disgraceful act in Israel by prostituting herself in her father's house. So you shall purge the evil from Israel" (Dt 22:21). As is clear from this passage, a woman engaging in adultery was a dishonor, a disgrace to her "man," whether the man was her father or the person she might marry in the future.

While Jesus was teaching, the scribes and the Pharisees brought in a woman who had been "caught in adultery." Adultery was a violation of God's law; thus, violators were guilty of sin. However, the woman had been *caught* in her sin. This moved her sin from guilt to shame. What had been private is now public. John tells us that, after she had been caught, the religious leaders made her "stand before all of them" (8:3). What before may have remained limited to personal guilt now is widened to become an issue of public honor and shame. The guilty one is "made" to stand in front of everyone. She is shamed by her religious leaders.

Now that she is exposed "before all of them," her trial begins. The first action on the part of her prosecutors is to accuse her: "Teacher, this woman was caught in the very act of committing adultery. Now in the law Moses commanded us to stone such women" (8:4-5a). The Greek word used to describe her act of adultery is a technical legal term. The leaders' use of legalese reinforces the trial-like setting of the scene.

The scribes' and the Pharisees' selective use of the law exposes their sexist, patriarchal double standard. First of all, if the woman was not just *caught*, but *caught in the very act of committing adultery*. It is clear that she had to be involved in the sex act with a man. Where was the man? The reader might question why he hadn't been brought forward along with the woman so that, as the law truly said, they both might be found guilty and stoned. However, the blindness of the religious leaders to their own sexist selectivity leads them to selectively interpret the law itself. It applies only to her. They lay down their challenge to Jesus, setting him up with two "nows": "Now in the law Moses commanded us to stone such *women*. Now what do you say?" (8:5).

That they are selective in their interpretation and application of the law to the woman alone is evident insofar as Leviticus 20:10 makes it clear that both the adulterer and the adulteress should be stoned. Why they would choose to apply the law only to the woman or why similar double standards continue through the interpretation of "the law of Christ" by today's religious leaders are matters that we will not take up here. We do need to ask, however, if there may not be other contemporary instances of this type of double standard based on selective interpretation of scripture.

That there are became clear to me not too long ago as I participated in a faith-sharing on the gospel of John.

At 8:00 on Friday mornings all sorts of people gather together in our friary. These people, who are usually white, are of different Christian denominations and from various professional and economic backgrounds. What unites them is a common ministry: they all minister to prisoners who live in the Milwaukee County Jail across the street. They gather weekly in our friary to listen to the scriptures for the following Sunday and enter into a kind of "audience-response" interaction with the texts and each other that might help them as they share their faith with the inmates and the guards on Sunday mornings.

On one such Friday, to prepare for the Fifth Sunday of Lent, we reflected on this passage from John. Our reflections were colored by our awareness of the fact that many in the Wisconsin State Legislature were working to reinstate the death penalty that had been abolished for more than a century. Members of our group had spent many hours speaking before gatherings, testifying in Madison against the proposed bill, and writing letters to editors offering their reasons against the bill. All these efforts, however, seemed to be getting nowhere. Polls showed that the number of people in Wisconsin wanting the death penalty was growing daily rather than decreasing.

While highly populated by Lutherans, Wisconsin is one of the most "Catholic" states in the country. This led us to wonder why people professing to be identified with Jesus—who suffered the death penalty (18:38–19:16)—could be so much in favor of such a sentence. How could this be? In searching for reasons, one group member asked how you can expect people to go beyond "the law" when they have been taught that it is "enough" to obey rules and regulations to "get into heaven." Another brought up fear of the "other" (usually poor and non-white), the type of deep-rooted emotion that makes rationality impossible.

Finally Nancy Moews spoke. Nancy taught basic English at Milwaukee Area Technical College, a couple of blocks away. "I'm not one bit surprised that Catholics want the death penalty in Wisconsin," she said matter-of-factly. "After all, they've been members of an institutional church that imposes a kind of ecclesiastical death penalty on all sorts of persons. If you are divorced and remarried, you are cut off from the church's life. If you are gay, you are defined as unnatural. If you practice artificial birth control, you are in mortal sin. And if you publicly state that women should have full participation in all the sacraments of the church, you cut yourself off with the ultimate death penalty: excommunication. So why should we be surprised?"

We sat there stunned. The room had never been so quiet after an application of a scripture passage to our contemporary life. Then we began to wonder why we allow our religious leaders to define dynamics that scapegoat others when they themselves might be questioned. But this line of thought took us beyond what we are now in considering the text.

Jesus "on Trial" for Threatening "Their" System (8:6-7)

The scribes and the Pharisees challenge Jesus, quoting the law and asking whether he agrees with it, including how he would apply it in this concrete situation. However, a deeper issue lies behind their questioning. John tells us that "they said this to test him, so that they might have some charge to bring against him" (8:6).The leadership group of *hoi Ioudaioi*, represented by the scribes and Pharisees, have created a "set up." The real issue has little or nothing to do with the woman or her adultery. Their objectification of her has just been a ploy to get at Jesus. Her adultery is merely a chance to put on trial the one they really want to kill: Jesus. They could care less about her being stoned; it's him they want out of their lives. This same type of dynamic was evident in the late 1990s when the sworn enemies of President Bill Clinton used the alleged adulterer,

Monica Lewinsky, in their effort to impeach him and get him out of their lives. She proved just a pawn in their larger scheme of things. Any shame connected with her they wanted to put on him.

It has continually amazed me that, although the scriptures themselves state that this story is about "testing" Jesus or putting him on trial, our social location and biases keep getting in the way of our understanding. Thus the stress by the commentators on side issues, such as the persons of Jesus and the woman, or her adultery as a grave sin, or the realization that all of us are sinners, even while the text itself says that the scribes and Pharisees not only said what they said, but did what they did "to test" Jesus "so that they might have some charge to bring against him."

Less than ten verses earlier Nicodemus, who "was one of them" (7:50) had asked, "Our law does not judge people without first giving them a hearing to find out what they are doing, does it?" (7:51). Even though they responded by attacking him personally and questioning his credentials, he does seem to have made a point. Now his question is answered in their plan to put Jesus to such a test so that, according to the law, he can be accused for violating it. Why? "Testing" Jesus is their way of putting him on trial, of undermining his increasing influence over the crowds (8:2b), of dishonoring him and re-establishing their authority.

If they are to remain in power, he has to be eliminated. The reason why they want to kill him, as Jesus already had told *hoi Ioudaioi*, is that he "performed one work," the sabbath-healing of the invalid (7:19; see 5:18). His cure on the sabbath had made them *cholan*, biliously angry. Such anger is envy-tinged; Jesus threatens their power.

In the presence of the woman standing before them all, Jesus is now the one being tried. They begin by interrupting his own teaching (probably because they consider themselves the real teachers). They speak to him in words of seeming honor and respect, acknowledging his position as a teacher. However, by calling him "Teacher," they are obviously being hypocritical, since they have previously made it clear that they don't know where he is from or where he has obtained his learning (7:15). After all, he is a layman; they are the teachers. Having addressed him insincerely, they begin their interrogation with a seemingly innocuous question regarding the action of the woman and the law of Moses. Her adulterous affair has been defined. The law about stoning such people is clear. If Jesus says she should not be stoned, he stands as one who violates the law of Moses and community tradition. If he argues in favor of stoning her, he will not only disown his healing way of being present to others in their need, but will be accused of usurping the power of the Romans (since John will later make clear that the Jewish people had no right to sentence anyone to capital punishment [18:31]). This would make Jesus a revolutionary in the eyes of the Romans.

Unlike Augustine's understanding which grouped the scribes and Pharisees with the woman and saw them all as sinners, our view here links the woman and Jesus as test cases which, if successful, will result in capital punishment for both of them. By framing the dilemma before Jesus in terms of the law of Moses and the life of the woman, the scribes and the Pharisees are raising a genuine legal point. However, as Hisako Kinukawa notes, "the woman and Jesus are turned into objects for this technical legal discourse. The woman becomes a point of law, and Jesus is to give the final judgment. No concern is paid to the social or religious circumstances that have brought about such consequences for this woman. And the woman has no right or power to defend herself except to keep silent."[18]

Jesus' honor has been challenged. The goal is not just to shame him but to use his response, one way or another, to find him guilty so that the religious leaders might proceed with their desire to eliminate him. Jesus, however, responds with silence. The fact that silence as a form of shunning is probably a typical cultural response to hostility becomes evident when John notes that "they kept on questioning him."

The Religious Leaders on Trial for Their Testing of Jesus (8:7b-11)

Jesus does not rise to their bait. To respond would have been to fall into the trap set for him by the religious leaders who framed their question in terms of what the woman had done (8:4) and what the law demanded (8:5). He refuses to allow them to set such terms. Consequently, his response neither condones the behavior of nor exonerates the woman; it neither denies nor acknowledges the law. Meeting the challenge of their continued queries, "he straightened up and said to them, 'Let anyone among you who is without sin (*anamartētos*) be the first to throw a stone at her'" (8:7). The word *anamartētos* is used only here in the whole Second Testament.

Jesus' declaration totally turns the tables.

The story has taken place within the trial-like setting of chapters 7 and 8. A woman caught in adultery is brought like a criminal to stand in front of everyone to be tried. However, as the reader realizes, this is not the real trial taking place. The real trial is that of Jesus, who has been set up so that the judgment already made by his enemies can be confirmed. But Jesus now turns everything around by asking a question that effectively puts all his accusers—as well as hers—on trial themselves.

Their own duplicity is now unmasked before "all the people." The "Teacher" has posed an even greater dilemma to his accusers (as well, it seems, as to the onlookers): "Let anyone among you who is without sin be the first to throw a stone at her." Each person's guilt is now threatened with exposure in a way no less shameful to each than the original accusation was to the woman. She stood accused by the religious leaders before all. Now all—especially the leaders—stand challenged by Jesus.

Who or what has Jesus just put on trial here? The scribes' and Pharisees' own sexual pecadillos or their more serious crimes? Hardly. Their abuse of the woman and their discriminatory ways? Possibly. What is really at issue, however, is a deeper infidelity. This is their own insincerity and hypocrisy. They are exposed as those who live by the lie and need a masked environment of "concern" to keep it from being brought to light.

I found a similar insight in a column by Anthony Lewis at the time I was writing this book. In 1997, then Secretary of Defense William Cohen had just forgiven a top Air Force general for his past adultery. Cohen's action produced a fire-storm of controversy, much of it condemning him for having a double standard. In commenting on the incident and public reaction to it, Anthony Lewis of *The New York Times* wrote an article entitled "The First Stone." He noted (in a way that showed how far our culture has moved from that of Jesus):

> Adultery remains a sin. But it is also a fact of life in contemporary American society. One of the all-time best-selling books in this country, "The Bridges of Madison County," romanticizes— you could really say celebrates—adultery.
>
> Despite that reality, the armed forces have become more and more agitated about adultery. In 1985 the services instituted just six courts marital for adultery without other charges. By last year [1996] the figure had grown to 168.[19]

In his final paragraph, Lewis went on to expose the deeper sin of the situation. As I read the article, I couldn't help but think that this was the deeper sin that Jesus also unmasked:

> We could do with a little less piety, too. When some Congressman or commentator deplores adultery in the forces, you have to wonder whether he is in a position to cast a stone. The true American sin is not adultery but hypocrisy.[20]

Hypokrisis in the scriptures involves injustice. While the word is not used in John, injustice is definitely the reality that Jesus—who previously challenged the religious leaders to "judge with right judgment" (7:24)— has exposed in them. Their judgment is not just, because they have not sought God's will in this situation but their own (see 5:30). It is especially unjust in light of the fact that this judicial "testing" seems to be the response of the religious leaders to Nicodemus's concern that they not try Jesus, or anyone, "without first giving them a hearing" (7:51).

Now, however, with Jesus setting the terms of the inquiry (and ensuring that these terms are non-negotiable by "once again" bending down and writing on the ground), all the accusers, judges, and juries will be themselves.

The challenge has been made. The word John puts on Jesus' lips (used only in this gospel and but once) for "without sin" (*anamartētos*) does not refer to sexual sin. The sin that they must be without in order to throw a stone is sin in general, sin in the sense of missing the mark of wholeness and integrity.

The ball is now in their court. What will they do? Will the guilt they each bear for the sins they themselves have committed now be exposed before all within the temple itself?

"When they heard it," John says simply, "they went away, one by one, beginning with the elders; and Jesus was left alone with the woman standing before him" (8:9). Instead of trapping Jesus into condoning violence against this woman, they walk away, thus showing that they have no response to his challenge. Unlike their challenge, his was not meant to cause more shame in those who were already guilty by exposing them to further public humiliation. By their own response, however, his hearers publicly admit their guilt and, in the process, publicly shame themselves —beginning with the elders who walk away.

With everyone dispersed, "Jesus was left alone with the woman standing before him" (8:9). As she was made to "stand before all of them" in her shame, she now stands before him alone. In her guilt? We aren't told. In her shame? Not as far as Jesus is concerned. Guilt is something that Jesus must address, but shame does not enter into his dealings with someone like her. It seems to be a need only for those who would have made her their scapegoat to keep from having violence done to them. Straightening up, he said to her: "'Woman, where are they? Has no one condemned (*katakrinein*) you?'" (8:10). The word for condemn (Wis 4:16; Est 2:1) refers to a judicial death sentence (Dn 4:37a). While it is used only here in John, the Synoptics use it in reference to a judgment having to do with another death (Mt 20:18; 27:3; Mk 10:33; 14:64; 16:16) or destruction (Mt 12:41, 42; Lk 11:31, 32). The word is based on *krinein*, the word for "to judge," which is used twice as much in John as in all the other gospels put together.

When she responds to his question with a title of respect and reverence: "No one, sir (*kyrie*)," the only one (according to the NRSV translation) left to condemn her is Jesus himself. Now Jesus passes his own judgment, clearly and concisely: "Neither do I condemn you. Go your way, and from now on do not sin again" (8:11).

As children of the tradition, it would be easy to focus only on Jesus' mercy toward a recognized sinner. However, as I have tried to point out, while this is an emotional and gripping part of the story, the underlying theme is the ongoing conflict between Jesus and the religious leaders. Here he has won the day. They have all gone off, one by one.

But they will return more united than ever. They will have their day— in the courts and in the courtyards.

SIX

DO YOU BELIEVE
IN THE SON OF MAN? (9:35)

The Question of John 9:1-41

In chapter 8, in the context of the light ceremonies of the feast of Booths, Jesus declared himself not only to be the temple's illuminating power but "the light of the world" (8:12). In chapter 9 he will heal one born blind in a way that exposes the temple leaders' blindness. These leaders include the ones in chapters 7 and 8 who so identified themselves with Moses and Abraham that they rejected the One these patriarchs had anticipated.

The story of the blind person in chapter 9 deals with light in two forms. The first is literal and physical: Jesus' intervention enables the invalid to see. The second is metaphorical and spiritual: Jesus enlightens the once-blind man's understanding.

While the healing of this blind person leads some of the rulers to acknowledge that "Never since the world began has it been heard that anyone opened the eyes of a person born blind" (9:32), the unwillingness or inability of the group as a whole to recognize the deeper structural significance behind this sign exposes their group-inspired blindness.

Significant parallels exist between the the invalid described in chapter 5 (5:1-8) and the man born blind depicted here in chapter 9 (9:1-41). Both individuals are anonymous and both need healing. In addition, their healing exposes the deeper sickness in a system that refuses to recognize its disease.[1]

By examining the stories of these two disabled people in a diseased system, we disciples/readers are enabled to deepen our own understanding of how human and corporate disabilities can be transformed by an encounter with the person of Jesus Christ.

Paul Duke and Gail R. O'Day show that chapter 9 of John is organized in a chiastic structure of seven parts.[2] I have adapted their structure to fit the themes of this book:

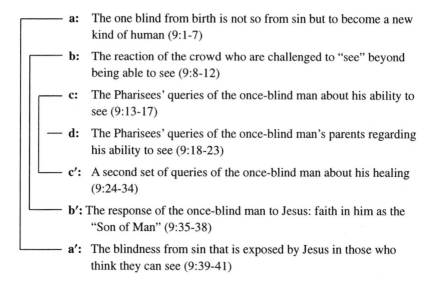

a: The one blind from birth is not so from sin but to become a new kind of human (9:1-7)

b: The reaction of the crowd who are challenged to "see" beyond being able to see (9:8-12)

c: The Pharisees' queries of the once-blind man about his ability to see (9:13-17)

d: The Pharisees' queries of the once-blind man's parents regarding his ability to see (9:18-23)

c′: A second set of queries of the once-blind man about his healing (9:24-34)

b′: The response of the once-blind man to Jesus: faith in him as the "Son of Man" (9:35-38)

a′: The blindness from sin that is exposed by Jesus in those who think they can see (9:39-41)

a. The One Blind from Birth Is Not So from Sin but to Become a New Kind of Human (9:1-7)

The chapter begins with John noting of Jesus that "as he walked along, he saw a man blind from birth" (9:1). What the NRSV (which remains closest to the original Greek) fails to communicate in this opening sentence is the absence of the article "a" (*ho*) in front of the word for "man" (*anthrōpos*). Instead of *ho anthrōpon* it just says *anthrōpon*. A literal translation would have it read that "humanity" was there, "blind from birth."

In this one human being, humankind itself—blind from birth in original sin—is about to have an encounter with the Human One, the Son of Man. As a result of this engagement, the blind one will experience not just the ability to see physically, but the ability to see with the eyes of faith. The importance of what happens to this anonymous one is enlightening for readers of every sex, race, creed, and persuasion who not only identify with this character in his sickness but also try to see with eyes of faith when their belief may be undermined by the distorted vision of *hoi Ioudaioi* and the blindness of "the world."

We have already noted that first-century Mediterranean culture saw a "who" rather than a "what" behind every disease. People believed that blindness was caused by some kind of separation from God or by sin (Gn 19:11; Dt 28:28; 2 Kgs 6:18).[3] Jesus' own disciples reflected this culturally defined ideology. They asked Jesus: "Rabbi, who sinned, this man or his parents, that he was born blind?" (9:2). In a society that identified sickness with sin, as in the "case" of the one sick for thirty-eight years, Jesus makes a clear break from the prevailing religiously-legitimated medical model. He answers: "Neither this man nor his parents sinned" (9:3:).

In John's mind, this one's blindness is meant to expose humanity's distorted vision, to make it possible for God's work in the world to bring forth light. This representative of humanity who has remained in darkness since birth "was born blind so that God's works might be revealed in him" (9:3b). Since Jesus is the Father's apprentice, sent to continue God's work of making all whole, he cannot rest until this work is achieved. Thus Jesus says (interlinking the "I" and the "we"): "We must work the works of him who sent me while it is day; night is coming when no one can work. As long as I am in the world, I am the light of the world" (9:4).

Just as in the beginning, when darkness covered the earth and God's word brought light into the world (Gn. 1:1-3), so now in another creation-dynamic directly connecting the original work of God in making humankind from "the dust of the ground" (Gn 2:7), Jesus set about performing a little folk medicine.[4] He "spat on the ground and made mud with the saliva and spread the mud on the man's eyes, saying to him, 'Go, wash in the pool of Siloam (which means Sent)'" (9:6-7a). By doing the work of making the mud and spreading it on the man's eyes, Jesus indicates that he is accepting responsibility to do something about this invalid's condition.

As in the case of others whom the reader has watched accepting the force of Jesus' word in their condition of need and darkness (2:1-12; 4:46-54; 5:2-9), the only thing asked of this person is that he obey: "Then he went and washed and came back able to see" (9:7). Now made well, the once-blind one no longer can be objectified or labeled in terms of sin; he has become a man made whole. This new life is light for someone who heretofore lived in darkness (1:4). By framing the healing in this way, John is clearly declaring that a new chapter in the story of creation has begun. It is, however, only a prelude to an even more significant chapter in creation's unfolding story through its main character, the one called "Son of Man."

b. The Reaction of the Crowd Who Are Challenged to "See" Beyond Being Able to See (9:8-12)

The author now states: "The neighbors and those who had seen him before as a beggar began to ask, 'is this not the man who used to sit and beg?'" (9:8). John has described this human being as "blind from birth." However, his neighbors seem locked into describing him in terms of the former marginalization that resulted from his blindness. They "had seen him as a beggar (*prosaitein*)." His blindness had made him not only an invalid but, consequently, also a beggar. This is how society "saw" him. In his "world" he might now see, but he still was perceived as marginalized.

In Jesus' culture, anyone with a physical disability was not just afflicted by a disease. Since everything pertaining to an individual had communal implications, an individual's disease or problem became a familial and/or communal illness or problem. Furthermore, those beyond the immediate family or kin—the "neighbors"—saw individual disabilities as a social sickness, a deviation from the social order. This person may have been blind, but society saw him as a beggar.

Being involved in a ministry in Milwaukee dedicated to serving people with various disabilities and needs, I find a contemporary parallel to the attitude displayed in this gospel story. Many people called "beggars" by today's society come to St. Benedict the Moor because they have personal problems. Insufficient income brings people to our door for bus tickets. Unemployment sends people to our clinic. Various disabilities lead them to our meal program. Many persons come because of some kind of dis-ease within themselves. People driving by on State Street who see the lines waiting to get in for a meal perceive "those people" as beggars. I've heard some observers say that the sight of the people at our place makes them "ill." By labeling such human beings "beggars," society can easily make of them its scapegoats. It can ignore the deeper disease, things like corporate downsizing and runaway jobs created by Milwaukee's businesses, the underlying social sickness that gives rise to many of the situations our ministries try to address.

Like some contemporary civil servants who see their clients as statistics rather than human beings, the "neighbors" in the gospel story debate among each other about the now-cured person. Throughout the discussion he remains anonymous. Their inability to identify him by name indicates that they must have kept themselves at arm's length from him; none had come close enough to him to know his name. Like the disciples, they too viewed him as someone identified with sin, someone to avoid for fear of contamination.

"Seeing him" as a beggar would be hard to change, even though he now had vision. So he tried to tell them: "I am the man" (9:9). The once-blind man now not only has sight, he is gaining insight. He who has been touched by Jesus is now not only cured of his blindness, is now not only healed, he has been made well. He now can image the creative power of the one who made him whole. In words recalling the divine name, "he kept saying 'I am [*egō eimi*] the man'" (9:9).

Egō eimi is the closest to a name the once-blind one will ever receive in this gospel. Placing these words on the man's own lips "*egō eimi*," (the only time in John's gospel that someone other than Jesus utters them), seems to be John's way of moving the man's identity from that of an anonymous beggar who now can see to one whose work is now clear. He must witness to the light for others in their darkness.

The depth of the people's darkness is revealed when John says he had to "keep" telling them "I am the man." In response, "they kept" querying him some more. In fact, now that the healed one has made clear that his identity is linked to the "I AM," their queries increase: "They kept asking him, 'Then how were your eyes opened?'" (9:10).

He tells them about "the man called Jesus" and what he has done. He explains that, in the process, "I went and washed and received my sight" (9:11). Rather than evoking awe or new insight, his testimony and witness elicit only another query: "They said to him, 'Where is he?'" To this he answers simply, "I do not know" (9:12). It is now becoming clear that the issue is not the blind person and his sight, but the person who enabled him to see.

c. The Pharisees' Queries of the Once-Blind Man about His Ability to See (9:13-17)

John says "*They* brought to the Pharisees the man who had formerly been blind" (9:13). *They* seem to have been the "neighbors" who had been disputing previously over his identity. Now they bring him to the masters of religious dispute. These religious leaders are beginning to "see" his healing as a threat to the religious observance of the people which they control. An even deeper reason for their concern becomes evident when John notes after the cure: "Now it was a sabbath day when Jesus made the mud and opened his eyes" (9:14).

Nowhere else in all the gospels, except in 5:9 and here, are we told *after* the healing the day of the event: it took place on the sabbath. Not only do Jesus' actions show the need for sabbath-breaking when its observance has become an obstacle to divine activity, his work of enabling the blind one to see is Jubilee-proclaiming. It is *shalom*.

As I indicated in the chapter on the previous sabbath healing, if sick people are those who have fallen from the human condition of wholeness, Jesus' healing of sickness on the sabbath is John's way of noting the arrival of that wholeness promised by *shalom*. In the words of Guillermo Cook:

In God's plan the Sabbath and the Shalom are inseparable. The Sabbath was more than a weekly day off from work. It was meant to be rest for God's entire creation—His people, the animals and the land. The Jubilee Year—liberty to the captives and lands returned to their original owners—was intended to communicate Shalom in the realms of work, natural resource conservation and of social relations, as well as at the level of our relationship with God.[5]

What now confronts the Pharisees is not just an isolated sabbath-healing; it is the real possibility that a whole new order, that of shalom itself, has broken into their "world." If this kind of creative restoration of humanity spreads, they could become powerless and uncessary.

Now a deeper pathology is about to be diagnosed. The problem, as we have noted, is not so much this anonymous one who has been healed on the sabbath. The problem has to do with the person who did the healing on the sabbath. Already the Pharisees have suspected Jesus and his words and deeds (4:1; 7:32, 45-53; 8:13). Now they query the man about what was done and who did it. He is familiar enough with Jewish law to know that Jesus could be accused of violating the law, so, as a good client, he protects his benefactor. He refuses to tell them that Jesus has done things that are not allowed on the sabbath—that he formed clay, anointed his eyes, and told him to wash in the Pool of Siloam. Instead of saying he "made clay" (which would have been against the law as found in *Shabbat* 7:23; 8:1), he states: "He put mud on my eyes. Then I washed, and now I see" (9:15). The man's simple narration of the facts evokes only more queries.

The Pharisees realize that what has happened cannot be easily dismissed or hidden. This results in division (*schisma*) within their ranks. The first group (representing for a contemporary reader the pre-Vatican II way of teaching in the Roman Church) argue deductively: No good can come from a violation of a law. Nothing divine comes from deviation from the divine law. An objective law has been disobeyed. Jesus is wrong. Error has no rights. The second group represents people who think more inductively. They consider the data and then ask questions as to its implications for faith. While opening the eyes of one blind from birth on the sabbath would seem to make Jesus a sinner, these others are not so sure. They ask: "How can a man who is a sinner perform such signs?" (9:16b). The Pharisees are now "faced with only two options: their own doctrinal-cultural tradition or the well-being (Shalom) of the needy person."[6]

Unable to agree, the factions look to the now-sighted one for an answer. They ask: "What do you say about him? It was your eyes he opened" (9:17a-b). As the blind man was, in the beginning, simply "humanity" (*anthrōpos*), so now he acknowledges Jesus simply as "prophet." By not using any article (*prophētēs*) that would particularize Jesus as one in a long line of prophets, the man identifies Jesus in terms of what the prophets before him only envisioned. The sighted one is now moving into ever-deeper insight and ever-deeper expression of that insight in his own prophetic proclamation.

d. The Pharisees' Queries of the Once-Blind Man's Parents (9:18-23)

Isaiah had prophesied that Israel's deliverance would be linked to the opening of the eyes of the blind (Is 35:5-6; 29:18-19) in the midst of others whose eyes would be closed "so that they may not look with their eyes... and comprehend with their minds, and turn and be healed" themselves (Is 6:10; see Jn 12:38-40). Now, in the presence of the sighted-one, yet blinded to its implications for their own belief, "*hoi Ioudaioi* ... called the parents of the man who had received his sight." They queried the parents: "Is this your son, who you say was born blind? How then does he now see?" (9:18-19). These are the same parents whom Jesus had earlier exonerated from any sin-inducing-sickness that society thought might have created the son's blindness (9:3). However, now they too are shown to be suffering from their own kind of blindness, the blindness that rises from fear. In John's words, "*hoi Ioudaioi* had already agreed that anyone who confessed Jesus to be the Messiah would be put out of the synagogue (*aposynagōgos*)" (9:22). In a society in which proper social standing was viewed as imperative, the parents—who must have been overjoyed at the miracle that had taken place in their son—could not witness to what had happened for fear of losing their status in the eyes of others.

No evidence exists that people who testified to Jesus at this time were being excommunicated from Judaism, its temple, or its synagogues. If Jesus himself was never rejected from the temple, how could those who followed him during his lifetime on earth suffer this fate? But, if people were not really persecuted in this way for professing their faith in Jesus during his public life, why did John place such an apparently untruthful statement in the sacred text?

According to a theory first identified with Louis Martyn, it seems quite clear that John was retrojecting into the story a situation facing his community (or recently faced by it). Martyn and later exegetes like Raymond Brown point out that the ongoing division between the Jewish community and Christians came to a head when a group of Jewish leaders introduced into synagogue worship the so-called *birkat ha-minim*. This "benediction of the heretics" was a prayer that invoked a curse upon "heretics," who included the Nazarenes, an early name for Christians. While various elements of Martyn's thesis have been disputed,[7] it does seem that, after 90–95, Christians were barred from the synagogues if they openly confessed Jesus to be God's Messiah. The procedure involved some kind of trial and resulted in ostracizing the believer. The banishment included separation from one's own parents and wider family. Anyone professing belief in Jesus was considered outside the "world" of Jewish belief. The "them" and "us" of alienated groups took on an institutionalized expression. These dynamics of the late 80s and 90s were read into the text as though they were occurring in the 30s.

With this as background, it should not be surprising that the parents of the now-sighted son are depicted as being "afraid" of the religious leaders. Their fright is representative of a large number of characters in John who believe in Jesus but who won't openly profess their faith in him for fear of elements of *hoi Ioudaioi* (7:13; 12:42; 19:38; 20:19; see 3:1-10). It also reflects the experience of the early church with crypto-Christians, who secretly believed in Jesus but feared professing their faith publicly. With religion embedded in the warp and woof of the culture, rejection by the leaders of that entity which meant life itself would mean virtual death, social and cultural alienation.

On the one hand, the parents are willing to admit the hard data about their son: he is theirs, he was born blind, and "now he sees." On the other, they are afraid to acknowledge how he has come to see or who it is that enabled him to see. They can describe the "what" but not witness to the "who." Fear blinds them from professing their faith. Unwilling to take a stand on behalf of the one who has made their son whole for fear they will be diminished in the sight of their religious leaders, they can only conclude: "He is of age, ask him" (9:23).

I find it understandable that John could have "doctored" the text to retroject the situation of the Johannine community into it. But what I find difficult to understand is why we are so reluctant to recognize contemporary situations in our own religious temples where fear keeps people from saying what they believe to be true. We can easily give homilies on history and discuss the fear of being rejected from the first-century temple. Yet rarely do I find scripture scholars even suggesting parallel instances in our age when people fear being ostracized for professing their faith in ways that might prove unacceptable to today's religious leaders. Perhaps the parents' situation is not all that uncommon today, especially when we may be blinded by the fear of being labeled "unbeliever," rejected as "uncatholic," or excommunicated as "outside the church." Maybe we need to consider whether our own fear keeps us from declaring what we know in our hearts to be true. If we are grounded in truth, we should have no fear of speaking that truth, even when it must be addressed to those in power. We are "of age"; we must give evidence of the faith that grounds us in the truth.

By now it is becoming clear to the reader that continued participation in the status quo of the synagogue compromises faith in Jesus Christ. How might this apply today to continued participation in contemporary religious institutions whose dynamics compromise people's faith in God? Many people "leave" the church because they no longer believe their God would allow for discrimination, such as the sexism they experience in

Catholicism. For these people, faith in God demands non-participation in what they consider a sin.

c′: A Second Set of Queries of the Once-Blind Man about His Healing (9:24-34)

For a "second time they [probably the Pharisees] called the man who had been blind" (9:24a). Using a stock phrase used for oath-taking ("Give glory to God"), they continue the trial. They attest that they "know (*oida*) that this man is a sinner." The man responds to their infallible way of knowing by stating: "I do not know whether he is a sinner." What he can be sure of is "that though I was blind, now I see" (9:25). The leaders' way of knowing keeps them from seeing; the once-blind person's sight is leading him to know. Gail R. O'Day notes that, while John uses two words for "to know" (*ginōskein* and *oida*),[8] in chapter 9 he uses only *oida*, never *ginōskein*. She continues by speculating as to why this may be the case:

> It is even more striking when one realizes that *oida* is actually derived from a Greek root for seeing (*id-*). In chapter 9, the Fourth Evangelist is establishing an intimate connection between sight and knowledge. His use of the verb *oida*, which is semantically linked to verbs of seeing, is not unrelated to his use of words with an innate double meaning in John 3. Thus, by the very language that the Fourth Evangelist uses in chapter 9 to speak of knowledge, he signals the reader that there is a connection between knowledge and sight. What that connection is will be revealed as the narrative moves to its conclusion.[9]

The once-blind one's certainty regarding what has happened only elicits more queries about what Jesus did to him and how he opened his eyes. If they can discover what Jesus did to him and how he did it, they can determine if he violated sabbath. There is no doubt now that the issue is not the man who has been made well but Jesus who made him so.

Aware of their maneuvers, the man turns the tables. In a second riposte, stronger and more sarcastic than the first, he challenges them with his own query: "Do you also want to become his disciples?" (9:28). The reader must wonder whether this implies that the man born blind has now "come and seen" in a way that makes him identified with Jesus. The Pharisees suggest that this is in fact the case when they "revile" him by saying he is a disciple of Jesus. At the same time, they justify their position by an appeal to Moses' teaching, probably in the same way that we today defend ourselves by identifying ourselves with our own teachers (which, depending on our way of "seeing" can range from Mother Angelica to Richard McBrien). They revile him for being connected to this person whose origin eludes them: "We do not know where he comes from" (9:28-29). Then, as now, "where you are coming from" represents something much more than a place; it reveals the source of your identity.

The man has matched every one of the leaders' challenges with a riposte of his own. There have been three challenges and responses in all. With each, as he has grown in his insight and articulation, they have become more blinded and intransigent. Finally, exasperated with their "know it all" teaching "the man answered, 'Here is an astonishing thing! You do not know where he comes from, and yet he opened my eyes. We know that God does not listen to sinners, but he does listen to one who worships him and obeys his will. Never since the world began has it been heard that anyone opened the eyes of a person born blind. If this man were not from God, he could do nothing'" (9:30-33). Here a layperson lectures the clerics, a once-blinded man exposes the ongoing blindness of the leaders.

Despite what Jesus has already declared about the non-linkage of sin and sickness, the leaders resort to the argument of last resort, the personal attack. "They answered him, 'You were born entirely in sins, and are you trying to teach us?'" (9:34a). How can a born sinner teach those who are ordained for "holy" work? Their attitude seems to be much like that of religious leaders today who "hold" a teaching office and believe that God somehow gives them possession of the truth. They see their vocation as teachers. The role of the laity is to willingly embrace whatever they teach.

When the teachers have convinced themselves that they possess all truth, those who are not teachers have nothing to offer. In effect, they are "entirely in their sins." When religious teachers have become so convinced of their own ideology that they believe that whatever they teach is of God, their teaching gets cloaked in the mantle of infallibility. When infallibility displaces humility, ideology becomes idolatry. Now God must stand behind their interpretation. The ultimate expression of this is found in the religious leader who is so certain of his own position that he is convinced that, even if it is wrong, God will make it right. Rather than consider the possibility that some truth, that some teaching, that some theology mysteriously may be beyond their control, the last resort of such "teachers" is to reject the messenger, especially when the message can't be countered with sound data. Consequently, John tells us of the now-insightful sighted one, "they drove him out" (9:34b). The man may have survived the challenges of the Pharisees with his own ripostes, but his battle has found him invalidated totally: he has been cast out from the temple, the center of his "world." In their fear, his parents have saved face (and their religious hides). Now, because of his courage and their culture, he has become estranged from them as well.

b': The Response of the Once-Blind Man to Jesus: Faith in Him as the "Son of Man" (9:35-38)

When "Jesus heard that they had driven him out," he found him (9:35a). Having been elusive in the story since the time of the healing, Jesus seeks out the one driven from the institution because of what he has said. Now Jesus asks him the question that must be answered affirmatively by anyone who is to be made well: "Do you believe in the Son of Man?" (9:35b).

We have watched the man progress in his ability to profess publicly his faith. In a pattern similar to the Samaritan woman's growth in faith, we have observed him referring to Jesus with a series of titles. Each manifests a deeper insight into Jesus' identity. First he referred to him the way everyone else did, as "the man called Jesus" (9:11). Further challenged in his faith, he declared, "He is a prophet" (9:17). "Reviled" and doubted even more, he testifies to Jesus as one from God empowered with an astonishing gift of healing (9:31-33). Driven from the temple for being a "martyr" on his behalf, he still does not confess Jesus as anything beyond a respectful "*kyrios*" (["sir"] 9:36) despite the fact that Jesus has just defined himself as the "Son of Man." Seeking to connect this title with a person, he now indicates the depth of his quest: "And who is he, sir? Tell me, so that I may believe in him" (9:36).

The meaning of "Son of Man" in John 9:35 and elsewhere[10] (to say nothing of its use in the other gospels) has been much debated among scripture scholars. They argue about the term's meaning in John, whether it means the same thing in the Synoptics, and whether it was a term actually used by Jesus. Some think it is another instance of retrojection by the early church.[11] We can safely say, however, that whenever John uses the term (with the possible exception of 12:34) it appears as a self-identification by Jesus. No other human but Jesus uses it as a reference to himself. It is another way of saying "I am."

Despite the debates, it also does seem true that, from the perspective of the rest of the gospel, "Son of Man" is not only Jesus' self-description. It is a unique expression of his "work" on behalf of humanity in the "world" as well. It thus refers both to his identity and his mission. In this sense, I much prefer a translation that uses a contemporary image, such as "Child of Creation." Having descended into the created world from the "Father" (3:13), this one will be lifted up (3:14; 8:28; 12:34) by the world in a sign of rejection (his crucifixion). However, because of his fidelity to "the Father," what the world considers his defeat will redound for his glorification (12:23; 13:31) insofar at it will ensure his ascent back to "the Father" (6:62). His death/resurrection will not just be a personal glorification. It will be the drawing-source of all to him (3:14). Those who believe in him (9:35) will not only be drawn to him, they will feast on his word (6:27) and eat of his flesh (6:53). While all will be drawn to him, not all will remain with him. Yet those who remain faithful will be judged worthy (5:27).

In summary, "Son of Man" in John, while being a self-reference of Jesus, also appears to be a representative image. In his descent/ascent, "the Child of Creation" draws all to himself so that he will be the power at the heart of all creation and all creation will be one in him. "Son of Man," Margaret Pamment writes, "while referring to Jesus, draws particular attention to his representative humanity, that is, Jesus is pictured as representing not what every man is, but what man could and should be."[12] In this case, every man and woman is to be one who, in being drawn to him, will confess faith in him and remain with him. With the once-blind one, all people can progress in their faith in Jesus to the point of adoration. They can worship him (9:38).

a': The Blindness from Sin That Is Exposed by Jesus in Those Who Think They Can See (9:39-41)

In 8:21, Jesus had said to the Pharisees within the hearing of "some of *hoi Ioudaioi*: 'You will look for me but you will die in your sins.'" Now chapter 9 concludes with Jesus declaring that the very reason why he came into the world "for judgment" was so that "those who do not see may see, and those who do see may become blind" (9:39). On its surface, the narrative of the cure of the one born blind in John 9 tells of a miraculous physical healing by Jesus. But underlying the account is a deeper spiritual healing that Christ brings to those who are open to him in faith. The story concludes with Jesus condemning the Pharisees for their spiritual blindness.

In a final query, some of the Pharisees who heard Jesus say this "said to him, 'Surely we are not blind, are we?'" (9:40). Jesus responds by saying: "If you were blind, you would not have sin. But now that you say, 'We see,' your sin remains" (9:41). As the once-blind man's vision has brought him to faith, so the Pharisees' blind "knowing" keeps them—willfully—from that same faith. This is the blindness that reflects sin. The "seeing" that equates with "sin" represents a willful choice to resist Jesus' person and message. The Pharisees are worse than blind because they refuse to see. Their infallible way of knowing has blinded not only their eyes but also something deeper, their hearts and souls. Such resistance represents sin in its deepest form. In John, sin blinds people. When found in individuals or institutions, such blindness is characterized by denial and darkness as well as deception and delusion. Yet, like all suffering that results from being controlled by these dynamics, those who are blinded think they see. They are firmly convinced their "vision" is perfect.

This chapter has highlighted ways in which the blindness with which Jesus contended can be expressed in today's equivalents of *hoi Ioudaioi*. But such blindness can be expressed in other ways also. It is endemic throughout the whole wider "world," especially where people are indifferent to the disabilities and disabling forces suffered by others. Legion are its manifestations. One of the chief of these is the way the ideology supporting materialism and consumerism blinds people to the disastrous effects on other persons and the planet itself. The consequence is indifference.

In his weekly column, "Herald of Hope," my Archbishop, Rembert G. Weakland, O.S.B., noted how John's ninth chapter made clearer to him this blindness of indifference:

> Probably when the listeners heard this story of the man born blind for the first time, that is, when John first wrote it down, they understood it a bit differently [than we hear it today]. They knew of the tensions between the disciples of Christ and the leaders of the synagogue and were not surprised that the blind man was tossed out of the latter...
>
> Fine, I understand how this passage was interpreted by the catechumens in the time of St. John. I can imagine what it meant to the catechumens a few centuries later when the bitter persecutions took place; I can even imagine what it means to many today who, when they accept baptism, are rejected by their family and friends. All that makes sense to me as historical precedents, but it says little to me today.
>
> What does it mean to me and to other cradle Catholics in my capitalist culture? No organization has thrown me out; I do not know about you.... What parallel is there in my life?
>
> I can assure you that I may not get tossed out of any group by being a disciple of Christ; yet...I pick up subtle remarks that could be interpreted as others saying things like: "Who are you to teach us about such things? Do you have a doctorate in economics? What do you know about the 'law' of supply and demand?" And on it goes. Followers of Christ today are not thrown out of the synagogue; they are simply dismissed by our society as irrelevant or naive.
>
> If you talk about the disparity between the rich and the poor at home and around the world, if you are concerned about the sanctity of all human life everywhere on this globe, if you say that the system is to serve the person and not vice-versa, if you affirm the need for respecting the property and goods of others, if

you say that the capitalist system leaves many people out in the cold, you are simply dismissed as irrelevant: "Who are you to teach us?"...

I have come to accept that sometimes it is more Christian to be naive than to have all the answers to the world's problems according to the world's criteria. Let them dismiss me if they will. I simply must go on thinking that what Jesus said was light.[13]

Archbishop Weakland's reflections now bring me to to conclude this chapter by examining the different ways of "seeing" in chapter 9 and the rest of John's gospel and how these are manifested in other contemporary expressions.

The Different Ways of "Seeing" in John

"Seeing" in its various forms in John is closely related to believing. An examination of John's words for "seeing" reveals four different words: *eidenai* (used thirty-six times), *oran* (thirty-one times), *blepein* (seventeen times) and *theōrein* (six times). "Seeing" is used ninety times while *pisteuein*, the word for faith, is used ninety-eight times. How they connect (and don't connect) in John can have much significance for the reader in today's "world."

In 1:14 John writes: "And the Word became flesh and lived among us, and we have *seen* his glory." Similarly, 1 John begins:

We declare to you what was from the beginning, what we have heard, *what we have seen with our eyes*, what we have looked at and touched with our hands concerning the word of life—this life was revealed, and we have seen it and testify to it, and declare to you the eternal life that was with the Father and was revealed to us—we declare to you *what we have seen* and heard so that you also may have fellowship with us; and truly our fellowship is with the Father and with his Son Jesus Christ. We are writing these things so that our joy may be complete. (1 Jn 1-4)

Building on the development of the story-line in John's gospel, especially in chapter 9, I find four kinds of seeing and non-seeing in humanity:[14] (1) those who are "blind from birth;" (2) those who see (and even believe) as the result of a physical encounter; (3) those who are blind for reasons not related to physical health, and (4) those who see with the eyes of faith. The man highlighted in chapter 9 is the only one who fits the first and the second categories. In the way his eyes were opened we find the development of someone who freely makes a commitment of faith. However, because the object of his faith is visible, his seeing does not represent the fourth kind of faith-sight.

Those Who See (and Even Believe) as the Result of a Physical Encounter

1. *Physical eyesight.* When I studied Greek, the verb used for conjugation was *blepein,* "to see." It refers to the physical act of "seeing" with one's eyes. In chapter 9 it refers exclusively, except with regard to the Pharisees (9:41), to the physical act of seeing, as happened with the once-blind person (9:7, 15, 19, 21, and 25). This kind of seeing is done with the senses.

2. *Seeing as "knowing."* This kind of "seeing" refers to knowledge that aids understanding. When we understand something or someone, we often say "I see" or "I know." Thus, in the second encounter of the once-blind person with the Pharisees, they debate about what they "know" regarding the action of Jesus and their understanding of the law (9:24, 25, 29 [2x], 30, and 31). Their "knowing" includes the sense of being quite sure of things.

3. *Shaped seeing* refers to viewing someone or something for such an extended period that it becomes habitual. It is how we interpret the familiar things around us. This kind of "seeing" (*theōrein*) is expressed in chapter 9 in the "neighbors and those who had seen him before as a beggar" (9:8). Oftentimes, as when we read a sentence and miss a misspelled word, this impaired vision results from not really "seeing" reality, but only what we expect to see. Sometimes such seeing reflects what is; sometimes it doesn't. In this sense, "shaped seeing" also fits under a form of blindness that is not "from birth."

4. *Insight.* This seeing-by-making-connections is manifested in the way the one who was once blind perceived Jesus. It was not that he called Jesus "prophet" that made him have insightful seeing, it was that he had made the connections to reach this conclusion. Thus, in response to the Pharisees' question: "'What do you say about him? It was your eyes he opened.' He said, 'He is a prophet'" (9:17).

5. *Faith in something observable.* The fifth way of seeing expressed in chapter 9 is the seeing that believes—when the object of one's belief is visible. This faith-filled seeing is evident when Jesus finds the man driven from the synagogue and asks him: "Do you believe in the Son of Man?" After the man indicates that he would like to know who this is, Jesus says to him, "You have seen him, and the one speaking with you is he." In response, the man professes his faith in a simple creed: "Lord, I believe" (9:35-38). Another example of this kind of physical sight and authentic believing can be found in the resurrection experience of Thomas:

Thomas (who was called the Twin), one of the twelve, was not with them when Jesus came. So the other disciples told him, "We have seen the Lord." But he said to them, "Unless I see the mark of the nails in his hands, and put my finger in the mark of the nails and my hand in his side, I will not believe."

A week later his disciples were again in the house, and Thomas was with them. Although the doors were shut, Jesus came and stood among them and said, "Peace be with you." Then he said to Thomas, "Put your finger here and see my hands. Reach out your hand and put it in my side. Do not doubt but believe. Thomas answered him, "My Lord and my God!" (20:24-28)

Those Who Are Blind for Reasons Not Related to Physical Health

This kind of "blindness" arises not from physical causes, but from other sources: inherited notions and attitudes about others, ideologically biased viewpoints, attitudes controlled by past images and experiences, over-identification with rules and regulations, fear, rage, and what the scriptures call "hardness of heart." All these are found in the ninth chapter of John.

1. *Inherited notions and attitudes about others.* Jesus disciples' express this kind of blindness when they speak from their received tradition which holds that disease arises from personal or communicated sin: "Rabbi, who sinned, this man or his parents, that he was born blind?" (9:2). The received tradition is also reflected in the leaders' response to the blind one's testimony about Jesus (9:34).

2. *Ideologically biased viewpoints.* "There is none so blind as those who will not see," or, as Guillermo Cook notes: *spiritual blindness often has ideological roots.*[15] This kind of "blindness" is grounded in cultural stereotypes that are not easily changed. It evidences wrong notions that, while not supported by facts, remain ingrained. In contemporary language, it is reflected in the kind of bias that comes from fundamentalism on the one hand and "political correctness" on the other. In the latter case, I am reminded of a time when I preached on this passage at St. Benedict's Parish in Milwaukee. It is a haven for people disaffected with the institutionalized Roman Church. The members consider themselves very open to all people, especially those marginalized by church and society. They fondly refer to themselves as a "wildlife refuge."

Trying to develop an audience-response approach to the reading on a Sunday which featured John's chapter 9, I invited the parishioners to consider where they might be blinded, but they couldn't "see" where this could be. After all, weren't they the very ones who were working for justice and trying to confront the ideology in the church that did so much harm to so many? At that I asked them how they would react if a man came into the church wearing a clerical collar. How would they "see" such a person: as a priest or minister of some sort or as one of "them" who had to hide behind a collar? Then I asked them what they'd do if a nun were to show up in full habit. The community might not excommunicate such a person, but the welcome might be somewhat strained! To their credit, they "saw" what I was trying to say.

3. *Attitudes that are controlled by past images and experiences.* The man born blind was identified by his blindness, so much so that the townspeople were unable to see him healed. He was not defined by his own "I am." Rather, an identity was imposed on him by others who were locked into seeing him in the condition of one in that culture who suffered a disease: he was a beggar. "Is this not the man who used to sit and beg?" (9:8).

4. *Over-identification with rules and regulations.* Because they were convinced that righteousness could come only from a rigorous fulfilling of all points of the law, the Pharisees could not see in the breaking of the law the possibility that the original law-giver was in their presence (9:16).

5 *Fear.* This is what kept the parents of the once blind man unable to see with eyes of faith. Their fear kept them locked in a temple that had actually excluded their own son. Once he was healed—and back in the temple—they still could not acknowledge this in faith (9:20-23).

6. *Rage.* Rage arises from a sense of being disrespected or challenged. It can also spring from fear. When the man born blind challenged the Pharisees, they "reviled him" (9:28). They were right and he was wrong (9:29).

7. *Hardness of heart.* This is the worst kind of blindness. It is the kind of blindness to which Jesus refers when he says of the religious leaders: "I came into this world for judgment so that those who do not see (*mē blepontes*) may see (*blepōsi*), and those who do see (*blepontes*) may become blind" (9:39). In John's gospel, Jesus "departs" from and "eludes" those who are blind in this way. As John goes on to note in chapter 12:

Although he had performed so many signs in their presence, they did not believe in him. This was to fulfill the word spoken by the prophet Isaiah:
"Lord, who has believed our message,
and to whom has the arm of the Lord been revealed?"
And so they could not believe, because Isaiah also said,
"He has blinded their eyes and hardened their heart,
so that they might not look with their eyes, and understand
with their heart and turn—
and I would heal them."
Isaiah said this because he saw his glory and spoke about him.
(12:37-41)

Those Who See Only with the Eyes of Faith

No one has ever seen (*oran*) God (1:18a; 5:37). According to biblical tradition, God cannot be seen. The closest anyone came to "seeing" God in the Hebrew scriptures was Moses' experience on Sinai. In fact, in using images like "angels" or other visual apparitions experienced by people, the scriptural writer actually is trying to describe an experience of the invisible presence of God (Gn 12:7a; 17:1; 18:1; 26:2; 26:24; 35:9; 48:3).

John continues this tradition by saying that no one has seen God, "except the one who is from God; he has seen the Father" (6:46 [2x]). The closest anyone else will come to seeing God (= "the Father") is in "seeing" Jesus (14:7). Thus, we have already heard the substance of Jesus' response to Philip's request: "Lord, show us the Father, and we will be satisfied" as "Whoever has seen me has seen the Father. How can you say, 'Show us the Father'? Do you not believe that I am in the Father and the Father is in me?" (14:9-10). Here "seeing" is linked to "believing." Those who believe in Jesus, the Word of God, "see" God.

I often think of my Mother's fear of "getting to heaven" and realizing that one of us, her sons, might not be there. "How can this be heaven if I won't see you?," she often mused. Such thinking still identifies "heaven" with a place and considers God someone physically visible. For this reason, Pope John Paul II said at a 1999 general audience that heaven is not a place but an intimate relationship with God and that, when we live in intimacy with one another, we experience part of heaven on earth.[16]

In terms of this way of "seeing," the only way God becomes visible is in the sense of what the fox said to the Little Prince: What is real is invisible to the eye.

As John wrote in his first letter:

> No one has ever seen God; if we love one another, God lives in us, and his love is perfected in us. By this we know that we abide in him and he in us, because he has given us of his Spirit. And we have seen and do testify that the Father has sent his son as the Savior of the world. God abides in those who confess that Jesus is the Son of God, and they abide in God. So we have known and believe the love that God has for us. God is love and those who abide in love abide in God, and God abides in them. (1 Jn 4:12-16)

In John's theology, the love one has for another is the measure of one's love of God. If we love one another, God lives in us and God's love is perfected in us. In other words, the only way to see God is to recognize another by a life of care, even to the point of being willing to lay down one's life for the other. This theological truth is echoed in the wonderful phrase from *Les Miserables*: "To love another person is to see the face of God."

The final kind of seeing, the kind that receives the highest endorsement from Jesus in John's gospel, is that of those who "have not seen but have believed," in contrast to the man born blind and Thomas who, as Jesus said, "believed because you have seen me" (20:29).

Jesus' ultimate blessing is given to those whose seeing is based not on any physical or visual "siting," but on faith alone. Not to see the risen Christ and yet to believe in him constitutes the highest form of "seeing" possible. With this kind of seeing, one lives only by faith. A powerful example of this can be found in the story of Sr. John Vianney, a School Sister of Notre Dame in the congregation's Milwaukee province.

As I have heard the story from those who knew her, she was diagnosed at an early age with a debilitating nervous condition that would lead to increasing paralysis. She was told that she would begin having trouble walking, then need a cane, move to a walker, be confined to a wheelchair, and, finally, be virtually bed-ridden for decades, unable to move herself.

One day after receiving the diagnosis, when she was still able to pray the Stations of the Cross, she experienced a powerful light coming toward her. Within it, a figure came closer and closer. She felt the presence of the Risen Lord. At that, she heard words: "John Vianney, you know what is in store for you. Before it comes, would you like to enter into my glory?" She surprised herself by replying, as spontaneously as Thomas, but not using his words: "No Lord, because you said, 'Blessed are those who have not seen and yet have come to believe.' Just help me believe." With that, she said, she never again had an experience of Christ in any form. However, while she lived in darkness, which included deep depression, she became one of those who witnessed to the Risen Lord in such a way that others came to believe.

Living in/by Faith

One of the best descriptions of the Johannine meaning of *pisteuein* ("faith") can be found in Rudolf Bultmann's piece in the *Theological Dictionary of the New Testament*. Bultmann makes it clear that, for John, faith is hardly ever a noun. It is a verb. And while it might involve acceptance of certain faith-statements, its deeper expression has to do with becoming engaged with another. Thus, Johannine faith involves an embrace of the Jesus and his proclamation directly or through others. Acceptance of Jesus is impossible without acting on his message. "To believe in Him" is "to come to Him" (5:40; 6:35, 37, 44f, 65; 7:37), "to receive Him" (1:12; 5:43), "to love Him" (8:42; 14:15, 21, 23f, 28; 16:27).[17]

At the same time, *pisteuein* demands a "renunciation of the world," insofar as the world stands opposed to faith in the message of Jesus Christ about turning from self-centeredness to self-sacrifice (see 3:17). This is what Bultmann calls "an act of desecularisation" in that the person believing in Jesus Christ has separated from, turned from, lost faith in the "world."

> Desecularisation is not to be regarded as a flight from the world but as the reversing and destroying of worldly norms and values. Similarly, it would be a misunderstanding to think that the believer is to be taken out of the world (17:15). His turning from the world is a turning from evil (17:15). "World" for John is not a natural entity.... It is a historical entity and power constituted by the men who turn from the light, from God, and who through their own conduct all share in its force and power. For this world, revelation is an offence because it calls this world in[to] question; it is the judgment of the world (3:19; 12:31). Faith is an act of descularisation in the sense that it overcomes the offence and banishes all the autonomous power of man. Positively it is a grasping of the revelation which comes in the Word.[18]

A faith limited to "a personal relationship with Jesus Christ" is something quite individualized and subjective. While *pisteuein* does contain elements involving personal relationship and commitment, it also demands an embrace of the message of Jesus Christ in the power of his Spirit. In the case of the believer (the reader), witnessing to that message in one's own life, in the reality of one's own "world," attests to the authenticity of one's faith. In John, the deeds of the "world" represent darkness and evil: "And this is the judgment, that the light has come into the world, and people loved darkness rather than light because their deeds were evil. For all who do evil hate the light and do not come to the light, so that their deeds may not be exposed. But those who do what is true come to the light, so that it may be clearly seen that their deeds have been done in God" (3:19-21).

SEVEN

FOR WHICH OF THESE
ARE YOU GOING TO STONE ME? (10:32)

The Question of John 10:1-39

Chapter 10, well-known for its "good shepherd" passages, is pivotal for the entire gospel of John. Herein the forensic exchange between Jesus and his opponents finds him leveling a new charge at them. In the previous chapter he accused *hoi Ioudaioi* of "not seeing." In this chapter he declares that the leaders are not hearing. Since Johannine seeing and hearing involve people's basic faith stance, what John declares here is that the religious leaders were simply closed to Jesus himself. They lacked faith.

Since chapter 5, hostility between Jesus and *hoi Ioudaioi* has been building. There, within the context of a festival (5:1) and in response to his first truly "public" sign of healing the invalid on the sabbath (within the temple territory), *hoi Ioudaioi* "were seeking *all the more* to kill him" (5:18). In chapter 6, when the festival of Passover is near, various groups "complain" or are "divided" among themselves regarding Jesus. Their internal conflict has arisen from his teaching about their need to make not only his word but his very body and blood part of themselves. "After this," in chapters 7 and 8—in the context of the "Jewish festival of Booths"—we find charges and countercharges flying in the courts of the temple yard as public opinion swings back and forth regarding Jesus' identity and mission. In the midst of all this, "the scribes and the Pharisees" objectify a woman in sin as a way of "testing" Jesus so they can put him on trial. Jesus turns the tables and exposes the deeper sin of their lack of just judgment (7:53-8:11). In chapter 9, he performs his second sabbath healing. Though the blind person now sees, John uses the occasion of his healing to expose the sickness of the systems' leaders whose confidence reveals their deeper blindness.

In chapter 10, the conflict between Jesus and *hoi Ioudaioi* broadens to include Jesus' concerns about leaders "within the flock." Unlike previous chapters which highlighted Jesus' conflicts with hostile forces outside the community (*hoi Ioudaioi*), chapter 10 concentrates on a new kind of alien leadership. He focuses on powerful forces within the community, the community's leaders (= shepherds) who have failed sufficiently to identify with Jesus' person and vision. John's Jesus puts enmity between him and them. He labels them "thieves," "bandits," and "strangers." They act like mere functionaries—"hired hands"—who have no real care for the flock. Unlike Jesus' relationship to "his" flock, "their" exercise of authority is leading the people astray.

Because its sections are quite loosely related, chapter 10 seems to be a composite of different traditions. These seem to have been brought together to address the kind of internal leadership problems faced by the Johannine community.[1] That chapter 10 is a composite is reflected in the fact that the two main sections of the chapter deal with events that took place at different times. The first part of the chapter occurs during the feast of Booths.[2] This event takes place in autumn. The second section of the chapter occurs at the "time the festival of the Dedication took place in Jerusalem. It was winter" (10:22). Despite the different time frames, there are parallels in the themes of the two sections. The first parallel in each section revolves around the notion of plain speaking (see 10:6; 10:24); the second has to do with the shepherd and sheep (10:1f; 10:27-29). The most important parallel, however, is found in the use of the "I am" statements (10:7, 11, 14; 10:38).

First Section: John 10:1-21

Notions related to shepherding dominate the chapter. In Jesus' time, while the agrarian notion of shepherd and sheep had economic implications as well as deeply embedded spiritual implications, cultural identifiers relating to images of shepherd and sheep seemed to have dominated. In such a culture, John Pilch has pointed out, "animals are interpreted and treated as symbols of the internal differences peculiar to this world." While sheep symbolized honor, shepherds were associated with shame.[3] Shepherds represented a lower class, below day workers and artisans. Because of their work with sheep, they were considered unclean—"bad" people. Society considered them outcasts and ostracized them. They were labeled, invalidated, and rejected. This was aggravated by the fact that their "long absences from home made it impossible for them to protect the womenfolk as they ought." All of these factors contributed to "the shameful reputation of shepherds in the first century."[4]

Cultural notions of honor and shame make it easier to understand some of the dynamics taking place in the first part of this chapter. Jesus declares that the only way to access the sheepfold is through the gate. To try to relate to the sheep in any other way makes a leader who tries to do so "a thief and a bandit" (10:1). The shepherds of the people, the leaders

who have labeled and ostracized others, are themselves thieves and bandits. The only one with ultimate access through the gate is the one and
only shepherd, Jesus himself (10:2). Jesus' reference to himself as both
gate (10:7) and shepherd appears consistent with texts that scripture
scholars find reflecting the final edition or redaction of John's gospel.
These verses make an appeal to a community divided into factions to
focus on Jesus as the core of their lives, despite their conflicts with their
leaders. As the Johannine community was witnessing the rise of a way of
thinking that "accentuated . . . the importance of institution and office" of
Peter and the apostles, these words served as a reminder that Jesus is the
absolute shepherd, and that the significance of all other forms of shepherding is relative (see 10:15f).[5]

Jesus says the shepherd "calls his own sheep by name and leads them
out" (10:3). Being a city boy, I found it difficult to believe that a shepherd
could actually call sheep by name, much less even desire to do so. However, this all changed for me in 1997 when I traveled to Mongolia. The
raising of sheep is central to Mongolia's culture. While visiting a ger I
learned that, although shepherds may have hundreds of sheep, all are
given names honoring them for their uniqueness. There, in a foreign land,
John's image of Jesus being willing to lay down his life for the sheep (see
10:15f) became clear to me for the first time. Because of this kind of intimacy and care, John notes, the shepherd "goes ahead of them, and the
sheep follow him because they know his voice" (10:4).

"The voice" represents more than a vehicle for words; it connotes a
person whom sheep know and with whom they can identify without fear
or intimidation. Anyone else will be a "stranger" (10:5). In John, "knowing" involves seeing and hearing that leads to belief. The one who
"knows" another loves and abides in that one. Whoever "knows" hears
the voice and obeys what is said.[6]

Because they did not grasp what he meant when he used such images,
John's Jesus switches to another literary device: the use of metaphors. He
no longer speaks about any anonymous gatekeeper; now he becomes the
"gate for the sheep" (10:7). No longer does he talk about a "shepherd of the
sheep"; he is "the good shepherd" (10:11, 14). His unique goodness as a
shepherd will be evidenced in his willingness to "lay down" his life for the
sheep" (10:11; 10:17-18). By calling himself "the good shepherd [who]
lays down his life for the sheep" Jesus shows that he has come "that they
may have life and have it abundantly" (10:10). The abundant life available
in Jesus for believers was being undermined by the various divisions within
the Christian community. This led Jesus to call for other sheep to come to
the fold "so there will be one flock, one shepherd" (10:16).

Despite their differences with the Petrine approach to leadership, the
Johannine community knew that Jesus' vision for the flock was inclusive

rather than divisive; it had to remain united. Anthony Blasi notes: "The passage appears to recognize other Christian groups and to call for a formation of a single identity for all of them. This implies that the Christian group in the image—presumably the Johannine—was not or had not been in any unity with one or more other Christian groups but was in the process of merging or at least contemplating a merge with the other groups."[7] I would add the distinct possibility that (at least for the contemporary reader), in face of the increasing influence of the hierarchical dynamics associated with the Petrine community, the Johannine expression of Jesus' person and message was in decline. As 1 John makes clear, while the Johannine community saw itself as distinct from this other type of expression, it was struggling with regard to its understanding of the unity and self-sacrificing love that was to be its hallmark. Its very life—which was rooted in self-sacrifice—was at stake.

It is in this sense that Jesus declares: "No one takes it [my life] from me, but I lay it down of my own accord. I have power to lay it down, and I have power to take it up again. I have received this command from my Father" (10:18). What exactly is this "command from my Father" related to Jesus' laying down his life of his "own accord"?

It would be wrong to conclude from these words that God was commanding Jesus to lay down his life; in fact I believe it would be blasphemous to say that God willed Jesus to do so. Why, then, do so many Christians find meaning in an atonement theory that somehow makes God demand "infinite reparation" for original sin, for humanity's rebellion against God? Why do so many bow before a God who sanctions killing?

In his dissertation on John's notion of salvation, the Canadian Basilian, J. Terence Forestell, observes that, while the most prominent theology of salvation in the New Testament has interpreted Jesus' death as an expiation for humanity's sins in a way that restored it to friendship with God, the gospel of John seems relatively free of such notions as satisfaction and expiation. Thus, when Jesus says he is the good shepherd and that "I lay down my life in order to take it up again" (10:17),

> the cross which resulted from this must be evaluated precisely in terms of revelation in harmony with the theology of the entire gospel, rather than in terms of a vicarious and expiatory sacrifice for sin. Revelation and the sacrifice of the cross are not two parallel or complementary theologies of salvation in Jn. On the contrary, the evangelist understands the cross as the culminating act of a revelatory process in which God manifests himself to men and bestows upon them his own divine life. The cross has this revelatory meaning in Jn because it is the exaltation and glorifi-

cation of the Son of Man; it is the way by which Jesus passes from this world to the Father; it is the supreme revelation of the love of God for men because Jesus effectively lays down his life for his sheep; it is both a symbol of the gift of eternal life and the means whereby the sources of divine life are finally opened for men.[8]

Rather than Jesus' laying down his life on the cross as an expiation for sin, it is the expression of Jesus' self-sacrificing love, and it reveals the world's sin of refusal to live in this love. As for the reference to Jesus as "the Lamb of God who takes away the sin of the world" (1:29), Forestell notes that the notion "is not developed in a characteristically Johannine fashion and may simply reflect a cultic interpretation of Jesus' death in the eucharistic celebrations of the Johannine community,"[9] much as it does today in ours.

"The Father" could not have commanded Jesus' death, especially his death by crucifixion, for various reasons. God could not have commanded (in the sense of willing it) that Jesus lay down his life in a way that would require someone or some group known as "enemy" to kill him. First of all, if God actually "willed" the death of Jesus, no matter for what worthy cause, it would make God at least implicitly guilty in his death. As any good Catholic knows, to kill someone is evil. However, to *will* that someone be killed by others is evil as well and makes the one who wills the killing as evil as the perpetrator. If God were to have commanded Jesus to lay down his life in the sense of actually directly willing it or intending it, that would have made God responsible and, therefore, guilty of murder. Second, if God wanted others to kill Jesus, it would mean that God willed people to violate the fifth commandment: "You shall not murder" (Ex 20:13). God's "command" is not that Jesus be killed. Rather, God's "command" is invested in Jesus' "power" to lay down his life. This he will do voluntarily, knowing full well that the consequence of his words and deeds in an alien "world" will bring him to death at the hands of his enemies.

When Jesus compares himself to the religious leaders in a way that labels them not only as estranged from the sheep but as thieves, bandits, and mere hired hands who don't really "know" the sheep, the response from *hoi Ioudaioi* is further division in their own ranks (10:19). Some continue to demonize him; they cannot find anything "good" in him. Yet others, recognizing the "good" he was doing for people, were saying, "These are not the words of one who has a demon. Can a demon open the eyes of the blind?" (10:20-21). Although John says that Jesus' words divided *hoi Ioudaioi* "again," this is the chapter's first direct reference to this group of Jesus' main opponents.

Second Section: 10:22-39

Making a transition from the feast of Booths, which set the context for the first section of this chapter (see 7:2-14), John notes that, "at that time the festival of the Dedication took place in Jerusalem" (10:22a). In keeping with John's pattern, some kind of conflict between Jesus and those leaders who presided over the temple feasts can be expected to take place. This time, on the feast of the rededication of the temple, *hoi Ioudaioi* create a confrontation by asking: "How long will you keep us in suspense? If you are the Messiah, tell us plainly" (10:24). With this challenge, Jesus declares that he has already told them and they don't believe. Furthermore, more than his words, his works (*erga*)—done in the name of his Father—testify plainly as to his messianic origins.

Until this point in the chapter, *hoi Ioudaioi* have pressed Jesus to speak to them "plainly" if he is "the Messiah" (10:24). Jesus' response makes it clear that the real issue is not his speaking. Neither is it a question of his speaking plainly, because his works make his words perfectly clear (10:25). The real issue is their hearing. The problem rests in the fact that, because they are not his sheep, they do not hear his voice (10:26-27). Therefore, they are impostors.

Now, escalating his challenge to them to a higher level, he implies directly that he considers their resistance to him a futile effort to "snatch" the sheep not only from his hands (10:28) but from his Father's (10:29). At the same time, he makes it clear that they will not be successful. The reason? They are archetypal of those religious leaders of any age whose interests are not grounded in their own hearing of the voice of God, but in insisting that their own voices be heard by the flock. Unlike their way which results in division (10:19f), Jesus' way promotes unity: "the Father and I are one" (10:30).

With Jesus' statement that he and the Father "are one," *hoi Ioudaioi* took up "stones again to stone him" (10:31). The leaders' enraged response elicits from Jesus two questions. First, after noting that "I have shown you many good works from the Father," he asks, "For which of these are you going to stone me?" (10:32). At this *hoi Ioudaioi* retort: "It is not for a good work that we are going to stone you, but for blasphemy, because you, though only a human being, are making yourself God" (10:33). They cannot link his doing God's "work" with Jesus' showing that he indeed is the son apprenticed to the "Father." In this work he is "one" with the Father.

It seems evident that neither John, as narrator, nor Jesus was speaking of any kind of essential, metaphysical, or ontological unity between Jesus and God as Father as we understand this today. Jesus is one with God insofar as he is fully in accord with God's will in a way that enables God to continue to accomplish in creation the divine activity. Now Jesus, as Messiah, represents God's presence and work in the people's midst. His God-oriented works expose as bankrupt the self-serving works of the religious leaders who are frustrating God's purposes in the world.

If the first question revolved around what Jesus does (his works [*erga*]), the second has to do with his very identity (his self [*egō eimi*]). When *hoi Ioudaioi* respond that they feel justified in stoning him because he, who is "only a human being is making himself to be God" (10:33), Jesus retorts with a question based on the words of Psalm 82: "Is it not written in your law, 'I said, you are gods'?"

According to Jesus, in the past those people who received God's living word into their lives were empowered, to this degree, to be "gods." Now the Word itself has become enfleshed in the midst of all people. This Word stands before them and their leaders as the sign of God's presence, totally dedicated to remaining in union with God. How, then, he asks, can they say that he is "blaspheming" because he said, "I am God's Son" (10:36)? Further articulating his unique relationship with God, he declares: "The Father is in me and I am in the Father" (10:38b). At this point, rather than reacting with a considered response or even demeaning ripostes, they try to eliminate the one whose words have convicted them. The section ends with *hoi Ioudaioi* trying "to arrest him again, but he escaped from their hands" (10:39).

How the "I Am" Statements of Jesus Help Define Who "We Are" to Be (10:1-18)

The particular statement of Jesus that seems to have triggered the violent response of *hoi Ioudaioi* was his "I am" declaration. The image connected him intimately to God as Son (10:36). In the koine Greek of the New Testament, "I am" is *eimi*. When one wanted to place emphasis on the *eimi*—or some attribute of it—the first person pronoun, *ego*, would be added. *Egō eimi* thus could be translated as "I am myself." On the lips of Jesus "*egō eimi*" echoed the divine name (Yahweh) revealed in Exodus 3:14: "God said to Moses: 'I am who I am (*egō eimi*).'"

Most scripture scholars agree that Jesus' *egō eimi* statements in John are more than mere points of personal emphasis. Rather, they point to something deeper: his divine connectedness. While John's community did not have the benefit of ecumenical councils to define the nature of this connectedness as the ontological unity we believe in today, it did recognize something of God's own divinity in how Jesus functioned. In a world where Greek, Egyptian, and Roman "gods" were given that name (and fought for power among each other), John is saying: Whatever other claims you may have heard, Jesus is the true divine revealer. At the heart of Jesus' revelation is his unique union with God's power.

Recently there has been a rash of books trying to describe the uniqueness of Jesus and the kind of impact he had on the lives of people in his society. Following Albert Schweitzer and the "quest for the historical Jesus," Marcus Borg has interpreted him to be a "holy person" and "subversive teacher of wisdom" whose vision of life centered on spirit.[10] Borg's colleague in the Jesus Seminar, John Dominic Crossan, has sketched Jesus as a "revolutionary Jewish peasant" whose healing and table fellowship subverted society's categories.[11] John Meier proffers a Jesus who appeared as a "marginal Jew" and whose message alienated him from his co-religionists.[12] E. P. Sanders has found in Jesus the image of an "eschatological prophet" committed to the restoration of Judaism.[13] Elisabeth Schussler Fiorenza sees Jesus as a "wisdom prophet" intent on creating an alternative model of community that would challenge the existing patriarchal forms in favor of something more egalitarian.[14] Rudolf Schnackenburg, one of the greatest Johannine scholars in the world today, portrays Jesus as "our friend" who created a circle of friends which we call church.[15]

Despite the solid and helpful work of these scholars, I find their approach appeals more to my head than my heart. Somehow I haven't been able to translate their reflections into my spirituality, especially when it comes to developing a more intimate connectedness to the one who called himself the "I am" in a way that might impact my own "I am." However, inspired by chapter 10, I've discovered a simple and appealing insight: rather than reading descriptions about Jesus, an authentic reader-response approach to the word must let Jesus speak for himself—through his own images. If I allow the Jesus of John's gospel to speak to *me* as I engage the text, something might get triggered in my person that could lead to greater intimacy with him and, through him, with the God he called Father. Indeed, if it is true that "Johannine mysticism is based on the oneness between Jesus and the Father and on abiding in Jesus and that the Father and Jesus are perfectly one while remaining two," then it might be equally true that my abiding in Jesus might also characterize my "relationship with the Son, which is the source of mystical experience." [16]

In John's gospel, Jesus defines himself more than thirty times with the "I am" statement in one form or another. References without an image connect Jesus' personal identity with that of God. Those with an image point to the singular way in which he manifests his divine power in relationship to humans.[17]

Each "I am the . . ." statement takes place at or around the time of some "festival of *hoi Ioudaioi*." That Jesus identifies himself with the most religious of all images ("I am") during these feasts appears to be John's way of making it clear that, in the person and proclamation of Jesus, the old order centered in the temple and its feasts is not only being subverted, it is being replaced in the person of God's authentic presence revealed in the Word itself. The subversive dimension of the "I am" statements represents a way in which a subculture like the Johannine community could identify its own uniqueness in contrast and as an alternative to the wider Petrine church.[18]

As the early Johannine community developed, it discovered itself to be a conscious alternative to the dominant and dominating patterns around it. The alternative way of viewing and identifying one's social location in an alien environment is called antilanguage. Metaphor is the vehicle of communication of antilanguage. Thus it is not surprising that Bruce Malina would argue that a unique expression of the antilanguage of the Johannine community would be expressed in the metaphors connected to the "I am..." statements where Jesus says of himself: "I am bread, light, a gate, the good shepherd, the resurrection, the way, the truth, the life, the vine."[19] In John's gospel, Jesus communicates himself through metaphors and invites the community to discover its own identity and uniqueness through these metaphors. All nine metaphorical references point to a specific dimension of Jesus' "I am." Each involves four elements:

(1) The predicate nominative of each identifies a characteristic of Jesus flowing from First Testament images. These metaphors make clear those with whom Jesus is identified and those who stand opposed to him.

(2) By identifying who he is, Jesus reveals a dimension of "the Father." In the process he shows how far away from God are those who stand opposed to him.

(3) In the metaphor, Jesus sets the terms regarding how those who remain with him will have access to God. As they identify with Jesus' "I am" in its metaphorical expression, his true disciples will come to find themselves separated from others who claim to be the light, life, truth, etc.

(4) The disciple identifying with Jesus in the specific "I am..." statement is invited to go deeper into the metaphorical meaning behind to the metaphor, i.e., life, including eternal life. Those cutting themselves from this source (i.e., life) do so at the risk of their lives.

In the remaining pages of this chapter, I will offer suggestions for understanding and approaching Jesus Christ through his own metaphorical images. I have found these images helpful in "enfleshing" his divine identity, thus making possible a deeper intimacy with him. The goal is that suggested by Michael Willett Newheart: that "the encounter projected onto these images is now projected onto Jesus, with the result that the bond between him and the reader is cemented."[20]

I Am the Bread of Life (6:35, 48); I Am the Bread Come down from Heaven (6:41)

In chapter 6 Jesus refers to himself as "I am" with a predicate nominative related to bread in two different ways. In the first he is "the bread of life" (6:35, 48) itself; in the second he is "the bread of life come down from heaven" (6:41). Recognizing the source of his identity in the Father who gave *hoi Ioudaioi* all the bread they needed when they "ate the manna in the wilderness" (6:31), Jesus declares that this same Father now offers us "the true bread from heaven. For the bread of God is that which comes down from heaven and gives life to the world" (6:33). In a "world" where a nation like mine can be demographically subdivided by advertisers according to what people eat[21]—to the point that "We Are What We Eat"[22]—the bread that comes from heaven is the true bread of life.

When the crowds ask Jesus for "this bread always" (6:34), Jesus declares, "I am the bread of life" and "whoever comes to me will never be hungry, and whoever believes in me will never be thirsty" (6:35). If Jesus is to be this bread for us readers, how are we to identify with him through this metaphor? If we allow him to be bread for our life, what implications might this have for us who live in a world where so many still go hungry?

This last question reminds me of a "holy card" I designed while in the seminary. It was 1967. For Holy Thursday, my first as a priest, I took a 6" x 5" card and folded it in half. On the front, on the bottom and right side, I painted various-sized circles to evoke the kind of colors found on the wrapper for Wonder Bread. On the left side I penned the saying attributed to Mahatma Gandhi: "If Christ would ever come again, he would have to come as bread, for there are so many people who are hungry." On the inside I wrote: "On the night before he died, Jesus took the bread, blessed God, broke the bread and gave it to his disciples saying: 'Take this and eat it; this is my body for you.'"

Jesus' opponents perceived him only as a human being. Thus, when he used the metaphor about being bread, the very substance of life itself, the source of eternal life itself (6:47-51), they could only complain (6:41, 61) and dispute (6:52). Today, despite mandates from the religious leaders of the Roman Church not to complain and dispute about the present rules which effectively limit access to the bread of life because of their insistence on maintaining a male, celibate, clerical model for the one who pre-

who presides over the Eucharist, many people have "turned back" to "the world" and "no longer" identify with Jesus through this metaphor in the Roman Church (see 6:66). Still others, instead of finding alternative ways to ritualize Jesus' life-giving presence in their midst, rely on non-available clerics and miss the possibility of experiencing the real presence as broader than its clerical expression. This metaphor invites us to ask about those times when we may be more concerned about preserving crumbs than maintaining access to the loaf itself.

I Am the Light of the World (8:12)

Jesus' statement about being "the light of the world" is best contextualized in the very first words of John's gospel: "In the beginning was the Word, and the Word was with God, and the Word was God. He was in the beginning with God. All things came into being through him, and without him not one thing came into being. What has come into being in him was life, and the life was the light of all people. The light shines in the darkness and the darkness did not overcome it" (1:1-5). In an energy-cheap society which itself produces the "darkness" of greenhouse gases, the light identified with Jesus invites us to another "bottom line."

While Jesus defined himself as "light of the world," he recognized the Father as the source of any light that was in him. The source of this light/glory he revealed to human beings (1:14). St. Catherine of Siena supposedly said that, if we could get only a glimmer of the presence of Christ within us, its light would blind us. Through the Word in the beginning of creation, God's first utterance had been, "Let there be light" (Gn 1:3). This light had come through darkness to make the first day. Now, with Jesus saying that he is "the light of the world," all past days, all present days, and all future days are to be lived in his light.

What does it mean for readers to hear Jesus say, "I am the light of the world"? I believe it involves following him in such a way that we "will never walk in darkness but will have the light of life" (8:12; see 1 Jn 1:5-7). Identifying with Jesus as "light of the world" means that those faithful to him must live in this world aware of its darkness, its areas of opposition to him, and be illumined by his word that we hear and his works that we see. With his light informing us, we should not be afraid or ashamed to confront the darkness in the world of our culture and church, even if their response is to call us the children of darkness (see 1 Jn 2:9-11).

Light has always been associated with the divine. People who claim to have had heavenly apparitions often mention images of light connected to them. Having grown up in the 1940s and 1950s, I heard many stories about Our Lady of Fatima. I can still vividly recall various accounts of the "sun whirling in the skies." Indeed, during the time when I was a child in

Wisconsin, the Blessed Virgin was said to be appearing to Mrs. Van Hoof in Neceedah. Our neighbor went there (against the "orders" of the bishop) and returned insisting that she had seen the sun spin in the sky.

While we thank God for the light of Christ as we stand around the Easter candle, we are also called to make sure that its brightness shines even more powerfully within us when we remain in Jesus Christ. As his followers we are called to expose the shadows and darkness of the forces that stand opposed to the light of Christ within us. We must thus make sure that the light within us is seen as a flame rather than a flicker.

I Am the Gate for the Sheep (10:7)

John's Jesus identified himself as "gate" for the sheep (10:7) because he understood that his Father was the source of the metaphor's reality in him. And, while no image of God being the gate for the people exists in the Hebrew scriptures, it is clear that God is the source of life itself and, therefore, *the* gate. Jesus contrasts his way of being "gate" with that of "all who came before me," meaning those leaders in the Jewish community or the Petrine Christian community who were putting themselves in front of him. These are thieves and bandits. The sheep don't listen to such thieves and bandits (10:8), even those who may insist that their way is the only way.

The first thing the sheep find by coming through the gate ("whoever enters by me") is salvation. I have already made it clear that this "salvation" (a word used but once in John, and by Jesus in reference to *hoi Ioudaioi* and not himself [4:22]) is not really what people carrying "John 3:16" banners would have us believe. The verb "to save" (*sōzein*) is used only four times (3:17; 5:34; 10:9; 12:47; see also 11:12; 12:27). It doesn't mean salvation from sin and death as much as the believer's way of entering into the fullness of God's life.

When any religious institution, religious group, or interpretation identifies itself as the only entrance by which humans can access Jesus rather than Jesus himself being the gate, something is askew. Instead of life in abundance there will be the death and destruction. Rudolf Schnackenburg writes:

> The door-word is meant to show...that, because of Jesus's self-revelation, all other claimants are usurpers through being convicted of a false claim to being saviors. So long as Jesus, the shepherd, is installed in his function as door, every illegitimate claim in respect of revelation, leadership and the bringing of salvation falls to pieces when it comes into contact with him. There is but one entrance to the sheep, and it is "occupied" by Jesus.

There is but one bringer of salvation, one way to the Father (cf. 14:4-6)—Jesus, the "door."[23]

Many of us find it easy to become preoccupied with the "religious bandits" whom we identify with those stealing life from the sheep rather than giving it. When this happens, we need to ask ourselves if we might perhaps have become so centered on the leaders' threat to the sheep that we miss the gate ourselves—not to speak of where our true pasture might be found.

I Am the Good Shepherd (10:11)

John contrasts the good shepherd with those hired hands whose identification with the sheep arises merely from function rather than relationship. When "the wolf" comes, they flee. They do not "care for the sheep" (10:13). If the image of shepherd is seen as a symbol of authority, the fact that the hirelings (or hierarchy?) do not truly *care for the sheep* will be evidenced in dynamics and structures more defined by control than care, more by caprice than compassion.

We have seen that this part of the shepherd discourse may have served as a warning to leaders within the Johannine community that found itself at odds with the Petrine/Apostolic group to remain within the flock of Jesus.[24] Care characterizes the concern of the Shepherd-God immortalized in Psalm 23: "The Lord is my shepherd, I shall not want. He makes me lie down in green pastures; he leads me beside still waters; he restores my soul. He leads me in right paths for his name's sake" (Ps 23:1-3). If God is the Shepherd who cares for the flock, those who serve in God's name must be ministers of care rather than control. This is the whole concern of Ezekiel who railed against those false shepherds who fed themselves rather than the sheep (Ez 34:1-3). The result of this, as Ezekiel made clear in his prophecy, was that "they were scattered, because there was no shepherd; and scattered, they became food for all the wild animals" (Ez 34:5).

In this context Jesus proves that he is the "good" shepherd by his commitment to lay down his life for the sheep. In order to ensure the lives of the sheep, to keep them from being "scattered over all the face of the earth" (see Ez 34:6), a good shepherd is willing to put his own life on the line. Instead of running for his life in face of threats (from synagogal or Petrine leaders?), the good shepherd lays down his own life "so that" there may be but one flock and one shepherd (10:16).

If Jesus declares that he himself is the "good shepherd," what does this mean for us, John's readers? Ezekiel's prophecy may suggest an answer: "As for you, my flock...I shall judge between sheep and sheep, between

rams and goats. Is it not enough for you to feed on the good pasture, but
you must tread down with your feet the rest of your pasture? When you
drink of clear water, must you foul the rest with your feet?" (Ez 34:17-18).

Our political economy is driven by cost-benefit calculations. While I
was writing this book, it was revealed that the nation's largest corporation
stood behind marauders who had decided that, since the company would
have to spend less money by settling with accident victims who sued over
a defective part than by changing the part, they would not change the defective part. This despite the fact that changing the part would have saved
lives—and would have cost only $2.40 per vehicle.[25] For those identified
with the Good Shepherd and thus willing to lay down their lives for one
another, an important question might be: Where am I willing to deny life
to others so that my lifestyle might continue?

I Am the Resurrection and the Life (11:25)

In the Lazarus, Martha, and Mary story, Jesus fuses his declaration:
"I am the resurrection and the life" with two promises: (1) those who believe in him will live and (2) those who live in him will never die. These
strong affirmations need to be heard in a culture of death where the
stench of individualism mixed with consumerism saps the lives of so
many, even believers. They also need to be heard in a church that has
buried more of its members in cemeteries called "Calvary" than in cemeteries called "Resurrection."[26] We must ask ourselves whether we Catholics are more preoccupied with Jesus' death (and our own) than with his
resurrection (and our own).

Until now all the "I am" statements of Jesus link his "I am" with the
source of his life—in the "I am" he calls "Father." And, even though this
passage contains but one reference to God as Father, it is a critical reference. As the people removed the stone from the grave that held Lazarus,
"Jesus looked upward and said: 'Father, I thank you for having heard me.
I knew that you always hear me, but I have said this for the sake of the
crowd standing here, so that they may believe that you sent me'" (11:42).

What might such words mean for those of us today who struggle with
these words of Jesus: "I am the resurrection and the life" and "those who
believe in me, even though they die, will live, and everyone who lives
and believes in me will never die. Do you believe this?" (11:25-26). Resurrection belief can only be a free response given by those who acknowledge the power of the resurrection in their lives and choose that life over
all cultural forms of death: personal and communal as well as economic,
political, and even religious.

This reminds of a story a nun told me some time ago. It seems that, in
the late 1960s and into the 1970s, when all sorts of "renewal programs"

were occurring, some community members went to a particular conference. They returned very enthused. "What did you learn?" asked one of the nuns who had been having problems with the changes that came after Vatican II.

"Well, we don't need to believe in the resurrection of Jesus any more," one of them replied.

This was the last straw for the other nun. She left the order.

As the nun speaking with me recounted the story, she commented: "People have been saying there's no resurrection for two thousand years. So I don't see why the sister got so upset. It's nothing new." But then she added something very new, but also very basic: "The resurrection isn't something you *have to believe* in—it's just something you *do*."

To *have to believe* in the resurrection takes it out of the realm of mystery, out of the realm of faith. Belief in the resurrection cannot be forced, or mandated, or legislated. It is something freely embraced and witnessed to in one's life of faith. "I am the resurrection and the life. Those who believe in me, even though they die, will live, and everyone who lives and believes in me will never die. Do you believe this?" The question invites a faith response. It doesn't insist on it.

I Am the Way (14:6)

In his Farewell Discourse Jesus declared himself to be the way, the truth, and the life. Having promised a place in one of the many dwelling places in his Father's house (14:1-4), Jesus invites us to find in him and in his Spirit the entrance to our eternal abode. But our future entrance is found by identifying with him now as the way, the truth, and the life. While Jesus defines himself as the way, the truth, and the life for us, he recognizes that the Father is the source of everything for him.

If Jesus is to be the one around whom our lives are to be centered, what does this mean for the reader who lives in a world which often promotes its own institutions as the ultimate source of meaning? What does it mean for those of us living in the Petrine-oriented church, where some leaders insist that it is a matter of faith that they alone know the way, that only they possess the fullness of truth, and that ultimate access to sacramental life depends on being obedient to their mandates?

First of all, Jesus clearly declares himself to be "the way." Also, because Jesus fulfilled in his person the purposes of God's Torah, he became recognized as "the way" (*hē hodos*). It is interesting to note that, before Christians were ever called by that name, those who identified with the person of and path Jesus chose for himself were identified as followers of "the Way" (Acts 9:2; 18:24-28; 19:9, 23; 22:4; 24:14, 22). Jesus being "the Way" has important implications in a culture where more people know the way to the mall than to a church.

For the Jewish people, following the way meant living in fidelity to God. Faithful living according to God's vision was expressed through the metaphor of a journey: "I have chosen the way of faithfulness; I set your ordinances before me. I cling to your decrees, O Lord; let me not be put to shame. I run the way of your commandments, for you enlarge my understanding. Teach me, O Lord, the way of your statutes, and I will observe it to the end. Give me understanding, that I may keep your law and observe it with my whole heart" (Ps 119:30-34).

Immediately after declaring himself to be the way, Jesus says, "No one comes to the Father except through me" (14:6b). These words have created much division. In more fundamentalist interpretations, Jesus says here that he alone gives access to God and that only by identification through him, with him, and in him can that access be ensured. History sadly narrates the violence done by those who created religious systems which limited Jesus' "way" to their institutional expressions of it. Such an approach then—or now—has various consequences. Sometimes it results in the exclusion of all those who have never heard of Jesus, or who, having heard of him, have not been able to believe in him. At other times those who profess such beliefs make serious searchers give up, as in the case of Gandhi, who reportedly said he'd like to follow the way of Jesus but Jesus' followers made him change his mind. Others end up rejecting Jesus because of their inability to accept the ways of faith-adherence prescribed for them by those who purport to speak in Jesus' name. In effect they say: "If that's what it means to follow Jesus, I don't want to have anything to do with it."

What about those followers of "the way" who interpret literally Jesus' words about not being able to have access to God save through him (and, by extension, through their unique institutional or interpretative expressions of him)? Franz Rosenzweig provides insight for us when he notes that "No one comes to the Father if one does not need to come to the Father because one is already there."[27] Many people are "already there," because their steps have taken them on paths to God following the way of Jesus, if not his person. As long as these paths have been centered on God as *their* way, their source of life, their ground of being, their "bottom line," the fact that Jesus—the human revelation of God for readers like us—may not be their guide is secondary to the fact that they are on (or "in") the way itself.

Trying to probe the deeper meaning of Jesus' metaphor of being the way invites all of us to ask if and to what degree we have made Jesus our way. Is it possible that our individual and/or institutional interpretations of this proclamation of Jesus—interpretations which make us "the way" —may have put other people off the path? I know of several people who have tired of the internecine battles within Roman Catholicism and have sought the way of Jesus in more inclusive denominations or religions.

I Am the Truth

By using this "I am" metaphor, Jesus shows that truth is not an object of inquiry but a person who is the object of a life's quest. In a militaristic culture such as ours, where planning for war as well as paying for it and its consequences take more from the economy than any other item, "truth is the first casualty"[28] and cynicism often results. In a world where people ask "What is truth?" and need "truth in advertising" laws to guide them, one who is truth itself offers a hopeful alternative.

In the First Testament, truth characterizes an essential quality or attribute of God (Ps 31:5; Jer 10:10). The Hebrew word for truth originally involved notions of *emet*, or fidelity. Truth and steadfast love (*hesed*) characterized God's fidelity and justice or right way of ordering life. The two notions connect in Genesis 32:10 and Psalms 25:10 and 108:4. Truth as mercy is the basis of God's justice: "For he is coming to judge the earth. He will judge the world with righteousness, and the peoples with his truth" (Ps 96:13).

Scripture scholars debate the meaning of the Greek word for "truth" (*alētheia*) in John's gospel (1:14, 17; 3:21; 4:23-24; 8:31-47). According to Ignace de la Potterie, John's notion of *alētheia* involves the original Hebrew notion of *emet* as loving kindness, fidelity, and righteousness. In this sense there exists the way *of* truth. To be *of* truth is to cultivate an interior disposition, to bring oneself into harmony with *hē alētheia*. When this occurs, one remains in truth and under its influence, acquiring a co-naturality and affinity with it. It affects one's whole way of being.[29]

In three different places, John's Jesus is described or refers to himself in terms of what is "true." He is the true light (1:9), the true bread (6:32), and the true vine (15:1). Being truth and being true, in John, are virtually synonymous. According to Jerome Neyrey: "Truth and true are also important claims in the growing forensic imagery of the Fourth Gospel, as Jesus' claims are tested in court and his testimony is subjected to close scrutiny. Being truthful (7:18), witnessing to the truth (5:33), and being true testimony (5:31-32; 8:13-14) reinforce the sense of exclusivity and authenticity by Jesus, especially over against the synagogue."[30] This sense of authenticity also applies over against any religious expression that too easily identifies what might be its own ideologically-biased "truths" (something) with the truth of Jesus (someone).

Too often, in Catholicism, truth is a possession; in John' gospel, truth is the person of Jesus. In Catholicism, truth is frequently a commodity; in John, truth is the Christ. In Catholicism, truth can be objectified in faith-statements and moral imperatives; in John, the only source for truth is Jesus Christ who invites identification and imitation. In Catholicism, truth can be found in statements uttered as infallible pronouncements; in John, there is but one word that speaks truth: "I am." In Catholicism, truth requires an intellectual assent; in John, it demands a moral commitment. De la Potterie says *alētheia* in John is "not an object of intellectual research, but the essential principle of the moral life, of sanctity."[31]

I believe that the letters of John place so much stress on this kind of "truth" because it is essential to the moral life. In fact, "living in truth" seems to be the chief characteristic of authentic life in the community. This truth is not intellectual. It involves one's entire way of being. Jesus' followers "walking in truth" (2 Jn 4; 3 Jn 4) was the greatest source of John's joy.

An understanding of Jesus as "truth" and his followers "walking in truth" invites us to ask ourselves when we may have allowed ourselves to develop our moral lives, indeed our very understanding of holiness itself, on articulations of the truth in dogmas and *fiats* (or reactions to these) rather than in the one who is the very source of truth.

I Am the Life

While the Synoptics mention the word for life (*zōē*) fourteen times, John uses it thirty-four times, usually in reference to Jesus' self-communication of life to those who believe in him. This life is the promise to all who believe in Jesus Christ, the unique promise of Jesus in John's gospel.

G. R. Beasley-Murray has pointed out "a major difference" between the meaning of "life" in John's gospel and its meaning in the First Testament, early Jewish literature, and the Synoptic gospels: "In all these latter writings 'life' or 'eternal life' is a future hope, since it is life in the kingdom of God that is to come; in the Fourth Gospel, however, it is characteristically the gift of God given in the present time."[32] In our culture of death where "Life" has been so trivialized that it refers to a children's cereal or even a board game, Jesus' proclamation that he is Life itself serves as a startling counterpoint. When human beings feel they have a right to deny life to others—especially the unborn, the unwanted, and the "undesirables"—Jesus' identification of himself with Life can be truly subversive to such a culture.

I find the best way to understand how John viewed Jesus' identifying himself with Life and the implications of this for us in the opening lines of 1 John:

> We declare to you what was from the beginning, what we have
> heard, what we have seen with our eyes, what we have looked at
> and touched with our hands, concerning the word of life—this life
> was revealed, and we have seen it and testify to it, and declare to
> you the eternal life that was with the Father and was revealed to
> us—we declare to you what we have seen and heard so that you

also may have fellowship with us; and truly our fellowship is with the Father and with his Son Jesus Christ. (1 Jn 1:1-4)

Jesus' source of life is God. Their relationship itself is life: "For just as the Father has life in himself, so he has granted the Son also to have life in himself" (5:26). For the believer, "eternal life" means abiding in this relationship, in experiencing or "knowing" the "only true God, and Jesus Christ" (17:3) whom God sent into the world to give it life, even though "the world" was intent almost from the beginning on taking Jesus' life from him.

Morton Kelsey tells a story about something that occurred at the end of World War II. When Russian peasant soldiers left Vienna to return home, many took with them the marvelous faucets from the quarters in which they had been billeted. Somehow they failed to realize that these would be of no use without some kind of reservoir and a pipe system for conducting the water. Learning from this story, Kelsey notes, "Jesus says that our lives are as useless as these uncoupled faucets if we are not linked with him. The purpose of our lives is that his life may stream through them and activate them, just as the purpose of the pipes and faucets in a house is that they may be connected to the main line so that water may flow through them." Kelsey then asks: "Is it possible to make such a connection?" His response is simple and clear: "I am sure that it is. Deep in every human soul there dwells the Spirit of the living God, the Spirit of power and light and life.... Every normal human life is ... a whole water system ready for the water of life."[33]

When I was young I thought of the sacraments as "faucets" that transmit life to the believer. Now, with John, I realize that any such "faucet" must be connected to Jesus himself, the one who provides water springing up for eternal life (4:14).

I Am the True Vine (15:1)

In a final metaphor related to life, Jesus identifies himself with the image of the vine. By describing himself as the "*true* vine," John's Jesus contrasts himself with bogus, impostor, or alien forces that promise life but cannot deliver. Unlike these forces, which do not rely on a life-source beyond themselves for their own power, Jesus acknowledges that the life he gives to the branches has a source beyond himself. This is the Father, the ultimate source of life for himself as well as the branches. Since the Father is the "vinegrower" (15:1), any life in the branches must also be grounded in this life-source.

What does it mean for us, as readers, to be identified with Jesus as the vine and the Father as the vinegrower? First of all, it demands that we "remain" connected to our life-source at all times. Then, if we are to bear fruit on this vine, we must be pruned. The vinegrower "removes every branch...that bears no fruit," while "every branch that bears fruit he prunes to make it bear more fruit."

I got a glimmer of what this "pruning" might involve for Jesus' followers when I met a woman while I was ministering in her parish. She told me that she had been quite "down" for several years. First, she realized that her husband no longer loved her. Then her job became a chore. Finally, her twenty-six-year-old daughter—her only child and the pride of her life—developed schizophrenia. She was told that there was no cure, that her daughter would be afflicted for the rest of her life.

Depressed, the woman decided to get into her car and just drive. After several days of traveling, she found herself at the Grand Canyon. There she beheld the awesome beauty sculpted into the earth's surface. Deeply moved by the geological majesty of that sight, she was struck by a parallel in her own life. She found herself saying: "We are made beautiful by what is taken away." This woman had experienced many "losses" in relation to her husband and daughter, as well as her job. Many things had been taken away. But here she realized that she had been pruned in a way that not only made her beautiful in the eyes of God, but also empowered her to relate to others in their losses in a way that might help them bear fruit. So she decided to get professional training as a grief counselor. She's been at peace ever since.

"Whoever does not abide in me is thrown away like a branch and withers; such branches are gathered, thrown into the fire, and burned" (15:6). In a culture that seems more at home with silk flowers than with flowers cut from the garden, with plastic plants from K-Mart and vines made from vinyl, Jesus' words about being the "true" vine might fall on deaf ears. Yet, now as at the time of Jesus, the role of an authentic disciple is to abide in God's life, to proclaim the truth of God's love to the "world," and to practice it joyfully even in face of the "world's" misunderstanding and persecution (15:9-18).

Being a disciple, then, cannot be limited to the therapeutic or even communal dimension of discipleship. Remaining on the vine that is Jesus demands witness in "the world." In this sense I can conclude with Pheme Perkins: "'Abiding' is not simply concerned with remaining in the community. Christians must glorify God by 'bearing much fruit,' apparently a reference to the fact that they will have to witness to Jesus before the hostile world (cf. 15:27). Thus, the community is being entrusted with continuing Jesus' own mission."[34]

The mission ultimately will be enhanced to the degree that the metaphors of Jesus' "I am" become our own—in the power of his Spirit.

EIGHT

DID I NOT TELL YOU THAT IF YOU BELIEVED, YOU WOULD SEE THE GLORY OF GOD? (11:40)

The Question of John 10:40–12:19

The raising of Lazarus from the tomb is the seventh "sign" performed by Jesus. Given Jesus' previous challenges to the existing religious order, this most powerful sign elicits a formal plan and decision by the highest religious authorities to have him killed. In the way John structures this story, John's readers are challenged to find what may be tomb-like in their own lives, their religion, and their "world," and to hear Jesus' voice inviting them to come forth from those tombs into newness of life.

John sculpts the Lazarus story through the medium of a chiasm. This chapter follows the structural outline proposed by Peter F. Ellis:[1]

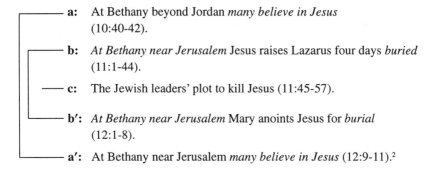

a: At Bethany beyond Jordan *many believe in Jesus* (10:40-42).

b: *At Bethany near Jerusalem* Jesus raises Lazarus four days *buried* (11:1-44).

c: The Jewish leaders' plot to kill Jesus (11:45-57).

b': *At Bethany near Jerusalem* Mary anoints Jesus for *burial* (12:1-8).

a': At Bethany near Jerusalem *many believe in Jesus* (12:9-11).[2]

Chiastically centered on the Jewish leaders' plot to kill Jesus, these verses in John highlight the event which led to the final decision of *hoi Ioudaioi* to move, in an organized fashion, to completely eliminate Jesus from their system. While this executive decision was made for more than one reason, the final straw, that which brought formerly disparate interest groups together to agree that he must die, was the fact that he raised a dead man, Lazarus, to life.

a. At Bethany beyond Jordan Many Believe in Jesus (10:40-42)

To elude *hoi Ioudaioi* who wanted to stone (10:31) and arrest him (10:39), Jesus left Judea for a town called Bethany, in an area across the Jordan (10:40). His time in Judea, particularly in the context of various Jewish feasts celebrated at the Jerusalem temple there (5:1; 7:14, 37; 10:1f), had elicited resistance and even efforts by *hoi Ioudaioi* to kill him. Consequently he seems to have abandoned the possibility that people of this territory would hear his message. Hence his move across the Jordan.

Jesus' transition "across the Jordan" was not just a geographic relocation. In the context of the sharp contrast between the Galilean peoples' evident belief in Jesus and the resistance of the Judaean Jews, especially those Jewish leaders whose position was predicated on maintaining the people's belief in *the leaders'* teaching and interpretation of the rules and regulations, John uses the image of Jesus moving across the Jordan to reveal a deeper movement. To the degree that Jesus was gaining the people's loyalty, the Jewish leaders were losing their influence over them. The more the people entered Jesus' sphere of influence through their belief, the less loyalty the leaders could expect to claim from them. Another way of charting the geographical/ideological parallels could be:

Geography = Territory = Terrain = Boundary = Sphere of Influence =
Side(s) = Position = Ideology

b. At Bethany near Jerusalem Jesus Raises Lazarus Four Days Buried (11:1-44)

Beginning: Jesus outside Judea (11:1-16)

While he is "across the Jordan," word comes to Jesus that Lazarus, his friend, is sick. The evangelist (who already knows what the outcome will be) tells us that upon hearing this, Jesus says: "This sickness does not lead to death; rather it is for God's glory, so that the Son of God may be glorified through it" (11:4). Jesus uses this statement about sickness to relativize all forms of sickness and "invalidity," including those that will lead to death, in light of a deeper glory. From Jesus' perspective, the sickness would not end in death. Rather, two things were about to be revealed through it: the glory of God as well as his own glory. How these two forms of glory affect the characters involved and their various forms of belief will be detailed as events proceed.

After having heard that Lazarus was ill, despite the fact that "Jesus loved Martha and her sister and Lazarus very much,... he stayed two days longer in the place where he was" (11:5-6). Then Jesus said to his disciples, "Let us go to Judea again" (11:7). Aware of the dangers that Jesus had just eluded (10:31f, 39f), they said: "Rabbi, *hoi Ioudaioi* were just now trying to stone you, and are you going there again?" (11:7-8). Experiencing rejection and threats from the religious leaders is one thing; going back for more is another. Jesus responds with the first question in this section: "Are there not twelve hours of daylight? Those who walk during the day do not stumble, because they see the light of this world. But those who walk at night stumble, because the light is not in them" (11:9-10).

The anthropology of Jesus' time included the belief that all people contained a spark of divine life within them. The eye was the outer organ of this inner light in each person. Thus, when John's Jesus refers to people stumbling, he invites the reader to realize that he is pointing to a much deeper kind of light for illumination: the light that he is in his "I am" (8:12) and the light of faith that enables people to see and believe (1:7-9). The "daylight" refers not so much to the natural light of day, but to the inner light of faith by which believers keep from stumbling (1 Jn 2:10). Such a light cannot be found within or among those defined by the "world" (1:5).

Jesus then uses a phrase that indicates his and his disciples' closeness to Lazarus: "*Our* friend Lazarus has fallen asleep (*koimasthai*) but I am going there to awaken him." At this the disciples counter: "Lord, if he has fallen asleep, he will be all right (*sōzein*)" (11:11-12).

In the Synoptics, *sōzein* often refers to recovery from illness or sickness. But in John it has a deeper connotation. It represents the fuller recovery of being "made well" that brings with it liberation or salvation (3:17; 5:34; 10:9). While the evangelist is aware of the connotation, the disciples do not grasp the fuller meaning of the sickness that will be to Lazarus' liberation and salvation. This leads Jesus to speak directly: "Lazarus is dead. For your sake I am glad I was not there, so that you may believe" (11:14-15a).

Lazarus' situation once again connects the stance of Jesus' disciples to the stance of John's reader. Jesus' comments with regard to his sick (and now dead) friend are—at the surface level—quite incredible in the fullest meaning of unbelieve-able. But for those with the right light inside of them, his word and the work about to be identified with it are meant to elicit a deeper faith. Upon hearing Jesus say, "'Let us go to him,' Thomas . . . said to his fellow disciples, 'Let us also go, that we might die with him'" (11:15b-16).

The identity of the "him" to whom Thomas refers has been a source of confusion. Is he speaking of Lazarus who is now dead or of Jesus who is being threatened by *hoi Ioudaioi* with death? Jesus' earlier withdrawal from Judea seems to have been based on the fact that *hoi Ioudaioi* had only recently been trying to stone him (11:8). This, combined with the previous concerns of the disciples, makes it seem quite clear to me that Thomas is referring here to Jesus' impending death.

Middle: Jesus outside Bethany (11:17-37)

Upon arriving in another town called Bethany, near Jerusalem, Jesus "found that Lazarus had already been in the tomb four days" (11:17). Since Jews believed it took three full days for the soul to totally depart from the body, Lazarus' "four days" in the tomb may have been John's way of letting the reader know that Lazarus was truly dead! Acknowledging the sisters' loss, "many of *hoi Ioudaioi* had come to Martha and Mary to console them about their brother" (11:19). Around this time "Martha heard that Jesus was coming, [so] she went to meet him, while Mary stayed at home" (11:20). The word used by the NRSV translators for Mary's being "at home" was *sitting*.

In various cultures, including parts of Jewish culture to this day, at times of mourning, people "sit" with the members of the family for a number of days after the family member has been buried. In this "sitting"-setting, when she hears that Jesus is close by, Martha leaves Mary sitting with the group and seeks out Jesus. She greets him with the statement: "Lord, if you had been here, my brother would not have died. But even now I know that God will give you whatever you ask of him'" (11:21-22). Acknowledging his power, Martha holds out hope that Jesus can do something for her brother.

"Jesus said to her, 'Your brother will rise again.' Martha said to him, 'I know that he will rise again in the resurrection on the last day'" (11:23-24). For a second time, Martha tells Jesus that she *knows*. First she knows that Jesus could have done something so that Lazarus would not have died (11:21). Now she says she knows Lazarus will rise again, but "on the last day." Such a response was not unique. It reflected the popular belief of many of the people at that time.[3] While a final resurrection of the dead was debated among the religious leaders (see Mk 12:18-27), rank-and-file folk like Martha didn't need to wait for a fiat from them to believe in it.

In response, Jesus says to her, "I am the resurrection and the life. Those who believe in me, even though they die, will live, and everyone who lives and believes in me will never die" (11:25-26a). Belief in this "resurrection" offers the possibility of a new, transformed way of life. Gail R. O'Day writes that, here, it involves "the most radical narrative embodiment in the Fourth Gospel of one's willingness to be transformed and of Jesus' ability to transform."[4] This transformation comes through the one who refers to himself as the "I AM," the one who is resurrection and life itself.

Although Jesus has just defined himself as "resurrection" and "life," Martha's understanding still is clouded by the prevailing view of "believers" like herself. The most her faith can muster is to call him "the Messiah, the Son of God, the one coming into the world" (11:27). In the Synoptics it is Peter who utters these high-christological titles (Mt 16:16; see Mk 8:29; Lk 9:20). By placing the words on Martha's lips, John is preparing the reader to realize that authentic faith must go beyond even what Martha (and Peter in the Synoptics) envisioned.

After professing her "faith," Martha "went back and called her sister Mary." Mary, having heard that Jesus was asking for her, "got up quickly and went to him" (11:28-29). When she meets him, Mary repeats (11:32) exactly what Martha has previously said (11:21), without adding Martha's final words: "But even now I know that God will give you whatever you ask of him" (11:22). Furthermore, before she greets him, she does something that Martha did not do: she kneels at his feet (11:32) in a gesture of deepest honor reserved for a god or an emperor or one believed to be a savior.

Why these different approaches to and encounters with Jesus? Simply stated, John shows Martha's and Mary's as two different kinds of belief. Martha's "faith," while identifying Jesus as someone special with God, still views Jesus as a kind of peer. Thus, when she greets him, she begins by asking him to ask God for Lazarus's life. Mary's faith goes deeper. She believes in *him*. First she kneels before him in recognition of his being a power unto himself. Then she acknowledges without any additions that if he had been present, Lazarus would not have died.

Now *hoi Ioudaioi* who had been sitting with Mary arrive. When Jesus sees his opponents following the weeping Mary "also weeping, he was greatly disturbed in spirit (*tarassein*) and deeply moved (*embrimasthai*)" (11:33). The two weeping (*klaiein*) entities—Mary and *hoi Ioudaioi*— elicit *tarassein* and *embrimasthai* in the depths of Jesus' spirit (11:33).

The two words that describe Jesus' reaction to the weeping are not used often in John. *Tarassein* is used to describe people's emotions only four other times (12:27; 13:21; 14:1, 27), while *embrimasthai* is used only one other time—in 11:38. Rather than suggesting a romantic and sympathetic image of mourning and grief, the words, especially *embrimasthai,* have overtones of fury and frustration. For this reason, Rudolf Schnackenburg and George R. Beasley-Murray, following the Eastern tradition, marshal a great amount of evidence to show that John's description indicates that, in reaction to the weeping he encounters, Jesus *became angry* in spirit.[5] *Tarassein* has a similar sense, as it refers to a "stirring up" of something or that which disturbs. It is important to recall the meaning of these words as we read what Jesus does next.

In the midst of all the weeping, Jesus asks the question that is dreaded by all mourners when they get near the place where the body of the dead person rests: "Where have you laid him?" (11:34). Jesus' question echoes that first question asked by him in the gospel ("What are you looking for?" [1:39]). The response to both questions is the same: "Come and see" (1:39; 11:34b). Reacting to their response "Jesus began to weep (*dakruein*)" (11:36).

I've often wondered why John notes that Jesus wept, especially when we know from the beginning of the story that Jesus realized full well that Lazarus's sickness and even his entombment would not "lead to death." Why would Jesus weep about Lazarus's death if he knew what was going to happen? Why the tears if this dead man was about to come alive? Certainly, his weeping would have to arise from a source other than sorrow at the thought that a wonderful friendship would be no more. Wes Howard-Brook offers some thoughts that make much sense to me:

> Given that Jesus has actively set up Lazarus's death by his delay and claimed that it would be for the glory of God, it misses the point of the entire story to attribute Jesus' tears to the ordinary experience of death. Indeed, allowing this interpretation to be put in the mouth of Judeans greatly undercuts its likelihood. It is as if the narrator *expects* readers to come up with this interpretation and refutes it through the ironic role of the Judeans. Another clue to the prospect of a deeper meaning is that the Judeans speak of Jesus' "affection"(*ephilei*) as something from the past, while the narrator tells us that Jesus' love for all three siblings is ongoing (11:5). Finally, even those among the Judeans who acknowledge in verse 37 Jesus' previous opening of the blind one's eyes only think of his ability to help Lazarus as an opportunity whose time had passed: "Wasn't this one able...to prevent this one from dying?"[6]

We can get a some insight into the reason for Jesus' tears when we examine the Greek John uses for "weeping." The weeping of Mary and *hoi Ioudaioi* is described as *klaiein*; *dakruein* describes Jesus' weeping. This is the only time the latter word appears in the New Testament. It would be safe to conclude that the two words in John indicate a different source and context for each kind of "weeping." *Hoi Ioudaioi* followed Mary "because they thought that she was going to the tomb to weep there" (11:31). Later Jesus saw their weeping as well as Mary's (11:33). The weeping of Mary at the loss of her brother would be seen as sincere. However, given how John has, up to now, described "*hoi Ioudaioi* who had accompanied her," it is safe to say that they were "weeping" crocodile tears. Her weeping represented the normal reaction to a loss of a loved one; theirs came from a source estranged from love.

Given the difference, Howard-Brook notes that "it seems that Jesus' feeling and tears come not from grief at the fact of death but at the *unbe-*

lief [of the leaders] that accompanies it."[7] Howard-Brook's insight rings especially true when we recall the other emotion Jesus evidenced as he witnessed the behavior of *hoi Ioudaioi*: being troubled in spirit (11:33, 38). It was not the death of Lazarus that made Jesus weep or that now troubled him. It was the more profound spiritual entombment of the institutional corpse of an entrenched religious system and its leaders that elicited the reaction on his part.

This type of entrenched resistance became clear to me in a contemporary Lazarus-story I experienced as I shared a reflection week with Catholic campus ministers. The entire group's dynamics were being overshadowed by the dynamics taking place among three of the participants, a young priest and the young couple working with him. While the priest was very popular with the students, the couple were even more successful in their programs and in getting students involved. In addition, the young woman was an outspoken feminist. By the time study week came, the handwriting was on the wall. He who had the power was about to decide the future of her ministry: she'd have to go. During breaks in the meeting the scuttlebutt was not if, but when, she would be fired.

In my presentation, I had stressed how our institutions, with their "isms" and ideology, get bureaucratized and, therefore, resist change. As alternatives to this institutionalization, I suggested, we need to promote parallel, alternative communities within the clericalized church, communities that reflect ongoing conversion. In particular, I talked about sexist structures in the Roman Church and what the group might do when these become overly burdensome in their ministries. When the last morning came, as people gave conclusions from their small groups, I sat in the back of the room and listened to ideas about where they'd go, given the input of the study week.

Previous to my coming to that gathering, I had been under much pressure. I had also worked very hard to make my structural analysis understandable to the campus ministers. Thus, at the point when I realized in listening to their reports that their journey would not be taking them into the alternative way (which I will be calling the "Community of the Beloved Disciple") but acquiescing to the patriarchal clericalism that enveloped them all, I experienced *tarassein*. Sensing what was about to come from my depths, I knew I needed to leave the room as quickly as I could. Once outside, I began to weep.

At this, two things happened. First, the image of Jesus weeping in the face of his institution's death came to me. That image brought me much consolation. At almost the same moment, however, the young priest (who must have been waticing me) approached me and said, "But Mike, I can't change."

I only could respond: "Well then, you'll have to live with your reasons for the rest of your life."

Today my reply to those like him (including myself) would be to add, "If we can't change the institution, can we change the way we act within it? If we can't change that, we will remain controlled by it. And if we remain controlled by our fears, we will never experience the hope and comfort of the resurrection of God's power in us that has been promised."

Seeing Jesus weep, *hoi Ioudaioi* said: "'See how he loved him!' But some of them said, 'Could not he who opened the eyes of the blind man have kept this man from dying?'" (11:37). When our tears arise from our love, including our love of those who are our *hoi Ioudaioi* today, then we'll have a glimpse of what Jesus must have felt.

End: Jesus outside the Tomb (11:38-44)

At this point the *tarassein* erupts again in Jesus as he approaches the tomb. The tomb was a cave that had a stone "lying against it." The reality is clear: Lazarus, well within the tomb, had been sealed from life outside. Jesus said, "Take away the stone." Hearing Jesus' order, "Martha, the sister of the dead man, said to him, 'Lord, already there is a stench because he has been dead four days'" (11:39). Again Martha *knows* what is going on—at the surface level. Lazarus is truly dead (it's been four days). Even though you are here, Jesus, nothing will change the fact of his death.

Jesus now repeats what he said upon hearing of Lazarus's illness: (1) that it would not be unto death and (2) that it would be for God's glory (11:4). In addition, he asks her another question: "Did I not tell you that if you believed, you would see the glory of God?" (11:40). When Martha does not respond, they take away the stone. At that, "Jesus looked upward." Instead of asking God, as Martha had "known" he could do to keep Lazarus from dying, Jesus *thanked* God (11:41).

Jesus' anticipatory thanks to God was based not on faith, but on *knowing*: "I knew that you always hear me, but I have said this for the sake of the crowd standing here, so that they may believe that you sent me" (11:42). Now John concludes: "When he had said this he cried (*kraugazein*) with a loud voice, 'Lazarus, come out!' The dead man came out, his hands and feet bound with strips of cloth, and his face wrapped in a cloth. Jesus said to them, 'Unbind him, and let him go'" (11:43-44). Jesus' crying out ("to cry out," *kraugazein*) to give Lazarus life against death would be echoed later by the people as they cried out (*kraugazein*) for Jesus' death (18:40; 19:6, 12, 15).

The scene is dramatic. The once comatose body has been energized; that which was without life has been resuscitated.[8] Whether this event ever took place is not as important as what it means. Even more important for us readers than recalling the powerful story of how Jesus stood in front of the tomb, addressed the reality of death it contained, and called forth from its stench a revitalized reality is the fact that the one who once was dead and entombed has been given life. But he has been given life not just for his own sake, but that "you [us, the readers] may believe" (see 11:25, 40).

How we who "remain with Jesus" today are called to maintain our faith in the resurrection as we face the many collective tombs around us has never been made so clear to me as in a talk given by a friend, the late Sr. Lauretta Mather, O.S.F. As she struggled with her own terminal illness, Lauretta gave the presidential address to the twenty-fifth anniversary gathering of the Leadership Conference of Women Religious (1981). She called her talk, "Come Forth: Naming the Tombs, Making the Daybreak."

Lauretta began her remarks by reminding the leaders of the women's congregations: "Ours has been a courageous struggle to name tombs that have bound persons—including ourselves. There have been prophetic voices among us these years that called us and our Church and society to *come forth*. There has been a commitment to make the *daybreak*—to create the new order, to respond to new issues, and to new needs."[9] She continued by inviting her audience to name the tombs that might be holding them, to unbind themselves from all that kept them unfree, and to step out again to make the daybreak. She declared: "For Christians the tomb may never be a dwelling place. We are not to abide there, grow comfortable there. We are not tomb people but Easter people and, therefore, over and over again—through our history and into our future—we hear the cry: 'Come forth.' That call is a summons to decision. Naming the tomb we must leave it to make the daybreak."[10]

Then this person who had also been president of one of the largest congregations of women religious in the United States and who had witnessed the violence of some entombed and bound-up religious leaders in the Vatican imposing their unilateral and arbitrary will on her own congregation[11] invited the members "to reflect upon six tombs: dehumanization, legitimization of evil, violence, fear, idolatry, and isolation" and stated:

> Out of my own experience of trying to name and free myself from these tombs, I make five assumptions that undergird my reflections. First, that we do not leave tombs once and for all. We return to some tombs over and over; sometimes we step out of one into another. So I believe that while we have certainly named some of these and while we have been, and are, in the process of unbinding ourselves, still for us, for our Church, and for society these tombs continue to be places of darkness. Secondly, I believe that if Jesus were here, the tombs would be empty. "If you had been here my brother would be alive." If the person and the message of Jesus had sufficiently transformed us, our Church,

and our society, we would be outside these tombs; we would be with Jesus to make the daybreak. Thirdly, I believe that when we step out of tombs we become an enormous threat to the tomb-dwellers, because we then take up the cry: "Come forth." "Then the chief priests decided to kill Lazarus too, for it was because of him that many of the Jews had deserted and believed in Jesus." When we are responsible for the emptying of the tombs, we will be killed. Fourthly, our tombs are those of the Church and of society as well as ours. As we are, so is our world. I assume, then, that a justice agenda for the world and for the Church requires a justice agenda for our own hearts as well; neither is without the other; both are a response to: "come forth." Fifthly, to make the daybreak is God's work; we are simply summoned to collaborate. The mystery is that what is required of us is, in fact, beyond us.... Outside the tomb, we experience the promise that the one who has called us can be relied upon to give us strength for the struggle for the daybreak.[12]

The prophetic vision and challenging words of Sr. Lauretta Mather, who was placed in a tomb herself some years later, are as true today as then. In the words of Gail R. O'Day on the Lazarus story: "The greatest wonder of this text may be that despite Mary and Martha's inability to understand what Jesus is about and to grasp fully what he has to offer, *Jesus offers life anyway*. To those who are open, to those who grieve, to those who know there is nowhere else to turn, to those who will risk the experience of being transformed by Jesus, Jesus offers life: 'Lazarus, come out...'"[13]

As we end this section, it might be helpful to show the parallel dynamics that can get revealed in the way John presents the story of the Word in the world thus far:

GEOGRAPHIC/IDEOLOGICAL TERRITORY	JESUS ENTERS TO BREAK BOUNDARIES
A SICKNESS THAT IS NOT UNTO DEATH	TO MANIFEST GOD'S GLORY
DARKNESS	DAYLIGHT
BEING ASLEEP	POWER TO AWAKEN
"KNOWING" THAT IS NOT BELIEF	BELIEF THAT IS AUTHENTIC
REAL DEATH	PROMISE OF LIFE
WEEPING OF MARY AND *HOI IOUDAIOI*	JESUS' WEEPING
ENTOMBMENT	JESUS' *TARASSEIN*
THE DEAD ONE COMES OUT BOUND UP	UNBINDING AND LETTING GO FREE

c. The Jewish Leaders Plot to Kill Jesus (11:45-57)

The reaction to Lazarus's coming forth from the tomb, the seventh sign of Jesus, was mixed. "Many" of those known as *hoi Ioudaoi* "believed in him" (11:45). Others, however, "went to the Pharisees and told them what he had done" (11:46).[14] The work that Jesus had performed was of epic proportions. Never, since the beginning of creation, had anyone witnessed a dead person come to life (see 9:32). Despite knowing that some of their followers, like these informants, would remain faithful to them, the leaders recognized that the more people came under Jesus' influence, the fewer they would have under their control. At this point, they had two choices: submit in belief by joining Jesus or resist him by protecting their institution, "isms," and ideology. John makes clear the path they chose:

> So the chief priests and the Pharisees called a meeting of the council, and said, "This man is performing many signs. If we let him go on like this, everyone will believe in him, and the Romans will come and destroy both our holy place and our nation." But one of them, Caiaphas, who was high priest that year, said to them, "You know nothing at all! You do not understand that it is better for you to have one man die for the people than to have the whole nation destroyed." (11:47-50)

The meeting of the Sanhedrin was not part of its regular business-as-usual calendar. It had to be convened. Jesus' "signs" (*sēmeia*), if not stopped, would lead to all the people believing. The signs he performed had to be stopped to preserve the peoples' faith—in the leaders. Consequently, this special convocation of the highest authoritative religious body resulted in a conspiracy to take Jesus' life, not because Jesus had empowered a dead person to live, but because a dead system controlled by *hoi Ioudaioi* would not come forth from its self-made tomb. Its leaders, fearful of being buried themselves, had to act. The more honor Jesus received from the people, the more shamed and dishonored they felt. As Jerome Neyrey writes:

> They too perceive Jesus' success and interpret his gain as their loss in public worth (11:47-48). . . they act agonistically and in envy to destroy Jesus (11:49-53). Both Mark and Matthew indicate that "it was out of envy that they handed Jesus over" (Mark 15:10//Matt 27:18). They acted in a fashion true to their culture in envying Jesus' success and taking steps to reduce his stature and even crush him. Jesus' gain means their loss, and they do not feel mandated by God to allow this.[15]

As the public increasingly bestows honor on Jesus, his adversaries become bolder. The adversaries organize against Jesus in "a meeting of the council" and their decision to follow the insight of Caiaphas adds another dimension to Jesus' death. The evangelist adds, as a matter of explanation, that Caiaphas "did not say this on his own, but being high priest that year he prophesied that Jesus was about to die for the nation, and not for the nation only, but to gather into one the dispersed children of God" (11:51-52). From that day onward, John concludes, "they planned to put him to death" (11:53).

The plan to kill Jesus arose from the leaders of his own religion. They were so preoccupied with maintaining their status that they agreed to the rationale of Caiaphas: "It would be better." Just as today we find ecclesiastical leaders defining themselves as "the church" as though they could exist without the people, so too these religious leaders defined themselves as doing the right thing—for themselves, for the preservation of their own group, which they equated with "the nation." It would be "better" that this man die than to see the structure of Judaism as they knew it collapse.

The Sanhedrin, the highest authority among the Jewish people, not only decided on the death penalty for Jesus, they developed "a plan...to kill him." The death penalty was imposed on Jesus by the Sanhedrin because it would be "better" for them, the leaders, if he were to die. Were everyone to follow this dissident, their whole system of control could collapse.

A parallel situation comes to mind for contemporary Catholics. It involves the dynamics that led to the decision in 1968 by Pope Paul VI to reaffirm the traditional teaching of the institutional church with regard to birth control. Rejecting the overwhelming consensus of the majority of his hand-picked experts that the "church's position" had to change, he endorsed the advice of the minority. Catholics would continue to be told that their practice of artificial birth control was mortally sinful. However, as some participants in the deliberations have noted, the decision to reinforce that teaching had little or nothing to do with sexual reproduction. The underlying reason—never stated publicly as in the case of Caiaphas—had everything to do with maintaining the clerical system of control.[16]

In a similar vein, with regard to the threatened excommunication of whoever publicly disagrees with the conclusion that women cannot be priests in the Roman Church, we find more parallels with the first believers who were threatened with excommunication from the synagogue for their faith-stance (9:22; 12:42). At the same time we discover that the real reason is not that it will be better for the universal church—which has fewer and fewer males willing to be celibate priests—but "better" for the leaders if the celibate, patriarchal, clerical system continues in control. *This* is the "whole nation," the "church," that must be preserved.

What began as a quest story involving Martha and Mary's faith now comes to an unexpected end with a rejection story.[17] Returning to the Lazarus setting, it becomes clear for the reader, as Schnackenburg notes, that "whoever accepts Jesus' revelation as 'resurrection and life,' as Martha did (11:25-27), is led in faith to life; whoever denies and opposes it, as the high priests and Pharisees did (11:47-53), is walking the way of death."[18] To ensure that their power will not be taken away, they set a plan in motion so that he will be taken away, so that he will be "lifted up."

The leaders' decision led Jesus to make another tactical withdrawal. This time it took him to "Ephraim in the region near the wilderness"(11:54). With the Jewish feast of Passover near, many were on the lookout for Jesus in the vicinity of the temple. Jesus had often visited the temple or its precincts. There he had confronted the leaders in their "beliefs" or worked his signs. Thus, while some might now be searching for him because they had come to believe in him, others were looking for him in order to collect some kind of reward. This is so, John tells us, because "the chief priests and the Pharisees had given orders that anyone who knew where Jesus was should let them know, so that they might arrest him" (11:57).

b'. At Bethany near Jerusalem Mary Anoints Jesus for Burial (12:1-8)

"Six days before Passover, Jesus came to Bethany, the village of Lazarus." There at the house Lazarus shared with his sisters, Jesus was hosted at a banquet. With Jesus as honored guest, Lazarus sat, Martha served (12:1-2), and Mary performs a ritual of great honor for a guest. She "took a pound of costly perfume made of pure nard" and "anointed Jesus' feet, and wiped them with her hair" (12:3a). Mary's action goes beyond a simple sign of respect. On the one hand, by describing Mary's anointing of the body of Jesus, the temple of God, John is letting the reader know that women are able to touch the "temple" as the levitical priest did, with all that implies.[19] On the other, it reveals the kind of intimacy she had with him—as well as the ease with which Jesus accepted such a gesture of intimacy.

Jesus' willingness to have his body-temple touched by Mary, the woman, as well as the generosity of her spontaneous expression were met with exactly the opposite reaction—one of threat and niggardliness—by Judas. The author reminds us, in the context of Mary's intimacy, that this Judas, though one of his disciples, was "the one who was about to betray him" (12:4). Unable to accept that Jesus had allowed her to touch his body, Judas reproached him (and her). He demanded, "Why was this perfume not sold for three hundred denarii and the money given to the poor?" Again bracketing his remarks as he did with the comment about Judas being the betrayer, John notes that "he said this not because he cared about the poor, but because he was a thief; he kept the common purse and used to steal what was put into it" (12:5-6). John's reminder helps the reader recall parallel cases in which leaders use an evangelizing approach that gives lip service to passages in the scriptures about identifying with the poor while doing little or nothing to change the system or practices that keep the poor in their predicament. Meanwhile, the underlying direction of their programming makes sure they will be able to be enriched (oftentimes by the very ones who exploit the poor)—all in the name of God.

Jesus' riposte to Judas' challenge is succinct and clear: "Leave her alone." Then John places on Jesus' lips one of his all-knowing statements: "She bought it so that she might keep it for the day of my burial" (12:7). Judas purported to be concerned about those in need; Mary anticipated the need of Jesus. Judas's words were said in the context of betrayal; Mary's work was performed in the witness of intimacy. Judas was the one whose betrayal would lead to Jesus' death; Mary was the one whose generosity would prepare him for it.

Mary's act of generosity elicited the niggardly and hypocritical response of Judas. In turn, this elicited Jesus' counter-response, which ended with a saying that has become one of the biggest excuses used by his followers throughout the ages for not being concerned about the poor: "You always have the poor with you, but you do not always have me" (12:8). Far from justifying non-concern for those in need, Jesus' statement (which flowed from the works he performed on behalf of those in need throughout his life) indicates that his "remaining" with us will be evidenced in the way we respond to the needs of those poor who will always be with us.

a'. At Bethany near Jerusalem Many Believe in Jesus (12:9-11)

Now the scene changes. John narrates: "When the great crowd of *hoi Ioudaioi* learned that he was there, they came" to the house (12:9a). They came fascinated by Jesus and also because of what he had done to Lazarus (11:38-45): "They came not only because of Jesus but also to see Lazarus, whom he had raised from the dead" (12:9). Their "coming" to Jesus (as well as Lazarus) results in an extension of the religious leaders' death decree for Jesus: "The chief priests planned to put Lazarus to death as well, since it was on account of him that many of *hoi Ioudaioi* were deserting and were believing in Jesus" (12:10-11). When the survival of the leaders' status and power is at stake, it does not matter how many may have to die to preserve that "nation."

As readers, we can ask to what degree, if any, the raising of Lazarus, not to speak of the resurrection of Jesus which John anticipates in this story, affects our own believing. After all, we have been told, these signs have been shown and the words about them have been written that we "may come to believe that Jesus is the Messiah, the Son of God, and that through believing" we who find so many forms of death within, among, and around us, "may have life in his name" (20:31). Do we truly believe in this new life, and to what degree?

While I was writing this book I happened to be flying standby on a plane from Detroit to Milwaukee via Chicago's O'Hare Airport. Since I had been the last person to board the plane, I was seated in the middle of the middle row of seats. I got settled and began reading an article on John. Then the young man next to me asked: "Are you doing Bible Study?"

"Well, you might say so," I responded. "Are you involved in study of the Bible too?"

"Oh yes," he said. "I go to my Bible Study group in North Chicago every week at 6:30 A.M."

As we discussed the scriptures, and after he found out that this Catholic actually knew a bit about them, he said, "Tell me, what do you believe for yourself?"

I hadn't been asked that question in a long, long time. But my response came quite spontaneously: "I'll tell you what I believe. I believe in God. For me God is the source of all life in our universe. And I believe that this God has been revealed to us in Jesus Christ. He came among us and was killed by religious leaders he threatened. I believe he rose from the dead and sent his own divine Spirit into all of us who believe. We now are members of his body, the church. Our goal in life is to continue the work of God that he came to do in the power of the Spirit: to love the way he did. Everything aside from this is gravy."

This chapter shows us again that all life is about relationships and that all relationships are about love. "See how he loved him," *hoi Ioudaioi* remarked of Jesus' care for Lazarus (11:36). Because of that love, Jesus raised Lazarus from the dead. Because of Mary's belief that Jesus himself had the power to do this, she witnessed her brother restored to life, to her life. Because of our belief that he did this in the case of Lazarus, Jesus is now the promise of our own resurrection. This same resurrection has been promised to us for one reason: that we may believe. In this sense, Wilhelm Wuellner is so right: the Lazarus story has been written not so much to record the last and greatest of the signs "which Jesus performed in the presence of the disciples," but in order to enhance and confirm our belief as its readers that Jesus Christ is the Risen One of God and that, by believing this, in a way only imaginable to Lazarus, Martha and Mary, we may have "life in his name."[20]

WHAT SHOULD I SAY—
"FATHER, SAVE ME FROM THIS HOUR"? (12:27)

The Question of John 12:20-50

John 12:20-50 serves as a transition piece[1] between sections one and two. It completes the first section (1:19–12:19) in which we find Jesus replacing Judaism's most sacred sites and rituals with himself. It also lays the groundwork for the second section (13:1–20:31). Here we find contrasted the persons (and communities identified with these persons) of Peter and the Beloved Disciple.

As John has developed his story-line, Jesus has transformed Judaism's feasts and festivals, its rituals and rites, its sanctuaries and sabbaths. John has taken many of Judaism's most sacred images and prophetic metaphors and identified them with Jesus' "I am." In effect, John has taken the core of what was most holy for *hoi Ioudaioi*, dismantled it, and relocated it in the person of Jesus. Because Jesus had come "to what was his own, and his own people did not accept him" (1:11), John lays ultimate blame for Jesus' rejection on the blindness of the leaders of a religious institution. They had stated that their whole raison d'être was to help the people prepare for the Messiah. However, as John has shown, their ideological entrenchment kept them from recognizing the Messiah when he came (12:39-43). Those who did accept him and confess their faith in him would be *aposynagōgos*, "put out of the synagogue" (12:42).

The step-by-step transformation of the underpinnings of Judaism's most sacred system into the person of Jesus began with his ritual cleansing of the temple at Passover (2:13ff). At the next Passover he declares himself to be the new living Passover bread for those who [will not be identified by the former celebration but who] believe in him (6:4ff). Then, at the Feast of Booths he proclaims himself to be living water for those who move from the water rituals of the former feast to belief in him (7:3-39). At the same time, he becomes not only the light of the temple itself, but the light of the world for all who would follow him—in contrast, by implication, to following the religious leaders (8:12). At this festival he identifies himself to those leaders who can only indirectly link themselves to God through their "father" Moses as the Child of the very Father (8:39-59).

Jesus' reconstitution of the Jewish feasts in himself through "his special relationship to the Father"[2] continues "at the time the festival of Dedication took place in Jerusalem" (10:22). Here John takes Jesus' God-connectedness one step further by having him declare two things: (1) the "Father is in me and I am in the Father" (10:38) and (2) "my sheep hear my voice. I know them, and they follow me" (10:27). Now Jesus' words are quite clear about religious leaders in Judaism and their Petrine equivalents who had proved and were proving to be bandits and marauders: the days of their kind of leadership are over. Speaking of those who once followed them but are now linking themselves with him, he says, "No one will snatch them out of my hand" (10:28).

Besides developing a replacement theology related to the feasts of Passover, Booths, and Dedication, John also begins the first of Jesus' sabbath healing controversies in chapter 5 by noting that it took place in Jerusalem on "a festival of *hoi Ioudaioi.*" So, whether in relation to a feast or to the most sacred day of the week, the sabbath, John portrays Jesus as making all things Jewish redundant in the person of Jesus Christ—for those who believe in him.

With crowds greeting Jesus in his triumphal Passover entrance into Jerusalem, the notion of those who would believe in him gets extended. The very religious leaders who earlier had conspired against Jesus (11:47-53) now know for sure that they have lost their control over the people. The Pharisees "said to one another, 'You see, you can do nothing [to stop this transfer of allegiance]. Look, the world has gone after him!'" (12:19).

The World Going after Jesus

What was this "world" that was going after Jesus? Given John's image of Jesus as the Son of Man (12:23, 34) and the image of "Child of Creation" that it represents,[3] it seems clear that this "world" is not just the world of the Pharisees or *hoi Ioudaioi* that is slipping from their grasp. In keeping with John's vision, it represents creation itself; belief in Jesus has cosmic implications. This "world" includes the Roman system; belief in Jesus has subversive implications in a world where there can be but one "savior" (see 4:42). At its most immediate level, it represents any form of institutionalized religion that gets so entrenched that it abandons its role as proclaimer of that Messiah it purports to announce. In the process, its hired-hand leaders lose their grasp on those who once listened to their voice (see 10:16). Having heard the voice of Jesus speaking to them by name, they separate themselves from the former leaders and link themselves to him.

Until now John's focus has been on the entrenched religious system that Jesus came to replace. Jesus' sheep, his closest disciples, were in the background. The basic plot revolved around Jesus' conflict with *hoi Ioudaioi* over his provocative words and the subversive activities through which he revealed the leaders' ingrained resistance. However, as we move through this transition section, and especially into the section that continues through 17:26, the focus shifts from anything connected to *hoi Ioudaioi* to the community of believers who seek to be identified with Jesus. Bruce Malina notes, "we are in the exclusive presence of the ingroup and privacy."[4] Despite the trials and crucifixion, this ingroup will become more public as the gospel concludes.

The movement of *hoi Ioudaioi* from "ingroup" to "outgroup" seems to mirror the movement of Jesus' disciples from the shadows to center stage. Why, we might ask, is this shift so significant?

It seems clear that John has used the first section to show Jesus transferring to himself that which *hoi Ioudaioi* considered most sacred. In the second section, he concentrates on those who would transfer their loyalty from anyone else (e.g., John the Baptist, Judaism's officialdom) to him. These, who included not just Judean Jews, constituted "the world" that was perceived by the leaders of the former "ingroup" as going after Jesus.

While they probably saw "the world" (*ho kosmos*) going after Jesus as the world they sought to control—namely the world of all things Jewish —John begins his transition noting that the "world" going after Jesus involved a larger group of people. "Now among those who went up to worship at the festival were some Greeks" (12:20). Even though, at the time of Jesus, these would have been Hellenist Jews, the sense of the term for "Greeks" clearly shows a difference that the years would have made more pronounced.

As noted above, John's use of *kosmos* seems to bear a typical dual meaning. This becomes clear in the twofold identity of the "Greeks" who come to "see" Jesus. We have been told at least three times about God's plan for the Gentiles (4:42; 10:16; 11:51-52), and these Greeks are its "first fruits." Johannes Beutler notes: "If John had intended only to include Greek-speaking Jews, the word *Hellenistai* would have been more appropriate. A universalistic sense of the *Hellēnes* in 12, 20 is also underlined by Christ's 'drawing all to himself' in v. 32."[5] The "Greeks" represent peoples beyond the Hellenists. They stand for the universe of all people who will be lifted up and glorified in Jesus' cross and resurrection. The Greeks seeking Jesus are thus the members of the Johannine community who never identified with *hoi Ioudaioi*. Once not of the fold, they now are equal members.

Since it is not recorded that Jesus spoke Greek, it makes sense that those seeking to "see Jesus," or communicate with him, would begin with those closest to him who could be liaisons to the non-Jewish world. They approach Philip, who is from Bethsaida in Galilee, a bilingual urban area. Philip tells Andrew and they both tell Jesus, who responds by saying, "the hour has come" for the whole world to be brought into the life-giving power of the Son of Man, the universal one (12:23).

With the transition, John means to show that Jesus' influence is about to extend beyond the traditional boundaries of Judaism. That influence is to have imperial and even cosmic repercussions. This is clear from Jesus' words later in this section: "Now is the judgment (*krisis*) of this world; now the ruler of this world will be driven out. And I, when I am lifted up from the earth, will draw all people to myself" (12:31-32). According to Schnackenburg, the exact *krisis* of the world that is expressed by this image continues the forensic or trial-like setting that runs throughout John's gospel. Only now it is cosmic. It represents the "cosmic lawsuit between God and the world"[6] that will result in Jesus' triumph over the world. His being lifted up in death through the efforts of the forces of evil will reveal God's decisive victory. The judgment of "this world" will be its defeat in word and deed[7] (16:33).

Seeing Jesus through Discipleship that Imitates Him

John says that the Greeks told Philip, who then told Andrew, that they "wished to see Jesus" (12:21). From the beginning of John's gospel— when Jesus said to Andrew and the anonymous disciple "Come and see" (1:39)—we have observed that the Johannine "seeing" of Jesus involves images of discipleship. These were the first words Jesus said to Andrew and the anonymous disciple after asking them: "What are you looking for?" (1:38). Paul Hinnebusch links the two groups who sought to see with discipleship open to all when he writes: "The desire of the little group of Greeks to see him symbolizes the desire of all the nations to see him. To all the nations, not just to those first two disciples, Jesus says, 'come and see!' All the nations are engaged in that same search expressed in the first words of Jesus in John's Gospel, 'What are you looking for?'"[8]

"They came and saw where he was staying, and they remained with him that day. It was about four o'clock in the afternoon" (1:39). That this "coming" and "seeing" are linked to "staying" and "remaining" is so important that even the hour in which it takes place is mentioned. That this is the heart of discipleship is clear in Jesus' response to Philip and Andrew about "the Greeks": "Whoever serves me must follow me, and where I am, there wil my servant be also" (12:26).

Jesus' response also includes another reference to the *hour* (*hōra*). Now the "hour" is identified with his impending death and resurrection that will bring about the total transformation of all life and relationships:

The hour has come for the Son of Man to be glorified. Very truly, I tell you, unless a grain of wheat falls into the earth and dies, it remains just a single grain; but if it dies, it bears much fruit. Those who love their life lose it, and those who hate their life in this world will keep it for eternal life. Whoever serves me must follow me, and where I am, there will my servant be also. Whoever serves me, the Father will honor. (12:24-26)

While this passage refers to Jesus himself, it is clear that he extends the honor the Father will give him for going through his death-unto-life to those who follow him and who remain in him. As everything in Jesus' culture revolved around familial relationships defined by honor, so now the family of God will be extended to embrace all of those followers of Jesus who will live in this "world" ready to lay down their lives to remain in him.

I am reminded of the martyrs of every age who willingly decide to remain identified with Jesus Christ in the face of a hostile world. One who particularly comes to mind at this point is Sr. Ita Ford. She was in the group of four U.S. churchwomen killed in El Salvador by soldiers whose leaders were trained by the United States in its effort to "keep the world safe from communism." She was killed, as was her Messiah, because she also was considered too subversive for the leaders of her "world." Like the leaders of Jesus' "world," those who commissioned these soldiers were upset about the churchwomen's works. The churchwomen were trying to convince people that they had dignity and that their God was a God of ever-widening liberation rather than ever-deepening oppression. In the way Sr. Ita Ford had made room in her heart for this word (8:37), the leaders felt threatened by her. Consequently it was decided—with "orders from above"[9]—that, to preserve the nations of El Salvador and the United States, this Maryknoll Missionary sister and her three companions would have to die.

Not long after her brutal death I happened to give a day of reflection at the Sisters of St. Joseph motherhouse in Brentwood, Long Island. Among those participating was Ita Ford's mother. She must have been in her eighties. She was walking around with a clip-board getting signatures on a petition asking Congress to reopen its investigation into the cause of the missionaries' deaths.

The gospel for that Sunday was the passage from this transition section of John's gospel that presents the image of the grain of wheat dying and rising to new life. So I went to Mrs. Ford and said: "Mrs. Ford, today's gospel is about the grain of wheat falling to the earth, dying, and bearing much fruit. Ita was the grain that came forth from you and fell in death. Would you be willing to preach the homily and tell us how her death has brought forth some fruit?" Without batting an eyelash, she said she would.

At the homily Mrs. Ford said something like: "When we heard that Ita had died I just took her death as something devastating for myself and my family. But then, almost immediately, we began receiving letters and telegrams from priests and nuns and all sorts of people. They told us how her willingness to follow Jesus even to death had challenged them to turn their lives around, especially in areas that were far from him because of their sin. It was then that we discovered that what we had thought was something personal to our family had national and international implications."

Her witness to her faith in Jesus and her daughter's faith in Jesus was so powerful that I don't think there was a dry eye in that church.

Mrs. Ford seemed to understand what John was trying to convey in this whole passage. It is about Jesus' death and its impact on those who believe in him. It is about those who believe the message of Jesus and are willing to suffer the consequences for it—even to the point of being excluded from the synagogue. Finally, it is about the honor that will come to those who find their identity in Jesus Christ in contrast to those fear-based "believers" who love "human glory more than the glory that comes from God" (12:42-43).

Jesus' Death Is the Reconciliation of the Suffering Servant

In the face of his impending death, Jesus again experienced *tarassein.* However, this *tarassein,* this visceral reaction, had more to do with the death represented in the religious system that would not receive him than with anything about to happen to him. Thus his statement and question: "Now my soul is troubled. And what should I say—'Father, save me from this hour'? No it is for this reason that I have come to this hour. Father glorify your name" (12:27-28). "This hour" is that messianic moment prefigured by Isaiah, especially in Isaiah 52:15 which speaks of the influence of the Servant on the rulers of this world and Isaiah 6:10 which speaks of the blindness of those who oppose the word.[10]

According to Gail R. O'Day, the first part of this transition section, 12:20-36, is not only the most concentrated collection of sayings on the death of Jesus in John but it is also a clear expression of the implications of that death for the believing community. "The world that lives in opposition to Jesus ('this world') is judged by Jesus' death, and its power is obliterated (vv. 25, 31). Jesus' death has this effect, not because it is a sacrifice that atones for human sin, but because it reveals the power and promise of God and God's love decisively to the world." In the newly-restored relationship through Jesus' death/resurrection, reconciliation is achieved: with God, self, others and the world. Thus, she concludes, "It is critical to believe in Jesus so that one can share in the gift of his life, the gift that leads to eternal life, to the confident assurance of God's and Jesus' abiding presence. For Jesus' death to effect reconciliation with God, then, one must make the decision to believe in Jesus."[11]

As will be shown in section two, John sculpts his gospel by highlighting the different ways of relating to Jesus that were exemplified by two heroes of the early Christian community: Peter and the Beloved Disciple. He wrote this as the community faced division among its members. One group's members identified themselves with Peter and the Apostolic group while the other linked their discipleship to Jesus by imitating the pattern of the Beloved Disciple. Section one dealt with *hoi Ioudaioi* and their unbelief. Section two deals with the differing dynamics of relating to Jesus as exemplified by these two groups, both of which, according to John, must represent authentic forms of belief. Of these disciples Jesus speaks in the final words of this transition section. Their mission in and to the world is to live in it as those who have accepted Jesus in their lives. In embracing him they show their ultimate faith in the one who sent him:

> Whoever believes in me believes not in me but in him who sent me. And whoever sees me sees him who sent me. I have come as light into the world, so that everyone who believes in me should not remain in the darkness. I do not judge anyone who hears my words and does not keep them, for I came not to judge the world, but to save the world. The one who rejects me and does not receive my word has a judge; on the last day the word that I have spoken will serve as judge, for I have not spoken on my own, but the Father who sent me has himself given me a commandment about what to say and what to speak. And I know that his commandment is eternal life. What I speak, therefore, I speak just as the Father has told me. (12:44-50)

What he has spoken in word is to find a home not only in the disciples' ears, but in their very hearts (8:31).

Part II

PETER AND THE BELOVED DISCIPLE

TEN

DO YOU KNOW
WHAT I HAVE DONE TO YOU? (13:12)

The Question of John 13:1-38

With this chapter John moves the reader into accounts of Jesus' last days before his passion, death, and resurrection. Everything related to these most important last days takes place in the context of a meal. John calls it a "supper" (13:3). While the Synoptics do not refer to the Eucharist as a supper, this is the reference used by Paul (1 Cor 11:20). It is important to recall this when making connections between the ritual ceremony of the Eucharist described by the Synoptics and John's ritual of the bread in chapter 6 and the foot washing in chapter 13.[1]

Chapter 13 revolves around the twin dynamics of "knowing" and "doing" vs. "ignorance" and "betrayal/denial."[2] The opening words refer to Jesus' knowing and doing: "Now before the festival of the Passover, Jesus *knew* (*oida*) that his hour had come to depart from this world and go to the Father. Having loved his own who were in the world, *he loved them to the end"* (13:1). Similarly, at the end, just before Peter and Jesus dialogue about his future betrayal, Jesus says: "By this everyone will *know* (*ginōskein*) that you are my disciples, if *you have love for one another"* (13:35). Between 13:1 and 35 there are at least five other dyads related to knowing and doing (13:3, 11, 12, 17; see 13:15, 19, 21) or not knowing and denial (13:7). True knowing defines true disciples.

With some adaptation regarding titles for its sections, I will examine this chapter according to the outline developed by R. Alan Culpepper: (1) introduction and the washing of the feet (13:1-5); (2) Jesus' first conversation with Simon Peter (13:6-11); (3) Jesus' washing of the feet as a model for the disciples (13:12-17); (4) Jesus' announcement of his betrayal and exhortation to the disciples (13:18-20); (5) Jesus and Judas (13:21-30); (6) Jesus' prediction of his departure and his "new commandment" (13:31-35); and (7) Jesus' second conversation with Simon Peter (13:36-38).[3]

Introduction and Washing of Feet (13:1-5)

The context for this and the rest of the Farewell Discourse is *before* "the festival of the Passover" (13:1a). In the period of Jesus' life covered by the gospel, this is the third Passover that Jesus has celebrated (2:13; 6:4). The fact that the location is not described indicates the non-importance of physical geography in the scheme of things. What is important is the fact that boundaries will be broken by Jesus' "knowing" and "doing." Because place is not as important as time, we are told not where it took place but when: it was the time when "his hour (*hōra*) had come to depart from this world and go to the Father" (13:1).

Having come from God to "his own," Jesus "knew that his hour had come to depart from *this world* and go to the Father." Past chapters have made it clear that "his own" (1:11)—represented in "the world" and *hoi Ioudaioi*—did not receive him. Now, "having loved his own who were in the world, he loved them to the end (*telos*)" (13:1). "His own" here are those who, unlike the "world" and *hoi Ioudaioi*, did receive him and remain with him (see 1:12-13; 10:3, 4, 12). Thus, in this simple opening sentence of chapter 13 we not only meet the first knowing/doing dyad, we are presented with a summary of the whole story of Jesus' life that culminates with the crucifixion/resurrection.

Almost as an aside, John tells us that "the devil had already put it into the heart of Judas son of Simon Iscariot to betray him" (13:2). While the reader already has been told he "is a devil" (6:70), this representation of Judas as demonic is different. Unlike the Synoptics, John does not portray "the devil" as an extra-terrestial or individualized force. Rather, the devil represents the cosmic concentration of what is evil. In Judas's person this force is directed against the "Son of God," Jesus. Judas has been given over to the father of lies; Jesus, the source of truth (14:6), knows his hour is at hand to "depart from this world and go to the Father" (13:1b). The powers of darkness are to be overcome with light.

Now we are presented with the second knowing/doing dyad. Here Jesus' *knowing* involves his awareness of his descent from God and his coming ascent to "the Father [who has] given all things into his hands" (13:3). His action of physically getting up from the table ("ascending") begins a whole series of *doings*.

At the supper he got up (*egeirein*) from the table, took off (*tithenai*) his outer robe, and taking (*lambanein*) a towel, he girded (*diazōnnynai*) himself (13:4). In these four words we find images of *rising* connected to death (2:19, 20, 22; 5:8, 21; 12:1, 9, 17), laying down in the sense of *laying down* one's life (as with the good shepherd [10:11, 15, 17, 18] or *burying* a body (11:34; 19:41, 42; 20:2), *tying*, and being *girded*—a word that will be used of Peter's form of death (21:18). John uses dramatic images to communicate to the reader the significance of the occasion.

This ritual of ascending is followed by one of descending. Jesus "poured water into a basin and began to wash the disciples' feet and to wipe them with the towel that was tied around him" (13:5). While other studies of John might ask whether Jesus actually washed his disciples' feet and whether he did this at the time of Passover, reader-response concerns itself with the image and theology behind the representation. It is not a matter of "whether" but of "why." Sandra Schneiders writes: "The primary question posed to the interpreter by the episode of the foot washing in John is not whether Jesus actually washed his disciples' feet or actually spoke the following discourse, but rather what interpretation of life and relationships does it present, is that interpretation true, and if so what are the implications for the interpreter's own self-understanding."[4] We begin to get a glimpse of the ritual's contemporary implications for us when we examine what it "said" in that culture.

For various reasons, Jesus' washing of the disciples' feet shocked those who witnessed it. First of all, Jews considered washing another's feet to be a demeaning task for anyone but a slave. Such menial behavior was not even expected of Jewish slaves; only Gentile slaves were called upon to perform this task. Second, in that culture defined by honor/shame codes, if a slave was not available, guests were expected to wash their own feet to preserve the honor of the host. It was inconceivable for the host to do this work. In performing this ritual, Jesus was performing a socio-drama that made it clear that the head of this Jewish band was willing—and desired—to do what only a slave would be forced to do. This represented a total reversal of expected roles, especially in relation to signs of welcome. He who had been "given all things into his hands," including power, now used his hands in a ritual that turned everything upside down.

Jesus' First Conversation with Simon Peter (13:6-11)

At the surface level of the dialogue between Peter and Jesus recorded in the next six sentences, we find typical examples of the challenge and riposte that characterized the male-dominated culture of that time. But at a deeper symbolic level we seem to find exposed a fear regarding the Petrine community experienced by members of the Johannine group. This fear had to do with their concern that Peter's interpretation of leadership as authority and function was being gradually distanced from Jesus' own witness and modeling.[5] By giving such play to this part of the story, John seems to be highlighting the "knowing" and "doing" of Jesus in contrast to Peter's reluctance to emulate the pattern of his Teacher and Lord.

In three exchanges Peter tries to set the rules, only to be countered by Jesus' responses which point to a way of relating in the community that goes deeper than Peter can see.[6] In all three instances, Jesus' way of knowing exposes Peter's lack of understanding. The dynamics invite the reader to move from Peter's surface way of "understanding"—which is tied to maintaining a status quo related to roles and hierarchies that serve only to preserve control—to Jesus' deeper understanding which is tied to service. Jesus' way of knowing is linked to doing what Peter's ignorance cannot fathom:

1. *First exchange.* Peter: "Lord (*kyrie*), are you going to wash my feet?" (13:6). Peter's question bespeaks a challenge. He cannot accept the way Jesus chooses to relate to his fellow disciples, especially himself: "Are *you* going to wash *my* feet?" Peter cannot accept the change in the power dynamics that are being ritualized here, much less the symbolic re-ordering of status implied. Culpepper writes:

> Given the assumptions surrounding foot washing in the first century, Peter's statement expresses a response that would be readily appreciated by first-century readers. Peter's first statement, resisting the foot washing, arises from his acceptance of the social norms which reinforce superior and inferior social standings. Jesus, by laying aside his garments and beginning to wash the disciples' feet, has displaced those norms and is responding to a different mandate, a different way of ordering his relationships with other persons.[7]

Jesus' stance of actual service, in contrast to talk about it, has challenged Peter and all Jesus' followers to a new kind of descent in order to ascend. At this point John articulates the third dyad of knowing and doing in Jesus' riposte to Peter: "You do not *know (oida)* what I am *doing*, but later you will understand (*ginōskein*)" (13:7). The "later" awareness of the disciples will come only with the resurrection (see 2:22; 12:16); for Peter it will come only upon being told by the Beloved Disciple (21:7; see 20:6-10).

2. *Second exchange.* Instead of grasping Jesus' response to his first question and doing something about it, Peter blindly challenges Jesus again: "You will *never* wash *my* feet" (13:8a). Peter is so tied to the culture's codes defining honor/shame rituals that he simply doesn't "know" what Jesus has said. His preoccupation with preserving the traditional role of the hierarchy which has made him a leader in the group makes him deaf to Jesus' words about how leadership in the group should be exercised. Somehow he seems to sense that Jesus' action is subverting not just his relationship with his disciples, but the way power is exercised by all religious leaders.

At the time of the gospel's final redaction, the way power was being used in the wider and growing ecclesial community seems to have become a concern for the Johannine community within it. Trying to be faithful to Jesus' pattern, it viewed power in terms of service. Now it was finding its sister community identified with Peter, and the apostles locked into a view of power that mimed the entrenched dynamics of *hoi Ioudaioi,* dynamics that Jesus had rejected. As Sandra Schneiders writes: "In some way, Peter grasped that complicity in this act involved acceptance of a radical reinterpretation of his own life-world, a genuine conversion of some kind which he was not prepared to undergo. Jesus confirms this by replying, 'Unless I wash you, you have no heritage with me' (13:8b)."[8] Jesus' retort to Peter reveals the cleansing he needed in his attitudes. It also prefigures the ultimate inheritance promised all those who will remain with Jesus as an alternative group within the wider church: a share in the eternal life to come (12:26; 14:3, 19; 17:24).

This is not the first time Jesus has uttered an "unless" (*ean mē*) statement. In fact, the first three uses of the phrase (3:3, 5, and 6:53) refer to the requirements for being born again in baptism and remaining in Jesus by eating his flesh and drinking his blood. The fourth relates to faith in Jesus himself (8:24). While their belief in Jesus might lead them to accept the need to be born from above (3:3) in water and Spirit (3:5) and to express their identity with him in the Eucharist (6:53), to change power relationships from control dynamics to loving service seemed too much to ask. It appears the Petrine community was finding it difficult to radically transform the way power would be exercised within it. With this "unless" statement, however, the Johannine community was implying that the only authentic exercise of authority had to be based on the pattern of Jesus. All the "unless" statements clearly define new ways of living. Jerome Neyrey calls them "status transformation rituals:"

> Most of these "unless" statements, then, describe moments of status-transformation passage in the Johannine group's identity. Some represent the radical change of status from that of outsider to insider (3:3, 5). Others indicate a change of insider status, from less complete to more complete disciple and from imperfect to perfect follower. Indeed, there seems to be a sense of escalation in these statements: first, mere membership (3:3,5); then, elite confession (8:24); then, elite behavior (12:24).[9]

The orthodoxy of true faith, baptism, and Eucharist must be accompanied by a new kind of orthopraxy for leaders, an orthopraxy that involves service to others rather than service by others. Any ascent to leadership in the community must be accompanied by a kind of descent in the exercise of power vis-à-vis its members.

3. *Third exchange.* Hearing these words, Peter again only understands them superficially. He responds: "Lord (*kyrie*), not my feet only but also my hands and my head!" (13:9). Jesus' retort lays bare the sterility of Peter's understanding: "One who has bathed does not need to wash, except for the feet, but is entirely clean. And you are clean, though not all of you" (13:10). The "you" that is unclean may be not only Peter's individual body but the corporate body identified with him.

In the culture of the time, the washing of feet was a ritual that acknowledged one's belonging to a certain group. It was a purification rite that signified membership in the group. Purification by bathing was a ritual symbolizing cleanness in the sense of wholeness or cleanness from legal impurity. Thus, by linking purification and cleanness (see 2:6; 3:25) and by moving the notion of cleanness from the individual body to the group, Jesus indicates that he is speaking about another source of impurity in the body itself, namely Judas.[10] What Judas was going to do would not just be unclean, it would alienate Judas from the whole, from the body itself.

Peter submitted to the ritual. Whether he did so enthusiastically or grudgingly is not known. However, given the Johannine community's concern about the Petrine community's predilection for hierarchical patterns rejected by Jesus, there may be reason to believe his acquiescence was more reluctant than fervent.

As I noted in the preface, the first time I gave a retreat on John's gospel occurred in 1996 at St. Stephen's Retreat Center in Dover, Massachusetts. While preparing for my conferences, I would often share my thoughts with a wise Dominican, Henry Gallagher. One day, as I talked to him about Peter's resistance to Jesus' foot washing, he said, "Mike, I've got the greatest picture for you." He proceeded to track down Ford Madox Brown's representation of the scene. This nineteenth-century British painter entitled his work: *Jesus Washing Peter's Feet.* The 1860s piece portrays a glum and dour Peter whose hands are closed upon each other and whose head is downcast as he submits to Jesus' drying his foot with his garment.[11] I have chosen it for the cover of this book.

Later on, when I got my own color reproduction of the piece, I decided I would share it with retreatants that they might get a sense of Peter's possible feelings of frustration as he submitted to Jesus' way of exercising power. On one particular retreat, after I passed around copies of the picture, a nun commented: "As I looked at the whole body stance of Peter and the frustration etched on his face, I immediately thought of the scene that's forever etched in my memory when Pope John Paul II heard Sr. Theresa Kane ask for dialogue about the role of women in church ministry." Theresa Kane was merely asking Peter for discussion in the church on the topic of power; Jesus was telling Peter that a total transformation was required.

While the first Peter submitted to Jesus, it seems that those who define their identity by an appeal to him often seem unwilling to take the implications of the washing of the feet to their logical conclusion. That logical conclusion would be a total reordering of roles and structures that perpetuate hierarchical and patriarchal stances. In the words of Sandra Schneiders,

> Because of the human situation in which we find ourselves, Jesus' action was subversive of the sinful structures in which not only Peter, but all of us, have a vested interest. This deep contrast in understanding and commitment was suggested as being more than sufficient to explain both Peter's refusal and Jesus' ultimatum as well as establishing the meaning of the text for the contemporary reader.
>
> The conclusions followed directly, viz., that at least one meaning of the foot washing for contemporary disciples lies not in an understanding of Christian ministry in terms of self-humiliation or individual acts of menial service but as a participation in Jesus' work of transforming the sinful structures of domination operative in human society...[12]

Jesus' Washing of the Feet as a Model for the Disciples (13:12-17)

Now Jesus performs an ascending ritual. Before, he had descended by taking off "his outer robe." Now he "put on (*elabe*) his robe, and ... returned to the table" (13:12b). Once he is at the table, he makes a solemn declaration. The fourth dyad related to "knowing"and "doing" is articulated. Jesus asks the question that represents the heart of this chapter: "Do you know what I have done to you?"

The reader knows that the rest of the disciples are like Peter: they don't know. His ignorance is theirs as well. Thus, before they can hazard a guess, Jesus himself expands on his rhetorical question. In the process he shows that those who know what he is saying and doing will be those who do what he does: "You call me Teacher and Lord—and you are right, for that is what I am [not *egō eimi* here but *eimi gar*]. So if I, your Lord and Teacher, have washed your feet, you also ought to wash one another's feet. For I have set you an example (*hypodeigma*), that you also should do as I have done to you. Very truly, I tell you, servants are not greater than their master, nor are messengers greater than the one who sent them. If you know these things, your are blessed if you do them" (13:13-17).

In explaining why they should follow his example, Jesus does not challenge the honor rightly due him as "Lord" and "Teacher." What he does
challenge—and also subvert—is the traditional way in which the power
and authority connected to those titles have been exercised. If the disciples
recognize his power and authority, they should pattern their own lives according to his behavior. Such patterning has more to do with the reversal of
roles they should exhibit in the exercise of their authority than with the actual ritual of the foot washing. This is the example he has given.

The word for "example" (*hypodeigma*) used here by Jesus (13:15) is
unique in all the gospels. Its use in the First Testament involves an invitation to others to emulate an exemplary way of dying (Sir 44:16; 2 Mac
6:28, 31). Jesus' ritual of getting up, laying down, and taking up is representative of his freely-chosen decision to go through the Passover process
himself in a way that will bring everyone from death to life; it will result
in transformed relationships that give life rather than take it.

The ritual Jesus performed in the foot washing (13:6-11) was to be
reenacted in the ceremonies and dynamics of the Johannine community
(13:12-17).[13] The ritual was meant to distinguish this community from
other Christian communities, especially those of the Petrine/Apostolic
groups. According to Blasi, "Once the Johannine Christians had articulated
the symbols with which to express their identity, it became possible for
them to focus on themselves as a community."[14] In the case of foot washing, the community "knew" that by "doing" this ritual, it was establishing
its identity. However, the community also knew that the ritual had deeper
meaning having to do with patterns of relating. Jesus' washing of his disciples' feet was an invitation to a community for loving service. The community could not perform this ritual without living out what it meant. This involved an ongoing "laying down" of expectations of each other defined by
hierarchical roles in favor of loving service toward each other (1 Jn
3:11–4:21).

The "I have set you an example, that you also should do as I have
done to you" in John is the equivalent of "Do this in remembrance of me"
(Lk 22:19; 1 Cor 11:24). Just as the "do this" in reference to the Eucharist
refers not only to the ritual of taking, blessing, breaking, and giving but
also to the whole pattern of Jesus' "doing," so, in John's version of the
Passover meal the night before Jesus died, "Do as I have done to you" in
this "sacrament of the Last Supper" does not refer simply to the foot
washing, but to the underlying transformation of relationships in the community, a transformation that the foot washing represents. In John, the
foot washing is the archetype of the way a community will be sacramental; it will be an outward sign intended to give grace. The grace will enable the disciples to remain with Jesus through the way in which they
serve and love one another. In this sense, John Meier is correct when he

states: "One will find the definition of a sacrament verified much more in the foot-washing" than in some other sacraments such as matrimony or confirmation. "The foot-washing, and not the eucharist, is quite pointedly made the sacrament of the Lord's Supper by the Fourth Evangelist."[15]

John is stating that the example of the Lord and Teacher must be translated in the lives and ministry of the followers. This is clear from Jesus' remarks about servants not being "greater than their master" and messengers not being "greater than the one who sent them" (13:16). Jesus' final words in this section provide a fifth connection between "knowing" and "doing." Addressing his disciples, he says, "If you know these things [in the sense of what the symbolic activities truly are to mean in the community] you are blessed if you do them" (13:17).

Jesus' Announcement of His Betrayal and Exhortation to the Disciples (13:18-20)

In the culture of Jesus' time, table fellowship defined relationships, especially in terms of the dynamics of trust (or lack of it) that character- ized belonging or not belonging to a group. To be betrayed by one with whom you broke bread violated the core integrity of the ceremony of bread-breaking. It also undermined the integrity of the community itself.

At this juncture in the meal, Jesus refers to what will be his betrayal by a tablemate: "To fulfill the scripture, 'the one who ate my bread has lifted his heel against me'" (13:18). In quoting Psalm 41, the Johannine Jesus has changed the word for "eating" from *esthiein* to *trōgein*. This is quite possibly for the sake of making the eucharistic connection with chapter 6:54, 56, 57, 58. While his quotation of Psalm 41:9 is not exact, the issue is not so much the accuracy of the scripture quotation but that John's Jesus himself is shown to be using a kind of reader-response ap- proach in finding the scriptures fulfilled in his own experience. And that experience has to do with what scripture says about betrayal in the con- text of the "bosom friend in whom I trusted, who ate of my bread."

Francis Moloney considers this passage so important to the Johan- nine text that he makes it central to his structuring of the chapter itself (between 13:1-17 and 13:21-38).[16] For him, everything revolves around the Johannine use of the *egō eimi* formula statement in 13:19: "I tell you this now, before it occurs, so that when it does occur, you may believe that I am (*egō eimi*) he." While we have been analyzing this chapter in terms of the notions of "knowing" and "doing," it cannot be denied that Jesus' prediction of his betrayal is critical to our understanding of Jesus' freedom regarding the events that will follow. By quoting the psalm, Jesus prophesies that whatever is to follow will fall within the divine purview.

Now, using another familial theme—that of hospitality—John's Jesus says that those receiving the disciples sent by Jesus will be welcoming him as well as the one who sent him (13:20; 17:18; 20:21). Foot washing was the proper way in which hosts would greet their guests to prepare them for table fellowship. It was a welcoming ceremony that conferred honor upon those who would sit at the table as well as upon those who had sent them to the household. To "receive" or welcome through ritual signs those sent by Jesus is a way of indicating that room is being made for them in one's life. Receiving them in this ritual way is to welcome "him who sent me" (13:20). The one who sends is the one who is received.

The notion of being sent is central to John's understanding of Jesus' identity. The notion of receiving the one sent is central to the Johannine community's self-understanding. Mark never uses the word "sent" *(pempein)*. Matthew uses it but once (Mt 11:2), and Luke uses it four times (Lk 4:26; 20:11, 12, 13). John uses it thirty-two times. Here being "sent" parallels the dynamics of "receiving" *(lambanein)* the one being sent. This is the same word used in chapter 6 when the disciples received Jesus in the boat. "Receiving" someone sent by an authority involved certain protocols. Not to receive the one sent was to reject the person who had done the sending.

At the heart of relationship between sender and sent is trust. One never invests in an emissary powers that will be abused. When the vice president is sent on behalf of the president, the impression is given that "one who hears the one sent hears the sender." In our time an example of this can be recalled in the relationship between Bill Clinton and his vice president, Al Gore. However, when trust doesn't exist between the sender and sent, there is distancing. This was the case between George Bush and Dan Quayle. The repercussions of not receiving Dan Quayle were different from those of not receiving Al Gore. In the case of the former, there was no certainty that in hearing Dan Quayle one was hearing George Bush.

Jesus and Judas (13:21-30)

"After saying this," John notes (making a transition back to previous images of betrayal [13:10, 18]), "Jesus was troubled in spirit *(tarassein)*." The word *tarassein* has been used this way once before—describing Jesus' reaction when he saw Mary "weeping, and *hoi Ioudaioi* who came with her also weeping" at the death of Lazarus (11:33). There as well as here the word represents an emotion that arises in the face of a crisis. The next chapter will show that it expresses a reaction from one's depths in the face of actual or impending death. At the same time, it serves as a kind of protest against all those diabolical forces that are aligned with death. Jesus' *tarassein* was not his reaction to his own impending death, but to the death represented by the underlying dynamics of evil which he faced. For the Johannine author this *tarassein* also referred to what was happening within the community divided between the approach of those identified with the Beloved Disciple and those who identified with the Petrine group. Thus the fuller dimension of Jesus' emotion expressed in his next declaration: "Very truly, I tell you, one of you will betray me" (13:21).

Hearing these words, "the disciples looked at one another, uncertain of whom he was speaking" (13:22). The literal meaning of "looking at" is "looking into." Looking into each other, they tried to determine who Jesus' betrayer might be. It is at this point that "one of his disciples—the one whom Jesus loved" clearly enters the story for the first time.[17] As the Beloved Disciple reclines next to Jesus, the author has the hard-of-understanding Peter motion in order that the Beloved Disciple might let him know the identity of the betrayer. The all-knowing Jesus is aware of what Judas is about to do and he shares his knowledge with the Beloved Disciple.

While the Synoptics make an effort to describe the motivation for Judas's betrayal and while the reader knows that he is a thief, since he was stealing from the common purse (12:6), John makes no effort to suggest psychological or economic reasons for Judas's betrayal. He has already made it clear that Judas is but a representative of greater forces defined by "evil" itself in the form of the "devil" (see 8:44; 1 Jn 3:8, 10). For John, "the devil" is not an autonomous entity; it merely represents those forces that are aligned against Jesus and seek his destruction. For a community experiencing its own betrayals, Culpepper explains, Judas personifies any defecting disciple. Hence, our term today of someone being "a Judas":

> More than betrayer, however, Judas represents *the disciple* who betrays Jesus, for John emphasizes that Judas was "one of the twelve" (6:71), one of his disciples (12:4; cf. 6:64, 70). He is introduced in the context of mass defection. John's characterization of Judas is given greater depth by his assertion that Judas was given to Jesus by the Father along with the other disciples (17:12; cf. 6:65). His loss, therefore, is Jesus' failure (17:12); however true a son of perdition Judas may have been, Jesus was not able to make him clean (13:11) or alter his course by the gesture of love (13:26). Like later members of the Johannine community, Judas went out into the world and its darkness (13:30; 1 John 2:19; 4:1). He is a model of the many "antichrists" (who were also once within the community—1 John 2:18-19). Judas is the representative defector.[18]

For the first time we are given a time reference for the Farewell Discourse. As though to make more ominous the dynamics of betrayal taking place, John adds: "And it was night" (13:30b). The image of darkness not only stirs up archetypal notions of chaos, it makes clear that Judas represents those cosmic forces which prefer to remain in darkness because their deeds are evil (3:19).

I got a sense of how such betrayal can be found in our church today some years ago in Pittsburgh. During a retreat session, as I shared with the group my reflections on this passage, a woman in attendance experienced what I would call *tarassein*. Her agitation arose from her memory of an incident that had taken place years before at the time of the Holy Thursday foot-washing ceremony presided over by the bishop.

She recalled how the bishop announced that he would wash only the feet of men at the traditional Holy Thursday foot-washing ceremony. His decision created an uproar. Though the incident would never be repeated, the pain felt by this woman at that time was palpable again as she recalled: "I felt betrayed by the bishop." Her eloquent expression of *tarassein* that day made it clear to the whole group of us that those so identified with Peter's resistance to Jesus' foot washing of all the disciples have yet to understand or embrace the implications of that ritual.

Jesus' Prediction of His Departure and His "New Commandment" (13:31-35)

This section begins with an emphatic "now" (*nun*).[19] Shame has characterized the two earlier sections of this chapter, beginning with Peter's reluctance to have his feet washed and moving to Judas' betrayal. Now Jesus will transform all shame into the highest honor and glory (see 12:41, 43). "When [Judas] had gone out, Jesus said, 'Now the Son of Man has been glorified, and God has been glorified in him. If God has been glorified in him, God will also glorify him in himself and will glorify him at once'" (13:31-32). The glory of God, God's *doxa*, is reflected in Jesus' divine mode of being. As Jesus would enter his glory by laying down his life, so his followers will share in that glory to the degree that they abide in it through their sacrificing love. Their communal code of honor will be to imitate Jesus' behavior as a prelude to their own glory. By playing on the notion of human honor (5:41, 44; 7:18; 8:50, 54), John shows its double meaning. As Craig Koester writes: "The term *glorify* (*doxazein*) can mean to honor or praise someone (5:41, 44; 7:18; 8:50, 54); but the term can also mean to manifest the power and presence or 'glory' (*doxa*) of God (11:4, 40; 17:4, 6). In the Gospel of John, the crucifixion of Jesus is the locus of divine revelation, for through it the glory of God was brought within the realm of human experience."[20]

At this point, Jesus lovingly addresses those around him as "little children." People often use terms of endearment when they are close to death. I remember that, before my own father died, the last reference he made to me was "darling." Using the term "little children," (which 1 John uses of the community seven times), Jesus warns that "where I am going, you cannot come" (13:33). Then he gives them something by which they can be assured they will be able to remain with him in the meanwhile: "I give you a new commandment, that you love one another. Just as I have loved you, you also should love one another" (13:34). This commandment, which is given just after the washing of the feet, is not just something to be known in one's head. It is to be "done" in such a way that "everyone" will be able to recognize the disciples of Jesus: "Love one another. Just as I have loved you, you also should love one another. By this everyone will know that you are my disciples, if you have love for one another" (13:34-35). Even though he is going to a place where they cannot come, through their love for one another they will manifest to the world his abiding presence.

This soliloquy brings the chapter full circle. It began with Jesus, who knew that his hour for glorification was at hand, manifesting his love for "his own who were in the world" (13:1) by the foot washing. This was followed by his asking his disciples if they knew what he had done to them (13:12). The "knowing" and "doing" now come to the point where "everyone will know that you are my disciples, if you have love for one another" (13:35).

"Structurally, the foot washing and the new commandment are identical," Craig Koester writes. "Both anticipate the love Jesus shows for his disciples through his death on their behalf and make it an example of the love his disciples would show to one another. The statement 'if I then, your Lord and Teacher, have washed your feet, you also ought to wash one another's feet' is another way of saying 'love one another even as I have loved you' (13:14, 34)."[21]

Love was the chief characteristic of the Johannine community that identified with Jesus through the Beloved Disciple. In contrast to the Apostolic Christians who found their connection to Jesus through Peter, the Johannine group seems to have had no clear hierarchical structure or detailed delineation of roles and functions of a few vis-à-vis others. Rather than coveting rank and status, all members were simply called to love. Needless to say, this did not make for strong structures of accountability and evident roles for authority as could be found in the growing Petrine/Apostolic community.

Bruce Malina finds in the dynamics of the Johannine community a stance which represented "full disregard for existing institutions," particularly those from which it felt itself estranged.[22] Love would indicate the members' of the Johannine community's attachment to it. Love also would be the antilanguage that would make this community unique. According to Molina and Rohrbaugh:

> In sum, the social function of antilanguage and its in-group and out-group labels is to support and cement relationships within the in-group. Such group attachment... is called "love," the basic requirement of Jesus in this Gospel. The author thus expresses the in-group dimension of social relationship in terms of reciprocal love. Group attachment enables members to experience the abiding presence of Jesus, notably through the Spirit or power of God.[23]

The "new commandment" given by Jesus was really a nuanced version of an old one, articulated much earlier in the book of Leviticus: "You shall love your neighbor as yourself" (Lev 19:18). In John the "neighbor" (*plēsion*) who is to be loved becomes "one another" (*allēlous*). While this might initially appear to be a limiting of love to one's own group, it is actually a broadening of that love. Love was to be so concretized in the community that "everyone" (*pantes*) might come to know the antilanguage of Jesus' love through that of his followers. Any "newness" in this commandment has to do with the fact that, while the old commandment was identified with the law, this "new" commandment is to be modeled on Jesus' self-sacrificing love. The reason? If Johannine discipleship means "remaining" with Jesus, love of others is the way the "remaining" will take place. Mutual love, therefore, is the concrete mission of Jesus' disciples in the world.[24] As Jesus got up and laid down his garments to wash their feet, so all disciples must be willing to lay down their lives for each other (see 15:12-13; 1 Jn 3:16).

Authors like Bruce Malina and Anthony Blasi, who have examined the Johannine text in terms of the social setting and structure of the community, point to Jesus' command about love as the guiding characteristic which would define membership in that community. While the Synoptics would put adjectives in front of "love" like "compassionate," "forgiving," "healing," and "merciful," such attributes cannot be found in the Johannine version. Love is love and that's enough, as John writes in his first letter: "God is love, and those who abide in love abide in God, and God abides in them. Love has been perfected among us in this: that we may have boldness on the day of judgment, because as he is, so are we in this world" (1 Jn. 4:16b-17). Commenting on Jesus' words about loving each other, Blasi writes:

> That command should be understood not only as a recommendation about the excellence of mutual charity and respect, but also as an encouragement of a common Christian society in the face

of relatively hostile non-Christians: "I am giving you a new command, that you love one another; as I loved you, you should also love one another. By this all will know that you are my disciples, if you have love for one another" (Jn. 13.34-35). The competitive situation called for not only different individual Christians to unite in accord, but also for different Christian communities to do so. The Johannine community, which heretofore seems to have had a tradition that was independent of those of other Christian communities, seems ready under pressure (and perhaps persecution) to make common cause with other Christian communities.[25]

As it found itself growing in its self-understanding, reflected in its redaction of the Johannine material, the community realized that, just as love had motivated Jesus to undergo his passion, love would have to direct the disciples in their relationships to one another (13:34-35; 15:12-13).[26] If the Johannine community found itself isolated from the Jewish community and at odds with the Petrine group, it had only its own membership to rely on. Love, not the law or the leaders, was what would keep it intact.

Jesus' Second Conversation with Simon Peter (13:36-38)

The final section of chapter 13 begins with Peter picking up on Jesus' words just before the "love command": "Where I am going, you cannot come" (13:33). Peter asked Jesus: "'Lord, where are you going?' Jesus answered, 'Where I am going, you cannot follow me now; but you will follow afterward'" (13:36). While the words regarding Peter's following "afterward" anticipate (or echo?) the final words of Jesus to him after the resurrection (21:18f), here they merely elicit from Peter another declaration of bravado: "Lord, why can I not follow you now? I will lay down my life for you" (13:37). Jesus responds to Peter with words that have profoundly affected readers through the ages: "Will you lay down your life for me? Very truly, I tell you, before the cock crows, you will have denied me three times" (13:38).

By asking "where are you going?" Peter shows his lack of understanding about Jesus and his immediate future, a lack shared by the other disciples as well (14:5, 8, 22). At this point all Jesus can say to counter Peter's declaration about following him "now" by laying down his life is that he simply is not ready for this "now." In fact, this hour is about to reveal how unready Peter is to follow Jesus.

Peter's misunderstanding about the implications of "following" Jesus will still be evident in the post-resurrection narrative and in the late addition of chapter 21. Besides being told what manner of laying down his life Peter would endure, the reader is reminded again of Peter's question about who would betray Jesus (21:20; 13:24).

While Judas may be the betrayer, Peter will be the denier. Both forms of separating one's self from Jesus indicate rupture in the relationship. Jesus makes it clear that the lack of knowing among his followers will result in a dangerous doing: a break in the intimacy he has established with them and exhibited toward them only shortly before in the foot washing.

This is the fourth time Peter's bravado is challenged with a riposte by Jesus. While the three previous times dealt with the ritual of foot washing and how Jesus and Peter would define their roles, this fourth time goes to the deepest point of relationship: its core of trust. In the testing soon to come, Peter will prove untrustworthy, despite his protestations to the contrary. The lead disciple will prove to be a dishonorable shepherd. Instead, he will be prone to be like any other hireling who sees the wolf coming and flees (10:12).

In his reflection on this passage, Jerome Neyrey points to dynamics also taking place among the members of the alienated Christian communities themselves. He writes of John's implication that Peter has become the hireling shepherd rather than the good shepherd: "If this is true, then the narrator issues a serious challenge to Peter's role vis-à-vis the group. According to Johannine logic, the hireling has no relationship with the sheep: 'he who is a hireling, whose own the sheep are not.... He flees because he is a hireling and cares nothing for the sheep' (10:12-13). Whatever the Johannine group knew of the traditional role and status of Peter, that would be severely challenged by Peter's association here with the hireling and not the shepherd."[27] In light of the fact that it was the Beloved Disciple who rested at the breast of Jesus, the implication is clear: the community attached with the former does not elicit trust; the one identified with the latter has been tested and not found wanting.

Conclusion: John 13 and Reader Response

In summary, John 13 articulates for the community identified with the Beloved Disciple a model of being church that will distinguish it from the Petrine style. One would reflect the kind of "knowing and doing" exemplified in foot washing; its adherents would remain as beloved ones at the bosom of Jesus. The other would reflect non-knowing and non-doing in the form of betrayal and denial; its adherents would remain locked into repeating the dynamics of *hoi Ioudaioi*, the very dynamics that Jesus had replaced.

KNOWING AND DOING	(NOT) KNOWING AND (NOT) DOING
FOOT WASHING	BETRAYAL AND DENIAL
Reversal of roles	Maintaining status
Changing relationships	Resistance to changed relationships
Service	Hierarchy
Laying down life	Laying down nothing
Remaining with Jesus at his bosom	Remaining with Peter in patterns of *hoi Ioudaioi*
Remaining in love	Going out. It was night.

As I conclude this chapter, I can't help but recall a contemporary incident of Peter and the Beloved Disciple. It has given me much hope that the two can find mutual ways of continuing the example of Jesus' way of relating in loving service.

I know a woman[28] who worked very hard to get a degree in religious education so that she might "work for the church" in a diocese nearby. For several years she worked as a team member in her childhood parish with a pastor who exercised authority in a very collegial manner. But then, as he got older and the parish grew, he asked for a transfer. The new priest functioned differently, as did his associate who was assigned a few years later when the numbers in the parish mushroomed.

Increasingly the woman felt herself alone and isolated as the two seemed to make plans without her input.

Committed to the people of the parish, she decided that she would stay and try to work on her own conversion. She felt herself called to "lay down her life" by giving up any desire or effort to control what was happening or to change the behavior of the two priests. After several years of living in this painful situation, she began to notice a change on the part of the priests. The change became evident at a Holy Thursday liturgy at the parish. She wrote to me:

This past Easter Tridium I was blessed with a real bonus gift from the Lord. I was struggling with some "political" stuff going on in the parish and let go of some more stuff.... Once again I kept hearing "Let it go; let it go. It really doesn't matter." ... As I was reflecting on all that on Holy Thursday, I felt the Lord was reminding me I'm to be a servant minister and really re-examine my motives. So my mind and heart were off thinking about all that, when it came time for the feet washing. The pastor washed and kissed my feet and then just looked me in the eyes with such compassion. It just melted away any bitterness or hurt I may have had.

After that, the associate pastor preached about living in love and sharing that love with others. As an example he turned to my friend and told her he loved her and asked if she loved him. Free of any pain, hurt, or bitterness she looked him in the eye and said: "Yes, Father, I love you." She concluded by telling me how *"very* powerful" the experience had been for her.

The example Jesus gave the whole church for all time is *very* powerful because it is meant to speak to the issue of power itself. When those in the church of Peter and the Beloved Disciple find ways of living under this higher power, *very* powerful things are bound to happen!

ELEVEN

IF I HAVE SPOKEN RIGHTLY,
WHY DO YOU STRIKE ME? (18:23)

The Question of Jesus before Annas in John 18:1-27

If examined free of comparisons with the Synoptic versions, John's narrative of Jesus' passion and death appears quite straightforward.[1] Beginning with Jesus' arrest (18:1-11), it moves to his interrogation at the court of the Roman-deposed high priest Annas, the father-in-law of Caiaphas (18:12-23). The hearing then adjourns to the location of the acting high priest, Caiaphas (18:24). While both proceedings are taking place, Peter denies Jesus three times (18:15-18, 25-27). The actual trial before Pilate is the longest section; it ends with Jesus being handed "over to them to be crucified" (18:28-19:16a). After Jesus is crucified and dies (19:16b-30), his side is pierced and he is laid in the tomb (19:31-42).

The various scenes covering the hearings and trials of Jesus, his passion, and his death can be structured into three sections of quite equal length: (1) 18:1-27 (the arrest and hearings before Annas and Caiaphas), (2) 18:28–19:16a (the trial and conviction before Pilate) and (3) 19:16b-42 (the crucifixion, death, piercing, and burial). While all three sections are critical to the story, this chapter will reflect only on the first of the sections and the questions Jesus asks (us) in it.

I am limiting myself to the scenes before Annas and Caiaphas for two reasons. First, everything that takes place before the high priest with Jesus and in the courtyard with Peter revolves around discipleship. Second, when Jesus is taken before the religious authorities Annas and Caiaphas, he responds to their queries and to the actions of their police with two questions of his own.[2] Since this book revolves around Jesus' questions of the church, this chapter will concentrate on the context for the questions Jesus asks.

18:1-11: The Arrest of Jesus and Peter's Reaction

At the conclusion of the Farewell Discourse presented in chapters 14-17,[3] John narrates that Jesus "went out with his disciples" (18:1). These words serve to introduce a powerful commentary on what happens to disciples under pressure. The first section of chapter 18 elaborates on John's vision of authentic discipleship and what it means to witness to Jesus when the world is against you.

It begins when one of his disciples, Judas, comes to "the Kidron valley to a place where there [is] a garden, which [Jesus] and his disciples [have] entered." He brings with him "a detachment of soldiers together with police from the chief priests and the Pharisees, and they [come] there with lanterns and torches and weapons" (18:3). The message behind John's description of the scene, in which Jesus' opponents come at night, could not be more clear. Guided by human-made instruments of light, along with instruments of violence, they come to confront the one who has declared himself "light of the world" (8:12). In contrast to Jesus' disciples who have "the light of life," those who follow Judas now "walk in darkness" (8:12; see 9:5).

In the garden (18:1-11), "the soldiers, their officer, and the Jewish police arrested Jesus and bound him" (18:12). The fact that Roman soldiers and their superior officer are working in consort with the "Jewish police" indicates something that would have been highly unusual at the time: they are in collusion. Only John mentions the soldiers being organized into a "detachment" (*speira* [18:3]). This could be as small as a section of a cohort, a maniple (200 men), or the whole cohort itself (600 men). In addition to the Roman officers there were the police deputized by "the chief priests and the Pharisees" (18:3), a definite Johannine allusion to the earlier pre-ordained sentence of the highest religious authorities (11:47). Under the guidance of Judas, the representatives of this unholy alliance come to arrest Jesus.

There has been much debate as to whether and why Romans would have been involved in the simple arrest of a Jew who was under suspicion by the religious authorities. The fact that only John's gospel notes the presence of the soldiers (who represented the interests of Rome) in collusion with the police (who represented the interests of the Sanhedrin, the highest official body in the Jewish religion) cannot be taken lightly. At the same time, we cannot give it more significance than the data suggests. While it might appear that these two forces represent "the world" at its apogee, John doesn't seem to be concerned about this fact in his interpretation, since he doesn't even use the word "Roman" in describing the soldiers. Raymond Brown says, "it is only by deduction that we realize that Pilate and thus the Roman authority must have been consulted."[4]

Despite the enormity of the forces arrayed against Jesus, John makes him director of his own destiny. Consequently, "knowing all that was to happen to him," Jesus comes forward to confront those bent on his destruction (18:4a). He identifies himself (*egō eimi*) before Judas can point to him (18:4b-8a). Then he sets the terms of his arrest in a way that will fulfill the scriptures: "If you are looking for me, let these men go free" (18:8b-9). Jesus' control of his destiny is further underscored when Peter resorts to the same violence about to be done to Jesus with an act of violence himself: "Then Simon Peter, who had a sword, drew it, struck the high priest's slave, and cut off his right ear. The slave's name was Malchus. Jesus said to Peter, 'Put your sword back into its sheath. Am I not to drink the cup that the Father has given me?'" (18:10). John shows here that Jesus does not need Peter's help, especially when that "help" only perpetuates more violence, whether in service to religion or the state.

This incident is not unique to John's gospel. It is recounted in the three other gospels as well (Mt 26:51-54; Mk 14:47; Lk 22:50-51). What is different, and significantly at variance in John's version, is not just that John names Malchus as the victim of Peter's violence, but that, while the Synoptics protect the anonymity of this disciple who does the violence, John identifies him as Simon Peter. It almost seems as though John has intentionally decided to break the Synoptic conspiracy of silence about Peter as the perpetrator of the violence. Why? And why do all three Synoptics seem intent on not revealing the perpetrator's name? In describing the incident, they simply refer to him as "one who was with" Jesus. Why does the author of the fourth gospel choose to expose the one who was with Jesus as Peter?

To uncover a possible rationale one must go beyond the narration to the intent and ideology behind all four gospels themselves. A purpose of the Synoptic gospels, especially the Matthean version (which gives a fuller description of this incident than do its counterparts), is to highlight the significance and role of Peter in the community. A purpose of John's gospel is to point out those places where Simon Peter's behavior alienates him from authentic discipleship, especially when that behavior is contrasted with the behavior of the Beloved Disciple. Peter may have been "with" Jesus physically, but he was far from understanding his identity and purpose in the world. As Arthur J. Droge explains:

> The answer to this question is not hard to discern, once Peter's action is seen in light of his characterization in the Fourth Gospel as a whole. By identifying the unnamed disciple as Peter, the author intended to draw attention again to his obtuseness and inability to comprehend who Jesus was and what he was about to do. Peter's misunderstanding compels him to draw his sword in a vain attempt to protect Jesus. But Jesus needs no protecting in the Fourth Gospel, nor will he be deterred from accomplishing his mission. Jesus' impending death (if it is even death he suffers) is not the arbitrary result of circumstance, or even tragic, but the work appointed him by the Father. "No man takes it [my life] from me,"

Jesus declares, "I lay it down of my own free will. I have authority to lay it down, and I have authority to take it again; this command I have received from my Father" (John 10:18). In the Fourth Gospel, Jesus' death is his glorification, not his humiliation, and it is precisely this that Peter fails to comprehend.[5]

John Reminds the Reader Why This Arrest Has Taken Place (18:12-14)

At this point in his scenario, John tells us that Annas, to whom the collaborators first "took" Jesus, was the father-in-law of Caiaphas. John also reminds us that Caiaphas was the one "who had advised *hoi Ioudaioi* that it was better to have one person die for the people" (18:14; see 11:45-53). With this reference, John offers the rationale for what will follow: Jesus must die to preserve the system. Violence must be done to protect the sacred order. John here exposes the shadow side of *hoi Ioudaioi* and of any religious system that allows itself to be seduced by the evil that consciously or unconsciously condones violence in the name of God to maintain not only religion's rituals and rites, but especially religion's rulers and regulators.

While Caiaphas's "prophecy" applied to that particular situation, its echo continues wherever religion invokes God in support of violence when its institutional interests are threatened. Thus we get crusades and conquistadors, inquisitions and inquests. Individual or group violence is legitimated to sustain a deeper institutionalized violence that rarely gets exposed or acknowledged. What is most frightening is that, because theology is used as an overlay, the result can be idolatrous.

The rationale for using violence to preserve any type of institutional order is easy to understand. Stanley Hauerwas writes:

> We love order, even order that is based on illusion and self-deception. When we say we want peace, we mean we want order. Our greatest illusion and deception, therefore, is that we are a peaceable people, non-violent to the core. We are peaceable as long as no one disturbs our illusions. We are non-violent as long as no one challenges our turf.... the order of our lives is built on our potential for violence.[6]

Our potential for violence seems embedded in our individual and corporate psyches. When conflicts arise among us, a desire to re-establish order is not far behind. Because order is that force in human relations that keeps us from killing each other, it is important to preserve order in the face of conflicts. Many anthropologists have shown that, when conflicts arise, they can get resolved by finding a scapegoat upon whom blame can be placed. Scapegoats keep conflicts among people from getting out of hand. Thus, in Caiaphas's wisdom, Jesus must die to preserve the system. "Order is always achieved at the expense of someone or some group," David Stevens has written. "The price that is paid for order is victimization."[7] Victimization demands scapegoats.

Building on the pioneering work on scapegoating of Rene Girard (who finds in this notion the basis of all culture and religion itself), Stevens argues that "societal conflict and the violence of individual against individual is transformed into a peaceful state when the scapegoat is expelled from the group, carrying with him [sic] everyone's violence and guilt. Violence is the ultimate weapon against disorder but it is used against the innocent scapegoat."[8] From John's perspective in chapters 7 and 8, scapegoating results from works that are evil. Those whose systems demand scapegoats are "children of the lie."

Having brought the reader to this point, John makes it clear that those claiming to be Jesus' disciples must decide whether they will witness to the world that they are disciples of the truth (Jesus) or follow Peter's self-interested way of seeking survival and become children of the lie. Everything will now evolve around being children of the lie or being disciples of Jesus, around those disciples who cower under threats and persecution and those who will faithfully witness to the truth. The stage is set. For the reader, the test will come whenever Jesus must be proclaimed. For Peter, the trial takes place in the courtyard of the deposed high priest of Judaism.

As we have seen, Jesus is very much in control of his life and destiny. The same will not be able to be said of Simon Peter, or of any of Jesus' disciples whose names we know. Only one, the anonymous disciple (the Beloved One?) remains with Jesus. This brings us to consider the next section of the text dealing with Peter's first betrayal.

Peter's First Denial (18:15-18)

After Jesus' arrest and transfer to Annas, "Simon Peter and another disciple followed (akolouthein) Jesus" (18:15a). The word akolouthein, which is not as common in John as it is in the Synoptics to describe discipleship (as "following"), is more than coincidental here. The context for the ensuing contrast is being established. John continues: "Since that disciple was known to the high priest, he went with Jesus into the courtyard of the high priest but Peter was standing outside at the gate. So the other disciple, who was known to the high priest, went out, spoke to the woman who guarded the gate, and brought Peter in" (18:15b-16).

With this passage about Simon Peter and "another disciple" following Jesus we are invited to go beyond the physical image related to "following" and consider the two kinds of "following" that constitute authentic discipleship in John. Here, as we will see in all the other passages that link this unique disciple and Peter, the former represents the disciple who remains with Jesus under pressure. Peter, concerned about his own survival, does not measure up when the testing comes.

This scene in the "courtyard (*aulē*) of the high priest" is filled with contrasts and questions. First the contrasts. The word for Annas's courtyard, *aulē,* is the same as that used for the sheepfold in chapter 10. The gate of this *aulē* is noted in both as well. In 10:1 the gate is that which is open for the sheep; here Peter stands "outside the gate" and has to be brought in by the "other disciple" (18:16). Meanwhile the "other disciple" goes in and out of Annas's *aulē* (18:15-16), just as the shepherd in chapter ten does (10:1-5). Whether beginning with the walled garden of Judas' betrayal in 18:1-11 or here in the *aulē* of Annas, Mark Stibbe finds a Johannine "satire of Peter." He writes:

> Through this subtle use of settings, the narrator equates the roles of Jesus, Judas, Peter and the beloved disciple with certain roles in the shepherd discourse of John 10. Obviously, Jesus plays the part of the good shepherd, and Judas of the thief in 18.1-11. In 18.15-27, however, the beloved disciple plays the part of the shepherd who walks in and out of the fold, and the girl at the gate plays the part of the gatekeeper. This leaves Peter, who runs away in the hour of danger in 18.15-27. Here the flight is not a literal desertion, but a metaphorical flight from confession. This means that Peter can only be equated with one role in the shepherd discourse: the role of the hired hand, who runs away in the hour of danger (10.12-13).[9]

Now that we have addressed the contrasts, we can begin to look at some of the questions. Who was this "other disciple" who followed Jesus with Peter? Did the high priest know this disciple was connected to Jesus? Why does John state that Peter was standing outside at the gate and that the gate was guarded by a woman? What kind of connection did this other disciple, who knew the high priest, have with this woman? What did this disciple say that made the woman allow Peter to come in?

The identity of this other disciple is debated. However, I believe it could have been the "beloved disciple" first mentioned in 13:23-26. Mark Stibbe and many other exegetes take this view. A major reason is that John tends to place the "beloved disciple" in situations which put him in contrast to Peter. The anonymous disciple is associated with Peter in all the other references to "the disciple who went by that name" (13:23-26; 19:25-27; 20:2-10; 21:7, 20-23). Raymond Brown argues that this anonymous disciple must have been the "beloved disciple" for two reasons: his accompaniment of Jesus in the high priest's palace and his accompaniment of Jesus during the passion, since "he appears at the foot of the cross" in 19:25-27.[10] For those of the Petrine orientation used to viewing Peter in terms of the status conferred on him in 16:16-18, Peter's role as one who, unlike the Beloved Disciple, does not "remain with" Jesus is not easy to swallow.

Returning to the dynamics taking place in the courtyard, we might ask: If this "beloved" or anonymous disciple was "known (gnōstos) to the high priest," did the high priest know of his connection to Jesus? If not, there would be no danger in his getting closer to the interrogation. But if the high priest did know of his ties to Jesus, why would this disciple not also be considered suspect? E. A. Abbott suggested long ago that, if this anonymous disciple was known by the high priest as part of the Jesus-group, the only one of that group who would have been safe in the high priest's presence would have been the one who had alienated himself from the group: Judas himself. This would mean that the two disciples who followed the progress of the betrayal to the courtyard were Peter and Judas.[11] Thus, Judas would be the anonymous disciple. This seems impossible, given the fact that, until now, John has had no problem clearly identifying Judas and describing his devious behavior (see 6:71; 13:26-30; 18:2-4). Why then would John not have clearly identified him here? It seems much more likely that this anonymous disciple was the Beloved.

The next concern has to do with the woman. How could a woman be guarding the gate leading to access to the high priest? If women were not allowed inside the temple precincts, how could they be trusted to be its guards? And, if women were among the guards, why would one of this "weaker sex" be doing guard duty at this most dangerous time—night? Some exegetes think this is John's mocking way of imaging the underlying fraudulent nature of the entire interrogation scene before Annas, a deposed high priest. Others believe it was his attempt to harmonize his version with the Synoptic tradition that referred to a maidservant as a challenger of Peter.[12]

John makes a point of telling us that Peter was warming himself "with" the slaves and the police who had made the fire (18:18); he is part of the reality that opposed Jesus. We have seen that, in John, discipleship involves "remaining with" Jesus and finding one's ultimate security in that relationship. Through this image John shows that Peter is finding his security with the very ones who are protecting the religious system that is about to do violence to Jesus—this Jesus he has privately said he would never betray. The contrast between discipleship and security is made clear in the woman's question asked of the one who is to be the gate and its guard (see 10:1-7): "You are not also one of this man's disciples, are you?" (18:17a). At the very time when he is called upon to bear witness to the truth of the one who has said "I am" (egō eimi) "the truth" (14:6), Peter tells his first lie: "I am not" (ouk eimi).

John uses this first contrast between the lie of the lead disciple and the truth of the Lord and Teacher (13:13) to bring the reader to another interrogation: that of Jesus himself before the "high priest" the reader knows as Annas.

The Hearing before Annas (18:12-14, 19-24)

Annas became high priest in 6 C.E. and got deposed about ten years later. During his reign he succeeded in establishing a family dynasty known for its wealth, greed, and tyranny. Though he had been deposed, his influence continued in five of his sons, each of whom became high priests. His son-in-law was now acting high priest. That Annas is called "high priest" several times (18:15, 16, 19, and 22) need not indicate that John has his historical facts wrong. It could evidence an example of the anti-Roman feelings of the Jewish people. Even though Rome had deposed their high priest, they continued to bestow on him the title since, in their eyes, the position of high priest was for life (see Num 35:25).

It would not surprise the Johannine audience that Jesus would be brought to Annas before being brought to Caiaphas, especially since the leadership group, the Caiaphas-dominated Sanhedrin, had already been swayed by his counsel: "Caiaphas was the one who had advised *hoi Ioudaioi* that it was better to have one person die for the people" (18:14). The result of this "trial" was that Jesus would die (11:50).

The die determining Jesus' destiny has been cast long before chapter 18. But the semblance of judicial impartiality must continue. Thus, Annas, "the [other] high priest questioned (*erōtan*) Jesus about his disciples and about his teaching" (18:19). As noted earlier, *erōtan* connotes queries arising from concern about one's own and one's group's self-interest. Subtly, John reveals the motivation behind the questioning.

The inquisition of Jesus by Annas in chapter 18 is best understood by recalling the dynamics between Jesus and his opponents in chapters 7 and 8. Pointing to 7:46-49 and the series of sharp exchanges between Jesus and *hoi Ioudaioi* in 8:19-39, Donald Senior notes: "Throughout John's Gospel, Jesus' personal identity as the unique revealer of God is the stumbling block for the leaders."[13] Annas's questions of Jesus here go beyond the specifics of Jesus' identity. His interests have to do with the impact of Jesus' identity and message on his followers.

The first concern of Annas, the leader of leaders, is Jesus' disciples, the members of the Jesus-movement. If Annas's role was to help preserve his own religious group's stakes, it would be natural that he would be concerned about any other possible claimants for the people's loyalty. The questions that interested Annas were: How big was this group? Was it big enough to constitute a real threat? Was it organized, or was it simply a ragtag bunch of naive folk?

The second line of questioning involved teaching. While Annas wanted to "know" about the teaching, Jesus' disciples had come to "know" the person beyond the teaching. Sadly, because he was entrenched in his "knowledge" of the law, Annas could not come to this way of "knowing." He knew only that Judaism had had its share of many religious reformers and zealots. Many had Maccabean-like messages and platforms designed to deliver Israel from Rome's bondage. What was the nature of Jesus' message? Perhaps Annas knew full well what it was and just wanted to hear it from Jesus himself now that he had him under investigation. We will never know Annas's motivation, much less Jesus' answers. As in so many religious interrogations throughout the ages, almost everything remains unknown or is kept secret to "protect the people."

The fact that Annas was not sincere in his probing seems evidenced by Jesus' response to the queries about his followers and his message. Directly responding to Annas's questions about his disciples and teaching, Jesus begins by addressing the last query first: "I have spoken openly (*parrēsia*) to the world; I have always taught in synagogues and in the temple, where all *hoi Ioudaioi* come together. I have said nothing in secret" (18:20). Ignace de la Potterie has pointed out that four times in this scene with Annas (18:20 [2x], 21, 23), "John uses the Greek word *lalein*, generally translated, for want of something better, by 'speak'. But in religious language the word *lalein* has acquired a higher significance: in biblical Greek it is one of the terms signifying divine revelation: the revelatory word of God . . . it is *par excellence* the word of him who is himself the Word of God."[14] His self-revelation is made, not just for a few, but for the whole world. This is one of those times that John does not use the term "world" in a negative sense.[15]

Jesus attests that he has spoken openly. Speaking "openly" here is not simply a matter of speaking publicly, in a way that can be witnessed by everyone. It is also a matter of speaking truthfully. According to Donald Senior, John again is linking this interrogation scene with the forensic dynamics of chapter 8. "There too," he writes, "the atmosphere was charged with confrontation between Jesus and the Jewish leaders, and there, too, were references to Jesus' arrest and his Passion (see 8:20, 28, 59). Jesus proclaimed himself to be 'the light of the world,' the Revealer whose very being discloses the ultimate truth of God's presence in the world (8:12)."[16]

In chapter 8 Jesus had declared to his entrenched religious opponents: "You are from your father the devil, and you choose to do your father's desires. He was a murderer from the beginning and does not stand in the truth, because there is no truth in him. When he lies, he speaks according to his own nature, for he is a liar and the father of lies. But because I tell the truth, why do you not believe me?" (8:44-45).

The question is direct: "If I tell the truth, why do you not believe me?" (8:46). The answer is clear to anyone who knows the motivation of people preoccupied with preserving their control over others, especially when that control is reinforced by a kind of collective narcissism that is blind to truth: their lack of faith arises not only because they are children of the lie, but because their works are evil as well.

Probably no popular American writer has more clearly expressed the connection between evil and the lie than M. Scott Peck. Some of his insights have helped me better understand the dynamics behind the debates between Jesus and his opponents in chapters 7 and 8. At the heart of his theory is the notion of individual and/or collective narcissism. In order to preserve one's self or a group that feels threatened, a scapegoat must be found. This results in works that are evil and that are rationalized through the lie. Peck's words regarding the connection between people who do evil and "people of the lie" should challenge all of us who have some kind of religious authority:

> The words "image," "appearance," and "outwardly" are crucial to understanding the morality of the evil. While they seem to lack any motivation to *be* good, they intensely desire to appear good. Their "goodness" is all on a level of pretense. It is, in effect, a lie. This is why they are the "people of the lie."
>
> Actually, the lie is designed not so much to deceive others as to deceive themselves. They cannot or will not tolerate the pain of self-reproach. The decorum with which they lead their lives is maintained as a mirror in which they can see themselves reflected righteously. Yet the self-deceit would be unnecessary if the evil had no sense of right and wrong. We lie only when we are attempting to cover up something we know to be illicit. Some rudimentary form of conscience must precede the act of lying. There is no need to hide unless we first feel that something needs to be hidden.[17]

Unlike his questioner, Jesus has nothing to hide. He has not taught in secret places. He has preached openly and has preached the truth. Further, there are witnesses to what Jesus has said in the synagogues and in the temple: those who heard him. Thus he responds to Annas's query with his own question: "Why do you ask me? Ask those who heard what I said to them; they know what I said" (18:21).

The Johannine response of Jesus to Annas's queries is all the more powerful when we recall that there are none around who will come to Jesus' defense. Certainly there are no members of the Sanhedrin who will openly defend him. The crypto-believers like Nicodemus are still hiding in the dark. The crowds are nowhere to be found and Jesus has few if any followers left who can be asked about "his disciples and about his teaching" (18:19). Instead of bearing witnesses to him and his message, his closest associates have abandoned him. One has already betrayed him (6:70-71; 12:4; 13: 21-30) and another—the acknowledged spokesperson of the now-dispersed group (see 6:68-69)—is in the process of denying any kind of relationship with him (18:15-18, 25-27). Except for the anonymous disciple (see 18:15), the rest of the disciples are missing from the scene.

On hearing Jesus' words, "one of the police standing nearby struck Jesus on the face, saying, 'Is that how you answer the high priest?'" (18:22). In response to this challenge from Annas's gendarme, Jesus says: "If I have spoken wrongly (*Ei kakōs elalēsa*), testify to the wrong. But if I have spoken rightly (*ei de kalōs elalēsa*), why do you strike me?" (18:23). Jesus' response to the soldier's violence exposes and shames the religious system. When confronted by the truth, the institution's representative can only strike back in anger.

Ignace de la Potterie has shown that the blow, which takes place at the center of this section on Jesus before Annas, is a symbolic gesture. It is a response to Jesus' self-revelation (*lalein*) by "the high priest's servant [who] becomes to some extent the representative of all those who have rejected the revealing word of Jesus to the world."[18] But, if this soldier is representative, what is there in us that makes us strike another in face of what is good and right? Why did the guard abuse Jesus, especially when his life and words represented the way, the truth, and the life (14:6)? In the words of Donald Senior, "The blow struck by one of the officers is another sign of the opponents' failure to recognize 'Truth.' Jesus is slapped because his answer is taken as disrespect for the high priest (see Exodus 22:28) but Jesus' words reassert his witness to the truth."[19] In this first slap, one of the police of the religious authority abuses the representative of truth while the authority looks on in silence. It will happen again when Jesus is slapped before Pilate (19:3).

Earlier, the Pharisees had said to Jesus: "You are testifying on your own behalf; your testimony is not valid" (8:13). Now, under interrogation, Jesus issues a direct riposte to such thinking: "If I have spoken wrongly," if I have spoken untruthfully, "testify to the wrong." Since there are no "witnesses" that will testify one way or another, Jesus is left with his own person and message as his witness.

If Jesus did speak rightly, if his words were truthful, did the soldier strike him merely because of his concern for maintaining the prestige of the priesthood? I agree with Donald Senior that the policeman slapped Jesus because his opponents were unable to "recognize 'Truth,'" but I also believe that there is something deeper here. Jesus immediately moved to stop the violence of one of his "lieutenants" when "Simon Peter, who had a sword, drew it, struck the high priest's slave, and cut off his right ear" (18:10). Here, Annas is silent (if not supportive) in the face of violence on the part of one of his liutenants. Jesus' "why" deserves further probing by readers who find themselves similarly confronted by the "police" who represent today's religious authorities. In trying to understand why the policeman would be willing to do this violence to Jesus (and keeping in mind de la Potterie's insight that the soldier is a personification of all the forces that stand opposed to Jesus' self-revelation), Scott Peck again provides helpful thoughts.

In *People of the Lie* Peck considers individuals whose works were evil. He then analyzes how systems themselves are reinforced by those "police" or corporate "soldiers" who see themselves as guardians of the system they feel compelled to protect. It is true that the soldier who struck Jesus did so without clearly stated authorization. However, in state-sponsored violence it is also true that such activities are part and parcel of the system itself. This is why the policeman was not reprimanded for using his power in an abusive way. Individual violence is in some sense representative and reflective of systems of violence. Peck makes this clear when he moves from examining evil done by individuals to considering evil in systems. He points to the violence done by the U.S. military to the people of MyLai, Vietnam as an example of "group evil."

On March 16, 1968, elements of Task Force Barker moved into a small group of hamlets known collectively as MyLai in the Quang Ngai province of South Vietnam. The province was considered to be a Vietcong stronghold. It was often difficult to distinguish combatants from noncombatants and it was assumed that the civilians there were aiding and abetting the enemy. As Peck notes, "the Americans tended to hate and distrust all Vietnamese in the area."[20] Despite the fact that the only people found there were unarmed women, children, and old men, the troops of C Company killed at least 500 of these unarmed people. Later this would be justified with a saying that has become part of the American cultural tradition: "We had to destroy this village in order to save it."

Caiaphas felt justified in destroying Jesus in order to save the religious system that had come to serve him so well. It is not surprising that a temple policeman, like all but one soldier at MyLai, would feel that he was only doing his duty by slapping Jesus. His kind had to be destroyed in order to save the people. Today, many in the Roman Church seem to have a working ideology that parallels what we heard our political and military leaders say during Vietnam. In effect, with the decrease in the number of priests because of the leaders' limitation of the priesthood to only one kind of candidate, the landscape of the Catholic Church seems to be experiencing a kind of saturation bombing. In the process, it sometimes appears that the Vatican and the bishops seem ready to destroy this church in order to save it in its male celibate expression.

Peck notes of contemporary police or soldiers in the military that: "Triggers are pulled by individuals. Orders are given and executed by individuals. In the last analysis, every single human act is ultimately the result of an individual choice."[21] However, at the same time, he shows that something happens to that individual choice if one has previously chosen to be part of a group with its rewards for compliance and benefits for protecting the system:

> The individual adult as individual is master of his own ship, director of his destiny. But when he assumes the role of follower he hands over to the leader his power: his authority over himself and his maturity as decision-maker. He becomes psychologically dependent on the leader as a child is dependent on its parents. In this way there is a profound tendency for the average individual to emotionally regress as soon as he becomes a group member.[22]

Individuals change when they join a group, especially if that group uses control as its normal form of exercising power. In the case of the Roman Church, it often seems that, after being appointed to the college of bishops, a man will exchange his own way of thinking for group-think. While this does not always happen, it does happen often enough, especially when "thinking with the church" is taken to its extreme. Adding to the problem is the fact that the appointment process itself selects for conformity. Thus, what Scott Peck writes of people selected for leadership in the military has many parallels in church leadership:

> It is an old maxim that soldiers are not supposed to think. Leaders are not elected from within the group but are designated from above and deliberately cloaked in the symbols of authority. Obedience is the number-one military discipline. The dependency of the soldier on his leader is not simply encouraged, it is mandated. By nature of its mission the military designedly and probably realistically fosters the naturally occurring regressive dependency of individuals within its groups.[23]

There are bishops who pride themselves on being "company men." They consider it an honor if they are recognized by the Vatican for "toeing the line" in their diocese, especially in the face of challenges from groups of people who see dissidents everywhere. Like Nicodemus, many of these men are very good people; they seem sincere. However, once they are part of the group, something invariably happens to their ability to reason or to speak their own truth. Obedience becomes the ultimate virtue. Those who obey without questioning are considered loyal and rewarded with promotions.

Peter's Second and Third Denial (18:25-27)

Having established Jesus as the one who speaks truthfully to the point of being willing to suffer violence as a result, John now returns the reader to the courtyard. Here Peter is challenged again, only to lie again. In this second and third of Peter's denials, he is pictured as still warming himself. Only now an anonymous group called simply "they" by John (but known to the reader as the official religious representatives, *hoi Ioudaioi*)[24] ask him about his being a disciple of Jesus (18:15) and being "with him" in the garden (18:25). "Again Peter denied it" (18:27a).

In the garden across the Kidron Jesus had boldly declared, in the face of clear and imminent danger from his questioners: "I am he" (*egō eimi* [18:5, 8; see 18:6]). In the high priest's garden, Peter capitulates in fear. Peter declares twice that he is not Jesus' disciple (*ouk eimi* [18:17b, 25b; see 18:27a]). In the Johannine "synchonization" of Jesus' trial and Peter's denial,[25] the contrast between Jesus' bold proclamation and Peter's pathetic witness could not be stronger.

Mark Stibbe develops this contrast in clear strokes when he notes that, while Jesus is very much in control throughout, Peter is not. In fact, he loses control (18:1-27):

> Peter, on the other hand, seems to be very much controlled by them. In the heat of the moment, he brandishes a sword and cuts off Malchus's right earlobe (v. 10), thereby evoking a sharp rebuke form Jesus. In vv. 15-16, Peter relies on the beloved disciple to get him into the courtyard of Annas' house. In v. 17, his bravado with Malchus turns into timidity before a servant girl. In vv. 25-27, he again fails to declare his allegiance to Jesus, this time on two occasions. At the end of the section, a cock crows, reminding us of Jesus' prophecy of Peter's denials in 13:36-38. Everywhere... there are indications of Peter being controlled by his circumstances. His conduct is the very opposite of Jesus'.[26]

At the very moment when Jesus, the "Teacher and Lord" (13:13-14), is boldly challenging those who would question him, Peter peters-out in fear. The implications for members of the Johannine community who claim allegiance to Jesus through their connection to the Beloved Disciple are clear. To be faithful to the Lord and Teacher as disciples, they will have to bear witness to him even when it might result in their being brought to trial themselves. Those disciples called to fidelity will not be found only among those who were the first to receive these words of John; they are those who, through these words, believe in this Lord and Teacher—in every age.

TWELVE

DO YOU LOVE ME? (21:15, 16, 17)

The Threefold Question of John 21:1-19

There is much debate among scripture scholars with regard to John's chapter 21. A major element of the controversy relates to the chapter's placement in the gospel: was it always part of the gospel or was it added later? If it was always part of the gospel, how does one explain the final words of chapter 20? They appear to be a conclusion for the gospel: "Now Jesus did many other signs in the presence of his disciples, which are not written in this book. But these are written so that you may come to believe that Jesus is the Messiah, the Son of God, and that through believing you may have life in his name" (20:30-31). If the gospel originally ended at this point, why the add-on? And, if it was added, what should it be called? An appendix, an attachment, an addition, an epilogue, a supplement, a postscript?

Arguments for a later addition arise from seeming inconsistencies with chapter 20. If the risen Jesus had been experienced twice by key male disciples,[1] why, in chapter 21:4 did the disciples "not know that it was Jesus" calling to them from the shore? Was this way of describing this appearance an effort to show him manifest in yet another form? Or, if Jesus had already appeared to "the disciples" except for Thomas (20:19-24) and then "a week later" to "his disciples," including Thomas, one would assume that Peter had been there too. Why wouldn't Peter recognize Jesus this third time?

It is hypothesized that chapter 21 was added to John's gospel in order to address issues not covered in the first twenty chapters. Specifically, this chapter was meant to address concerns related to the way the Johannine community would participate in the wider church. During this time the Johannine community was witnessing an increasing emphasis on the role of Peter in a way that seemed to vitiate its own self-understanding of what it meant to "remain" with Jesus. While members did not seem to look upon the Petrine community with much favor, at the same time they realized they were part of the wider church that could never be divorced from Peter. Thus, they had to find ways to witness to their vision of being

identified with Jesus in love as they watched the Petrine/Apostolic group
take on patterns that seemed reflective of the very things Jesus had resist-
ed in *hoi Iouaioi*. In particular, the Petrine/Apostolic community's stress
on their leaders seemed to be undermining the centrality of Jesus Christ
and his love in the community.

It is generally agreed that Peter is treated in a more positive light in
this final chapter than in the rest of the gospel. Indeed, if one were to rely
only on the representation of Peter given in the first twenty chapters, his
primacy would be in grave doubt. Chapter 21, therefore, seems to have
been added to restore Peter's reputation and affirm his position in the
community. Thus, many scripture scholars, including the late Raymond
E. Brown, have proposed Peter's "rehabilitation" as a main reason for the
addition of the chapter.

Apart from canonical considerations, a compelling argument for the
acceptance of chapter 21 as part of the whole gospel is the fact that there
is no extant manuscript of John's gospel that does not contain this ending.
While it may have been added later, it is clear that its thrust fits into the
overall scheme of John's gospel. Thus, we can conclude with Brown that
the writer of John 21 was "a Johannine disciple who shared the same general world of thought as the evangelist and who desired more to complete
the gospel than to change its impact."[2] Within this context of inclusion-
conclusion, we can apply reader-response theory to explore what the
chapter might mean for us today.

The chapter can be divided into three sections (21:1-14; 21:15-19,
and 21:20-25).[3] In its first and last sections, Simon Peter and the Beloved
Disciple are highlighted and contrasted. The Johannine community or
final redactor, both of which identified with the Beloved Disciple, seems
to have felt it necessary to address Peter's role in the community of believers. The Petrine order in the wider church had to be elaborated for the
Johannine believers. The implications for us who struggle to believe in
Jesus Christ within an ecclesiastical system that has become overly clericalized and institutionalized through its appeals to Peter and his "office"
seem obvious.

More and more scholars believe that John's gospel in its final form
arose in a context of what we today would call growing clericalization and
institutionalization. The clericalization was expressed by those "ordained"
as leaders who gradually came to see themselves as possessing the truth in
such a way that their exercise of authority disempowered members of the
wider church. Of this institutionalization P. J. Hartin writes:

> Institutionalization had started within the early church as is evi-
> denced by the Pastorals. At the same time some leaders were ex-
> ercising their authority in a dominating manner as both 3 John

and 1 Peter bear witness. Against this background the Fourth Gospel emerges and shows two important lessons. Firstly, the way in which the claim to authority should be exercised, and secondly the fact that another eventually important authority exists in the early church, the authority of the Beloved Disciple.[4]

Because of the role of Peter in chapter 21 and because much of the Johannine understanding of Peter is presently overshadowed by the Synoptics' stress on Peter (especially in Matthew), we need to take a closer look at his place and function in John. This chapter will concentrate on the first two sections of chapter 21. The final chapter of this book will discuss 21:20-25. The first section (21:1-14) revolves around fish and a meal; the second (21:20-25) has to do with sheep and shepherding.

Simon Peter's Role in John's Gospel

Unlike the Synoptics, John never names the "twelve"[5] or calls them "apostles." Yet, among all the named disciples, Simon Peter gets a kind of primacy in John. John describes Peter's call (1:40-42), his confession of faith (6:66-70), his role in the foot washing, and the prediction of Peter's denial (13:1-38). John also makes note of Peter's presence in the garden where he cut off the right ear of Malchus (18:10-11), at Jesus' interrogation before Annas (18:15-18, 25-27), with the Beloved Disciple at the empty tomb (20:1-10), and by the Sea of Tiberias (all of chapter 21). While Peter's appearance (especially after chapter 13) occurs in some relationship or comparison to the Beloved Disciple, Peter definitely does have a significant role, mixed as it may be.

Scripture scholars are divided as to how the fourth gospel characterizes Peter. The division relates, in the main, to the dynamics occurring between Peter and the Beloved Disciple or, more significantly, between the Petrine community and that identified with the Beloved Disciple. There seem to be four different perspectives regarding Peter.

One group of scholars finds a strong anti-Petrine thrust in John. No positive significance is given to Simon Peter. A. H. Maynard notes that, while chapter 21 might present Peter as being superior in authority and the Beloved Disciple as being superior in intimacy with Jesus, "in the body of the Gospel Peter is made to appear in very bad light, indeed. This gospel apparently came from a community that wanted nothing to do with the primacy of one man, not even Peter!"[6] Although Maynard does acknowledge that Peter is in some way rehabilitated in chapter 21, in his overall "deprecation" of Peter, Maynard is joined by a formidable group of exegetes. This includes earlier writers like B. W. Bacon and E. C. Hoskyns as well as more recent ones like Eric L. Titus and Graydon F. Snyder.

Another group of scholars distinguishes between the roles of Peter and the Beloved Disciple and, while attributing a more important role to the Beloved Disciple, these exegetes find no explicit or direct anti-Petrine tenor in the gospel. Representative of this group is Raymond E. Brown. While admitting a secondary role for Peter, he writes: "Peter is not the special hero of the Johannine writer. The BD [Beloved Disciple] has that role; and the writer takes special interest in showing the Beloved Disciple's 'primacy of love,' a superiority that does not exclude Peter's possessing another type of primacy."[7] Others who agree with Brown's approach are Oscar Cullmann and those of the Lutheran-Roman Catholic dialogue group[8] as well as Raymond F. Collins who finds Peter "superseded" by the Beloved One.[9] Jerome Neyrey takes a more anthropological approach in reaching the same conclusion. Building on the insights of the cultural anthropologist Mary Douglas, he writes:

> As a type of traditional, apostolic leadership, Peter represents an ascribed leadership based on fleshly and earthly criteria. The beloved disciple, in contrast, is a charismatic figure whose status does not depend on ascribed authority but on achieved legitimacy. He is supremely in the know.... His leadership, I suggest, represents a spiritual or charismatic emphasis seen in the Fourth Gospel as better or higher than what Peter represents. The contrast, moreover, is developed in terms of heaven/earth and spirit/flesh dichotomies. In this case, downplaying Peter signals a rejection of what Peter stands for and implies devaluation of the traditions about the earthly Jesus and structures and roles the earthly Jesus is credited with establishing. With his special knowledge, his remarkable belief, and his extraordinary following of Jesus in crisis, the beloved disciple represents a posture above and against what Peter represents.[10]

A third group views Simon Peter and the Beloved Disciple as two figures whose distinctiveness flowed from their separate functions in the early church. Rather than concentrating on their differing personal identities, these scholars stress their corporate meaning and complementary roles. R. Alan Culpepper and Kevin Quast represent this balancing approach, as does P. J. Hartin, who writes: "For Peter the function is that of exercising a pastoral authority. For the BD [Beloved Disciple] it is an exercise of discipleship of love and witness. For Peter one could speak of a primacy of pastoral leadership; for the BD it is a primacy of a discipleship of love and witness."[11]

A fourth group, composed mainly of Roman Catholics, sees John's portrayal of Peter in a positive light. R. Mahoney finds that John shows no major differences, much less rivalry, between Peter and the Beloved Disciple. If there is any contrast between them it exists at the level of discipleship.[12] Francis J. Moloney notes that, while there "can be little doubt that the Beloved Disciple provides the model for discipleship in the Johannine Church," Peter is still the primate: "There is enough evidence in the Johannine narrative to inform the reader that Simon Peter has a position of primacy in the hierarchy of Jesus' disciples." Even more, he concludes, the two are at least equal insofar as both are "those who have heard him."[13]

I find myself in the third group. My own reflections have led me to conclude that John's gospel highlights two main figures in the post-resurrection community: Peter and the Beloved Disciple. Both have pride of place, and the purposes both serve are at the service of one reality: remaining in the love that Jesus said would characterize his followers (13:35). The Beloved Disciple exemplifies this reality and patterns his behavior on it. Peter resists this reality and is never shown patterning his behavior on it. It is only in this added chapter that Peter seems to be transformed in love.

As Jesus' followers expressed their discipleship in the wider church, those claiming to be of the Petrine group and those identified with the Beloved Disciple found that they had increasing differences. Both claimed they were faithful to Jesus' intent. John wrote his gospel and accompanying letters to make it clear that a vibrant, unified church needed both dimensions. To have one approach without the other would be destructive not only of the church, but of the plan and prayer of Jesus himself. While deferring to Peter's place of primacy in the church, John highlighted the approach of the Beloved Disciple as the ideal. Defined by love, this approach was to take precedence over any other form for all members of the church—including its Petrine/Apostolic advocates. This is a major reason why we find John concerned with issues of discipleship rather than apostleship. All disciples are to witness to what authentic love is to be.[14]

Peter Returns to Fishing Only to Experience the Risen Jesus (21:1-14)

John's introduction to chapter 21 states: "Jesus showed himself again to the disciples by the Sea of Tiberias" (21:1). By naming the Sea of Tiberias, John aims to do two things. First, he wants the reader to recall another setting where food was multiplied and Peter's faith was tested (6:1-69). The allusion to chapter 6 evokes the memory of another affirmation of the real presence of Jesus in the community, again in the context of a meal (21:12-14).

Second, by mentioning the Sea of Tiberias, John seems to want to portray Peter as not having heard of the resurrection appearances of Jesus, much less having experienced them. John notes that, in the company of six other disciples (with two being unnamed), "Simon Peter said to them, 'I am going fishing'" (21:3a). Peter's words seem to indicate that he is unaware of the resurrection and so is returning to business as usual. He appears to have no other option but to return to the trade by which he made his living previous to meeting Jesus.[15] Without resurrection faith, what else is there to do? His fellow disciples found themselves in the same predicament. Thus, "They said to him, 'We will go with you.' They went out and got into the boat, but that night they caught nothing" (21:3b).

By saying they "got into the boat," John is creating another link with chapter 6. Here the "boat" describes something more than a vehicle used for fishing; it represents the community, particularly the community of the church. Peter is the one who organizes the group to do the fishing. However, the fact that this group lacks the real presence of Jesus is made clear by John's note that it was night and "that night they caught nothing." Without the experience of the presence of the risen Christ, nothing seems to work.

When Jesus made his "daybreak" appearance, the disciples did not know (*oida*) it was he (21:4). Responding to this stranger's invitation from the beach to "Cast the net to the right side of the boat, and you will find some [fish]," they threw their net. Now they were "not able to haul it in because there were so many fish" (21:5-6). This incident brings to mind an experience I had in Nicaragua.

The year was 1978. I was in a leadership position in my province which, since 1938, had ministered on the Caribbean side of Nicaragua in the State of Zelaya. Our men had developed a pastoral approach based on the Medellin Documents and the development of basic Christian communities. However, the regime of Anastasio Somoza felt threatened by the formation of community leaders. Catechists, delegates of the word, and deacons were often harassed; some even "disappeared." One of our friars who publicly challenged the system of Somocismo had to leave the country.

It seemed that all of the U.S.-born friars might be expelled. If they were expelled, it would end the Order in this part of Nicaragua. Now, in the darkness of this period, it became clear that something had to be done or the decades of labor would not continue to bear fruit. At the same time, it became even more clear that, if we wanted the Order to continue here in Nicaragua, the style of the missionary friars from the United States would have to change to allow for the formation of communal "holding environments" to attract young Nicaraguans to the Order.

A "Franciscan Week" meeting was called to discuss the issue. As it began, one could feel the tension among the men. They knew that, if a decision were made to create communities that would be able to receive the young men, some friars would have to leave their apostolic activity to enter formation work. Others would have to take their place or double up. On the first night, when the facilitator asked participants to name their hopes and fears, the fears outnumbered the dreams three to one!

As the days progressed, it seemed that almost every time the group got close to deciding to make the move, one or another friar would find a way to derail the action. One friar in particular seemed to find very creative ways of doing this. Such were the dynamics until mid-week when the friars were given this scripture passage from John for their reflection.

After a half-hour of private prayer the group returned to do faith-sharing around the passage. After some had spoken, "Father Bonaventure" shared his insight. The gist of his words was something like this:

"You know that I have been resisting what's being discussed these days. But I have been doing this because I somehow assumed that this meant we haven't been doing a good job all these years and I know we have. I thought people were saying we were being stupid for fishing all night and for not getting any human catch for the Order. I know that we've all tried. However, as I tried to imagine myself in the boat fishing all night and my frustration increased, I heard Jesus calling to me—and to the rest of us in this boat—'Lads, you have no fish, have you?' We've had some, but they've all gotten away, so we too have had to answer, 'No.'

"But then," he said, "I heard Jesus simply say, 'Cast the net to the other side of the boat and you will find some.' He didn't stand there telling us how stupid we were, that we had been doing things all wrong, that we had fished all night in vain, that we hadn't done any good. All he said was that it's time to throw the net on the other side. I'm ready to do that. And if we do this together, I think we will be very blessed."

After hearing his faith-sharing, the entire group was ready to throw its net to the other side. A whole new direction for the pastoral presence of the North American Capuchins in Nicaragua was embraced. And, in a short time, it became clear that the Order was being "implanted" in Nicaragua. The numbers are nothing like the "so many fish" that "they were not able to haul" in, but they are enough to sustain day breaking forth from the night (see 21:6).

With the original experience of the huge catch, "that disciple whom Jesus loved said to Peter, 'It is the Lord!'" (21:7a). Again, as at the tomb, this disciple rather than Peter was the one who understood the implications of what had happened. Peter and this disciple had run to the tomb together. Yet, while both entered and saw, only the Beloved Disciple "saw and believed" (20:3-8). Now, although Peter and the "disciple whom Jesus loved" are in the boat, only the Beloved Disciple recognizes the real presence of the risen Jesus in the multiplication of the fish.

Upon hearing the Beloved Disciple proclaim, "It is the Lord," Simon Peter "put on some clothes, for he was naked, and jumped into the sea"

(21:7b). This detail about Peter's clothing—or, more accurately, the lack
of it—might make one ask: Why does John provide such a detail related
to Peter's nakedness? I've read all sorts of commentaries on this. Some
take the passage literally: Peter's honor demanded that he clothe himself.
Others speculate as to why he would dress and jump into the water when
everyone else would undress to enter the water. Still others, building on
Peter's image presented in the Synoptics, stress his impulsiveness. None
have satisfied me, especially since I know that John's images always
mean more than they appear to mean. I get some glimpse of what John
might have been symbolically communicating by Peter's nakedness when
I recall my own reaction to someone I had betrayed.

The first and immediate (and, therefore, impulsive) normal human reaction of one who has publicly abandoned and betrayed or openly denied
and deserted a close companion, not to speak of one considered a Teacher
and Lord (13:13), is shame. When shame overwhelms someone, the first
impulse is to want to hide, to cover up. This is particularly so in a culture
in which relationships are defined by bonds of honor and shame. By denying any connection to Jesus, Simon Peter had dishonored himself more
than Jesus. By being ashamed to publicly identify himself as a one of
Jesus' disciples (18:17, 25, 27), Simon Peter had exposed himself to
ridicule by others as well as rejection by Jesus. It's little wonder, then, that
he would be ashamed of himself. In general, the first reaction of someone
who is ashamed is to hide. Simon Peter, who is "naked," needs to "cover
up." Thus, John tells us, the embarrassed one "put on some clothes."

In a wonderful study of this passage (21:7-8), D. H. Gee offers various reasons why the traditional notions connected with Peter's impulsive
reaction to the presence of Jesus don't seem to work. After spending six
pages offering exegetical reasons to support what I've noted here from
my own personal experience, Gee concludes:

> Peter sprang into the water when he heard it was the Lord, be-
> cause he was ashamed and did not wish to face him. He took his
> upper garment because, whatever means he might adopt to avoid
> the encounter, he would need his clothes. He skulked in the water
> while the others came in the boat, dragging the net behind them,
> and gathered round the fire; but yet he could not bring himself to
> swim away, when his chance to do so came as the boat was
> beached. As in the courtyard of Annas he kept his distance; he
> could neither bring himself to approach Jesus, nor could he bring
> himself to leave.[16]

Gee's points are well taken, especially if we accept the fact that chapter 21 may have been an independent tradition detailing the first resurrection experience of Peter with Jesus.

I have a vivid memory of my own experience of what Peter must have felt that morning. My memory has to do with how an invitation to breakfast offered the possibility of a new way of relating.

When I was a junior in high school, I belonged to a "gang" that had no name. We did, however, have our regular rituals. For example, when we got together, we would invariably go to Bob Kremer's house and make plans there. We were allowed there any night of the week between 6:45 and 7:30. There was no need to call, because the ritual was a nightly one; it never changed.

One Tuesday morning at breakfast, before my mother left to teach, I asked her if I might use her car the following night.

"What for?" Mother asked.

"Well, you know I'm in charge of planning the Junior Prom this year. So a bunch of us are going to meet at Terry Kohlman's house to start figuring out what we might do."

"At Terry Kohlman's?"

"Yes," I responded.

My home town was Fond du Lac, Wisconsin. It is midway between Milwaukee and Green Bay, about 65 miles from each. Highway 41 serves as a kind of beltway around a good portion of the city. I lived inside the beltway; Terry lived on a farm on the other side of Highway 41.

"You're not going anywhere else, are you?" my mother asked.

"No, just to Terry's house."

"Okay," she responded.

Late the next afternoon, after my mother returned from school, I started getting some phone calls.

"Why are you getting all those calls?" Mother asked, aware that our nightly ritual never involved the telephone.

"Well, the guys know we're going to Terry's house, so they want to make sure I'm going to pick them up so I can get them there."

"Why aren't they going to Bob Kremer's like every other time and why aren't you picking them up there as usual?

"Because Terry lives on the other side of Highway 41 and they want to make sure I'm getting the car."

"Are you sure you're not going to do something else? Are you telling me the truth?"

"Mother, of course I'm telling you the truth. Why can't you ever trust me?"

"Well, it sounds a little fishy to me, that's all. But you can take the car."

I left the house and took her 1952 Chevy coupe to Bob Kremer's house. There everyone was ready. We got into the car and drove to Harry Zeim's grocery store on the corner of 6th and Park Avenue. There we bought our beer and then "liberated" the Pall Malls. I served as lookout

for the latter operation. Somehow I distinguished between the act of stealing and merely serving as the sentinel. It also seemed okay to smoke
them; you just couldn't steal them. Once we got the beer and the ciga-
rettes, we returned to the car, disconnected the speedometer (which could
be done in those days), and drove to Green Bay where we watched our
friends play a basketball game against Premontre High School. On our return, with only a mile left on Highway 41, I got picked up for speeding.
And, because I was underage, I needed a parent go to court with me. My
father, who was an insurance claimsman, was often away for extended
periods, so I had to tell my mother what had happened.

"I got into some trouble," I said as I checked in with her after arriving home.

"Are you okay? What happened?"

"Well, I was coming home from Terry Kohlman's house," I said,
"and a mile out on 41 I got picked up for speeding. And you or Dad have
to come with me to court when I appear."

"You were coming home from Terry's house?"

"Yes, and I got caught for speeding. And you've got to come with me
to court."

"From Terry's house?"

"Yes."

"Well, go to bed. We'll talk about it in the morning."

Needless to say, I did not sleep well that night, trying to figure out
how I could avoid seeing her in the morning. When morning did come, I
heard the familiar call:

"Mike, it's time to get up."

"Okay, I'll be right down," I answered, but I knew full well I would
not go downstairs while she was there, even if it meant missing school
that day.

Five minutes later came another call and another response from me.
This was followed by one more call, and a reminder that breakfast was
getting cold. "I'll be right there," I said as I stayed right there in my bed.

A few minutes later, my mother came to my room and sat on my bed.
"Okay, Mike," she said: "Why don't you tell me what really happened
last night?"

I told her the essential facts: that we had disconnected her speedometer and gone to Green Bay for the game.

At that, she gave me a kind of love-tap on the side of the head and
said, "I'm glad you weren't afraid to tell me the truth. Now come down
and have a good breakfast."

Exegetes write about why Jesus, who already had fish on the grill,
would ask the disciples if they had any fish. Raymond Brown and others
can write about Peter's rehabilitation in this scene. For me, however, it is

about more than this. What Jesus' words, "Come and have breakfast," imply for me is a unique form of reconciliation and even communion with another who has been alienated because of one's self-imposed shame due to personal betrayals and denials. The word *aristan* means to "eat breakfast." Such a meal entails the kind of restoration to relationship that liberates you from your shame and frees you from your guilt. It also invites you to begin a new, restored, re-established friendship. If the denial took place around a charcoal fire, it is around a charcoal fire that the reconciliation can take place as well. It is at a meal that Jesus forgives us who repent. The breakfast, the meal, is what takes away the sin. It is in this context, then, that we can move to the second of the three main parts of this chapter.

The Threefold Love Request (21:15-19)

After describing the breakfast of reconciling communion between Simon Peter and Jesus, John elaborates on the threefold interchange between the two. Each step of the interchange involves three movements: Jesus' question about Peter's love, Peter's response assuring Jesus of his love and, finally, Jesus' authoritative command to Peter to care for the lambs/sheep (21:15-17). The triad of triads begins with Jesus' opening question to Peter. It is meant to remind us of Peter's earlier call to discipleship (1:40-42). "When they had finished breakfast, Jesus said to Simon Peter, 'Simon son of John, do you love me *more than these?*'" (21:15a). Who or what are the "these"?

The Greek word for "these" (*toutōn*) can be masculine or neuter. While Jesus may be asking "Do you love me more than you love these others?" or "Do you love me more than you love these other things (such as fishing)?" his question is more likely "Do you love me more than the other disciples do?" Peter's response is not that he loves Jesus "more than the other disciples do." Humbled by his earlier shame, Peter simply responds: "Yes, Lord; you know that I love you" (21:15b). The author, reflecting the love of the community of the Beloved Disciple, knows that Peter's love can be no match for that of the Beloved One; thus Peter's honesty in his unwillingness to say that he can do what he can't.

Returning to a theme developed in the first chapter, the notion of the "bottom line," Jesus is now asking Peter about his bottom line. To whom or to what is he ultimately oriented? Forgetting the past, what will be the basic priority of his life now, and for the future?

Many exegetes and even more popular preachers interpret the threefold dialog in this section (21:15-17) by comparing it with the threefold denial of Jesus by Peter in the courtyard of Annas (18:15-18, 25-27). Linking the two scenes leads them to see this story as having to do with reconciliation. The fact that both take place around a charcoal fire seems to support their rationale (18:18, 25 and 21:9).

However, as noted above, it was in the section immediately before this (21:1-14) that reconciliation took place. The breakfast itself was the reconciliation. What follows in the threefold challenge-response-command in 21:15-19 must therefore be something more.

We could perhaps get some insight into what this "something more" might be by taking a closer look at Peter's threefold denial of Jesus. First of all, it took place in the courtyard of the deposed high priest (18:15). Second, it involved a public witness in which he refused to acknowledge his identification with Jesus (18:17, 25, 27). Finally, its threefold expression indicated an absolute rejection of being connected to Jesus Christ in any way. If this is what is involved in this denial, its opposite at the Sea of Tiberias cannot be just the "rehabilitation" that many scripture scholars imply.

While I would agree with the statement of Peter Ellis that "this triple commissioning of ch. 21 may reflect Peter's triple denial of Jesus in ch. 18,"[17] I would add that, instead of the "Peter, do you love me" simply counterbalancing the earlier denial, the whole passage (do you love me, you know that I love you, feed my sheep/lambs) is meant to make sure that Peter's triple commission will always be as grounded in love as the earlier denial was grounded in fear. Only this kind of love will drive out fear (1 Jn 4:18). If once, in the context of a meal, Peter strongly proclaimed a loyalty only to disclaim it when he was challenged, now, forgiven in another meal, his embrace of Jesus must imply a following that will take him where he would not go but where he must remain in order to maintain his fidelity. Where once Peter's denial and renunciation of Jesus separated him from Jesus, now his profession and annunciation of him will identify him as a true witness. Because he faced Jesus in his embarrassment and shame for disowning him, he can now be honored by being welcomed back as a true witness. If once he repudiated Jesus and disavowed any connection to him, now he must acknowledge and testify on his behalf. Because he had retracted his promise to be willing to lay down his life for Jesus (13:37), now his promise of love for Jesus must include a sharing of that love with Jesus' other disciples that will lead him, as it led Jesus, to the cross (21:18-19). Thus, building on the knowing and doing of chapter 13, Peter is transformed for service when he finally can say to Jesus: "Lord you know everything; you know that I love you" (21:17).

Many have made much of the different Greek words for "love" (*agapan* and *philein*) used by Jesus and Peter, the different words for "know" used by Peter (*oida* and *ginōskein*), and Jesus' different words for tending and feeding (*boskein* and *poimainein*) the lambs and sheep (*arnion* and *probaton*). It seems that all are used interchangeably—here as throughout John's gospel. In other words, the triad is not meant to be analyzed in terms of the different meanings and implications of words. It is, instead, quite straightforward: a question is asked by Jesus, an answer is given by Peter, and a command is given Peter by Jesus, the chief shepherd.

By using a threefold question, response, and commission, John is suggesting that a whole new reality is now being established. Not only does the threefold dynamic describe a newly-constituted relationship between Jesus and Peter, but, as Jerome Neyrey notes, John uses the ritual of the meal and the repartee to indicate a changed role for Peter as well. It is a transformation of status bestowed on Peter by the one who has questioned him and to whom he has responded.[18]

From this perspective, Peter is not given a position—as would be the interpretation of those of the Petrine group—as much as a program. If he is to have any power, authority, or prestige in the wider community among the sheep, he cannot stand on status. His call must be fulfilled by his fidelity. In the exchange, Jesus is not just giving a commission to Peter. He is changing Peter's very status by empowering him to do what Jesus has declared to be core to his mission. Jesus' ultimate charge to Peter is not a role but a responsibility. In imitation of Jesus, the good shepherd (10:15), Peter is to feed the flock by being willing to lay down his life (21:18-19). Once, he did not "know" what Jesus was doing during the meal at the Last Supper; now he has been forgiven at another meal, the Resurrection Breakfast. This demands that he make Jesus' example his own. He is to feed the flock in the way Jesus did—not by restricting them access to the meal but by using it as a sign of their reconciliation.[19] As Neyrey notes, Jesus

> addresses Peter in a way that signals a radical transformation of his status. Readers know that Peter failed thrice in loyalty (13:38; 18:17, 25-27). Despite his claims to the contrary (13:36-38), he has been presented neither as "noble" nor as "shepherd" but as a hireling or sheep. Now Jesus questions Peter, and in doing so transforms his status to that of loving/loyal disciple and publicly acknowledges his role as shepherd.

Question:	Answer:	Status Transformation:
"Simon, son of John, do you love me more than these?" (21:15a, 16a, 17a)	"Yes, Lord; you know that I love you." (21:15b, 16b, 17b)	"Feed my lambs" "Tend my sheep" "Feed my sheep" (21:15c, 16c, 17c)

This Gospel labors to affirm that Peter finally becomes the group's shepherd. Through ritual loyalty oaths, the status transformation of Peter is accomplished. Jesus himself acknowledges

it as he invests Peter with the role and status of Shepherd of all
the sheep ("Feed my lambs...Feed my sheep"). It is now legiti-
mate for Peter to act as "shepherd."[20]

The fact that the Johannine Peter now is legitimated as shepherd does
not mean that the other disciples or all the sheep are somehow to be sub-
ordinated to Peter in the legalistic sense found in Matthew. Rather, his authority as shepherd is to be one of "pastoral ministry to the already existing flock of Christ."[21] Having denied Jesus earlier (18:17, 25, 27) and
now having been reconciled to Jesus (21:12-13), Peter is ready to turn
around his life on behalf of the very sheep that were the objects of Jesus'
love. Only now, like the Beloved Disciple, his presence to the sheep must
mirror the way of love first shown by the one who alone is the good shepherd. He is called to imitate the good shepherd rather than the hired hand
who would flee when he sees the wolf coming (10:12). Like all the other
disciples, Peter too must come under the authority of the one teacher, the
Paraclete who will remain in the community forever within everyone who
loves Jesus and keeps his commandments (14:15-17); only this one will
be the "guide...into all the truth" (16:13).[22]
    In the face of the increasing emphasis on Peter, almost to the point of
making him more important than Jesus, all (including members of the
Petrine and Apostolic group) must never forget that, if Peter's pastoral
role is to be forever, Peter must always remember that the sheep are not
and will never be *his* flock; they belong to Jesus: "Feed *my* lambs"
(21:15), "Tend *my* sheep" (21:16), "Feed *my* sheep" (21:17). Or, as Raymond Brown, the only biblical scholar to serve on the Pontifical Biblical
Commission in the late 1990s, wrote before his death in 1998:

> As shepherd, Peter's authority is not absolute. Jesus is the model
> shepherd to whom the Father has given the sheep and no one can
> take them from him. They remain his even when he entrusts their
> care to Peter: "Feed my sheep."...[or] "Tend my sheep as mine,
> not as yours." Thus, one cannot think of Peter's replacing Jesus
> as the shepherd of the sheep. Once again I Peter (v 2-4) is har-
> monious with Johannine thought about shepherding: the flock of
> God has been given into the charge of Christian elders who are
> shepherds over it, but Jesus remains the chief shepherd (see also
> I Pet ii 25).[23]

If my theses about this chapter in John are correct—that the breakfast
meal on the shore is the moment of reconciliation between Jesus and
Peter and that the threefold denial of love has its counterpart in the threefold commission grounded in love—then the dynamics that take place in

chapter 21 involve much more than a simple "rehabilitation" of Peter. I find an evolution in Simon Peter from entrenchment to pastoral engagement, from religious resistance to acceptance of responsibility. While he was entrenched in his absolutes, Peter abdicated his responsibility to profess his connectedness to Jesus when the chips were down. In the process he became estranged from Jesus. Realizing that he would have to face the risen Jesus caused him deep embarrassment. He was liberated from his shame by Jesus' invitation to a meal; the sharing of that breakfast effected reconciliation. His entrenched ideas about roles had made him resist the foot washing, and his failure to admit his connection with Jesus had ruptured their relationship. Now, in the embrace of love, not only was he restored, but his very status was transformed. In the midst of the other disciples, Peter was empowered with a new role: he was to feed the community through the exercise of a pastoral authority that would not divide the flock but ensure its unity. Where once his role had been that of someone who makes promises but can't deliver, now his promise of love, grounded in Jesus' transforming words, would enable him to accept responsibility for the flock, even to the point of manifesting his love by laying down his life.

The whole process of Peter's movement from entrenchment to engagement:

ENTRENCHMENT   ESCAPE   ESTRANGEMENT   EMBARRASSMENT   EMBRACEMENT   ENGAGEMENT

and from resistance to responsibility:

RESISTANCE   RUPTURE   REPENTANCE   RECONCILIATION   RESTORATION   RESPONSIBILITY

serves as a model for everyone willing to follow Jesus to places where they would not go, even if this be to the cross itself.

Rather than providing some kind of scriptural grounding for Peter's status or authoritative office, verses 1-19 of this chapter highlight the role of Peter as representative of the process through which every believing disciple must pass if we are to be faithful to Jesus' words: "Follow me" (21:19). We too must free ourselves of our entrenched ideas and ideologies, including religious ones, that estrange us from Jesus Christ. If we are embarrassed because we have denied Jesus, we can embrace him again and be empowered, as was Peter, with the strength and courage to feed the flock ourselves.

In his reflections on this passage (including verses 20-25 which I reserve for consideration in the next and final chapters), Timothy Wiarda insists that the text of chapter 21 *"is more a vivid account of human experience than a collection of symbolic ecclesiastical statements."*[24] Seen in this light, Peter is more a model of all struggling believers than an authority figure to be used by contemporary religious leaders to preserve their control. Wiarda goes on to note that, rather than to highlight any articulation of Peter that isolates him from the community, *the writer's chief purpose in this narrative is to teach discipleship.*[25] If this is true, then, like Peter, we too will have to face those areas where we resist submitting to Jesus' way of discipleship. We too will have to admit where we have ruptured our relationship with him—often in promoting dysfunctional religious patterns. We will need to repent of our ways and be reconciled with Jesus anew, so that we might be restored to our resurrection faith in a way that will enable us to follow him, even to the cross itself.

Such is the model of discipleship everyone in the Petrine Community and the Community of the Beloved Disciple must never forget. It is a model that is particularly important for those ecclesiastical leaders who might be tempted to forget that this chapter's stress is on discipleship. As Kevin Quast has written, "the church is to consist of those who have decided, out of their love for him, to follow Jesus. This particularly applies to those who are in positions of authority in the church."[26]

The status transformation of Peter has implications for religious leaders who identify with him. Religious leadership means being engaged by Jesus with responsibility for feeding Jesus' flock; it means translating the very pattern of Jesus' life into one's own. By being willing to follow Jesus in this way, even to the cross, Peter now is assured that he can be the good, the noble shepherd:

> "Very truly, I tell you, when you were younger, you used to fasten your own belt and to go wherever you wished [mirroring the entrenched portrayal of Peter and resistance to be defined by Jesus]. But when you grow old, you will stretch out your hands, and someone else will fasten a belt around you and take you where you do not wish to go." (He said this to indicate the kind of death by which he would glorify God.) After this he said to him, "Follow me." (21:18-19)

Until this point in the gospel, Peter had often failed in his following of Jesus. Now he is empowered to be a faithful disciple of Jesus to the end. In the process he will become wholly clean, a transformed person. His divinely authorized pastoral function is to feed the sheep, to care for them, even to the point of laying down his life for them.

THIRTEEN

IF IT IS MY WILL
THAT THIS ONE REMAIN UNTIL I COME,
WHAT IS THAT TO YOU? (21:22)

The Question of John 21:20-25

In John's gospel both the first words of Jesus and his last appear as questions. At the end of the gospel we learn that Peter has been told he must be willing to be led by forces beyond his control—even to his death—if he is to faithfully follow Jesus (21:18-19). At this, Peter "turned and saw the disciple whom Jesus loved following them." So he said, "Lord, what about him?" (21:21). Jesus' response is a stinging riposte: "If it is my will" that this one[1] "remain (*menein*) until I come, what is that to you? Follow me!" (21:22).

At the time of the final redaction of John's gospel, unlike today, controversy revolved not so much around the identity and function of the Beloved Disciple as around the Beloved Disciple's death. The confusion seems to have arisen from the need to balance Jesus' words about the Beloved Disciple remaining "until I come" with the reality that the Beloved One had died. Trying to address this dilemma, the author noted: "So the rumor spread in the community that this disciple would not die. Yet Jesus did not say to him that he would not die, but, 'If it is my will that this one remain until I come, what is that to you?'" (21:23).

In this final chapter, I will discuss the Beloved Disciple and what Jesus' words about this one remaining "until I come" might mean for us contemporary disciples. Simply stated, because I view the Beloved Disciple as a representative figure primarily meant by the author to characterize authentic following of Jesus, the reason why "this one" will "remain until I come" is that each of us and our communities of faith are to find our identity and purpose in the model of "this one" in every place and every age "until" Jesus returns in glory. How I have reached this conclusion and the implications of faithfully identifying with "this one" in a wider church dominated by a Petrine imperative will be addressed in this chapter.

The Scriptural Sources Identifying the Beloved Disciple

To grasp what the Beloved Disciple meant in the early church and what the Beloved Disciple might mean to the contemporary church, we must consider the sources. A formal mention of this figure occurs in five places, with two less clear additional references. In every one of the five (or seven) passages, the Beloved Disciple is somehow juxtaposed with Peter and, in every one, comes off far more positively. Raymond Brown has declared: "Such contrasts cannot be accidental, especially since in several scenes John seems to have added the Beloved Disciple to establish the contrast."[2] Since this seems to be the case, the question as to why the Beloved Disciple is contrasted with Peter must be examined in light of dynamics taking place among the early Christian communities.

Let us begin by examining the scriptural references to the "disciple whom Jesus loved."

The Five Explicit References to the Beloved Disciple

In the five explicit references to the Beloved Disciple, all but the first refer to this one as *the disciple* whom Jesus loved (19:26; 20:2; 21:7; 21:20). The first simply refers to "one of his disciples—the one whom Jesus loved"(13:23). With this nuance, we can examine the context and reference for the term as used by the Johannine writer.

1. John 13:23 within 13:21-26

After saying this [regarding the need to follow Jesus' example by washing each other's feet] Jesus was troubled in spirit, and declared, "Very truly, I tell you, one of you will betray me." The disciples looked at one another, uncertain of whom he was speaking. *One of his disciples—the one whom Jesus loved—was reclining next to him.* Simon Peter therefore motioned to him to ask Jesus of whom he was speaking. So while reclining next to Jesus, he asked him, "Lord, who is it?" Jesus answered, "It is the one to whom I give this piece of bread when I have dipped it in the dish." So when he had dipped the piece of bread, he gave it to Judas son of Simon Iscariot . . .

In this first reference, the intimacy of the Beloved Disciple is contrasted with the ignorance of Peter. Peter, the spokesperson of the group, must ask the Beloved Disciple to find out from Jesus the identity of his betrayer. For readers used to seeing Peter as the intermediary between Jesus and the disciples, John makes it clear here that Peter needs an intermediary to understand what Jesus is talking about.

The text gives us no indication that when the one who rested on Jesus' bosom discovered who the betrayer was he communicated his knowledge to Peter. The author seems to be making two points: (1) The Beloved Disciple was closer to Jesus, not just physically, but intimately (he was reclining "next to" Jesus). He was "at the bosom" of Jesus. (2) The Beloved Disciple was the one to whom Jesus communicated his deepest thoughts. Not all of these were to be shared with Peter. Thus, whether through intimacy with Jesus or the sharing of information, the Beloved Disciple overshadows Peter, even if Peter is spokesperson for the core group of disciples.

2. John 19:26 within 19:25b-27

Meanwhile, standing near the cross of Jesus were his mother, and his mother's sister, Mary the wife of Clopas, and Mary Magdalene. *When Jesus saw his mother and the disciple whom he loved standing beside her, he said to his mother, "Woman, here is your son." Then he said to the disciple, "Here is your mother." And from that hour the disciple took her into his own home.*

This is the only passage which identifies the Beloved Disciple without any direct reference to Peter. The reason should be clear: Peter has not just denied Jesus, he is nowhere to be found at the time when Jesus is laying down his life—even though Peter had stated that he was willing to lay down his own life for Jesus (13:36-37). At the cross, it is the Beloved Disciple who "remains with" Jesus. Peter has separated himself from the side of Jesus.

From Jesus' earliest appearance in John's gospel, "remaining with" Jesus defines discipleship (1:35-39). For those used to interpreting this passage in a way that highlights the mother of Jesus, it is clear that it is the Beloved Disciple, not Peter, who has been chosen to make a dwelling for her. She is to "remain with" him, not with Peter and not even with Jesus' "brothers" (2:12; 7:3, 5, 10). Jesus' alter-ego with his mother is to be not Peter or those who once constituted Jesus' family, but the Beloved One. As Jesus' words from the cross to his mother and the Beloved One make clear, "remaining with" Jesus will now be defined more in terms of relationships than of blood. In the Spirit flowing from the side of Jesus (19:30-37), a new family—of those who believe in him and his name—is created. In this sense, Mary is much more the mother of the church of the Beloved Disciple than of the Petrine Church.

3. John 20:2 within 20:1-10

Early on the first day of the week, while it was still dark, Mary
Magdalene came to the tomb and saw that the stone had been removed from the tomb. *So she ran and went to Simon Peter and
the other disciple, the one whom Jesus loved, and said to them,
"They have taken the Lord out of the tomb, and we do not know
where they have laid him."* Then Peter and the other disciple set
out and went toward the tomb. The two were running together,
but the other disciple outran Peter and reached the tomb first. He
bent down to look in and saw the linen wrappings lying there,
but he did not go in. Then Simon Peter came, following him, and
went into the tomb. He saw the linen wrappings lying there, and
the cloth that had been on Jesus' head, not lying with the linen
wrappings but rolled up in a place by itself. *Then the other disciple, who reached the tomb first, also went in, and he saw and believed*; for as yet they did not understand the scripture, that he
must rise from the dead. Then the disciples returned to their
homes.

This passage revolves around a quest. According to John Painter, it is
the first quest since chapter 4 of John's gospel that does not involve some
kind of rejection.[3] It is also one of the most subtle depictions of the
Beloved Disciple eclipsing Peter.

Upon hearing Mary Magdalene's announcement about the empty
tomb, Peter and the Beloved Disciple both run to the tomb. The Beloved
Disciple outruns Peter. Here, in a sense, it is Peter who follows the
Beloved One, not the other way around. However, in an image of clear
deference to Peter, the Beloved Disciple—who has already looked into
the tomb—waits for him. When Peter arrives, he goes in and sees the images that indicate that Jesus is not there: the linen wrappings are lying
there and the cloth that had been on Jesus' head is rolled up separately.
Then the Beloved Disciple goes in and, having seen the same things Peter
has seen, believes.

In contrasting the three different words used in the text for "seeing,"
Arthur Maynard shows the Beloved One's vision to be superior to
Peter's: "These three words for seeing have been used with strict respect
for their variant shades of meaning. Before he enters the tomb the other
disciple 'sees' in a general sense, Peter when he enters only 'observes' the
physical scene, but the BD [Beloved Disciple] upon entering 'sees with
spiritual insight' and the result is faith."[4] At the tomb Peter only finds absence; the Beloved Disciple is first in faith in the Risen One.

4. John 21:7 within 21:4-8

Just after daybreak, Jesus stood on the beach; but the disciples
did not know that it was Jesus. Jesus said to them, "Children, you
have no fish, have you?" They answered him, "No." He said to
them, "Cast the net to the right side of the boat, and you will find
some." So they cast it, and now they were not able to haul it in
because there were so many fish. *That disciple whom Jesus loved
said to Peter, "It is the Lord!"* When Simon Peter heard that it
was the Lord, he put on some clothes, for he was naked, and
jumped into the sea. But the other disciples came in the boat,
dragging the net full of fish, for they were not far from the land,
only about a hundred yards off.

In this final resurrection appearance, Peter is once again contrasted
with the Beloved Disciple. Peter, who seems to have returned to his former ways before this encounter with Jesus on the shore, is unable to recognize the real presence of Jesus. The Beloved Disciple, who has accompanied Peter, is the one who witnesses to Peter that the one on the shore is
"the Lord." This is the second time that Peter's way of seeing is an obstacle to the expression of faith.

As the Beloved Disciple, in contrast to Peter, was the first to believe at the empty tomb, so in this scene it is this one again who utters
the proclamation that Jesus is risen: "It is the Lord!" The Johannine author makes it a point to note that the Beloved Disciple is the one disciple who must inform the unknowing Peter. Whether first to believe or
first to proclaim belief in the real presence of the risen Lord, the
Beloved Disciple not only outruns Peter; he outstrips in faith the acknowledged, yet naked, leader of the community of believers identified
with him.[5]

5. John 21:20 within 21:20-23

*Peter turned and saw the disciple whom Jesus loved following
them; he was the one who had reclined next to Jesus at the supper and had said, "Lord, who is it that is going to betray you?"*
When Peter saw him, he said to Jesus, "Lord, what about him?"
Jesus said to him, "If it is my will that he remain until I come,
what is that to you? Follow me!" So the rumor spread in the
community that this disciple would not die. Yet Jesus did not say
to him that he would not die, but "If it is my will that he remain
until I come, what is that to you?'

Having just proclaimed the kind of death Peter will experience and, indeed, how his death will involve a kind of crucifixion (which had occurred by the time of the final editing), John indicates Peter's own recognition and realization of the Beloved Disciple's significance for the future followers of Jesus. Hearing about his fate, he asks Jesus: "Lord, what about him?" Not only does Jesus declare that it just might possibly be his "will that he remain" until Jesus comes, he challenges the basis of Peter's question with his riposte: "What is that to you?" (21:22).

Acknowledging the discipleship of this one who has remained with him, Jesus now simply commands Peter to be faithful in terms used by the Synoptics to define discipleship: "Follow me" (21:22). This command becomes all the more an imperative in light of the fact that it was this same Peter who, in spite of the fact that he had sworn that his following of Jesus would be to the point of laying down his life (13:36-37), tried to save his skin later by denying Jesus.

The Two Possible References to the Beloved Disciple

1. John 1:37 and 40 within 1:35-42

The next day John again was standing with two of his disciples, and as he watched Jesus walk by, he exclaimed, "Look, here is the Lamb of God!" *The two disciples heard him say this, and they followed Jesus.* When Jesus turned and saw them following, he said to them, "What are you looking for?" They said to him, "Rabbi" (which translated means Teacher), "where are you staying?" He said to them, "Come and see." They came and saw where he was staying, and they remained with him that day. It was about four o'clock in the afternoon. *One of the two who heard John speak and followed him was Andrew, Simon Peter's brother.* He first found his brother Simon and said to him, "We have found the Messiah" (which is translated Anointed). He brought Simon to Jesus, who looked at him and said, "You are Simon son of John. You are to be called Cephas" (which is translated Peter).

According to the evangelist, two of the Baptizer's disciples *followed* Jesus to "remain with" him. Only one of them gets named—Andrew. The other remains anonymous. In the opinion of many, this anonymity contributes to the possibility that this other disciple may have been the Beloved.

After these two come and "remain with" Jesus to create the core of the newly-forming community, Andrew tells Simon Peter about Jesus. In this version, unlike the Synoptics which stress the Petrine/Apostolic image of the church, Simon is not even "called" by Jesus, but by Andrew.

Furthermore, unlike the Synoptic version, the anonymous (Beloved?) disciple, not Peter, is the first to embrace discipleship. It is this disciple, not Peter, who has been with Jesus from the beginning. Having been with him from the beginning, he loves until the end (see 13:1).

Also, with regard to Simon's being called "Cephas" or "Peter" (1:42), unlike the Synoptics who make of this name change a basis of Peter's primacy, John uses it to indicate Peter's rock-like density.

2. *John 18:15-16 within 18:15-18*

> *Simon Peter and another disciple followed Jesus. Since that disciple was known to the high priest, he went with Jesus into the courtyard of the high priest, but Peter was standing outside the gate. So the other disciple, who was known to the high priest, went out, spoke to the woman who guarded the gate, and brought Peter in.* The woman said to Peter, "You are not also one of this man's disciples, are you?" He said, "I am not." Now the slaves and the police had made a charcoal fire because it was cold, and they were standing around it and warming themselves. Peter also was standing with them and warming himself.

While some dispute whether the anonymous disciple in John 1:35-42 can be linked with the Beloved Disciple, an increasing number of exegetes identify the "other disciple" in the courtyard with Peter as the Beloved One.[6] This certainly seems clear from even a cursory examination of the authors considered in the previous chapter on this section of John's gospel. The Beloved Disciple is described as the leader; Peter follows. This disciple is the one who leads Peter; he brings Peter into the courtyard. This disciple evidences no fear in being identified with Jesus; in fact, he is "known to the high priest" as a disciple. In contrast, when queried about his discipleship by a woman (someone who in that society had absolutely no social standing), Peter can only say in fear: "I am not" (18:17).

Having examined the passages that directly and indirectly mention the Beloved Disciple, it seems quite safe to conclude that, for the Johannine community, Peter and the Beloved Disciple were the two most prominent disciples of Jesus. At the same time, it also seems equally safe to conclude that the latter was closer to Jesus than Peter, especially in terms of the Johannine sense of discipleship as "remaining with" Jesus in love. This Beloved One has always remained in that love. Peter, who failed miserably, can only make a promise to love in the future. History shows he was faithful to his final promise. The gospel shows the Beloved Disciple was faithful from the first.

Who Was/Is the Beloved Disciple?

Volumes have been and continue to be written about the identity of and Johannine purpose for the Beloved Disciple. None has been proffered without some controversy. Hence, any approach to the question of this disciple's identity and role will be speculative at best. Yet this does not mean that an effort to investigate this issue has no value. It is my contention that it has great value, especially for contemporary readers. In fact, it is almost mandatory and certainly critical for contemporary readers if we are to correct present church patterns of institutionalization and clericalization that have arisen from an understanding (which often is ideologically-oriented) of what it means to be a community identified with Jesus in what we now call "church."

Much of the confusion related to the identity of the Beloved Disciple—in early times as well as now—seems to arise from an assumption that the gospel never verifies or denies. The author says that Jesus' statement about the Beloved Disciple remaining until he was to come gave rise to a "rumor...in the community that this disciple would not die" (21:23a). This passage has been interpreted by exegetes in various ways. The most common interpretation is that this one died, leaving the community confused about the consequences for disciples who identified with the Beloved Disciple. However, 21:23 does not say that the Beloved Disciple actually died. As John Breck notes, verse 23 "does imply that this disciple is not longer alive; yet that is a supposition based on inference and is not clearly stated."[7] In my mind this is critical in our determining the identity of the Beloved Disciple and, more important, John's understanding of the function of the Beloved Disciple in the wider church. It is to this task that I now turn: Who was/is the Beloved Disciple?

The theories can be reduced to three possibilities: the Beloved Disciple was (1) a historical figure (such as John the Apostle, John the Evangelist, the Samaritan woman, or Lazarus);[8] (2) a historical figure who also was meant to be an ideal for the Christian community; and 3) an ideal figure representative of the community itself. Each of these possibilities needs to be considered if we are going to understand the implications of the Beloved One for faith in the church today.

The Beloved Disciple as a Historical Figure

That John's gospel fails to give any name to the disciple whom Jesus loved is considered by some to indicate that the first readers of the gospel knew the identity of this person and that, therefore, this person was a definite historical figure. In addition, the final verses in the fourth gospel have led many to believe that, by the time it received its present form, both Peter and the Beloved Disciple had died. This created a kind of crisis for both groupings of disciples who had identified themselves with these historical personages.

Two specific texts in the gospel have led many to believe the Beloved Disciple was an actual person. The first occurs as an aside by the author after the description of the blood and water that flowed from the side of the crucified Jesus. We read: "He who saw this has testified so that you [the audience/the reader] also may believe. His testimony is true, and he knows that he tells the truth" (19:35). A connecting reference is found in the final words of the gospel: "This [i.e., the Beloved One] is the disciple who is testifying to these things and has written them, and we know that his testimony is true. But there are also many other things that Jesus did; if every one of them were written down, I suppose that the world itself could not contain the books that would be written" (21:24-25).

Many authors link these passages from the redactor-evangelist with one of the disciples in the boat with Peter (21:2). Consequently, they equate the Beloved Disciple with the evangelist John and the evangelist John with the disciple (apostle) John. Because the evangelist identified himself as a disciple of Jesus, they named him John the Evangelist and thus identified the Beloved Disciple as John the Apostle.[9] This interpretation was formally affirmed (in face of mounting attacks to the contrary) by the Vatican in 1907.

In terms of the text, there is little doubt that the narrator is saying the Beloved Disciple is the apostle John and that this apostle is himself the narrator. A nuance of this view is found in Rudolf Schnackenburg's writings. He suggests that the gospel "grew out of the preaching of John the son of Zebedee which was gradually committed to writing" by a Hellenist (Greek-oriented) Christian. It was the apostle's disciples, not John himself, who substituted the expression "the disciple Jesus loved" for the original "I" of John, especially in those places where he refers to his personal testimony of what Jesus said and/or did.[10]

In the 1960s, when I first studied the gospel "according to John" in the seminary, this synthesis of the three figures—the Beloved One, John the son of Zebedee (or the "Apostle"—a word not used in this gospel), and John the Evangelist—was de rigueur. As I noted in the introduction, this view was enshrined in many Catholic churches (as well as in our minds) in the image of the crucified Jesus with his mother and John, the latter often portrayed as looking up at Jesus, quill-pen and book in hand. This view is still reflected in the writings of fundamentalist authors.[11]

However, there are problems related to conflating John the Apostle, John the Evangelist, and the Beloved Disciple as one person. In fact, as early as 1962, the Journal of Biblical Literature carried an article offering twenty-one reasons why John the Apostle could not have been John the Evangelist and, therefore the Beloved Disciple.[12] Probably the main rea-

son why many scholars reject the conflation of the three figures into one
comes from the text itself. John 21:24 speaks about the text from the perspective of its author: "This is the disciple who is testifying to these
things and has written them, and we know his testimony is true." How
could any eye-witness of Jesus' earthly ministry have written John's
gospel as we know it today, especially when it was written almost seventy
years after Jesus' death? Or, even if this were historically possibile, why
would the Beloved Disciple refer to himself in such portentous terms? Finally, if the Beloved Disciple had died, why would this gospel give the
impression that he was still alive?

Two of the twentieth century's most important Johannine scholars
were Rudolf Schnackenburg and Raymond Brown. Both began their ca-
reers convinced of the simple identification of the apostle, evangelist, and
Beloved Disciple. In time, however, both changed their positions and
concluded that the Beloved Disciple could not be John the Evangelist,
much less John the son of Zebedee.[13] A main reason for not accepting the
Beloved One as being John, the son of Zebedee, comes from the list of
disciples mentioned in 21:2. There, *among* the seven are "the sons of
Zebedee" as well as two unnamed disciples. Why would the Beloved Disciple not be named as one of these sons of Zebedee if he was John?[14]

The Beloved Disciple as Both Historical and Literary/Figurative Representation

One of the first Americans to investigate John's gospel from a liter-
ary-narrative perspective was R. Alan Culpepper. His analysis of the passages relating to the Beloved Disciple led him to conclude that this disciple was/is an "idealized characterization of a historical figure."[15] This real
historical person plays a representative, paradigmatic, and symbolic role
in John. The Beloved Disciple is the ideal disciple. According to Culpepper, the Beloved Disciple is the image of what a true disciple must be and
do, a characterization of what it means to follow Jesus Christ. As such, in
the thought of Barnabas Lindars, he is "a foil to Peter."[16]

It would be quite safe to say that the majority of recognized scripture
scholars are in agreement that the Beloved Disciple represents a historical
figure who serves a literary or paradigmatic function in John's gospel.[17] A
good articulation of their positions can be found in the Catholic-Lutheran
study on Peter in the New Testament. It concludes: "We accept as the
most likely working hypothesis that for the Johannine community the
Beloved Disicple was a real person whom they thought to have been a
companion of Jesus and whose career was dramatized so that he could
serve as a model for all disciples or believers."[18]

Probably the most interesting approach to this interpretation is that of
Rudolf Bultmann. He finds that in the first twenty chapters of John the

Beloved Disciple is a purely figurative character; in chapter 21 the Beloved Disciple becomes a "definite historical person."[19]

The Beloved Disciple as a Literary/Paradigmatic Figure

Because of unresolved issues related to the texts in which the Beloved One appears, a third group of scholars has concluded that the Beloved Disciple must be viewed as an idealized character created by the evangelist to highlight Johannine themes, especially those related to discipleship.[20]

While I recognize the importance of the fact that early Christian communities evolved from their identification with historical figures (Peter, Paul, Thomas, Apollo, etc.), I find myself increasingly in agreement with this third group of scholars. This is not only because of my efforts to develop a faith-based reader-response approach to John's gospel. My reluctance to view the Beloved Disciple as a historical figure arises from an examination of some of the texts in which this figure appears.

The first explicit mention of the Beloved Disciple takes place in chapter 13 at the foot washing. Here we find the Beloved Disciple lying close to the breast of Jesus, a position of great honor in a culture defined by honor/shame dynamics. When Jesus declares that "one of you will betray me" (13:21), "shame" enters the picture. The disciples immediately seek to know who the betrayer might be. "Simon Peter therefore motioned to him [the Beloved Disciple] to ask Jesus of whom he was speaking" (13:24).

Why would Simon Peter do this? From his characterization in this gospel as well as in the Synoptics, we know that he does not hesitate to speak for himself. Second, and more important, why is it that, once the Beloved Disciple discovers how the betrayer will be identified, this information is not communicated to Peter? Further, once Jesus dips his hand into the dish and gives the bread to Judas, son of Simon Iscariot, why doesn't the Beloved Disciple act immediately to forestall the betrayal? In that honor-shame culture, to defend the integrity of the master was a key function of the disciple. That the Beloved Disciple just sat there without intervening as Judas got up would counteract all of the existing codes of honor. Finally, after Jesus tells Judas, "Do quickly what you are going to do" (13:27), why does John say that "no one" at the table knew why Jesus had said this?

Reflecting on this scene, Rudolf Schnackenburg came to ask the same kinds of questions. He concluded that "the scene lacks all historical credibility."[21] My own view is that the scene represents an effort on the part of the evangelist to introduce and highlight the role of the Beloved Disciple, especially in contrast to Peter. That the Beloved Disciple took no action would suggest that he was as dense as Peter in understanding what Jesus meant. This does not seem credible, since the sign that Jesus used to identify his betrayer was unambiguous.

A second reason for considering the Beloved Disciple an idealized/ representative figure is found in the portrayal of this figure at the cross. The author informs the reader of an "historical" point: "Standing near the cross of Jesus were his mother, and his mother's sister, Mary the wife of Clopas, and Mary Magdalene" (19:25). We are not informed of the presence of the Beloved Disciple until the next verse: "When Jesus saw his mother and the disciple whom he loved standing beside her, he said to his mother, 'Woman, here is your son.' Then he said to the disciple, 'Here is your mother'" (19:26). As some women, such as Margaret Pamment and Sandra Schnieders, have noted, it seems odd that John would not have included the Beloved One in the list of those who stood near the cross of Jesus. It seems especially odd in a male-defined culture to list only women when the text in this instance indicates that the Beloved Disciple was a man.

Furthermore, it was expected that "sons" would take responsibility for their mother when the one who was originally responsible for her died. Where were "his brothers" (2:12; 7:3, 5, 10) when their mother needed them? Why this outsider? The author is stressing faith-relationships over blood ties and seems to be using the story as a literary device to demonstrate a new kind of discipleship that undermines cultural convention and social expectation. While seeing this scene as more ideational than historical, I agree with Craig Koester, who writes:

> The Beloved Disciple is a model of faith throughout John's Gospel, although there is no suggestion that he was part of Jesus' kinship circle. The words that Jesus spoke—"Behold, your son" and "Behold, your mother"—resemble to some extent the formulas used for rites of adoption in the ancient world. They are appropriate for a scene in which two people, who are connected by their common faith relationship with Jesus rather than by kinship ties, are brought together into relationship with each other, forming the nucleus of a new community.[22]

Unlike most exegetes, I see the last scene involving the Beloved Disciple as providing even more reason to view the Beloved One as an ideal, paradigmatic, representative figure rather than a historical person: the scene simply sums up John's notion of discipleship for every age.

Everything revolves around Jesus' saying to Peter regarding the Beloved One: "If it is my will that this one remain until I come, what is that to you?" (21:22). The author tells us that, although a rumor had consequently spread that this disciple would not die, "Jesus did not say to him that he would not die, but, 'If it is my will that he remain until I come, what is that to you?'" (21:23).

Those who take a historical-critical approach to the text have concluded that the Beloved Disciple had indeed died and that this death was not as "glorious" as that of Peter, who had died an ignominious death like that of Jesus. Consequently, they surmise, the author had to find a way to address the problem of the Beloved One's death.

A close examination of the text finds no mention that this disciple has died. Indeed we are told the contrary: *"that this disciple would not die"* but would remain until Jesus' return. If "remaining with" Jesus represents the essence of discipleship, and if John's gospel begins by describing those historical (and possibly representative) figures who "remained with" Jesus as disciples (1:39), why would John not want to assure readers—for all time—that Jesus would remain with them as long as they believed? After all, didn't Jesus also say that "those who believe in me, even though they die, will live, and everyone who lives and believes in me will never die" (11:25b-26)?

Thus, for the reasons offered in the last few pages, it seems much better for us as readers who struggle with our faith to read ourselves "written into" the text than to have to identify with some anonymous historical figure. Support for such an approach can be found in Jesus' prayer during his Farewell Discourse (the scene in which the Beloved Disciple appears for the first time): "I ask not only on behalf of these [the historical disciples], but also on behalf of those who will believe in me through their word [contemporary disciples who identify with the Johannine vision as they live within the Petrine/Apostolic church], that they may all be one" (17:20-21a). William S. Kurz concludes: "As the farewell dialogue itself looks forward to the Church's situation after the departure of Jesus, so the beloved Disciple exercises an important function in the Church after the founder's lifetime, which is the situation of the implied readers."[23]

As we have seen, it seems that the community that identified itself with the Beloved Disciple compared itself and its vision of discipleship with the Petrine/Apostolic church and its vision of discipleship and saw itself in a more positive light. As Brown concludes: "In counterposing their hero over against the most famous member of the Twelve, the Johannine community is symbolically counterposing itself over against the kinds of churches that venerate Peter and the Twelve—the Apostolic Churches, whom other scholars call the 'Great Church.'"[24]

If Jesus' farewell prayer was offered to God to include us who believe through their "word," how are we to be one, especially in light of the issues and concerns that face us in the Great Church overwhelmingly dominated by the Petrine/Apostolic approach? This question brings us to this book's concluding chapter.

WHAT DOES IT MEAN FOR US TO REMAIN AS BELOVED DISCIPLES? (21:23)

As noted in the preface, I gave my first retreat on John's gospel at St. Stephens Dominican Retreat Center in Dover, Massachusetts in 1996. One of the attendees was Jeanne Adams, a sister of the Holy Child. Jeanne and I had worked together some years before in the ministry of corporate responsibility. Since then she had ministered to people in Africa and the Caribbean. Now she was discerning where she might go in the future.

At the beginning of the retreat, I had spent a little time on the Beloved Disciple and how this figure was representative of a community whose approach differed from the increasingly Petrine/Apostolic thrust of the Great Church. Halfway through the retreat, Jeanne and I talked about some possible implications of this for what we face today: the ever-expanding reach of the Petrine church, with its ideology that sustains certain negative dimensions, including near-deification of the pope—almost to the exclusion of Jesus.

That this is no exaggeration is illustrated by a story I heard recently. A young priest I know told of attending a party at a college campus. One of the young women there spoke enthusiastically and at great length about the pope and his significance. Having heard her accolades, the priest said, "Nancy, as I listen to you, I can't help but think that, if you had to choose, you'd go with the pope rather than with Jesus."

"Oh yes," she replied without any hesitation.

"Why?" the priest asked.

"Because the pope is infallible."

More than ever, it seems, we need to grasp John's message: Jesus has to be the center, and his pattern—that of being willing to lay down one's life in love—has to be the model for our discipleship.

My conversation with Jeanne led me to consider a reader-response way of addressing our contemporary situation. I began to dream of what an ecclesial community might look like if it were to be based on the actual portrayal of the Beloved Disciple in John's gospel. If this figure was meant to be representative of discipleship and of the community of beloved ones for all time, what might we learn from the Beloved One regarding a Johannine meaning of "church" today?

Being a dreamer, I found myself in good company with the founder of my order, St. Francis of Assisi. He lived at a time when the papacy had reached the apogee of its political and military power. Within this setting he felt called by God to his vocation in the church and world as he prayed before an image of the crucified Christ in the abandoned Church of San Damiano outside the walls of Assisi. The image was an icon of Jesus on the cross surrounded by the figures mentioned by John in 19:25-26. From the cross he heard the words of Jesus: "Francis, go repair my house. You can see it is falling into ruin."

Today I find great consolation in realizing that it also is my calling to do what I can to rebuild this church which many consider to be falling into ruin. Part of the ruination has come, I believe, because of the myriad ways in which the Petrine/Apostolic dimension of the Great Church has all but eclipsed what it still means to be a gathering of Beloved Disciples.

Within the religious institution of my birth, along with its "isms" and ideology, I envision the creation of alternate communities dedicated to enfleshing a way of "remaining with" Jesus in the manner of the Beloved Disciple. Living within the existing ecclesiastical and social "world," but in a way that is grounded in the Spirit that poured forth from the side of Jesus on the cross (19:30-34), our vocation is to love one another in a way that will lead others to believe (19:35).

The Spirit of Jesus as the Source of Life in the Community of the Beloved Disciple

The members of the Johannine community knew that "we abide in him and he in us, because he has given us of his Spirit" (1 Jn 4:13). They were convinced that the abiding presence of Jesus was grounded in the Spirit that came to them from the side of the crucified/risen[1] Christ. In the Spirit they found their link to Jesus through the image of the Beloved Disciple who had remained with Jesus and had never been separated from him at the cross or at the resurrection. This Spirit enabled them to be faithful to Jesus because, in the words of Jesus, this Spirit will continually remind them "of all that I have said to you" (14:26).

The ultimate role of this Spirit is to convict the "world" of its sin (16:8-9). The role of the Community of the Beloved Disciple and of any community identified with the cause of Jesus Christ in the world is to be so faith-grounded in the word (as in the Johannine word) that their very lives testify to the Word being enfleshed in them. This idea is well summarized by Craig Koester:

The Gospel writer sought to disclose the abiding significance of what Jesus had said and done in the conviction that Jesus himself continues to abide among people through the Spirit or "paraclete" (14:15-17, 23). Like the belief that the world is God's creation, a sense of the ongoing work of the Spirit undergirds Johannine symbolism theologically. The Spirit did not bring new revelation on the same order as Jesus had already given but manifested Jesus' presence and disclosed the significance of his words and actions to people living after his ministry on earth had ended (14:26). The Gospel presents the paradox that the divine is made known through what is earthly and the universal is disclosed through what is particular. This gives Johannine symbolism a tensive, dialectical quality that conveys transcendent reality without finally delimiting it. The Gospel's testimony, given in symbolic language, is a vehicle for the Spirit's work; and it is through the Spirit that the testimony becomes effective, drawing readers to know the mystery that is God.[2]

Through reflection on the scriptures, our tradition has come to realize that the Advocate, the *paraklētos*, is the third person of the trinitarian household of God. As the divine domain and life-giving power of God,[3] this Spirit will enable disciples who have taken the mother of Jesus to their households (19:27) to have access to the many mansions of the Father of Jesus (14, especially 14:2, 25-26). At the same time, this Spirit will challenge them to reside in the wider community of the church, to resist the stumbling blocks of the "world," to challenge its ways and to invite it to be ever more human and humane.[4]

The many dwelling places in God's house promised in Jesus' prayer the night before his death (14:1-4, 15-26) become present through the Spirit's presence in the Johannine community. In the Spirit, any future experience of that promise is present now. John W. Pryor notes that this future-made-present enabled the disciples to be

> conscious of a new relationship with God by the presence of the Spirit in their lives, and this Spirit awareness was also felt to be the Spirit of Jesus, his ongoing presence with them. . . . Thus, while the Father and Son came to dwell (*menein*) with the disciples while they were still "in the world", this present dwelling is but an anticipation of the fuller, the perfected indwelling yet to be.[5]

At this point in my dreaming I found myself asking more specifically: How might our "remaining with" Jesus in the power of the Spirit get expressed? Above all—and for all—it means abiding in love (1 Jn 4:7–5:13). I have found it helpful, on a more personal level, to visualize myself at the cross with the mother of Jesus. And, if others join in this representative way of understanding the Beloved Disciple, we will be able to view ourselves gathered together, remaining with him, waiting for his return. At the communal level, I suggest we try to envision anew what it might be to truly represent this Community of the Beloved Disciple. This seems all the more imperative as increasing numbers of people become alienated from the institutional Roman Church because of its almost obsessive concentration on its Petrine expression. Only when we realize that the need to remain faithful to the vision of the Beloved Disciple demands that we do so within the dominant Petrine/Apostolic church—but in a way defined by self-sacrificing love rather than power dynamics —will the fullness of reader-response theory come alive.

Characteristics of a Contemporary Community of the Beloved Disciple

Building on the five certain references to the figure of the Beloved Disciple (13:23; 19:26; 20:2; 21:7; 21:20) and the less-clear mention in 18:15-16, I suggest the following principles for a contemporary Community of the Beloved Disciple grounded in self-sacrificing love:

1. Jesus must be central in the life of the Beloved Disciple, whether individually or communally.

The first appearance of the Beloved One in 13:23 portrays the disciple next to Jesus in an image of intimacy. This intimacy is built upon a relationship wherein Jesus is able to entrust his confidences to the one so loved. In the mainline churches today there is a critical need for disciples to recline "on the bosom" of Jesus, to make him central, the core of all life, and to be entrusted with his most secret thoughts.

If the central theme of the Synoptics is the reign of God, the whole focus of John's gospel is Jesus himself and what it means to abide in him and to remain in his love. This sense of being part of him, celebrating in his Spirit, requires a deep intimacy with him and a knowledge of his inmost thoughts—especially about where he is being betrayed and denied today by those who seem more intent on preserving old patterns than on awareness of his life-giving presence. Such intimacy does not mean we immediately go out and buy bumper stickers proclaiming: "I JUST ♡ MY JESUS!" It means, as we have tried to show, that we position ourselves at Jesus' bosom, attuned to the questions he asks us in our culture and church, questions that invite us to greater fidelity. It means having the kind of familiarity and intimacy in our lives that the first letter of John proclaimed as the sign that we have truly had the Jesus-experience.

The authenticity of our connectedness to Jesus will be expressed in love for others. Simply stated, "we love because he has first loved us" (1 Jn

4:19). If we remain in this love of God we will love one another. Any other way is not God's: "Those who say, 'I love God,' and hate their brothers or sisters, are liars; for those who do not love a brother or sister whom they have seen, cannot love God whom they have not seen. The commandment we have from him is this: those who love God must love their brothers and sisters also" (1 Jn 4:20-21). Even though we may differ seriously with those who seem to equate the church with its Petrine and Apostolic dimension, we must always be defined by the way we love.

A corollary of this is the realization that a life centered on Jesus in love does not always mean that Peter will get the kind of response he might like, a response that will satisfy his need for certainty. At the same time, this kind of "abiding" will make us aware of how easily we too can move away from resting on the bosom of Jesus to a level of intellectualization that actually keeps us from the kind of spirituality and intimacy with him we desire.

The consequence of an overly-intellectualized approach to my faith came home to me with a sudden awareness after a day's discussion with other like-minded U.S. Roman Catholics. After the interim elections of 1994, when the Republicans took over the U.S. Congress, many of us Catholic social activists felt quite devastated. A friend belonging to a religious community of women convened nine of us to discuss what options we might pursue. Although the group included people whose names are quite well known in Catholic circles, we agreed to remain anonymous and to be circumspect about our conversations.

It is safe to say that, the more we talked, the more we discovered that the Republicans really weren't the problem. The issue was deeper. We came to realize that, as Catholic disciples of Jesus committed to justice, we had too easily linked the gospel's social concerns with the agenda of the Democratic Party. In the process we had allowed ourselves to be blinded to its abuses of power with regard to such things as campaign finance reform and life-issues like abortion.

Then, just as we were unmasking the Democratic Party's own self-serving entrenchment, the religious right began linking itself with the Republican Party. With the ensuing proliferation of religious language used to portray the Republican Party as the Jesus-Party for the nation, we found ourselves embarrassed and unwilling to profess a faith-base or confessional stance for our political positions. The result was silence regarding the faith that motivated our justice efforts.

As we continued sharing and grew in trust, I discovered that my reluctance to speak publicly about the faith that grounded my justice efforts reflected a deeper malaise. I came to realize that, in my effort to be politically correct, I had become spiritually bankrupt. In my own way I could hear said to me Jesus' question raised centuries before: "Have I been with you all this time . . . and you still do not know me?" (14:9).

Others found themselves in a similar situation. Having spent many hours building up trust, we realized that we needed to come together again. The topic for each of us would be: Who is Jesus for me?

This question is the question every disciple—whether in the community of Peter or the Beloved One—must ask. But those who claim to be identified with the Beloved Disciple while living in the church of Peter had better make sure that their resting place is not one that will make them bosom-buddies of the Democrats, the Republicans, or any other human entity. The only place that will ultimately satisfy is at and from the heart of Jesus Christ.

2. If we accept our role as Beloved Disciples, we must find ways to take Mary into our home.

John 19:26-27 talks about "the hour" when the Beloved Disciple took Jesus' mother into "his own home." This does not mean that the Beloved One immediately left and took Mary to his house, supposedly in Jerusalem. On the contrary, the author makes it clear that a new kind of familial relationship is what must characterize the disciple identified in love with Jesus. In commenting on this passage, Raymond Brown wrote: "What is peculiar to the beloved disciple, what is *his own*, is neither his house nor his spiritual space but the fact that he is the disciple par excellence. *His own* is the special discipleship that Jesus loves."[6]

The implication is clear: from now on, there is no way we can be Jesus' Beloved Disciple—individually or communally, personally or ecclesially—without Jesus' mother in our home. For some of us, this might mean getting rid of crazy, pietistic notions of Mary which stress private revelation over divine revelation, words alleged to have been spoken by her to this or that visionary, in favor of listening to her final words to all who would be faithful to Jesus: "Do whatever he tells you" (2:5). For others, making room for Mary in our "homes" might mean greater imitation of this woman who helped inaugurate Jesus' ministry by getting him to respond to peoples' needs and embarrassment. For still others, it may mean a contemporary rediscovery and reclamation of Marian prayers and devotions that have been used for purposes other than the promotion of the greater good.

I believe there are many people waiting for a contemporary re-articulation of Mary that will speak to their hearts and their minds. I got an intimation of how many there might be in 1997 when I gave a talk at the national convention of Call to Action in Detroit. My subject was: "Mary, Model of Liberation." I was expected to give the talk twice. My venue was a room meant to hold about five hundred people. It was quite full for the first talk. However, after people heard about Mary as a model of liberation, a woman whose Magnificat is grounded in concern for those in need and a commitment to turn the world upside down to achieve a right order (Lk 1:46-55), the word got out that this "Mary" was someone to be grappled with. My second talk was standing-room only.

Today, as in the time of Luke and John, two of the most urgent issues facing our world today have to do with addressing peoples' needs and showing them mercy and compassion in a way that does not embarrass them. As we deal with these issues, I believe the witness of Jesus' mother can teach us much.

3. We must listen to the voices of women if we are to find that Jesus is risen from the dead.

In John 20:1-2 it is Mary Magdalene who informs both the Beloved Disciple and Peter that they need to pay attention to a new development: Jesus is no longer in the tomb. They not only listen to her—they act on her input. The contemporary implication of this is clear: as long as Peter does not listen to the Marys of the wider church, darkness will continue and the tomb will remain sealed. The fact that women need to be heard does not mean that there has to be competition between Peter and women. The text shows that this woman respected Peter; after all she told him first (20:2). At the same time, however, it is it also shows that Peter respected Mary and her insight; he acted on it.

Not to include the voices of women in the decisions of Peter will lead to death rather than life. Not to expose how Peter and those who identify with him may be doing violence to women in the way they abuse the sacred texts relating to Jesus' vision of leadership in the church is to protect a system of self-serving power rather than to foster a community of love. Not to recognize the equality of all in being born from above in baptism (3:3) is to make baptism a sign of exclusion rather than inclusion. Not to recognize that women have as much of a "right" as men to have access to all the sacraments is to do a disservice to the one who came to give life in all its fullness.

In the Roman Church of which I am a member, for years we had drilled into us the profession of faith made by Peter, "You are the Messiah, the Son of the living God" (Mt 16:16) as a justification for the papal power symbolized by the subsequent bestowal of the keys (Mt 16:19). The equivalent words of Martha were never offered as a reason for listening to the insights of women in our church. In response to Jesus' question asking her if she believed in him as the "resurrection and life" (11:25-26), Martha professed her faith in words even more detailed than Peter's: "Yes, Lord, I believe that you are the Messiah, the Son of God, the one coming into the world" (11:27). Even though, as we have seen, Martha did not really answer Jesus' question, why can't we also see that any infallibility claimed by Peter for proclaiming his faith in Jesus (Mt 16:16) must be balanced by an awareness of the fact that Peter can also be a "stumbling block" to the designs of Jesus (Mt 16:21-23)?

4. In the face of the empty tomb, we must find our own faith, especially when it seems Peter does not "see."

John 20:3-10 is a key passage in the gospel. It describes various reactions to Jesus' resurrection. The author notes that, while the Beloved Disciple has arrived at the tomb first and looked in, this one awaits Peter. Peter is the first to enter. There he "sees" but does not believe. The "seeing" that is accompanied by "believing" is reserved for the Beloved Disciple.

Rather than making comparisons regarding the two ways of "seeing" in this story, it seems appropriate to let the text speak for itself. It is clear that we cannot always depend on Peter's way of seeing if we are to live in faith. While those seeking to be defined by the discipleship of the Beloved One must defer to Peter and even wait for him to arrive, we cannot abdicate our faith to Peter's way of seeing. Peter's vision may not encompass authentic faith.

Pope John Paul II was among the first to admit that the Petrine way of "seeing" throughout the history of the church has not always been grounded in truth. He did this in his apostolic letter, *Tertio Mellennio Adveniente*, of November 14, 1994. This Pope, who was willing to acknowledge and ask pardon for past mistakes more than any other (in spite of the misgivings of some of his advisors), alluded to the ideology that can blind even people of good will. Such good will, he noted, does not "exonerate the church from the obligation to express profound regret" for the weaknesses we now realize motivated such actions. He wrote:

> It is true that an accurate historical judgment cannot prescind from careful study of the cultural conditioning of the times, as a result of which many people may have held in good faith that an authentic witness to the truth could include suppressing the opinions of others or at least paying no attention to them. Many factors frequently converged to create assumptions which justified intolerance and fostered an emotional climate from which only great spirits, truly free and filled with God, were in some way able to break free.[7]

A further implication of not relying on Peter alone to help us "see" is that our faith cannot be limited to Peter's vision, to his way of seeing—especially when it does not lead to deeper faith in the Risen One. In front of the empty tombs about us, our response must always be authentic faith.

5. In the midst of what might seem barrenness, we must not be ashamed to say: "Jesus is Lord."

John 21:7 is set in the context of a fishing scene with disciples who seem to have abandoned the dream that had sustained them regarding

Jesus as Messiah. They have given in to the temptation to go back to "business as usual." They have fished all night in vain, without any catch.

Those of us who have grown discouraged because we have been trying to fish in waters that have provided little or no catch must develop a humility that can admit to Jesus that we have "caught nothing." It is precisely in this powerlessness, in this barrenness, in this night, that we will be able to hear Jesus question us, inviting us to daybreak. Openness to his questioning implies being committed to a power that may take us in directions beyond traditional waters and tested ways. Jesus' question may lead to an invitation to throw our nets to the other side.

When we find manifestations of this higher power, of the divine in our lives, we should not be ashamed to witness to Jesus as Lord. This proclamation—"Jesus is Lord"—cannot be allowed to be associated only with Protestant fundamentalists. While we might be uneasy expressing our faith publicly in these exact words, we must find some way to proclaim our faith in a way that makes it clear that we are trying to center our lives around Jesus Christ.

For many of us, such professions might begin as embarrassed stuttering. I found this out for myself while writing this book. As I noted earlier, I have been spending much time recently searching for some kind of intimacy with God through the Spirit of Jesus. In the midst of this search, I encountered a resigned priest one day in our parking lot. He is very active in various ministries to the poor, some of which take place where I live at St. Benedict the Moor in Milwaukee's downtown area. This man has creative ways of trying to engage people in conversation beyond the typical, "How are you?" Thus, upon seeing me, he said: "What's giving you life these days, Mike?" To this I could only respond, "Well, to be really honest, it's my search for deeper intimacy with Jesus Christ."

While I did give witness to my faith, I don't think it was the kind of response that would have made for more conversation. He just looked at me and didn't really know what to say.

A corollary of our need to proclaim "It is the Lord" is the duty to remind Peter and those identified with him of where ultimate power in the church rests. Thus, there may be times when we will have to make it clear to Peter that Jesus is the Lord and that the church must always be oriented to the person of Jesus rather than a cult of the Pope.

6. We must realize that, until he returns, we are to remain in the world to continue the "works."

John 21:18-23 intimates how Peter will die and how the Beloved Disciple will remain until Jesus' return. The assumption from everything that has been articulated in John thus far is that Jesus' followers who "remain" in the world must do in it what he came into the world to accomplish. He came into the world to do the "works" of the one he called "Father." Because we have been given a share in the Spirit of Jesus and this "Father," we also are to be God's apprentices. Unlike *hoi Ioudaioi* who could not accept Jesus' identification of his works with those of "the Father," each of us must be able to say, until Jesus returns, "Because we believe, we continue his works" (see 14:12).

Now the Beloved Disciple will be found in whoever "remains" in union with the living Christ, continuing the work of God to make creation whole, witnessing to the word to bring about *shalom*. We must find our identity at the bosom of Jesus. From this center we can follow and remain faithful to Jesus. Fidelity to his words and remaining in them will constitute for us—and for Peter—what it means to "follow me." Our following will lead us to become the final redaction of John's gospel itself; our words and our works will be its concrete translation. According to William Kurz:

> Like the beloved disciple, the implied readers are to realize that Jesus loves them intimately and reveals his secrets to them. Like the beloved disciple, the implied readers are entrusted to Jesus' mother (both Mary and the church), and his mother to them. Like the beloved disciple, they know and are to testify that blood and water flowed from the crucified Jesus, to believe that he truly has risen, to recognize the risen Jesus from his miraculous deeds among the community of disciples, the church, to remain until Jesus returns, and to bear true witness to the good news about Jesus.[8]

Peter need not feel envious or threatened at the thought of this Community of the Beloved Disciple rising again. Recalling Jesus' last words to Peter, "What is that to you?" we must be willing to make it clear that our task is not so much to define ourselves in relationship to Peter but to remind him that we will be around until Jesus comes. We won't go away because we know we must remain at the heart of the church even when its Petrine dimension would just as soon see us slip away. We will remain with Jesus until he comes, confident that we have done what we could, even to the point of laying down our lives.

7. Our "works" must be witnessed in such a way that the world's high priests will know who we are.

If we accept the verses in chapter 18 about Simon Peter and another disciple (who "was known to the high priest") following Jesus "into the courtyard of the high priest" as referring to the Beloved Disciple, this passage has important contemporary implications. We must witness with our lives in such a way that the world's high priests will take notice. In my ministry of corporate responsibility, I am continually amazed at how seldom the vision of creating an inclusive and just community of care gets expressed—even in veiled terms—when we need to speak our truth to those priests of the business world who seem willing to sacrifice people and the planet for the sake of short-term profit.

In this I think of Sr. Pat Daly, a Caldwell Dominican co-worker of mine. She had been a thorn in the side of Jack Welch, the Irish Catholic chief executive officer of General Electric.

For years Pat raised the issue of the consequences of G.E.'s release of PCBs into the Hudson River in New York. The company's contribution to the already polluted river had made it so contaminated that people could not eat its fish. In a 1998 piece, "In PCB Fight, It's the Nun vs. the C.E.O.," *The New York Times* described what had happened at General Electric's annual meeting:

> Sister Pat stood up to advocate a shareholder resolution on G.E.'s pollution of the Hudson River. She called on the company to publicize the danger of eating fish from the river and to stop fostering misleading studies. And she compared the company's claims that PCB's are harmless with claims made by tobacco industry executives about the harmlessness of smoking.
>
> That is when John F. Welch Jr., G.E.'s chairman and chief executive, blew up. "That's an outrageous comparison," he shouted at the nun. "You owe it to God to be on the side of truth."⁹

Pat, a Dominican nun whose charism is to "Live in the Truth," simply said, "I am."

Disciples of Jesus patterning their following of Jesus on that of the Beloved One must speak the truth to power—and to the forces of power when they violate people and the planet. The goal is not that we may be "known"; it is that society's high priests may be challenged by our witness to the truth.

That witness extends to the church too. At certain times when Peter says "never," he may have to be reminded that the Beloved Disciple is going to remain until Jesus comes. Those who identify with the vision of the Community of the Beloved Disciple in a Great Church dominated by a Petrine/Apostolic emphasis must remain faithful. Whether addressed to Peter or to ourselves, the call is ultimately the same: "Follow me!"

"What is that to" us, or to Peter?

Everything. Or, as Peter himself would say: "Lord, to whom can we go? You have the words of eternal life. We have come to believe and know that you are the Holy One of God" (6:68-69).

NOTES

PREFACE

1. Raymond E. Brown, *The Community of the Beloved Disciple: The Life, Loves, and Hates of an Individual Church in New Testament Times* (New York/Ramsey/Toronto: Paulist, 1979), 56.

2. Bruce J. Malina, "John's: The Maverick Christian Group: The Evidence of Sociolinguistics," *Biblical Theology Bulletin* 24 (1994), 181. Also Malina and Richard L. Rohrbaugh, *Social-Science Commentary on the Gospel of John* (Minneapolis: Fortress, 1998), 226.

3. Reader-response (and audience-response) theory will be explained further on pages xviff.

PROLOGUE: DO YOU NOW BELIEVE?

1. Jerome H. Neyrey, S.J., "Questions, Chreiai and Honor Challenges: the Interface of Rhetoric and Culture in Mark's Gospel," *Catholic Biblical Quarterly* 60 (1999), 658-59. I am indebted to Jerome Neyrey for making this paper available to me before its publication.

2. Gerald A. Arbuckle, S.M., Ph.D., "Obstacles to Pastoral Creativity," *Human Development* 16 (1995), 17.

3. Raymond E. Brown, *The Community of the Beloved Disciple: The Life, Loves, and Hates of an Individual Church in New Testament Times* (New York/ Ramsey/Toronto: Paulist, 1979), 62.

4. R. Alan Culpepper, *Anatomy of the Fourth Gospel: A Study in Literary Design* (Philadelphia: Fortress, 1983).

5. I follow Brown's approach to the authorship of the gospel and letters. While spread throughout *The Community of the Beloved Disciple*, the question of authorship is summarized on pages 94-97. In effect, Brown associates authorship not so much with individual persons as with the schools identified with these persons.

6. For more on the layers of John's gospel, see Brown; Culpepper; J. L. Martyn, *History and Theology in the Fourth Gospel*, 2nd ed. (Nashville: Abingdon, 1979). For a good summary of the three versions of the gospel (and the community that was/is reflected in these versions), see Urban C. von Wahlde, "Community in Conflict: The History and Social Context of the Johannine Community," in *Gospel Interpretation: Narrative-Critical and Social-Scientific Approaches,* ed. Jack Dean Kingsbury (Valley Forge, Pa.: Trinity Press International, 1997), 223-28.

7. The first redaction, made in response to the Johannine community's need to be legitimated by the synagogal community, views Jesus as a reformer, one trying to purify Judaism. Jesus' legitimacy arose from his ability to verbalize a religion that would represent renewal. The second redaction moved the notion of Jesus as reformer to a more radical stance: in the person (words and works) of Jesus, Israel's feasts and rituals were replaced; he is now the message itself. The first and second redactions dominate in the first half of the gospel where we find Jesus dismantling Israel's religion (and all religion that claims to be messianic but does not center on him). The final redaction, made in response to the Johannine community's expulsion from the synagogue and increasing alienation from the Petrine/Apostolic community, reflects a community trying to be faithful to the person and message of Jesus as it watched its fellow Christians returning to power dynamics Jesus seemed to want to overturn. It viewed itself as a minority group under siege by hostile forces beyond it and, quite possibly, within it. At this level, the author(s) of John portray Christ in increasingly godly terms on the one hand and, on the other, as increasingly inimical to opponents.

8. From the resurrection on it seems that the early disciples identified themselves with early leaders, as Paul himself makes clear (1 Cor 1:12), and grouped themselves into communities around those leaders. Conflicts arose among the various communities which appealed to the uniqueness of their various "founders." So extreme was their identification with their founders that some of these communities risked diminishing or even forgetting their ultimate foundation in Jesus Christ.

9. For insights into the conflicts between the communities identified with Thomas and with the Beloved Disciple, see Gregory J. Riley, *Resurrection Reconsidered: Thomas and John in Controversy* (Minneapolis: Fortress, 1995), 177.

10. Kevin B. Quast, "Reexamining Johannine Community," *Toronto Journal of Theology* 5 (1989), 293-95.

11. Again, I will not develop the technical differences between the "historical," "intended," "implied," or "real" readers. From now on I will just refer to the "reader" as the contemporary reader of John (academically, the "real reader"). For more on the distinctions, see Segovia and others in *"What Is John?" Readers and Readings of the Fourth Gospel,* ed. Fernando F. Segovia (Atlanta: Scholars Press, 1996).

12. Brown, 85.

13. In this I concur with the Australian Johannine scholar, Francis J. Moloney: "A reader does not respond to first and second editions" (*Signs and Shadows: Reading John 5-12* [Minneapolis: Fortress, 1996], 44, n. 54). Moloney does not note here any difference between the implied reader or the intended reader. The assumption seems to be, therefore, the contemporary reader.

14. Dorothy A. Lee, "Beyond Suspicion? The Fatherhood of God in the Fourth Gospel," *Pacifica* 8 (1995), 141.

15. Mary Rose D'Angelo, "*Abba* and 'Father': Imperial Theology and the Jesus Traditions," *Journal of Biblical Literature* 111 (1992), 623.

16. Ibid., 627-28.

17. Lee, 146. For this notion Lee acknowledges several other exegetes as well.

18. John W. Pryor, "Jesus and Israel in the Fourth Gospel: John 1:11," *Novum Testamentum* 3 (1990), 201-18.

19. R. Alan Culpepper, "The Gospel of John as a Document of Faith in a Pluralistic Culture," in *"What Is John?,"* 115.

20. Tina Pippin, "'For Fear of the Jews': Lying and Truth-Telling in Translating the Gospel of John," *Semeia* 76, 1996, 82.

21. Ibid., 83.

22. Daniel J. Harrington, "The Problem of 'the Jews' in John's Gospel," *Exploration* 8 (1994), 2.

23. Padraic O'Hare, *The Enduring Covenant: The Education of Christians and the End of Anti-semitism,* (Valley Forge, Pa.: Trinity, 1997), 15-16.

24. I also get the sense that this (non)way of "translating" *hoi Ioudaioi* is to be recommended from reading *Explorations,* the journal committed to "Rethinking Relationships among Christians and Jews." American Interfaith Institute/World Alliance of Interfaith Organizations, 401 N. Broad Street, Philadelphia, PA 19108, 215-238-5340. See David P. Efroymson (following Gerard Sloyan, *Commentary on John* [Atlanta: John Knox Press, 1988]), "Let Ioudaioi Be Ioudaioi: *When Less Is Better,"* *Explorations* 11 (1997), 5.

25. Elizabeth Harris, *Prologue and Gospel: The Theology of the Fourth Evangelist.* Journal for the Study of the New Testament Supplement 107 (Sheffield: Sheffield Academic Press, 1994).

26. Heinrich Schneider, "The Word Was Made Flesh: An Analysis of the Theology of Revelation in the Fourth Gospel," *Catholic Biblical Quarterly* 31 (1969), 348, 351.

27. Robert Kysar, *John: The Maverick Gospel*, rev. ed. (Louisville: Westminster/John Knox, 1993), 61.

28. Walter Wink, *Engaging the Powers: Discernment and Resistance in a World of Domination* (Minneapolis: Fortress, 1992), 51.

29. 1971 Synod of Bishops, Introduction, "Justice in the World," November, 1971 (Boston: St. Paul Editions, 1972), 3.

30. Ibid. Emphasis added.

31. Arbuckle, 17.

32. Gail R. O'Day, *The Word Disclosed: John's Story and Narrative Preaching* (St. Louis: CBP Press, 1987), 163.

1. WHAT ARE YOU LOOKING FOR?

1. In John, "What [or whom] are you looking for?" is repeated three other times: twice to those coming to arrest him (18:4, 7) and to Mary Magdalene outside the tomb (20:15). In all four cases, the words involve some kind of looking as well as a turning of some sort. With the two disciples, "Jesus turned and saw them" (1:38). With Judas, "the detachment of soldiers together with police from the chief priests and the Pharisees" who came looking for Jesus "stepped back" after he proclaimed, "I am he." With Mary, after asking her the question and hearing her respond, Jesus called her "Mary." "She turned and said to him in Hebrew, 'Rabbouni!' (which means Teacher)" (20:15-16).

2. John Painter, "Quest and Rejection Stories in John," *Journal for the Study of the New Testament* 36 (1989), 18. Painter finds eight elements in the basic quest stories. While not every quest story clearly contains all eight elements, the account of the royal official's quest for healing for his son (which concludes 1:19–4:54) does. (1) The royal official requests that Jesus heal his son. (2) His request for the healing dominates the story. (3) The official, recognizing Jesus' higher power, remains anonymous. (4) The son's being at the point of death leads to a task for Jesus: the father "went and begged him to come down and heal his son." (5) His request for his son's healing elicits Jesus' response about people's need to "see signs." (6) Seeing the sign in this healing, the people are invited to move to a deeper level of belief. (7) Jesus' response to the request is given when he declares: "Go; your son will live." (8) The implications are described in various results: "the man believed," "his child was alive," "he himself believed, along with his whole household." Finally, the author articulates the ultimate implication by linking this action with a major image used in the gospel: "Now this was the second sign that Jesus did after coming from Judea to Galilee." Painter has expanded on quest and rejection stories in his *The Quest for the Messiah: The History, Literature and Theology of the Johannine Community*, 2nd rev. ed. (Abingdon: Nashville, 1993).

3. For an early discussion of this, see Nils Wilhelm Lund, *Chiasmus in the New Testament: A Study in Formgeschichte* (Chapel Hill: University of North Carolina Press, 1942).

4. I have chosen not to elaborate on the Prologue in this book for two reasons. The first is that it contains no questions asked by Jesus, and such questions are the focus of this book. The second is that I believe 1:19 through chapter 4 is a reflection on the themes contained in the Prologue as is, indeed, the whole gospel. Michael Labahn notes that "In John 2-4 we can find some shadows of the conflict [found in John's gospel between Jesus and his opponents], which is already mentioned in John 1, 1-14." See his "Between Tradition and Literary Art: The Miracle Tradition in the Fourth Gospel," *Biblica* 80 (1999), 185.

5. For more on this, see Raymond E. Brown, *The Community of the Beloved Disciple: The Life, Loves, and Hates of an Individual Church in New Testament Times* (New York/Ramsey/Toronto: Paulist, 1979) and Martin Stowasser, *Johannes der Täufer im Vierten Evangelium: Eine Untersuchung zu seiner Bedeutung für die Johanneische Gemeinde,* Österreichische biblische Studien 12 (Klosterneuburg: Katholisches Bibelwerk, 1992).

6. J. Daryl Charles, "Will the Court Please Call in the Prime Witness? John 1:29-34," *Trinity Journal* 10 (1989), 71-83.

7. The allegations about our friars and comments made by claimants' main lawyer, who queried me, became local Wisconsin as well as national news. See "Secrets of St. Lawrence," *Time*, June 7, 1993, 44.

8. John 11:22; 14:13, 14; 15:7, 16; 16:23, 24 [2x], 26; see 4:9, 10.

9. John 16:5, 23, 30; 18:19, 21 [2x], 22. An exception is 14:16. I am indebted to Wes Howard-Brook for providing this insight. See his *Becoming Children of God: John's Gospel and Radical Discipleship* (Maryknoll, N.Y.: Orbis, 1994), 199.

10. See, for instance, A. E. Harvey, *Jesus on Trial: A Study in the Fourth Gospel* (Atlanta: John Knox, 1976). Harvey interprets the whole gospel around the image of trial with the appearances of various witnesses. Those for the de-

fense are John, the disciples, some of the "Jews," the works of Jesus and, above all these, the Father. Witnesses for the prosecution include other "Jews," especially their leaders. Chief among these are the Pharisees and the chief priests. The charges have to do with whether claims related to Jesus as Messiah and equal to God (blasphemy) have merit or not.

11. Paul S. Minear, *John: The Martyr's Gospel* (New York: The Pilgrim Press, 1984), xii-xiii.

12. For more on this, see Ernest Becker, *The Denial of Death* (New York: The Free Press, 1973), 7.

13. At the time of my writing this book, the Christian "witness" allegedly given to their potential killers by two high school students received much coverage —to the point that it too became a commodity to be marketed. See Lisa Miller, "Marketing a Columbine Martyr," *The Wall Street Journal*, July 15, 1999, B1, 4.

14. Mark W. G. Stibbe, *John's Gospel* (London and New York: Routledge, 1994), 15.

15. Lynda McCullough, "Divine Coverage," *Common Boundary*, November/ December, 1996, 12.

16. Wade Clark Roof, *A Generation of Seekers: The Spiritual Journeys of the Baby Boom Generation* (San Francisco: HarperSan Francisco, 1993).

17. Speculation exists as to this disciple's identity. The possibility that this might be the Beloved Disciple will be discussed in chapter 13. For comments on this unknown disciple as factually and theologically uninteresting, see Frans Neirynck, "The Anonymous Disciple in John 1," *Ephemerides Theologicae Lovanienses* 66 (1990), 5-37.

18. For more on this, see Peter Dschulnigg, "Die Berufung der Jünger. Joh 1, 35-51 im Rahmen des vierten Evangeliums," *Freiburger Zeitschrift für Philosophie und Theologie* 36 (1989), 427-47.

19. This experience took place in 1997. A powerful experience of a very Jesus/Christ-oriented bishop came to me in the person of William G. Curlin, Bishop of Charlotte, N.C. For almost two hours in February, 1998 I was humbled at the faith-filled, Jesus-centered reflections which he shared with me. The motto on his coat of arms sums up his inspiring Christocentrism: *"Sentire cum Christo"*: to feel with Christ. I know many very wonderful bishops; however, Bishop Curlin's sharing was something quite special. I will treasure it always.

20. Carolyn Osiek, "The Jesus of John's Gospel: A Breed Apart," *Church* 5 (1989), 24.

21. The local "mega-church" in Milwaukee has stated that one-fourth of its registered members are former Catholics. I find this statistic repeated in other "mega-churches" as well.

22. The title "Son of Man" will be examined more fully in chapter 6. While it also is a title of Jesus in the Synoptics, it seems to have an unique meaning in John.

23. See Bruce J. Malina, *The New Testament World: Insights from Cultural Anthropology* (Atlanta: John Knox, 1981), 95.

24. John Pilch, *The Cultural World of Jesus Sunday by Sunday, Cycle C* (Collegeville, Minn.: The Liturgical Press, 1997), 22.

25. C. K. Barrett, *The Gospel according to St. John* (Philadelphia: Westminster, 1978), 159.

26. James B. Twitchell, *Lead Us into Temptation: The Triumph of American Materialism* (New York: Columbia University, 1999), 20.

27. Andrew Duffy, "Non-Profit Sector Hooked on Gambling Money: Survey," *The [Saskatoon] Star Phoenix,* July 28, 1999.

28. Barrett, 202.

29. Religious News Service, "Poll: Christian Terms Are Greek to Most," *The Orlando Sentinel*, March 5, 1994, C-7.

30. See for instance, P. Trudinger, "Jesus' 'Comfortable Words' in John 3:16: A Note of Disappointment to Some?," *St. Mark's Review* [Canberra] 147 (1991), 30-31.

31. Mark W. G. Stibbe, *John* (Sheffield: JSOT, 1993), 58-59.

32. For more on this, see K. H. Thiessen, "Jesus and Women in the Gospel of John," *Direction* 19 (1990), 52-64.

33. For a fuller treatment of this difference, see R. G. Maccini, "A Reassessment of the Woman at the Well in John 4 in Light of the Samaritan Context," *Journal for the Study of the New Testament* 53 (1994), 35-46.

34. Rudolf Schnackenburg, *Jesus in the Gospels: A Biblical Christology*, trans. O. C. Dean, Jr. (Louisville: Westminster John Knox, 1995), 223.

35. Craig R. Koester, "'The Savior of the World' (John 4:42)," *Journal of Biblical Literature* 109 (1990), 665-80.

36. Pope John Paul II, quoted in Allesandra Stanley, "Stop Squabbling, Pope Tells Austria's Divided Bishops as He Ends His Visit," *The New York Times*, June 22, 1998.

37. Sandra M. Schneiders, IHM, "Women in the Fourth Gospel and the Role of Women in the Contemporary Church," *Biblical Theology Bulletin* 12 (1982), 40.

2. DO YOU WANT TO BE HEALED?

1. Rudolf Schnackenburg, *The Gospel according to St. John,* vol. 2, trans. Cecily Hastings et al. (New York: Crossroad, 1980), 97.

2. According to Maria-Luisa Rigato, this unnamed feast likely was the harvest-pilgrimage feast of Pentecost; see "'Era festa dei giudei' (Gv 5, 1). Quale?," *Rivista Biblical* 39 (1991), 25-29. Frederic Manns argues for Tabernacles in "La fête des Juifs de Jean 5, 1," *Antonianum* 70 (1995), 117-24.

3. Mary Douglas, *Purity and Danger* (New York: Frederick A. Praeger, 1966), 115.

4. Allan Young, "The Anthropologies of Illness and Sickness," *Annual Review of Anthropology* 11 (1982), 257-85.

5. Ronald Frankenberg, "Sickness as Cultural Performance: Drama, Trajectory, and Pilgrimage. Root Metaphors and the Making Social of Disease," *International Journal of Health Services* 16 (1986), 603-26.

6. Young, 270.

7. Frankenberg, 622. See also Margaret Lock, "Cultivating the Body: Anthropology and Epistemologist of Bodily Practice and Knowledge," *Annual Review of Anthropology* 22 (1993), 142-43.

8. Ronald Frankenberg, "'Your Time or Mine': Temporal Contradictions of Biomedical Practice," in *Time, Health and Medicine,* ed. Ronald Frankenberg (London: Newbury Park, Calif.: New Delhi: Sage, 1992), 8.

9. According to T. Thatcher, there are 191 such "asides" in John's gospel. He organizes these into four broad functions: staging asides, including the statement here about the pool (44), defining asides, including John's explanation of the Hebrew name of the pool (46), asides that explain discourse (48), and those that explain actions (53). See T. Thatcher, "A New Look at Asides in the Fourth Gospel," *Bibliotheca Sacra* 151 (1994), 428-39.

10. Craig Koester, *Symbolism in the Gospel of John: Meaning, Mystery, and Community* (Minneapolis: Fortress, 1994).

11. John Pilch, "Understanding Healing in the Social World of Early Christianity," *Biblical Theology Bulletin* 22 (1992), 31. Pilch is the author who has best helped me understand the cultural dimension of sickness and health. I am indebted to his insights and sources.

12. Mark W. G. Stibbe, *John* (Sheffield: JSOT, 1993), 75.

13. In all cases where people's names (actual or pseudonymous) have been used in this book, I have asked for and received permission to use their stories.

14. Jeffrey L. Staley, "Stumbling in the Dark, Reaching for the Light: Reading Character in John 5 and 9," *Semeia* 53 (1991), 63.

15. Laszlof Foldenyi, "Novel and Individuality," *Neophilologus* 73, 11. My thanks to Jeffrey Staley for including this passage in his article above, 55.

16. Jesus' equality with God will be discussed in chapters 6 and 7.

17. Raymond E. Brown, *An Introduction to the New Testament* (New York/Mahwah: Paulist, 1994), 122-123.

18. J. Duncan M. Derrett, "Circumcision and Perfection: A Johannine Equation (John 7:22-23)," *Evangelical Quarterly* 63 (1991), 217.

19. James Roche, *Spirituality and Health: What's Good for the Soul Can Be Good for the Body Too* (Ottawa: Catholic Health Association of Canada, 1996), 17, 20. Quote from Zach Thomas, *Healing Touch: The Church's Forgotten Language* (Louisville: Westminster/John Knox, 1994), 44.

20. Lucy Suddreth, quoted in Doug Levy, "Tobacco Report Decried Education," *USA Today*, July 3, 1997, 4A.

21. B. D. Napier, "Community Under Law: On Hebrew Law and Its Theological Presuppositions," *Interpretation* 7 (1953), 413.

22. Thomas W. Mann, "The Reclamation of Creation," *Interpretation* 45 (1991), 362.

3. DOES THIS OFFEND YOU? DO YOU ALSO WISH TO GO AWAY?

1. Some scripture scholars debate whether the sixth chapter of John is eucharistic at all. However, the majority of those who come from the Catholic tradition find it to be so.

2. Raymond E. Brown, S.S., *The Gospel of St. John and the Johannine Epistles*, New Testament Reading Guide, 2nd rev. ed. (Collegeville, Minn.: The Liturgical Press, 1965).

3. Some find no eucharistic overtones in any of the sixth chapter. Maarten J. J. Menken summarizes this understanding when he writes that, while having eucharistic overtones, this "does not mean that the passage is primarily about the Eucharist," and: "'To eat Jesus' flesh and to drink his blood' then means: to believe in him as the one who dies for the life of the world. Or, in slightly different words: to believe that in Jesus' violent death God is acting for the life of the world." See his "John 6, 51c-58: Eucharist or Christology?," *Biblica* 74 (1993), 23, 16.

4. Wes Howard-Brook, *John's Gospel and the Renewal of the Church* (Maryknoll, N.Y.: Orbis, 1997), 49.

5. John J. Pilch, *The Cultural World of Jesus Sunday by Sunday, Cycle B* (Collegeville, Minn.: Liturgical Press, 1995), 117.

6. Wes Howard-Brook, *Becoming Children of God: John's Gospel and Radical Discipleship* (Maryknoll, N.Y.: Orbis, 1994), 146, quoting Craig Koester, *Symbolism in the Gospel of John: Meaning, Mystery, and Community* (Minneapolis: Fortress, 1994), chapter 2.

7. Peter F. Ellis, *The Genius of John: A Composition-Critical Commentary on the Fourth Gospel* (Collegeville, Minn.: The Liturgical Press, 1984), 15; see 109-11. Ellis has credited his "friend and colleague, John Gerhard, S.J. with the chiastic structure of John that centers around 6:16-21." See "The Authenticity of John 21," *St. Vladimir's Theological Quarterly* 36 (1992), esp. 17-18.

8. See Raymond E. Brown, *The Gospel according to John*, vol. 1 (New York: Doubleday, 1966), 265.

9. Pilch, 125.

10. Francis J. Moloney, S.D.B., *Signs and Shadows: Reading John 5-12* (Minneapolis: Fortress, 1996), 58. Here, if I read Moloney correctly, he seems to have moved from an earlier stress on a purely eucharistic substratum. See his "John 6 and the Celebration of the Eucharist," *Downside Review* 93 (1975), 243-51.

11. Anthony J. Blasi, *A Sociology of Johannine Christianity* (Lewiston/Queenston/Lampeter: Edwin Mellen, 1996), 269, 270.

12. For more on this see A. Joseph, "John's Second Discourse on the Bread of Life: Implications for Reconsideration of Eucharist Theology," *Prism* 10 (1995), 64-70.

13. Pilch, 122.

14. St. Augustine, Sermon 272, quoted in *Catechism of the Catholic Church*, 1396 (New York: Catholic Book Publishing, 1994), 352-53.

15. St. John Chrysostom, Homily on 1 Corinthians, quoted in *Catechism of the Catholic Church*, 1397 (New York: Catholic Book Publishing, 1994), 353.

4. WHY DO I SPEAK TO YOU AT ALL?

1. Stephen Motyer argues, somewhat in vain, I believe, that exegetes do not give proper attention to the destruction of the temple and its effect on the Christian scriptures. I believe this is a given and that exegetes are struggling with what the Jamnian religious leaders sought to stress as a force that could replace the

temple's drawing power, the law. See his *Your Father the Devil? A New Approach to John and "the Jews"* (Carlisle, U.K.: Paternoster, 1997), *passim.*

2. Jerome H. Neyrey, S.J., "The Trials (Forensic) and Tribulations (Honor Challenges) of Jesus: John 7 in Social Science Perspective," *Biblical Theology Bulletin* 26 (1996), 107.

3. The Essenes also personified the forces of evil in the devil. Whether the Essenes and the early Christians influenced each other and to what degree is not known. It is clear, however, that the two movements evidence a similar theological stance. Pagels quotes from 1 QM 19:10-12: "The Prince of Light thou has appointed to come to our support: but Satan, the angel Mastema, thou has created for the pit; he rules in darkness, and his purpose is to bring about evil and sin." She also notes that the Essenes called themselves "sons of light." Elaine Pagels, *The Origin of Satan* (New York: Random House Vintage Books, 1996), 58.

4. Ibid., xviii.

5. Ralph K. White, *Nobody Wanted War: Misperception in Vietnam and Other Wars* (Garden City, N.Y.: Doubleday Anchor Books, 1970).

6. Roy F. Baumeister, *Evil: Inside Human Violence and Cruelty* (New York: W. H. Freeman, 1997), 135, 136.

7. Ibid., 377.

8. The concept was used by Cardinal Bernardin Gantin, the former head of the Congregation for Bishops (1984–1998) of those who pressured his congregation for advancement. See John L. Allen, Jr., "Cardinal Decries 'Amazing Careerism' of Bishops on the Hunt for Advancement," *National Catholic Reporter*, May 28, 1999.

9. Another dimension of my ministry is to advise investors in religious institutions on the social/moral aspect of their portfolios. The groups I represent are members of the Interfaith Center on Corporate Responsibility (ICCR) in New York. The value of the combined portfolios of the religious entities represented at ICCR is estimated at $100 billion. I coordinate ICCR's tobacco ministry.

10. Neyrey, 114-15.

11. National Conference of Catholic Bishops, "When I Call for Help: Domestic Violence against Women," *Origins* 22 (1992), 355.

12. We know that exceptions to this law exist with the acceptance of married men who come to the Roman Church as clergy from other denominations or who are ordained in certain Eastern rites.

13. Severino Pancaro, *The Law in the Fourth Gospel: The Torah and the Gospel. Moses and Jesus, Judaism and Christianity according to John.* Novum Testamentum Supplement 42 (Leiden: E. J. Brill, 1975), 82-83.

14. Neyrey, 118.

15. Carolyn Osiek, R.S.C.J., "The 'Liberation Theology' of the Gospel of John," *The Bible Today* 27 (1989), 210-11.

16. Michael Willett Newheart, "Toward a Psycho-literary Reading of the Fourth Gospel," in *"What Is John?" Readers and Readings of the Fourth Gospel*, ed. Fernando F. Segovia (Atlanta: Scholars Press, 1996), 43.

17. M. Scott Peck, *People of the Lie: The Hope for Healing Human Evil* (New York: Simon and Schuster Touchstone Book, 1984), 39-40.

18. Ibid., 73.

19. Willett Newheart, 55.

20. I don't agree with Bailie on the source of violence in society, which he finds in mimetic desire that leads to scapegoating. It seems to me its source lies in the abuse of power expressed in the need to remain in control (which, in turn, may lead to scapegoating as it ultimately will do here in Jesus' case).

21. Gil Bailie, *Violence Unveiled* (New York: Crossroad, 1995), 221-22.

22. Ibid., 222.

23. Ibid., 223.

24. Michael H. Crosby, *House of Disciples: Church, Economics, and Justice in Matthew* (Maryknoll, N.Y.: Orbis, 1988), 251.

25. Francis J. Moloney, S.D.B., *Signs and Shadows: Reading John 5-12* (Minneapolis: Fortress, 1996), 94.

26. Bishop Kenneth Untener, quoted in John McCoy, "An Interview with Saginaw's Outspoken Bishop," *The Progress*, June 18, 1992.

27. Robert J. Karris, *Jesus and the Marginalized in John's Gospel* (Collegeville, Minn.: Liturgical Press, 1990), *passim*.

5. WOMAN, WHERE ARE THEY? HAS NO ONE CONDEMNED YOU?

1. The only major codex containing it is D, a text that is known to have quite a few interpolations.

2. Rudolf Schnackenburg's thorough discussion of the various questions around the text has been most helpful from a historical and form-critical point of view. Gail R. O'Day has given me the most insight from a feminist perspective. See Rudolf Schnackenburg, *The Gospel according to St. John*, vol. 2, trans. Cecily Hastings et al. (New York: Seabury, 1980), 162-71. Also Gail R. O'Day, "John 7:53-8:11: A Study in Misreading," *Journal of Biblical Literature* 111 (1992), 631-40.

3. O'Day, 631.

4. Raymond E. Brown, *The Gospel according to John*, vol. 1 (New York: Doubleday, 1966), 335-36.

5. C. H. Dodd, *The Interpretation of the Fourth Gospel* (Cambridge: Cambridge University, 1965), 345.

6. Another person who finds that the chapters are a kind of hodge-podge is John W. Pryor. He describes them as "a confused mass of sayings with nothing to hold them together in unity." See John W. Pryor, *John, Evangelist of the Covenant People: The Narrative and Themes of the Fourth Gospel* (Downers Grove, Ill.: InterVarsity Press, 1992), 34.

7. For an elaboration on the Lukan connection, see Michael Gourgues, "'Moi non plus je ne te condemne pas': Les mots et la theologie de Luc en Jean 8, 1-11 (la femme adultere)," *Studies in Religion/Sciences Religieuses* 19 (1990), 305-18.

8. It appears to me that a mini-chiasm can be found if one sees the beginning (7:53) and the end (8:9-11) as referring to people going home or away singly ("each" or "one by one") with the challenge and response of Jesus being the core (8:1-8).

9. The main un-Johannine word "Teacher" is used by the scribes and the Pharisees to address Jesus. Nowhere in John does any person call Jesus by that

name as a greeting or a reference, although it is used in the Synoptics with regularity. John refers to Jesus as "Teacher" only when he translates the word "Rabbi" (1:38 and 20:16). For a list of other un-Johannine words, see Barnabas Lindars, S.S.F., ed., *The Gospel of John,* New Century Bible (London: Oliphants, 1972), 308.

10. Sandra M. Schneiders, *The Revelatory Text: Interpreting the New Testament as Sacred Scripture* (San Francisco: Harper, 1991), 71.

11. Ibid., 89.

12. Lindars, 308.

13. For more on this "fit," see John Paul Heil, "The Story of Jesus and the Adulteress (John 7, 53-8,11) Reconsidered," *Biblica* 72 (1991), 182-91.

14. Gerald A. Arbuckle, S.M., Ph.D., "Obstacles to Pastoral Creativity," *Human Development* 16 (1995), 15.

15. Although Neyrey's words actually refer to the Markan community, I believe that they can also be applied to the Johannine community. See Jerome H. Neyrey, S.J., "Questions, Chreiai and Honor Challenges: The Interface of Rhetoric and Culture in Mark's Gospel," *Catholic Biblical Quarterly* 60 (1998), 657-81.

16. Arbuckle, 18.

17. Hisako Kinukawa, "On John 7:53-8:11: A Well-Cherished but Much-Clouded Story," in *Readings from This Place: Social Location and Biblical Interpretation in Global Perspective,* vol. 2, ed. Fernando F. Segovia and Mary Ann Tolbert (Minneapolis: Fortress, 1995), 85.

18. Ibid., 90.

19. Anthony Lewis, "The First Stone," in Abroad at Home column, *The New York Times,* June 9, 1997, A23.

20. Ibid.

6. DO YOU BELIEVE IN THE SON OF MAN?

1. R. Alan Culpepper has charted an excellent comparison of parallel points in the story-lines of chapters 5 and 9. See his *Anatomy of the Fourth Gospel: A Study in Literary Design* (Philadelphia: Fortress, 1983), 139-40. See also Bruce J. Malina and Richard L. Rohrbaugh, *Social-Science Commentary on the Gospel of John* (Minneapolis: Fortress, 1998), 109.

2. Paul Duke, *Irony in the Fourth Gospel* (Atlanta: John Knox, 1985), 118. Although she doesn't refer to the seven-fold structure of chapter 9 as a chiasm, Gail R. O'Day divides the text into the same sections. See *The Word Disclosed: John's Story and Narrative Preaching* (St. Louis: CBP Press, 1987), 55-56.

3. The blindness of Tobit seems to be an exception to this pattern. See Tobit 2:9-10.

4. O'Day, 59.

5. Guillermo Cook, "Seeing, Judging and Acting: Evangelism in Jesus' Way according to John 9," *Evangelical Review of Theology* 16 (1992), 255.

6. Ibid., 256.

7. For a survey of this, see Stephen Motyer, *Your Father the Devil? A New Approach to John and "the Jews"* (Carlisle, U.K.: Paternoster, 1997), 92-94. Mo-

tyer rejects the Martyn hypothesis because he argues that the polemic, if understood in first-century categories, was actually an evangelistic tool to win over Jewish converts. He states that "There is now a healthy consensus that (a) the Yavnean sages did indeed introduce a curse on the *minim* towards the end of the first century, but (b) we cannot be sure who the intended *minim* actually were, nor (c) what the precise wording was, and (d) since the curse worked by self-exclusion...it must have functioned more as exhortation to Jews generally than as a specific means of social exclusion. This fits with (e) the insight that the Yavnean sages were more concerned to heal breaches than to reinforce them" (p. 93). I find Motyer's "arguments" unsatisfactory, especially since he agrees that there was in fact a curse on the *minim* toward the end of the first century. From 9:22, 12:42, and 16:2 it seems quite clear the author of John identified his community and readers with those so accursed.

8. O'Day, 66-67. For more on this, see Ignace de la Potterie, "*Oida* et *ginōskō*, les deux modes de la connaissance dans le quatrième evangile," *Biblica* 40 (1959), 709-25.

9. O'Day, 66-67.

10. John 1:51; 3:13-15; 5:27; 6:27, 53, 62; 8:28; 12:23, 34; 13:31.

11. For more on the background of "Son of Man," see John R. Donahue, *Catholic Biblical Quarterly* 48 (1996), 484-98.

12. Margaret Pamment, "The Son of Man in the Fourth Gospel," *Journal of Theological Studies* 36 (1985), 58.

13. Archbishop Rembert G. Weakland, O.S.B., "Born Blind," in "Herald of Hope," *[Milwaukee] Catholic Herald*, March 21, 1996, 3.

14. The original insight for this approach to "seeing" comes from Shannon-Elizabeth Farrell, "Seeing the Father (Jn 6:46, 14:9)." This was a three part series in *Science et Esprit*, 44 (1992), 1-24, 159-83, and 307-29.

15. Cook, 261.

16. Cindy Wooden, "Heaven: Pope Says Heaven Is Intimate Relationship with God," *Catholic Herald*, July 29, 1999, 1.

17. Rudolf Bultmann, "*Pisteuō*," in *Theological Dictionary of the New Testament*, vol. 6, ed. Gerhard Friedrich, tr. Groffrey Bromiley (Grand Rapids, Mich.: Wm. B. Eerdmans, 1968), 222-23.

18. Ibid., 225.

7. FOR WHICH OF THESE ARE YOU GOING TO STONE ME?

1. For more on this, see Miguel Rodríguez Ruiz, "El discurso del Buen Pastor (Jn 10, 1-18). Coherencia teológico-literaria e interpretación," *Estudios Bíblicos* 48 (1990), 5-45.

2. Some exegetes argue for a structuring of 9:1-10:21 so that the "seeing" of the first part (9:1-41) might be paralleled, within the feast of Booths, with the "hearing" of the second part (10:1-21).

3. See John Pilch, *The Cultural World of Jesus Sunday by Sunday, Cycle C* (Collegeville, Minn.: Liturgical Press, 1995), 77.

4. Ibid.

5. Raymond E. Brown, *The Community of the Beloved Disciple: The Life, Loves, and Hates of an Individual Church in New Testament Times* (New York/Ramsey/Toronto: Paulist, 1979), 87.

6. For the kinds of "knowing" in John, see K. James Carl, "The Idea of 'Knowing' in the Johannine Literature," *Bangalore Theological Forum* 25 (1993), 53-75. For "knowing" in antisocieties, see Bruce J. Malina and Richard L. Rohrbaugh, *Social-Science Commentary on the Gospel of John* (Minneapolis: Fortress, 1998), 32.

7. Anthony J. Blasi, *A Sociology of Johannine Christianity* (Lewiston/Queenston/Lampeter: Edwin Mellen, 1996), 267.

8. J. Terence Forestell, C.S.B., *The Word of the Cross: Salvation as Revelation in the Fourth Gospel* (Rome: Biblical Institute, 1974), 191-92.

9. Ibid., 16.

10. Marcus Borg, *Jesus in Contemporary Scholarship* (Valley Forge, Pa.: Trinity, 1994), 28.

11. John Dominic Crossan, *The Historical Jesus: The Life of a Mediterranean Jewish Peasant* (San Francisco: HarperSan Francisco, 1991).

12. John P. Meier, *A Marginal Jew: Rethinking the Historical Jesus* (New York: Doubleday, 1971).

13. E. P. Sanders, *Jesus and Judaism* (Philadelphia: Fortress, 1985).

14. Elisabeth Schussler Fiorenza, *In Memory of Her: A Feminist Theological Reconstruction of Christian Origins* (New York: Crossroad, 1983).

15. Rudolf Schnackenburg, *The Friend We Have in Jesus*, trans. Mark A. Christian (Louisville: Westminster John Knox), 1997.

16. Xavier Leon-Dufour, "Ouvertures johanniques sur la mystique," *Christus* 162 (1994), 180-88.

17. Those without an image are 4:26; 6:20; 7:29; 8:23 (2x), 24, 28, 58; 10:30, 38; 13:19; 14:3, 20; 18:5, 6, 8; those with an image are 6:35, 48, 51; 8:12, 23; 9:5; 10:7, 9, 11, 14; 11:25; 14:6 (3x implied); 15:1, 5; see 18:37. Different numerations arise from various ways of interpreting the "I am" statements.

18. See Michael A. K. Halliday, *Language as Social Semiotic: The Social Interpretation of Language and Meaning* (Baltimore: University Park, 1978), 171.

19. Bruce J. Malina, *The Gospel of John in Sociolinguistic Perspective*. Forty-eighth Colloquy Protocol (Berkeley, Calif.: Center for Hermeneutical Studies in Hellenistic and Modern Culture, 1985), 16. An update can be found in Malina's "John's: The Maverick Christian Group. The Evidence of Sociolinguistics," *Biblical Theology Bulletin* 24 (1994), 167-82. Also Malina and Rohrbaugh, 14.

20. Michael Willett Newheart, "Toward a Psycho-literary Reading of the Fourth Gospel," in *"What Is John?" Readers and Readings of the Fourth Gospel*, ed. Fernando F. Segovia (Atlanta: Scholars Press, 1996), 52.

21. Michael Bauer and Miriam Morgan, "The Bay Area Palate: We Eat Chic and Healthy," *San Francisco Chronicle*, April 30, 1999, 1. The *Chronicle* commissioned ACNielsen to study people's eating patterns. It tracked consumer buying habits for 152 products in large supermarkets nationwide. The result? Marked differences exist between regions of the U.S.A.

22. "We Are What We Eat: The Survey Seems to Confirm the Stereotypes," editorial, *San Francisco Chronicle*, May 3, 1999.

23. Rudolf Schnackenburg, *The Gospel according to St. John*, vol. 2, trans. Cecily Hastings et al. (New York: Seabury, 1980), 289-90.

24. Ludger Schenke, "Das Rätsel von Tür und Hirt. Wer es löst, hat gewonnen!," *Trierer Theologische Zeitschrift* 105 (1996), 81-100.

25. Andrew Pollack, "Paper Trail Haunts G.M. after It Loses Injury Suit: An Old Memo Hinted at the Price of Safety," *The New York Times*, July 12, 1999.

26. In a conversation with the office of Catholic Cemeteries for the United States, I was told that three images connected to Jesus' death (Calvary, Holy Cross, and Mt. Olivet) came before those called "Resurrection."

27. Franz Rosenzweig, quoted in Marie-Louise Gubler, "'Ich bin der Weg und die Wahrheit und das Leben' (Joh 14, 6)," *Diakonia: Internationale Zeitschrift für die Praxis der Kirche* 24 (1993). Summary in "'I am the Way, the Truth and the Life' (Jn 14:6)," *Theology Digest* 41 (1994), 150.

28. As I was writing this book, *The Wall Street Journal* reported that, contrary to earlier statements "throughout the 11-week air war against Yugoslavia, the North Atlantic Treaty Organization said it had no formal contacts with the loosely organized Kosovo Liberation Army, or KLA," but that, with the fighting over, "KLA and NATO officials say they worked more closely together than previously admitted." Matthew Kaminski and John Reed, "KLA Played Key Role in Allied Air War," July 6, 1999.

29. For these insights into "truth" in John's gospel, I am indebted to David J. Hawkin, "Johannine Christianity and Ideological Commitment," *Expository Times* 102 (1990), 74-77 who builds on de la Potterie, below. See also his "The Johannine Concept of Truth and Its Implications for a Technological Society," *Evangelical Quarterly* 59 (1987), 3-13.

30. Jerome H. Neyrey, S.J., *An Ideology of Revolt: John's Christology in Social-Science Perspective* (Philadelphia: Fortress, 1988), 131.

31. Ignace de la Potterie, "'Je suis la Voie, la Vérité et la Vie' (Jn 14:6)," *Nouvelle Revue Théologique* 88 (1996), 925.

32. George R. Beasley-Murray, *Gospel of Life: Theology in the Fourth Gospel* (Peabody, Mass.: Hendrickson, 1991), 3.

33. Morton T. Kelsey, "Vine and Branches," *The Pecos Benedictine*, October, 1995, 2.

34. Pheme Perkins, *Love Commands in the New Testament* (New York/Ramsey: Paulist, 1982), 109.

8. DID I NOT TELL YOU THAT IF YOU BELIEVED, YOU WOULD SEE THE GLORY OF GOD?

1. It is likely that this story, as is the case in many of the Johannine stories, underwent more than one redaction. See D. Burkett, "Two Accounts of Lazarus' Resurrection in John 11," *Novum Testamentum* (1994), 209-32.

2. Peter F. Ellis, *The Genius of John: A Composition-Critical Commentary on the Fourth Gospel* (Collegeville, Minn.: The Liturgical Press, 1984), 177.

3. I make my remarks about Martha aware that, where I find deficient faith in her, others find her an example of "discerning faith," in contrast to Mary. See,

for instance, R. Alan Culpepper, *Anatomy of the Fourth Gospel: A Study in Literary Design* (Philadelphia: Fortress, 1983), 141.

4. Gail R. O'Day, *The Word Disclosed: John's Story and Narrative Preaching* (St. Louis: CBP Press, 1987), 76.

5. Rudolf Schnackenburg, *The Gospel according to St. John,* vol. 2, trans. Cecily Hastings et al. (New York: Crossroad, 1980), 335-36 and George R. Beasley-Murray, *John,* Word Biblical Commentary (Waco, Tex.: Word, 1987), 67-68.

6. Wes Howard-Brook, *Becoming Children of God* (Maryknoll, N.Y.: Orbis, 1994), 262.

7. Ibid.

8. Most likely Lazarus's "raising" was more in the nature of a resuscitation than anything like a resurrection. For more on this, see Paul S. Minear, "The Promise of Life in the Gospel of John," *Theology Today* 49 (1993), 485-99.

9. Sister Lauretta Mather, O.S.F., "Come Forth: Naming the Tombs, Making the Daybreak," address given at the Twenty-fifth Anniversary Meeting of the LCWR, August 27, 1981, *Sisters Today* 53 (1982), 265.

10. Ibid., 266.

11. The Sacred Congregation dealing with religious communities had unilaterally separated the German province of the School Sisters of St. Francis, headed by Lauretta Mather, from her authority and placed it directly under its own jurisdiction. This created much pain and alienation in the world-wide order. At the time when this speech was given, the issue had not yet been resolved, so the pain was felt very keenly.

12. Mather, 166-67.

13. O'Day, 98.

14. C. K. Barrett notes of this reference to "the Pharisees" that "Here John seems to speak of them as an official body, like priests, magistrates, or councillors. If he did so speak of them he was ignorant of Judaism as it was before A.D. 70. This judgment is only partially palliated by the observation that the scribes formed one element in the Sanhedrin and that most of the scribes were Pharisees." See *The Gospel according to St. John,* 2nd ed. (Philadelphia: Westminster, 1978), 405.

15. Jerome H. Neyrey, S.J., "The Trials (Forensic) and Tribulations (Honor Challenges) of Jesus: John 7 in Social Science Perspective," *Biblical Theology Bulletin* 26 (1996), 118.

16. In 1966 Cardinal Alfredo Ottaviani noted that the status quo should be maintained regarding the teaching in order to protect magisterial authority. For more on this see Robert McClory, *The Turning Point: The Inside Story of the Papal Birth Control Commission, and How* Humanae Vitae *Changed the Life of Patty Crowley and the Future of the Church* (New York: Crossroad, 1955).

17. John Painter, "Quest and Rejection Stories in John," *Journal for the Study of the New Testament* 36 (1989), 38.

18. Rudolf Schnackenburg, *Jesus in the Gospels: A Biblical Christology,* trans. O. C. Dean, Jr. (Louisville: Westminster John Knox, 1995), 240.

19. Maria-Luisa Rigato, "Maria di Betania nella redaazione giovannea," *Antonianum* 66 (1991), 203-26.

20. Wilhelm Wuellner, "Putting Life back into the Lazarus Story and Its Reading: The Narrative Rhetoric of John 11 as the Narration of Faith," *Semeia* 53 (1991), 113-32.

9. TRANSITION: WHAT SHOULD I SAY—"FATHER, SAVE ME FROM THIS HOUR"?

1. Rudolf Schnackenburg says this passage represents "the work of the evangelist." See *The Gospel according to St. John,* vol. 2, trans. Cecily Hastings et al. (New York: Crossroad, 1987), 380.

2. Gale A. Yee, "The Day Was the Sabbath," *The Bible Today* (1990), 203.

3. For more on the "Son of Man," see chapter 6.

4. Bruce J. Malina, "John's: The Maverick Christian Group: The Evidence of Sociolinguistics," *Biblical Theology Bulletin* 24 (1994), 180.

5. Johannes Beutler, S.J., "Greeks Come to See Jesus (John 12, 20f)," *Biblica* 71 (1990), 343.

6. Schnackenburg, 2:392.

7. For more on this, see Judith L. Kovacs, "'Now Shall the Ruler of This World Be Driven Out': Jesus' Death as Cosmic Battle in John 12:20-36," *Journal of Biblical Literature* 114 (1995), 227-47.

8. Paul Hinnebusch, O.P., *"Come and You Will See!,"* St. *John's Course in Contemplation* (New York: Alba House, 1990), 23-24.

9. Larry Rohter, "4 Salvadorans Say They Killed U.S. Nuns on Orders of Military," *The New York Times,* April 3, 1998, A1.

10. The thesis of Beutler (337-47) is that this whole section revolves around Isaiah's notion of the Suffering Servant. Given John's stress on "seeing" as the core of discipleship, I'd lean away from too great a stress on the Suffering Servant notion. This seems more of a Synoptic view.

11. Gail R. O'Day, "Johannine Theology as Sectarian Theology," in *"What Is John?" Readers and Readings of the Fourth Gospel,* ed. Fernando F. Segovia (Atlanta: Scholars Press, 1966), 202. In this fine article, O'Day details the three main "conventional" atonement theories (ransom, substitutionary/sacrificial, and moral influence) and shows that "none of the traditional atonement theologies presents a soteriology that accords with that offered in the Fourth Gospel" which is really about humans being reconciled with God in a restoration of relationships.

10. DO YOU KNOW WHAT I HAVE DONE TO YOU?

1. John Meier, "The Eucharist at the Last Supper: Did It Happen?," The Kenrick Lecture of 1995, *Theology Digest* 42 (1995), 343-44.

2. For more on this, see R. Alan Culpepper, "The Johannine *Hypodeigma*: A Reading of John 13," *Semeia* 53 (1991), 133-49; Francis J. Moloney, S.D.B., "The Structure and Message of John 13:1-38," *Australian Biblical Review* 34 (1986), 1-16; and Yves Simoens, *La gloire d'aimer: Structures stylistiques et interprétatives dans le Discours de la Cène (Jn 13-17),* Analecta Biblica, 90 (Rome: Biblical Institute, 1981).

3. Culpepper, 133-49. I have divided his seventh section into two to highlight the "knowing" and "doing" in 13:35 and its connection to the first section (13:1-5).

4. Sandra M. Schneiders, I.H.M., "The Foot Washing (John 13:1-20): An Experiment in Hermeneutics," *The Catholic Biblical Quarterly* 43 (1981), 79.

5. See Raymond E. Brown, *The Community of the Beloved Disciple: The Life, Loves, and Hates of an Individual Church in New Testament Times* (New York/Ramsey/Toronto: Paulist, 1979), 81-91.

6. Writing from my own social location, which involves being a Roman Catholic cleric, I find it fascinating that many in my institution find no problem taking passages from the scriptures that elevate Peter's representative status, especially Matthew 16:16-18, but are silent regarding the other equally representative texts. This represents blindness at its best and an ideological bias at its worst.

7. Culpepper, 138.

8. Schneiders, 83.

9. Jerome H. Neyrey, S.J., "The Footwashing in John 13:6-11: Transformation Ritual or Ceremony?," in *The Social World of the First Christians: Essays in Honor of Wayne A. Meeks*, ed. L. Michael White and O. Larry Yarbrough (Minneapolis: Fortress, 1995), 203.

10. For an interesting connection between the plan to betray Jesus and impurity arising from Judas's alliance with religious forces aligned with a foreign power in the hope of financial gain in 13:11 (see 18:2-4) and their connection to various First Testament texts (Num 31:16; Ez 14:11; 16:34; 20:7, 30–31; 36:25), see J. Duncan M. Derrett, "Impurity and Idolatry: John 13, 11; Ezekiel 36, 25," *Biblical Origins* 34 (1992), 87-92.

11. For more on this, see Lucy Feiden Rabin, *Ford Madox Brown and the Pre-Raphael History-Picture*, dissertation (Bryn Mawr, Pa.: Bryn Mawr College, 1973/1978), 215-221. According to Rabin, the face of Peter reflects not frustration but intense concentration. I find that interpretation difficult, both from an exegetical viewpoint in terms of the text and from an aesthetic viewpoint.

12. Schneiders, 91.

13. Neyrey, 200. Here he refers to Bruce J. Malina, *Christian Origins and Cultural Anthropology: Practical Models for Biblical Interpretation* (Atlanta: John Knox, 1986), 139-43.

14. Anthony J. Blasi, *A Sociology of Johannine Community* (Lewiston/Queenston/Lampeter: Edwin Mellen, 1996), 268.

15. Meier, 344.

16. Moloney, 6.

17. The last chapter will be devoted entirely to the meaning and role of this Beloved One in the Johannine community and in successive Christian communities through the ages.

18. R. Alan Culpepper, *Anatomy of the Fourth Gospel: A Study in Literary Design* (Philadelphia: Fortress, 1983), 124-25.

19. For a very helpful elaboration on its meaning see Rudolf Schnackenburg, *The Gospel according to St. John*, vol. 3, trans. David Smith and G. A. Kon (New York: Crossroad, 1982), 49.

20. Craig R. Koester, *Symbolism in the Fourth Gospel: Meaning, Mystery, Community* (Minneapolis: Fortress, 1995), 210. For more on the honor/glory connection in John, see C. H. Dodd, *The Interpretation of the Fourth Gospel* (Cambridge: Cambridge University, 1970), 208.

21. Koester, 244.

22. "This aspect of Jn's story clearly indicates that those commentators who see Jn's group as recently broken away from (or ejected from) existing Jewish institutions are quite correct (e.g., Brown, 1979). For the 'Johannine community' previous lines defining and delimiting meaningful social relations and institutions are largely eradicated. Thus group members find themselves beyond ordinary limits, in a situation in which the individual can find him/herself in a restored and culturally unadulterated humanity based on the realization of the new values that emerged in the uniqueness of Jesus, the Messiah." (Bruce J. Malina, *The Gospel of John in Sociolinguistic Perspective*. Forty-eighth Colloquy Protocol, March 11, 1984 [Berkeley, Calif.: Center for Hermeneutical Studies in Hellenistic and Modern Culture, 1985], 10-11.) For an updated version of this, see Malina's "John's: the Maverick Christian Group. The Evidence of Sociolinguistics," *Biblical Theology Bulletin* 24 (1994), esp. 178-81.

23. Bruce J. Malina and Richard L. Rohrbaugh, *Social-Science Commentary on the Gospel of John* (Minneapolis: Fortress, 1998), 48.

24. For a full treatment of the love command in John's gospel and the letters, see Jorg Augenstein, *Das Liebesgebot im Johannesevangelium und in den Johannesbriefen* (Stuttgart: Kohlhammer, 1993). For more on the relationship between the love commandment and "remaining" with/in Jesus, see Malina and Rohrbaugh, 55, 234 and P. J. Hartin, "'Remain in Me' (John 15:5). The foundation for the Ethical and its Consequences in the Farewell Discourses," *Neotestamentica* 25 (1991), 341-56. As it is treated in 1 John, see Edward Malatesta, S.J., *Interiority and Covenant: An Exegetical Study of the* ménein en *and* enai en *Expressions in 1 John,* excerpt from his thesis (Rome: Pontifical Biblical Institute, 1974), esp. 10-35.

25. Blasi, 190-91. Blasi is following the best in Johannine scholarship when he indicates that the love commandment reveals the final hand of the editor. For more on this, see Schnackenburg, 3:53f.

26. Urban C. von Wahlde, "Community in Conflict: The History and Social Context of the Johannine Community," in *Gospel Interpretation: Narrative-Critical and Social Scientific Approaches,* ed. Jack Dean Kingsbury, (Valley Forge, Pa.: Trinity Press International, 1997), 223-28.

27. Neyrey, 210.

28. Some of the details in this story have been changed.

11. IF I HAVE SPOKEN RIGHTLY, WHY DO YOU STRIKE ME?

1. It is for those more expert than I to argue about comparisons of John's version of Jesus' trial and passion with those of the Synoptics, as well as historical issues that challenge John's version. For some of this see Rudolf Schnackenburg,

The Gospel according to St. John, vol. 3, trans. David Smith and G. A. Kon (New York: Crossroad, 1982), 218ff. and Raymond E. Brown, S.S., *The Gospel according to John,* vol. 2 (Garden City, N.Y.: Doubleday, 1970), 828ff.

2. I know that 18:34 also is a question asked by Jesus of Pilate. However, because the other two questions seem to relate to contemporary issues affecting the witness of disciples in today's church and world, I have chosen only this section for comment. Furthermore, I have also chosen not to comment on the three denials of Jesus by Peter (18:15-18 and 18:25-27).

3. Reflections on Jesus' Farewell Discourse can be found in the introduction. While these do not do justice to the richness of the theology presented in the Farewell Discourse, some of its themes are addressed in other chapters of this book.

4. Brown, 2:816.

5. Arthur J. Droge, "The Status of Peter in the Fourth Gospel: A Note on John 18:10-11," *Journal of Biblical Literature* 109 (1990), 309-10. This description of Peter's behavior and its rationale will be further expanded in the next chapters. Here it is mentioned only to remind John's readers, including those of us who are Roman Catholic, to be aware of *John's interpretation.* We need to free ourselves as much as possible from our own received ideology related to Peter, an ideology that has been handed down to us through a patriarchically and clerically motivated tradition based almost exclusively on the Synoptic interpretation.

6. Stanley Hauerwas, *The Peaceable Kingdom: A Primer in Christian Ethics* (Notre Dame, Ind.: University of Notre Dame, 1983), 144.

7. David Stevens, "Truth Confronting Power and Order," *Doctrine and Life* 40 (1990), 194.

8. Ibid., 195. I have a major difference with Girard regarding the source of violence. Where he finds it in mimetic desire and the conflict that arises from desiring not only to possess what someone else has but to be who the other is, I find violence arising from the notion of power itself when power is defined as the ability to influence others in a way that is an expression of control rather than of care.

9. Mark W. Stibbe, *John* (Sheffield: JSOT Press, 1993), 184.

10. Brown, 2:822. Jerome Neyrey ("The Footwashing in John 13:6-11: Transformation Ritual or Ceremony?," in *The Social World of the First Christians: Essays in Honor of W. A. Meeks,* ed. L. Michael White and O. Larry Yarbrough [Minneapolis: Fortress, 1995], 210-11) goes further in his comparison of Peter and the Beloved Disciple. In a novel approach, he links this passage with chapter 10 which talks about the good ("noble") shepherd who leads the sheep and is willing to lay down his life for them (10:4, 11). He finds in the link an example of a kind of ritual that gets worked out in ceremonial form in 18:15-18. In this dynamic, Peter becomes the sheep led by the shepherd, the Beloved Disciple. At another level, Peter is symbolic of the hireling who will not be willing to lay down his life; the Beloved Disciple becomes the "noble" shepherd who is willing to do so. Neyrey notes that, whatever "the Johannine group knew of the traditional role and status of Peter, that would be severely challenged by Peter's association here [in chapter 10] with the hireling and not the shepherd." Laying the foun-

dation between chapters 10 and 18, and the comparison between the Petrine reality and the Johannine vision, Neyrey continues:

> Returning to Jesus' parables of shepherds, doors, and sheep in 10:1-4 and 11-13, we learn that the true shepherd enters the door; the doorkeeper recognizes and admits him; and he calls the sheep by name. This fully describes what the Beloved Disciple does in 18:15-18:

Metaphorical Description of the Noble Shepherd	*Johannine Description of the Beloved Disciple*
1. *Shepherd Enters by the Door* "He who enters by the door is the shepherd of the sheep" (10:2).	1. *Beloved Disciple Enters By the Door* "As the disciple was known to the high priest, he entered . . . while Peter stood outside the door" (18:15).
2. *Gatekeeper Recognizes Him* "He who enters by the door is the shepherd of the sheep. To him the gatekeeper opens" (10:2-3).	2. *Gatekeeper Recognizes Him* "So the other disciple, who was known to the high priest, went out and spoke to the maid who opened the door" (18:16).
3. *He Leads the Sheep In/Out* "He calls his own sheep by name and leads them out. When he has brought out all his own, he goes before them, and the sheep follow him" (10:3-4).	3. *He Leads the Sheep In* "Peter stood outside the door. . . . The other disciple spoke to the maid who kept the door and brought Peter in" (18:16).

In fact, using the perspective of this study, we should label the actions described in 18:15-18 as a ceremony. The respective roles of Beloved Disciple and Peter are confirmed as shepherd and sheep. Far from being either shepherd or noble, Peter acts out the inferior role of the sheep.

11. Edwin A. Abbott, *The Fourfold Gospel, I,* Diatessarica 10 (New York: G. P. Putnam, 1913), noted in "Notes on Recent Exposition," *Expository Times* 25 (1914), 149-59.

12. Brown, 2:824, n. 17.

13. Donald Senior, C.P., *The Passion of Jesus in the Gospel of John* (Collegeville, Minn.: Liturgical Press, 1991), 60.

14. Ignace de la Potterie, S.J., *The Hour of Jesus: the Passion and the Resurrection of Jesus according to John: Text and Spirit,* trans. Dom Gregory Murray O.S.B. (Middlegreen, Slough, England: St. Paul, 1989), 65.

15. This position is against that of C. K. Barrett who sees "the world" and "*hoi Ioudaioi*" as the same in this passage. Otherwise little reason seems to be needed for the reference to the temple and the synagogue. Jesus' message is to the

world, the temple, and the synagogue. See Barrett's *The Gospel according to St. John*, 2nd ed. (Philadelphia: Westminster, 1978), 528.

16. Senior, 61.

17. M. Scott Peck, *People of the Lie: The Hope for Healing Human Evil* (New York: Simon and Schuster Touchstone Books, 1983), 75-76.

18. de la Potterie, 73-74.

19. Senior, 62.

20. Peck, 213.

21. Ibid., 215.

22. Ibid., 223.

23. Ibid., 224.

24. Schnackenburg, 3:239.

25. Ibid., 228.

26. Stibbe, 181.

12. DO YOU LOVE ME?

1. For John, the fact that Mary Magdalene was the first to witness the risen Christ (20:11-18) does not seem to "count" because women did not "count" in that culture. Only males could give valid testimony. Thus John refers to the incident to be discussed in this chapter—the fishing story—as "the third time that Jesus appeared to the disciples after he was raised from the dead" (21:14).

2. Raymond E. Brown, *The Gospel according to John,* vol. 2 (Garden City, N.Y.: Doubleday, 1970), 1080.

3. There is also debate as to the source of the three parts and what links there may be between these, or some of these, and the Synoptics, especially Lukan passages. M.-E. Boismard has argued that the final redactor of Luke was also the final editor of John's gospel and, therefore, of this chapter. See "Le Chapitre xxi de S. Jean: Essai de critique literaire," *Revue Biblique* 54 (1947), 473-501. While acknowledging the arguments about questions related to the three parts constituting this chapter, I will not elaborate on these arguments. It seems to me that such issues are more properly addressed by exegetes using the historical critical method or stressing source criticism.

4. P. J. Hartin, "The Role of Peter in the Fourth Gospel," *Neotestametica* 24 (1990), 59.

5. John refers to the group Jesus has chosen as "the twelve" in 6:70, 71 and 20:24.

6. Arthur H. Maynard, "The Role of Peter in the Fourth Gospel," *New Testament Studies* 30 (1984), 546.

7. Brown, 2:1006-7.

8. This group is represented in the work entitled *Peter in the New Testament,* ed. Raymond E. Brown, K. P. Donfried, and John Reumann (Minneapolis and New York: Augsburg Publishing and Paulist Press, 1973).

9. Raymond F. Collins, "From John to the Beloved Disciple: An Essay on Johannine Characters," in *Gospel Interpretation: Narrative-Critical and Social-Scientific Approaches,* ed. Jack Dean Kingsbury (Harrisburg, Pa.: Trinity, 1997), 209.

10. Jerome H. Neyrey, S.J., *An Ideology of Revolt: John's Christology in Social Scientific Perspective* (Philadelphia: Fortress, 1988), 165-66.

11. Hartin, 58.

12. R. Mahoney, *Two Disciples at the Tomb: The Background and Message of John 20:1-10* (Bern: Herbert Lang, 1974).

13. Francis J. Moloney, S.D.B., "John 18:15-27: A Johannine View of the Church," *The Downside Review* 12 (1994), 241, 242.

14. Raymond Brown notes that "Discipleship is the primary category for John; and closeness to Jesus, not apostolic mission, is what confers dignity." See *The Community of the Beloved Disciple: The Life, Loves, and Hates of an Individual Church in New Testament Times* (New York/Ramsey/Toronto: Paulist, 1979), 82, n. 154.

15. Whether this passage means what I indicate here—that Peter was returning to his previous occupation—is debated as well. It can be argued, for instance, that nowhere does John's gospel identify Peter with fishing as a trade. The implication comes from other sources in the Synoptics and in tradition. I think I am in good company, however, when I make the assumption that Peter was a fisherman prior to his encounter with Jesus. See, among others, C. K. Barrett, *The Gospel according to St. John*, 2nd ed. (Philadelphia: Westminster, 1955), 577; Brown, *The Gospel,* 2:1096; Rudolf Schnackenburg, *The Gospel according to St. John,* vol. 3, trans. David Smith and G. A. Kon (New York: Crossroad, 1982), 353; Donald Senior, C.P., *The Passion of Jesus in the Gospel of John* (Collegeville, Minn.: The Liturgical Press, 1991), 141; Mark W. Stibbe, *John* (Sheffield: JSOT Press, 1993), 210. Barrett and Schnackenburg are less sure about this interpretation—as are others. See, for example, Kevin Quast, *Peter and the Beloved Disciple: Figures for a Community in Crisis,* Journal for the Study of the New Testament Supplement Series 32 (Sheffield: JSOT Press, 1989), 139-40.

16. D. H. Gee, "Why Did Peter Spring into the Sea? (John 21:7)," *The Journal of Theological Studies* 40 (1989), 488. For others supporting the notion of Peter's leap into the water as the reaction of a shame-based person, see Stibbe, 211 and Pheme Perkins, *Peter: Apostle For the Whole Church* (Columbia, S.C.: University of South Carolina, 1994), 99.

17. Peter F. Ellis, "The Authenticity of John 21," *St. Vladimir's Theological Quarterly* 36 (1992), 19. Acknowledging that "the tendency to 'rehabilitate' Peter, after his triple denial, in the encounter with the risen one, is hardly to be doubted," Schnackenburg adds: "But this notion accepted by most exegetes is still in need of precision. It is not only a matter of exhibiting the pardon granted Peter by Jesus; over and above that, the scene expresses two important data of the Peter-story: his entrusting with the pastoral ministry and his death as a follower of Jesus" (362).

18. Jerome Neyrey, S.J., "The Footwashing in John 13:6-11: Transformation Ritual or Ceremony?" in *The Social World of the First Christians: Essays in Honor of W. A. Meeks,* ed. L. Michael White and O. Larry Yarbrough (Minneapolis: Fortress, 1995), 211ff.

19. I am indebted to Larry Novakowski, then program director at Queenshouse, Saskatoon, Saskatchewan, for giving me this insight as he made a retreat I gave on "Questions Jesus Asks Us," July 31, 1999.

20. Neyrey, 211-12.

21. Schnackenburg, 3:366.

22. Brown, *The Community*, 87.

23. Brown, *The Gospel of John*, 2:1115-16. In further reflections on this same passage, Brown notes that Vatican I cited John 21:15-17, along with Matthew 16:16-19 as biblical texts establishing Peter as "constituted by Christ the Lord as *chief of all the apostles* and as visible head of the Church on earth" (italics Brown's). However, Brown notes that this citation is one of the "few examples where the Roman Catholic Church has solemnly committed itself about the literal meaning of a biblical text, that is, about what the author meant when he wrote it." He concludes his reflection by declaring: "In our judgment, exegetes who think that Peter had authority over the other disciples cannot conclude this from John xxi 15-17 *taken alone* but must bring into the discussion the larger NT background of Peter's activities" (1116, 1117).

24. Timothy Wiarda, "John 21.1-23: Narrative Unity and Its Implications," *Journal for the Study of the New Testament* 46 (1992), 67. Italics his. I think Wiarda's statement has to be taken to mean that the portrayal of Peter is meant to be a model for authentic discipleship rather than an apologia for any office or function in the church.

25. Ibid., 68. Italics his.

26. Quast, 135.

13. IF IT IS MY WILL THAT THIS ONE REMAIN UNTIL I COME, WHAT IS THAT TO YOU?

1. Because of the way I will be discussing the identity and function of the Beloved Disciple, I believe it better to refer to this figure as "this one" to include all possible disciples rather than interpreting this one as "he." Hopefully, as the chapter develops, the reader will understand my rationale, if not agree with it! Sandra Schneiders has raised the possibility that the Beloved Disciple need not be classified as a male. She suggests the Samaritan woman as a possible candidate to serve as "the evangelist's *textual alter ego*." Sandra M. Schneiders, "'Because of the Woman's Testimony...': Reexamining the Issue of Authorship in the Fourth Gospel," *New Testament Studies* 44 (1998), 532.

2. Raymond E. Brown, S.S., *The Community of the Beloved Disciple: The Life, Loves, and Hates of an Individual Church in New Testament Times* (New York/Ramsey/Toronto: Paulist, 1979), 83.

3. John Painter, "Quest and Rejection Stories in John," *Journal for the Study of the New Testament* 36 (1989), 32-33. See also his *The Quest for the Messiah: the History, Literature and Theology of the Johannine Community*, 2nd ed. (Nashville: Abingdon, 1993), 213.

4. Arthur H. Maynard, "The Role of Peter in the Fourth Gospel," *New Testament Studies* 30 (1984), 540.

5. Mark W. Stibbe, *John as Storyteller: Narrative Criticism and the Fourth Gospel* (Cambridge: Cambridge University, 1994), esp. 96-105.

6. Among those who do not identify the anonymous disciple in chapter 18 with the Beloved Disciple are David J. Hawkin, "The Function of the Beloved

Disciple Motif in the Johannine Redaction," *Laval Théologique et Philosophique* 33 (1977), 148-49; Barnabas Lindars, *The Gospel of John* (Grand Rapids, Mich.: Eerdmans, 1972), 31-32; Margaret Pamment, "The Fourth Gospel's Beloved Disciple," *Expository Times* 94 (1983), 366; and possibly Rudolf Schnackenburg, *The Gospel according to St. John*, vol. 3, trans. David Smith and G. A. Kon (New York: Crossroad, 1982), 386.

7. John Breck, "John 21: Appendix, Epilogue or Conclusion?," *St. Vladimir's Theological Quarterly* 36 (1992), 33.

8. The best summary of the possibilities I have found is James H. Charlesworth's *The Beloved Disciple: Whose Witness Validates the Gospel of John?* (Valley Forge, Pa.: Trinity Press International, 1995).

The most questionable suggestions regarding historical figures who could have been the Beloved Disciple include a wide range of possibilities, such as one of the Buddha's disciples (Ananda or Arjuna), a Gentile disciple, or an actual apostle such as Matthias (the disciple who took the place of Judas [Acts]), Jude, the brother of Jesus (based on 14:22 and Mk 6:3), Benjamin, Andrew, Philip, Nathaniel, Thomas, or even Judas Iscariot. Raymond Brown posits an "apostle" but one who was not part of "the twelve." Others propose anonymous figures from the gospels such as the rich young man/ruler or, as mentioned above, Sandra Schneiders' suggestion of the Samaritan woman. Still others are more Pauline, suggesting Paul himself, a Paulinist or Apollos or even a second generation Christian leader. In 1996 Kevin O'Brien decided the time for hypothesizing was over. Thus he declared, using italics: *"Simon the Leper, the owner/host at the Last Supper and no other, not Apostle, not disciple, not any idealistic replacement such as what some exegetes call an 'ideal disciple', not Lazarus, not John Mark, nor any other real person must be 'the disciple Jesus loved' (John 13:23-25)!"*

In the middle range of possibilities one finds quite serious suggestions ranging from a disciple of John the Baptizer to John Mark, the associate of Paul mentioned in Acts. Others find a Qumran connection. Eugene Ruckstuhl says the Beloved Disciple was a monk of the Jerusalem Essene community. He had provided a room for Jesus and the Twelve in the guest house of the Essene monks and was probably a priest and friend of the Sadducean high priest (Jn 18:15-17). Papias identified the Beloved One with the "Presbyter" John, or John the Elder, who was a leader in the post-apostolic church of Asia Minor. This suggestion more recently has been promoted by Martin Hengel and Richard Bauckham, who also see the Beloved Disciple as the author of the gospel and of the three Johannine letters as well.

As the strongest possibility, Lazarus stands out. Because we don't hear about the Beloved Disciple until after we have learned that Jesus "loved" Lazarus (11:36), scholars like Malina and Rohrbaugh, J. N. Sanders, Vernard Eller, and Mark Stibbe argue for Lazarus, and that Lazarus was the inspiration behind the text as we have it today. For instance, Stibbe writes of the one he calls BD: "the narrator in 21.24 is pointing to the authority, authenticity and credibility of the written source material from which he or she has drawn, not to the nature of the chapter in its final form. Thus, the narrator informs us that the incidents in John 21 derive from the written reminiscences of the beloved disciple, Lazarus." (Mark W. Stibbe, *John* [Sheffield: JSOT Press, 1993], 215.)

9. A minority still identify the Beloved Disciple with both the apostle and the evangelist. See, for instance, B. Silva Santos, "A autoria do Quarto Evangelho," *Revista Biblica Brasileia* 5 (1988), 157-181. Silva Santos does not rule out later redactional activity on the part of others.

10. Rudolf Schnackenburg, *The Gospel according to St. John*, vol. 1, trans. Kevin Smyth (New York: Crossroad, 1987), 101-4.

11. Over 100 years ago, B. F. Westcott, the Lord Bishop of Durham, England, published "the authorized version" of *The Gospel according to St. John* (London: John Murrary, 1902). He began by citing "internal evidence" identifying the gospel's author. This evidence was divided into two parts. First, Westcott cited *direct evidence* from the text itself. This involved three texts: (1) "And the word became flesh and lived among us, *and we have seen his glory*" (1:14); (2) the author's attestation after the death of Christ: "*He who saw this has testified so that you also may believe.* His testimony is true, and he knows that he tells the truth" (19:35); and (3) "*This is the disciple* [the beloved disciple (21:20-23)] *who is testifying to these things and has written them, and we know that his testimony is true*" (21:24). After citing direct evidence from the gospel itself, Westcott drew five conclusions that he proffered as *indirect evidence*: (1) the author was a Jew, (2) this Jew was of Palestinian origin, and (3) he was an eye-witness. Furthermore, (4) this evangelist was an apostle, and (5) this apostle was St. John himself.

A contemporary Johannine scholar, Gary M. Burge, argues that, in the main, Westcott's conclusions still hold. He finds "John, the son of Zebedee, as the most promising candidate" because (1) *He was one of the Twelve*, indeed part of the inner circle of Jesus, which would explain the intimacy; (2) *in the Synoptics John most often appears with Peter* and this certainly is the case in the gospel of John; (3) *the gospel normally refers to disciples by name but John is not listed among them*; this points to the Beloved Disciple as John; and (4) *the logic of chapter 21 points directly to John. Interpreting the Gospel of John* (Grand Rapids, Mich.: Baker, 1992), 45, 44.

For those who raise the objection of how John could refer to himself as "the disciple whom Jesus loved," Burge argues that, if the gospel went through various redactions, with the final version edited by his disciples: "This would explains [sic] the gospel's final verses (21:20-24). By this account *the beloved disciple* became *a title of veneration* employed by John's disciples to revere their deceased leader."

See also Herman N. Ridderbos, *The Gospel according to John: A Theological Commentary*, trans. John Vriend (Grand Rapids, Mich.: Eerdmans, 1997).

12. The arguments relate more to the connection with John, the son of Zebedee, than to the connection with the Johannine author. See Pierson Parker, "John the Son of Zebedee and the Fourth Gospel," *Journal of Biblical Literature* 81 (1992), 35-43. For a more contemporary summary, see Joseph A. Grassi, *The Secret Identity of the Beloved Disciple* (New York/Mahwah: Paulist, 1992), 5-10.

13. Schnackenburg, 3:383ff; Raymond E. Brown, S.S., "The Gospel according to John—An Overview," *Chicago Studies* 37 (1998), 6-7. Surprisingly, Schnackenburg postulates another apostle as the Beloved Disciple, but this one is unnamed: "The anonymous figure introduced by the evangelist and the editors as the 'disciple whom Jesus loved' and brought in at the last supper, is a historical

person, an apostle, who, however, did not belong to the circle of the twelve, and was most likely to have been a man from Jerusalem" (3:385).

14. I cannot conclude this section on the identity of the Beloved Disciple without including two possible candidates that must be considered in a class by themselves. In his 1992 study on the identity of the Beloved One, Grassi dismissed some of the more common theories and concluded that the Beloved Disciple is a "composite portrait" of someone who had been a disciple of Jesus. Later "Jesus adopted the youngster as his own son in a strong affectionate relationship." Probably the most intriguing suggestion with regard to the identity of the Beloved Disciple comes from exegetes like Alv Kragerud, H. Sasse, and Heinrich Schlier. They have suggested that the Beloved Disciple actually was/is the Paraclete, the very Spirit of Jesus who continued in the community and served as a model charismatic figure.

15. R. Alan Culpepper, *Anatomy of the Fourth Gospel: A Study in Literary Design* (Philadelphia: Fortress, 1983), 47, 121.

16. Barnabas Lindars sums up his view: "To me the Beloved Disciple is a creation of the evangelist in order to serve a specific function. He is one of the Twelve, who at crucial moments gives expression to the evangelist's own views. He represents true discipleship, understanding the necessity of the death of Jesus when all others fail. He is... a foil to Peter." See his *John*, New Testament Guides (Sheffield: JSOT, 1990), 22.

17. Among the most notable whom I have cited in this book or used for reference are Gerard Beasley-Murray, Raymond Brown, Oscar Cullmann, Maurice de Jonge, David J. Hawkin, Craig R. Koester, Francis Moloney, John Painter, D. Moody Smith, Kevin Quast, Rudolf Schnackenburg, and Sandra Schneiders.

18. Raymond E. Brown, K. P. Donfried, and John Reumann, eds., *Peter in the New Testament* (Minneapolis: Augsburg and New York: Paulist, 1973), 134.

19. Rudolf Bultmann, *The Gospel of John: A Commentary*, trans. G. R. Beasley-Murray (Philadelphia: Westminster, 1971), 701.

20. Some of these scholars wrote decades—even more than a hundred years—ago and include A. Julicher, Jan Hendrik Scholten, E. F. Scott, and possibly Alfred Loisy. Contemporary writers who hold that the Beloved Disciple is more a literary convention than a historical person include Barnabas Lindars, Ernst Kasemann, Alvin Kragerud, Joachim Kugler, and possibly Margaret Pamment.

21. Schnackenburg, 3:30.

22. Craig R. Koester, *Symbolism in the Fourth Gospel: Meaning, Mystery, Community* (Minneapolis: Fortress, 1995), 215-16.

23. William S. Kurz, "The Beloved Disciple and Implied Readers," *Biblical Theology Bulletin* 19 (1989), 102.

24. Ibid.

EPILOGUE: WHAT DOES IT MEAN FOR US TO REMAIN AS BELOVED DISCIPLES?

1. In John's theology, the crucifixion and resurrection are the same event.

2. Craig R. Koester, *Symbolism in the Fourth Gospel: Meaning, Mystery, Community* (Minneapolis: Fortress, 1995), 3.

3. I am indebted to M. Hasitschka for the appellation of the Spirit as the "divine domain." I find a powerful link in the connection between the divine domain and the many mansions for the disciple. See his "Die Parakletworte im Johannesevangelium. Versuch einer Auslegung in synchroner Textbetrachtung," *Studien zum Neuen Testament und seiner Umwelt* 18 (1993), 97-112.

4. R. Karwacki, "Spiritus Paraclitus," *Collectanea Theologica* 59 (1989), 35-42.

5. John W. Pryor, "Jesus and Israel in the Fourth Gospel—John 1:11," *Novum Testamentum* 32 (1990), 211-12.

6. Raymond E. Brown, *The Death of the Messiah* (New York: Crossroad, 1994), 958.

7. Pope John Paul II, *Tertio Mellenio Adveniente*, no. 35 in *Origins*.

8. William S. Kurz, "The Beloved Disciple and Implied Readers," *Biblical Theology Bulletin* 19 (1989), 106.

9. Elizabeth Kolbert, "In PCB Fight, It's the Nun vs. the C.E.O.," *The New York Times*, May 25, 1998.

INDEX

Abbott, E. A., 175
Adams, Jeanne, 212
adulterous woman story, 73–77, 77–87
aitein (to question), 6
akolouthein (to follow), 173
alētheia (truth), 123–24
anonymous disciples, 145, 171–75, 179, 204–11, 245n6, 245n8
anonymous women, 13, 80, 173–75, 205
antilanguage, 115
Arbuckle, Gerald A., xv, xxv, 78–79
atonement, 110, 147, 238n11
Augustine (saint), 55

Bailie, Gil, 66–67
Barrett, C. K., 16
Baumeister, Roy F., 60–61
Beasley-Murray, George R., 124, 131
Beloved Disciple, 173–75, 200–211, 245n6, 245n8, 246n11, 248n16
Beutler, Johannes, 144
birkat ha-minim (benediction of the heretics), 93
birth control, 70–71, 138, 237n16
Blasi, Anthony, 51, 110, 158, 164–65
blepein (to see), 100, 103. *See also* "seeing"
blindness, xxv, 88–89, 93–94, 96, 102–4, 239n6
boat narrative, 45–48, 160, 220
Borg, Marcus, 114
bread of life discourse, 48–49, 49–53, 116–17
Breck, John, 206
Brown, Ford Madox, 156
Brown, Raymond E.: adulterous woman story, 74; courtyard scene, 170; Eucharist, 42, 52; identity of the Beloved Disciple, 174–75, 200, 208; John's gospel, xv, xxvii, 93, 164; nature of Jesus, 36; Peter's role, 184–86, 191, 196, 200, 211
Bultmann, Rudolf, 105–6, 208

canonicity, 73–77, 183–85
Catherine of Siena (saint), 117
Catholic Health Association of Canada, 37
Cattafe, Thomasina, xi
Charles, J. D., 5, 7
children of the lie, 65–66, 173, 178, 180
cholan (rage), 68–69
church, the: as an instution, xxv, 14, 62–63, 70–71, 172–73, 178–81; apostles and disciples distinguished, 39, 148, 158, 163–65, 183–87, 211–15; author's vision of, xxvi–xxvii, 133, 212–22; and violence, 62–63, 172–73, 178–81. *See also* discipleship
Cohen, William, 85
Collins, Raymond F, 186
Cook, Guillermo, 91–92, 102
Council of Trent, 76
courtyard story, 169–73, 173–82
Crossan, John Dominic, 114
Cullman, Oscar, 186
Culpepper, R. Alan, xvi, xxii, 151, 154, 161, 186, 208

dakruein (to weep), 132
Daly, Sister Pat, 222

Also by Michael Crosby

The Seven Last Words
ISBN 0-88344-938-2

Personal and poetic meditations on the seven last words
of Christ on the cross make a challenging resource
for Lenten reflection.

"The ancient familiar words are made to reverberate with
contemporary exegesis and illustrations. The result is a
moving reflection that reveals the depth of Jesus' words so
that they echo loudly in our own hearts and struggles for
justice and hope."

– *Megan McKenna*

Spirituality of the Beatitudes
Matthew's Challenge for First World Christians
ISBN 0-8834-465-8

"Michael Crosby has not only understood what Matthew
was saying: he has understood the mind of Matthew and
brought that to bear upon the world today. I hope this book
finds a wide audience, for it will help many Christians read
the Scriptures with new insight and challenge."

–*Donald Senior, C.P.*

Please support your local bookstore, or call 1-800-258-5838.
For a free catalog, please write us at
Orbis Books, Box 308
Maryknoll, NY 10545-0308
Or visit our website at www.maryknoll.org/orbis

Thank you for reading *"Do You Love Me?"*
We hope you enjoyed it.

Of Related Interest

John's Gospel & the Renewal of the Church
Wes Howard-Brook
ISBN 1-57075-114-5

In examining the Lenten readings from John, Howard-Brook shows how the evangelist issues a call not only to personal conversion but for the conversion of the church itself.

"Howard-Brook reads John's gospel as a call to radical discipleship to the risen Christ. It helps bring the gospel to life, and if taken seriously, could do the same for our church."
–*John Dear*

Long Have I Loved You
A Theologian Reflects on His Church
Walter J. Burghardt
ISBN 1-57075-296-6

"This intellectual autobiography is an amazing display of erudition in the cause of edification—an ever-inquiring mind, capacious spirit, and creative imagination open to all the ways the Spirit builds up the Church. . . Required reading for anyone who wishes to understand the theology lying behind Vatican II and carrying its vision forward."
– *Msgr. Philip J. Murnion*

Please support your local bookstore, or call 1-800-258-5838.
For a free catalog, please write us at
Orbis Books, Box 308
Maryknoll, NY 10545-0308
Or visit our website at www.maryknoll.org/orbis

Thank you for reading *"Do You Love Me?"*
We hope you enjoyed it.